# 101 THE NEW CRÊPES COOKBOOK

*101 Sweet & Savory Crepe Recipes, From Traditional to Gluten-Free, for Cuisinart, LeCrueset, Paderno and Eurolux Crepe Pans and Makers!*

ISABELLE DAUPHIN

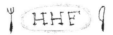

HHF

HHF PRESS

SAN FRANCISCO

# LEGAL NOTICE

The information contained in this book is for entertainment purposes only. The content represents the opinion of the author and is based on the author's personal experience and observations. The author does not assume any liability whatsoever for the use of or inability to use any or all information contained in this book, and accepts no responsibility for any loss or damages of any kind that may be incurred by the reader as a result of actions arising from the use of information in this book. Use this information at your own risk.

The author reserves the right to make any changes he or she deems necessary to future versions of the publication to ensure its accuracy.



ISBN-13: 978-1515139287
ISBN-10: 151513928X

Published in the United States of America
by Healthy Happy Foodie Press.

www.HHFpress.com

# DO YOU LIKE FREE BOOKS?

Every month we release a new book, and we offer it to our current readers first...absolutely free! This helps us get early feedback before launching a book, and lets you stock your shelf full of interesting and valuable books for free!

Some recent titles include:

- The Complete Vegetable Spiralizer Cookbook
- The Cast Iron Recipe Cookbook
- The Food Dehydrator Handbook

To receive this month's free book, just go to

www.healthyhappyfoodie.org/d1-freebooks

# Table of Contents

# INTRODUCTION

The wondrous crepe! Is there anything as delicious, versatile and easy to make? It is one of the most popular traditional foods of France. However, it has been adopted worldwide for its ability to provide a tasty vehicle for savory foods and sauces, or sweet and fruity concoctions. It can also be enjoyed as a fragrant and simple pleasure on its own, with a smear of sweet butter and a quick sprinkle of sugar. The crepe is the Queen of universally satisfying foods, and can conjure the delights of childhood or the romance of a Parisian night.

This simple yet thorough collection of recipes will enthrall your loved ones with mouthwatering recipes that anybody can easily make. Whether you are a mother preparing afterschool snacks for her children, a young man making his first candlelit meal to impress his fiancée, a high school student making breakfast for *maman* on mother's day, or a busy professor throwing together a quick and portable lunch to take to campus, there is something for everyone in this book! My tried and tested recipe for the essential batter is a breeze to learn, and becomes second nature very quickly with a little practice. Above all, my intent is that you have fun and get creative while making these 101 recipes—feel free to experiment with herbs, ingredients and combinations! After all, cooking is alchemy, and intuition can be your greatest tool in the kitchen.

# 1

# WHY YOU NEED THIS BOOK

## Learn How To Make Perfect Crepes

Congratulations! If you're reading these words, you are one step closer to making and enjoying delicious crepes. This book will teach you all you need to create perfect crepe batters for sweet and savory crepes. You'll also learn over one hundred delicious crepe fillings, from simple treats like crepes drizzled in lemon juice and dusted with powdered sugar to elaborate French haute cuisine like mixed seafood crepes San Tropez.

## Learn How To Use Your New Crepe Pan Like A Pro

Maybe you've seen crepes made. The process looks so fascinating: the chef pours the batter, swirls the pan, lifts the browning crepe edges, and, voila— perfect crepes. This book can turn you into a real crepe chef, too. Learn how to prepare your crepe pan and handle it just right, turning out mouthwatering crepes every time.

## Master This Simplest Form Of French Cooking

Many people consider French cooking the highest of the culinary arts. If you love crepes, you might be one of them. And you might think French cooking's too hard to learn. But consider the French crepe: delicious, suitable for a quick lunch or an elegant dinner, and, with a little practice, easy to make.

## Explore Traditional And New Crepe Recipes

Crepes have been, pardon the pun, a'round, for centuries. This book will show you how to make traditional French crepe recipes like la Bretonne, which originated in the homeland of the crepe, Brittany. You can also learn how to make delicious modern crepes — Nutella, anyone? — sold at crepe shops all over the world.

## Learn World Cuisine Using Crepes

Many cultures have a traditional flatbread or pancake recipe. Combining those local customs with French influence has led to millions of yummy meals all over the world. Explore African and India cuisines, and more, with the recipes found in this book. Some crepe batter recipes are altered with regional ingredients, like different flours or spices, while other recipes give you a chance to try new filling ingredients.

## Spoil Your Loved Ones By Making Delicious Crepes

For many of us, the foods we lovingly prepare by hand are the greatest gifts we give to friends and family. But sometimes, cooking for others can turn into drudgery, and the foods we prepare are boring and repetitive. Making crepes changes all that. The simple crepe has the power to lift the plainest ingredients to heights of elegance. Everyone feels spoiled by crepes!

## A Single Resource For Recipes From A Sweet Treat To A Full-Meal

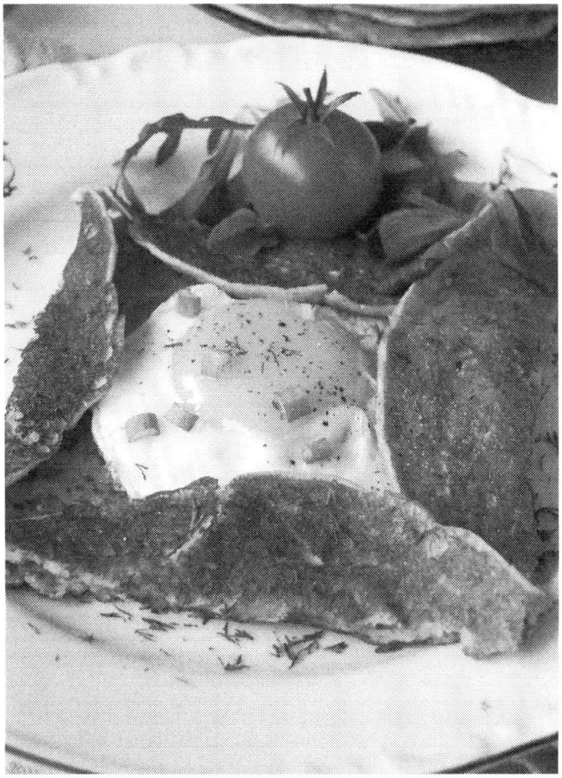

The crepe is endlessly adaptable because you can fill it with so many delicious ingredients. Swedish crepes with lingonberry jam is a quick and easy snack or breakfast, while crepe spanakopita covers most food groups and makes a complete dinner. Oh, and here's a secret: this book contains scores of recipes you can use even if, for some crazy reason, you don't feel like making crepes.

# 2

# BENEFITS OF MAKING CREPES

## Crepes Are Healthy, Natural, And Fresh

The crepe recipes in this book focus on the freshest, simplest ingredients. Crepes themselves are a delicious combination of barnyard basics: eggs, milk, butter, and flour. And they make healthy additions like fresh fruit, or gently steamed vegetables, into a special meal. Cooking with crepes opens a world of health options for you and your family.

## Prepare Ahead, Save Time

A great meal is the first casualty of a busy schedule. Crepes to the rescue! In a few steps, you can have basic crepe batter prepared. Refrigerate it for up to 24 hours, give it a stir, and you've nearly got dinner on the table. Cut down on prep time with filling ingredients from your supermarket deli case, like ham and cheese, or with mouthwatering slow-cooked pork from your crockpot. Already got a dinner plan? Enjoy crepes as an elegant dessert any night of the week.

## Perfect Dessert

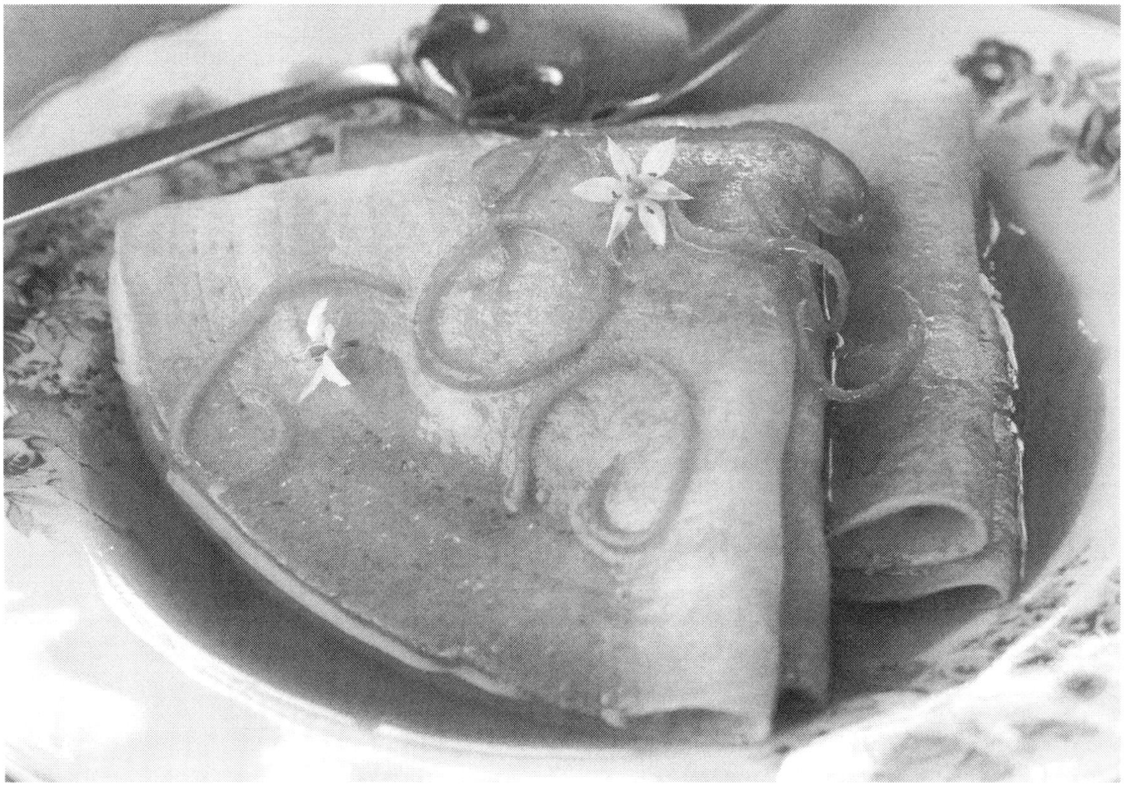

There are so many prepared desserts available at the grocery store that many of us have forgotten we can make them at home. When you learn crepe-making, that problem is solved. Many people love just the simplest crepe dessert, like a warm crepe drizzled in chocolate, or sprinkled with cinnamon and sugar. And fancier crepe recipes, like crepe suzette flambé, remind us that dessert is something to celebrate.

## Perfect Alternative To A Boring Sandwich

Ever since the Earl of Sandwich needed one hand free so he could keep playing in a marathon card game, the sandwich has been the Western World's most convenient meal. Now you can get a sandwich just about anywhere on the globe— which is why sandwiches, frankly, can be pretty boring. Enter the light, lacy, wrappable crepe. Fold it around any sandwich filling you can think of— ham and cheese, tuna salad, avocado and sprouts— and you've got a meal that beats the sandwich hands down.

## Impress Your Friends—Or A Date

Anyone can cook dinner, but not everyone can make dinner a special occasion. Crepes dress up your dinner menu so you can wow your friends, or make a great impression on your date. And with a little practice, you'll find them easy to make.

## Create Some Excitement

The preparation of many homemade meals is a drab affair for the senses. The sound of the microwave beeping mingles with the steam of boiling pasta water as defrosted chicken snaps and pops in the skillet. It doesn't have to be that way with crepes. Imagine golden crepe batter streaming from a ladle and subtly sizzling as it strikes the hot pan. The aroma of the fresh, simple ingredients draws curious visitors to the kitchen. You're creating something delicious and exciting— crepes for dinner (or breakfast or lunch) means no more dull meals, and no more dull cooking.

## Cook With Your Kids

Most of us have happy memories of kitchen time with our mothers and grandmothers, and would love to create memories for our own kids. Crepe making is a great way to do that. You usually have the ingredients for crepe batter right at hand, so no special shopping is required. And the simple recipe can be mastered even by the very young. Older kids can handle the hot pan on their own, and who knows, may even be making dinner for *you* someday.

## Simple Yet Elegant

Sometimes the most beautiful things are very simple. Elegant crepes simply wrap up deliciousness, whether in a La Vergeoise dessert crepe with jam and whipped cream, or a Francilienne dinner crepe, creamy with mushrooms and chicken.

## Perfect "To-Go" Food

Find yourself skipping breakfast because you just don't have the time? Crepes to the rescue. Fresh crepe batter keeps in the refrigerator up to 24 hours. Make some in advance, heat the pan, slice an apple, and you've got a handful of delicious, healthful food as you run out the door.

## Any Time of Day

Crepes are the perfect all-purpose, all-day meal-maker. Fill a breakfast crepe with fruit or eggs, warm a few slices of ham and cheese in a folded crepe for lunch, stir up some tangy ratatouille and crepes for dinner. And don't forget dessert— that bears repeating: With crepes you should never forget dessert. Few foods are as versatile, delicious, and as fun to make as crepes!

# 3

# SHORT HISTORY AND OVERVIEW OF CREPES AROUND THE WORLD

## Crepe Origins

The crepe began life as the food of humble farmers in the Brittany region of France. It was in Brittany's unwelcoming soil that buckwheat thrived and became a staple of the diet. The simple, broad, buckwheat pan-cakes crisped at the edges were called "crepe galette," crepe derived from the Latin for "crisp," and galette meaning a round flatbread.

Early crepes were served as bread, unfilled, to accompany a meal. Their virtue was that they were composed of simple ingredients available to most of the farming class, and that they required no time to rise.

No one really knows how long ago the first buckwheat crepes were made in France, but as wheat became a more common crop, cooks folded it into their crepe recipes. Today, we still use buckwheat for savory crepes because it gives body to hold heavier ingredients without adding much flavor to interfere with taste. Crepes made exclusively with buckwheat are gluten-free (surprise— buckwheat isn't wheat). White wheat flour provides a barely detectable but important finer texture for sweet crepes. Of course, in devising your own recipes, you might find you prefer wheat flour crepes for all your recipes, or that buckwheat galettes suit your palate (and maybe your digestion). There really aren't any rules, as the endless variety of recipes for crepe fillings attests.

That variety and the abundance of wheat crops have made crepes an elemental part of French cuisine. You'll find crepe stands on street corners and crepe pans in cafes and restaurants throughout France. Crepes are so significant a part of French culture they are included in the celebration of the holiday La Chandeleur. This February event of pagan and Christian origins warms the grey winter days with candlelight. Because the earliest wheat crops are not far in the future, crepes are prepared to use up the previous year's grain stores.

While the crepe is distinctly French, many other global cultures have flatbread recipes that adapt beautifully to make crepe dishes. India's dosa is made with a rice and lentil flour batter poured into a sometimes comically large pancake to hold a host of savory ingredients. The ancient flatbread of Ethiopian, injera, probably predates crepes. It is traditionally a risen and fermented batter, but can be easily adapted to a quicker formula to hold East African recipes. Closer to France, most European cultures have a traditional pancake. The Russian blintz, or blini, and the Swedish pannkakor are very similar to crepes, though more often eaten as dessert or breakfast food.

4

# HOW TO CHOOSE THE BEST CREPE – MAKING TOOLS

## Choose Your Crepe Pan

Crepe griddles and pans basically come in two types: griddles (like the Eurolux) that are kitchen-sized versions of classic crepe griddles; and pans that can also be used for other cooking tasks when crepes aren't on the menu (like Le Creuset pans and a host of others). If you have a small kitchen or a limited budget and your cookware needs to do double-duty, buying a crepe pan is probably the most practical choice. But crepe griddles are so easy (and so much fun) to use that they make nice "wish list" items.

## Cuisinart Crepe Pans

Come in three different varieties, with the Chef's Classic non-stick, 10-inch version being the most popular and best-reviewed.

### Advantages:

The shallow lip makes it easy to flip the crepes (or anything else you might be cooking in it) and it's easy to clean. The pan heats evenly, with no "hot spots." Also, the handle stay cool while cooking.

### Quirks:

Some users have complained about the pan's poor packaging, which allows it to be damaged in shipping. There are very few complaints about the pans themselves.

## Eurolux Crepe Maker

Comes in several sizes, including a cordless model that's significantly smaller than the original, 12-inch model. The classic batter-spreader—just like the ones used on the streets of Paris—is included. The surface of the pan/griddle has a non-stick coating, which makes cooking and clean-up easy.

### Advantages:

These crepe makers are lightweight and have little rubber feet to hold them steady while being used. They also have multiple temperature settings, which makes it easy to cook varying kinds of batter. (The griddles can also be used for cooking bacon or traditional pancakes.)

### Quirks:

Because this crepe maker has a number of plastic components, there may be a "plasticky" smell the first time or two it's turned on. Some users have also complained that the unit is slow to heat up, but for most users, that doesn't seem to be a problem.

## Le Creuset Crepe Pans

Are available in a range of sizes and in a range of prices—with a low of around $25

and a top price of more than $100 for those made of cast iron/enamel. The brand is the gold standard of cookware, and all their crepe makers are highly rated by users, so finding a pan to fit your budget and needs should not be difficult. In addition to pans made with their classic cast iron/enamel construction, Le Creuset also makes pans of heavy gauge forged aluminum that are extremely durable.

### Advantages:

These pans are completely oven safe at any temperature and very durable.

### Quirks:

Although the pans are dishwasher safe, hand-washing is recommended. Moreover, each time they're washed in the dishwasher, they need to be "reconditioned" by wiping down with vegetable oil before their next use, to preserve the non-stick quality of the coating.

## Paderno Crepe Pans

Come in three sizes and are made of carbon steel or professional-quality aluminum with a nonstick coating. (The nonstick varieties are two to three times more expensive.) The heavy-duty carbon steel pans provide excellent heat conduction but are not dishwasher-safe.

**Advantages:**

Lighter than cast iron, carbon steel is durable, won't chip and won't warp. Once it's seasoned, cooks have praised these pains for their nonstick quality, especially for vegan crepes, which tend to stick more than crepes made with eggs.

**Quirks:**

The metal handles on the aluminum crepe pan tend to heat up, and some have complained the lip is too low, but in general, both varieties of these pans come with very positive reviews.

## Norpro Nonstick Breakfast / Crepe Pan

Is a convenient 9.5 inches wide. Its low price may make you think it is a cheap option in more than one sense, but you may want to think twice.

**Advantages:**

This is the bargain, all-purpose pan. Light weight and durable, it heats evenly, and is easy to tilt when you're making crepes. Washed by hand, the surface should last.

### Quirks:

The nonstick surface can degrade if it's over-heated, and that could lead to the release of toxic chemicals. The range of heat for making crepes and cooking eggs should not cause that, but heating it empty could, so pay attention. If you use metal utensils on a nonstick surface, there's a good chance the surface will scratch. That could result in flecks of nonstick material in your food, which is unappetizing and might be toxic.

## Proper tools

Once you have your pan in hand, what else do you need to make crepes? It's really up to you. Farmwives in Brittany 500 years ago probably didn't have more than an all-purpose wooden spoon for stirring, ladling, and lifting. Some cooks today still advocate lifting the edges of the cooking crepe with fingers instead of a spatula. You might want to get a little more tooled-up than that. Some crepe-specific tools to consider:

### A Good Whisk

You probably own a whisk, but consider a stout, rust-proof one if you intend to make lots of crepes.

## A Plastic Or Wooden Spatula . . . Or A Crepe Spatula

You also probably already own plenty of spatulas. Just remember to avoid using a metal spatula with a non-stick pan, since it can scratch the surface. There's also a special crepe spatula useful if you are cooking crepes on a griddle. This is like a long, wide (completely dull) knife that slides neatly under the crepe and is just firm but flexible enough to flip it over.

## A Spreader

If you have a crepe pan, with edges, you don't need a spreader, since you can just tilt and twirl to spread the batter evenly, and it won't pour off (if you don't tilt too far). But if you're using a griddle, you can use a spreader to distribute the batter.

## Caring For Your Tools

The usual good kitchen hygiene rules apply to all your crepe tools— remember, you're working with raw eggs, so you have to keep everything clean. Scrub your tools in hot soapy water or throw them in the dishwasher unless the manufacturer warns against it.

# 5

## PRO TIPS FOR MAKING PERFECT CREPES

You learn to make perfect crepes the same way a piano player gets to Carnegie Hall: practice, practice, practice. The good news is that crepe-making practice is more delicious than Bach. For a faster track to perfection, consider some tips from the pros.

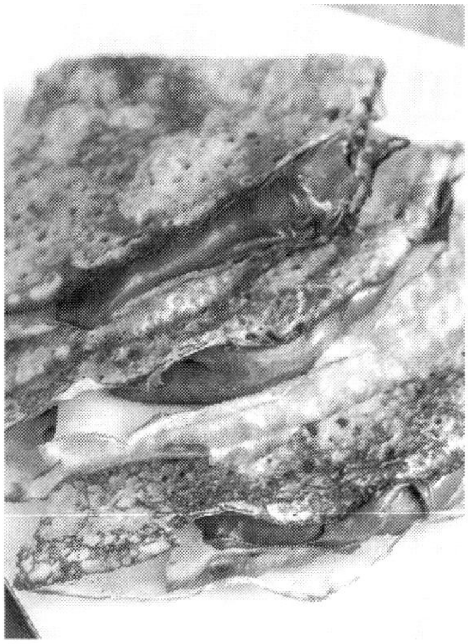

## Batter And Pan Prep Tips

### Start With All Ingredients At Room Temperature.

The exception to this rule is the butter; it gets melted, so will be a bit warmer. Of course, in general you don't want to leave eggs out too long, but 15 minutes to half an hour isn't going to spoil them.

### Add A Little Alcohol

Most traditional crepe formulas don't call for alcohol in the batter. But adding a Tbsp. or two of brandy to your batter can help tighten the crepe surface when the alcohol evaporates.

### Heating The Pan

Every pan, griddle, and stovetop is different. You'll learn the exact perfect setting for crepes after a couple of tries. Don't be concerned if your pan smokes— the true test of the right pan temperature is in how the crepes turn out. Give your pan at least five minutes to heat up. Ten minutes, even better.

### Time

The most important pro tip of all is really very simple: You must let the batter rest at room temperature for one hour.

If an hour isn't possible, then a minimum of 30 minutes is all right. Some kind of alchemy occurs when the batter is left on its own to breathe for a while. You will have a much better texture for your crepes if you religiously follow this step.

## Cooking Tips

### Batter Consistency

After the batter has rested, you should test its consistency to see if any additional flour is needed for thickening, or milk needed for thinning. To do this, quickly remix the batter with a handheld whisk or with a few pulses of your blender. Take a ladle, dip it into the batter, and slowly pour the batter back into the bowl. It should have the consistency of liquid cream— somewhat thick, yet fluid. If it looks too runny, add an extra Tbsp. of flour and beat again. If it looks too thick (which will give you too-heavy and awfully thick crêpes), add a dash of milk. After a few initial tries, you will quickly become accustomed to what a good batter should look like when you do the ladle test.

## Pouring, Cooking, and Flipping

After heating your pan, take a stick of butter and rapidly butter the hot pan surface by quickly rubbing the end of the stick over the entire pan surface. Immediately pour one ladle full of batter into the center of the pan. If you're using a griddle, gently push the batter out to the edges of the surface with a spreader. When using a pan, tilt it by the handle and turn it in a circular motion so the batter flows out to the edges all around the pan.

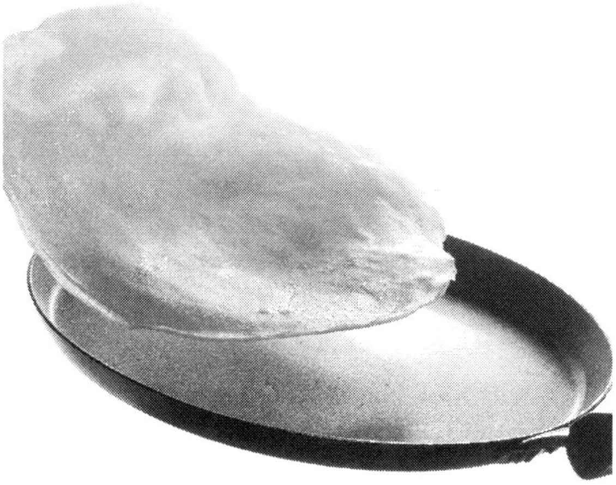

Now lay the pan flat onto the fire and wait approximately 1 to 2 minutes. The edges should start to brown and curl just a bit. When it looks like the crepe is starting to get golden spots or a nice golden sheen on the surface, take your spatula and flip it over rapidly. The second side will only take about half the time to cook. Remove the crepe with your spatula, and repeat the process of buttering the pan with your stick of butter. After making a few crepes when the butter starts to brown too much, you can wipe it off the pan with a paper towel and start again.

Use your first crepe as a test of the batter. It it's too thin, beat in another Tbsp. of flour. Too thick? Add just a Tbsp. of milk and try again.

As you finish your batch, keep the crepes warm in a 200 degree oven, stacked on top of each other with wax paper or parchment between each crepe. You can enjoy them immediately, or they'll keep at room temperature for a day or two, covered in plastic wrap or foil. You can keep crepes in the refrigerator, but they tend to dry out. If you do keep them in the refrigerator, reheat them in the crepe pan, or, better yet, in a microwave, covered with a paper towel.

## How To Fold Your Crepes

There are many ways to fold a crepe! Here are the most common, ranging from the traditional triangle-fold to the more elaborate star-fold.

# *Triangle fold*

1

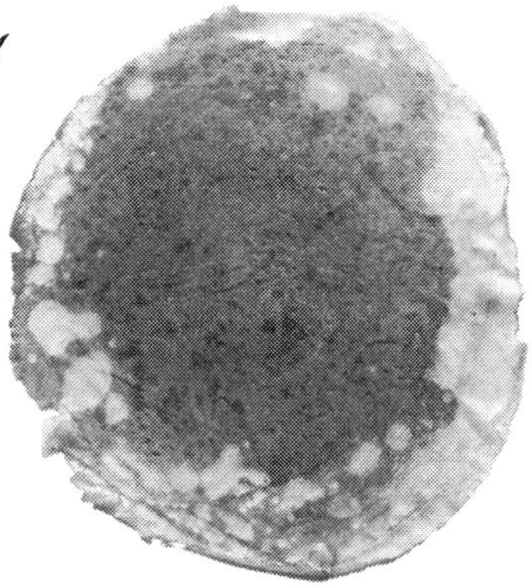

2

3

4

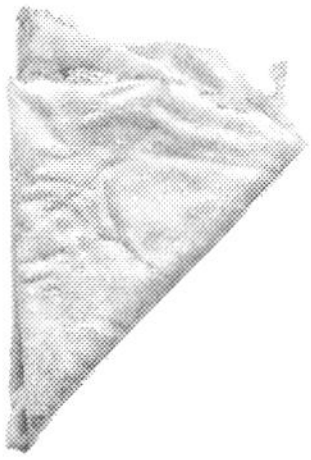

The triangle fold works for just about any type of crepe. It's easy to fold, and fits nicely into a napkin for eating on the go.

# *Roll*

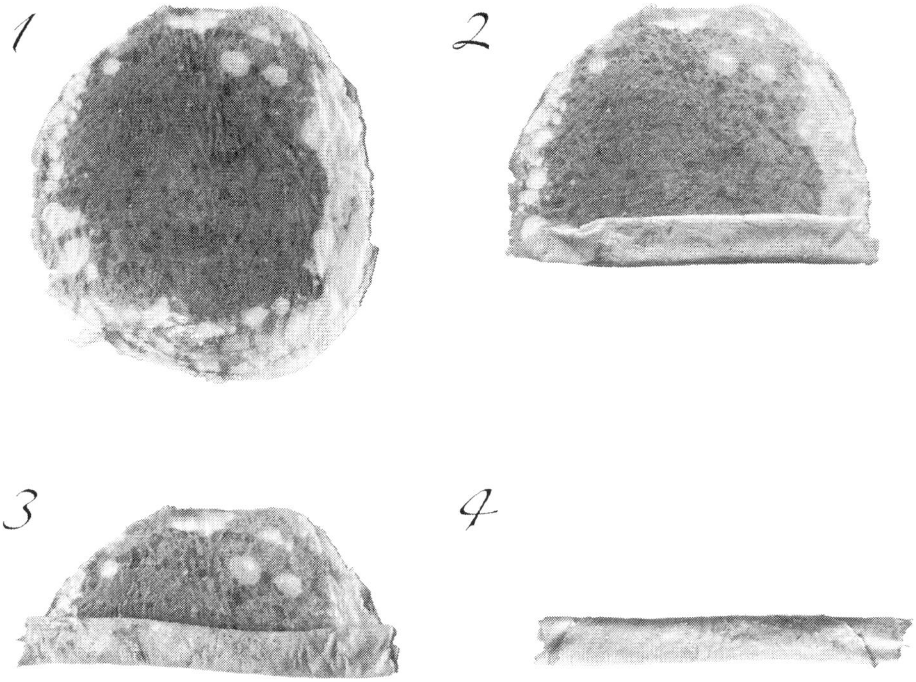


The roll fold is typically used for recipes that require eating with a fork on a plate. It's as easy as it looks: just put the filling into the middle of the crepe and roll it like a carpet!

# *Pouch fold*

1

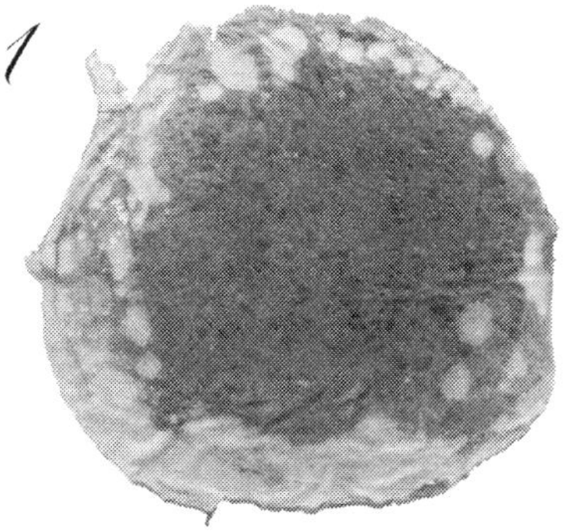

2

3

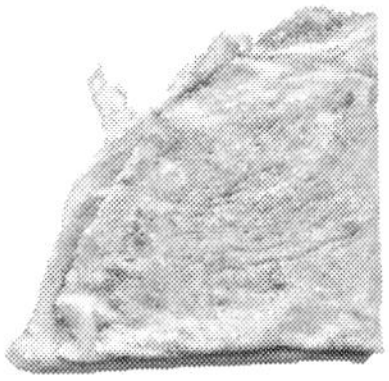

4

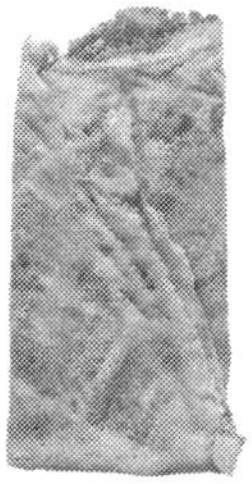

The pouch fold is often used for hand-held savory crepes because it keeps the filling nice and hot, like a little pouch.

# *Square fold*

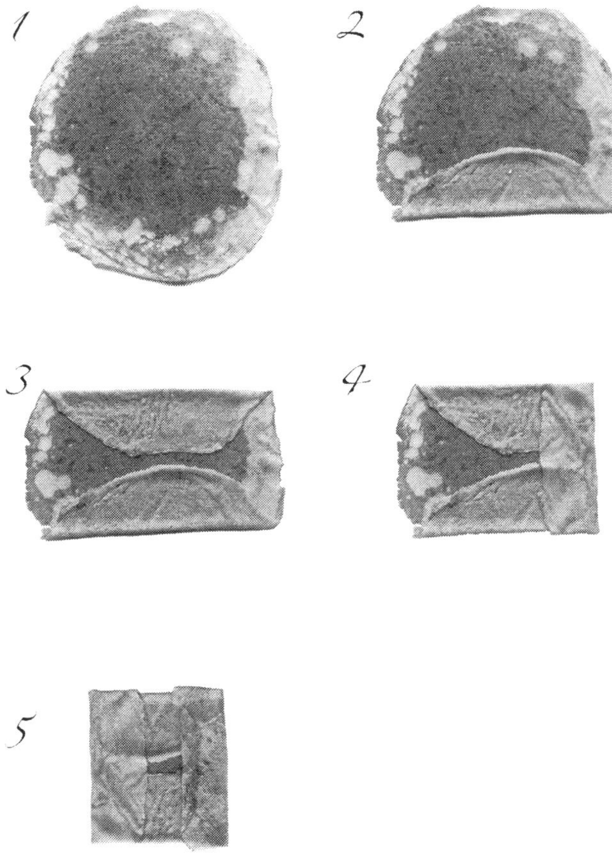


The square fold is typically used for savory crepes (especially egg recipes) served on a plate.

# Star fold

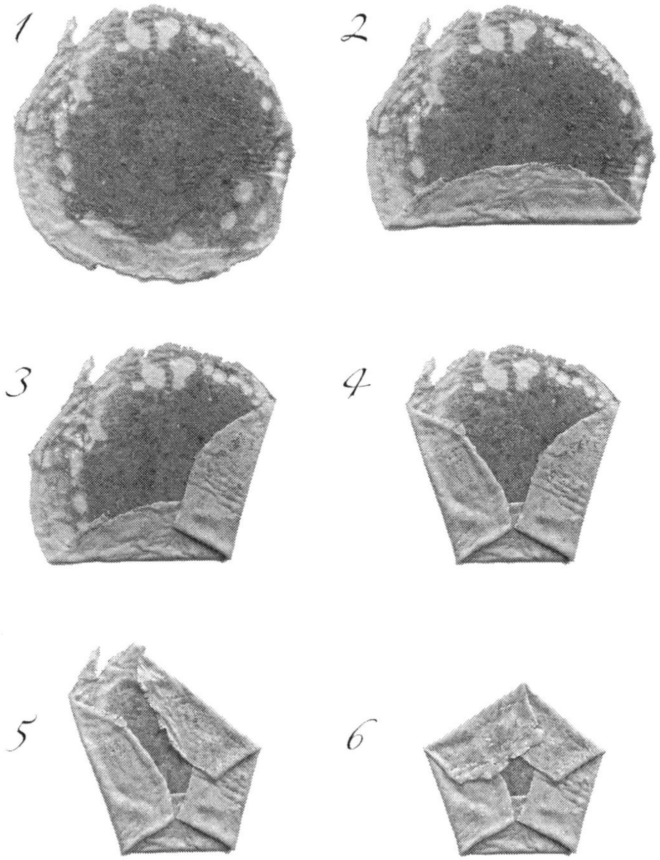


The star fold is a fancy variation on the square fold. Want to impress a guest? This is the fold for you!

6

# HOW TO USE THIS BOOK

Congratulations! You're ready to start exploring recipes and enjoying homemade crepes. To get the most out of this book, we suggest you:

## Explore Batter Recipes

Start here to develop your technique and learn which batters you like best.

## Begin With Kiosk Recipes

Crepe chefs working in street kiosks make mouthwatering crepes with minimal resources. If this is your first effort at crepe-making, or if you consider yourself a novice cook, satisfy your crepe-making and crepe-eating desires with simple recipes like sweet crepes with Nutella, before launching into more complicated dishes. The first few sweet or savory recipes in the French Crepes chapter feature kiosk crepes.

And in case it doesn't go without saying, *bon appetit*!

# 7

# CREPE BATTER RECIPES

# Classic Sweet Crepe Batter

## THE CLASSIC FRENCH SWEET CREPE

*This batter has been handed down in my family for generations. It represents the epitome of French crepe cuisine — simple, delicate, flavorful, amazing. It can be eaten immediately, right off the pan, or served with toppings. Either way, this basic crepe recipe is redolent of late summer nights in Paris, or a walk through an ancient French village.*

---

### INGREDIENTS:

*2 cups whole milk (do not use skim or low-fat milk as this will ruin the consistency of the batter).*

*4 eggs, beaten*

*1 Tbsp. melted salted butter*

*1 Tbsp. cognac, orange liqueur, vanilla extract, or orange juice*

*1 Tbsp. sugar (if you have vanilla sugar, this is good too)*

*1 tsp. grated orange rind or lemon rind (optional, but gives a nice touch)*

*1 1/4 cups white all-purpose flour*

*A few Tbsp. flour or milk to get consistency right*

### *Servings:*

*Servings: About 20 crepes*

*Prep time: 5 minutes plus 1 hour of inactive time*

*Cooking time: 30 minutes*

### *Nutritional Info:*

*Calories: 66, Sodium: 26 mg, Dietary Fiber: 0 g, Total Fat: 2.3 g, Total Carbs: 7.8 g, Protein: 2.7 g*

## Directions:

1. In a bowl or blender, mix milk, butter, eggs, liquid flavoring or juice, sugar and rind. Add the flour a little at a time, in three or four scoops, blending well between each spoonful.
2. Cover with a dishcloth or plate and set aside. Leave the batter to rest at room temperature undisturbed for one hour if possible, or at least 30 minutes.
3. After the rest period, re-blend the mixture once more with a few whisks or pulses, then check for the appropriate thickness. Adjust if necessary with up to 2 Tbsp. of flour or milk.

# Alternative Sweet Crepe Batters

## CHOCOLATE CREPES

*Chocolate-flavored crepes are so versatile that they count as a basic and they're very easy to make. Dust them with powdered sugar and they're delicious, or stuff them with a more complex filling and enjoy.*

---

### INGREDIENTS:

*1 cup of milk*

*1/2 cup half and half*

*2 oz. semisweet chocolate morsels*

*2 eggs*

*1 cup flour*

*2 Tbsp. unsweetened cocoa powder*

*1 Tbsp. granulated sugar*

### *Servings:*

*Servings: About 12 crepes*

*Prep time: 5 minutes plus*

*1 hour of inactive time*

*Cooking time: 30 minutes*

### *Nutritional Info:*

*Calories: 101, Sodium: 24 mg,*

*Dietary Fiber: 0.6 g, Total Fat: 3.9 g,*

*Total Carbs: 13.9 g, Protein: 3.2 g.*

### DIRECTIONS:

1. Combine milk and half-and-half in a small saucepan and heat over low. Add the chocolate morsels, stirring until the chocolate is melted.
2. In a bowl or blender, mix milk and chocolate mixture with eggs. Blend together the dry ingredients and them a little at a time, in three or four scoops, blending well between each spoonful.

3. Cover with a dishcloth or plate and set aside. Leave the batter to rest at room temperature undisturbed for one hour if possible, or at least 30 minutes.
4. After the rest period, re-blend the mixture once more with a few whisks or pulses, then check for the appropriate thickness. Adjust if necessary with up to 2 Tbsp. of flour or milk.

*Note: If you want to make gluten-free chocolate crepes, almond and coconut flours make the yummiest substitutes for wheat flour.*

## GINGERBREAD

*This is a lovely, seasonal variation. Make it at the holidays or enjoy making your home smell like the holidays anytime of year. As you can imagine, these crepes are perfect with vanilla ice cream. They also go well with stewed apples or— holidays, again— mincemeat.*

---

### INGREDIENTS:

*1 cup milk*

*2 large eggs*

*2 Tbsp. melted salted butter*

*2 Tbsp. + 2 tsp. dark molasses*

*1 tsp. vanilla extract*

*1 cup flour*

*1/4 cup granulated sugar*

*2 Tbsp. unsweetened cocoa powder*

*1 1/2 tsp. ginger*

*1 tsp. cinnamon*

*1/3 tsp. nutmeg*

*1/4 tsp. ground cloves*

*1/8 tsp. salt*

### *Servings:*

*Servings: About 8 crepes*

*Prep time: 5 minutes plus 1 hour of inactive time*

*Cooking time: 30 minutes*

### *Nutritional Info:*

*Calories: 165, Sodium: 91 mg, Dietary Fiber: 1.1 g, Total Fat: 5.1 g, Total Carbs: 26.1 g, Protein: 4.5 g.*

## DIRECTIONS:

1. In a bowl or blender, mix milk, butter, eggs, molasses and vanilla. Combine the dry ingredients thoroughly and add them a little at a time, in three or four scoops, blending well between each spoonful.
2. Cover with a dishcloth or plate and set aside. Leave the batter to rest at room temperature undisturbed for one hour if possible, or at least 30 minutes.
3. After the rest period, re-blend the mixture once more with a few whisks or pulses, then check for the appropriate thickness. Adjust if necessary with up to 2 Tbsp. of flour or milk.

# Alternative Savory Crepe Batters

## Gluten-Free and Vegan Batters

Traditional savory crepes, made with buckwheat as in the recipe above, are gluten-free. But savory crepes these days are often made with a blend of wheat flour and buckwheat flour, so don't assume all savory crepes are gluten-free.

The batter recipes in this section are free of gluten or contain no animal products, or both. Make special note of recipe directions that are a bit different from traditional crepes. Non-wheat flours behave differently than wheat— for example, requiring more leavening, or less time to blend with other ingredients.

# Coconut Flour

## (GF)

*In addition to being gluten-free, these crepes are also suitable for low-carb and Paleo diets, making this recipe triply good for you.*

*Yes, you read that number of egg whites right: nearly all coconut flour crepe recipes call for a large quantity of eggs and/or egg whites. You may want to use liquid egg whites in this recipe.*

---

### Ingredients:

- *1/2 tsp. lemon juice*
- *3/4 cup unsweetened almond milk (may also use soy milk)*
- *16 egg whites*
- *1/2 cup coconut flour*
- *1/4 tsp. baking soda*
- *1/8 tsp. salt*

### *Servings:*

*Servings: 6 crepes*

*Prep time: 5 minutes plus 1 hour of inactive time*

*Cooking time: 30 minutes*

### *Nutritional Info:*

*Calories: 128, Sodium: 56 mg, Dietary Fiber: 0.5 g, Total Fat: 6.4 g, Total Carbs: 9.5 g, Protein: 7.2 g.*

## Directions:

1. Combine the lemon juice and almond milk and let rest for five minutes.
2. Mix together the coconut flour, baking soda, and salt. Add these dry ingredients to the almond milk a little at a time, blending thoroughly.
3. Whisk in the egg whites.
4. Set aside for 10-15 minutes to thicken.

# Almond Flour

## (GF)

*Almond flour baked goods can be a little more fragile than those made with wheat flour, but that should not be a problem for crepes. These have a distinct rich flavor that goes well with many sweet fillings. If you'd like to enjoy them as savory crepes, drop the vanilla and honey.*

---

### Ingredients:

*1/8 tsp. salt*

*5 eggs*

*2 Tbsp. water*

*3 tsp. honey*

*1 tsp. vanilla extract*

*1/2 cup almond flour*

### *Servings:*

*Servings: About 8 crepes*

*Prep time: 5 minutes plus 1 hour of inactive time*

*Cooking time: 30 minutes*

### *Nutritional Info:*

*Calories: 59, Sodium: 76 mg, Dietary Fiber: 0.2 g, Total Fat: 3.6 g, Total Carbs: 2.8 g, Protein: 3.8 g.*

### Directions:

1. Beat the eggs with the salt.
2. Beat in honey and vanilla extract.
3. Blend in almond flour a little at a time, stirring with a fork or whisk to prevent lumps.

4. Add the water, using more if the batter is too thick.
5. Refrigerate for 20 minutes before using.

## VEGAN SWEET CREPE

*Here's a sweet crepe you can enjoy by itself or with any filling that melds well with the sweetness of maple. These crepes are very delicate so it may be easier to simply spread the batter thin enough they don't have to be flipped to cook thoroughly. Note the extra wait time.*

---

### INGREDIENTS:

*1/2 cup soy milk*
*1/2 cup water*
*1/4 cup melted margarine*
*2 Tbsp. maple syrup*
*1 cup flour*
*1 Tbsp. granulated sugar*
*1/4 tsp. salt*

### *Serving:*

*Servings: About 12 crepes*
*Prep time: 5 minutes plus 2 hours of inactive time*
*Cooking time: 30 minutes*

### *Nutritional Info:*

*Calories: 56, Sodium: 55 mg, Dietary Fiber: 0.3 g, Total Fat: 0.3 g, Total Carbs: 11.8 g, Protein: 1.4 g.*

### DIRECTIONS:

1. In a bowl or blender, mix soy milk, water, margarine and maple syrup. Blend the dry ingredients and add them a little at a time, in three or four scoops, blending well between each spoonful.
2. Cover with a dishcloth or plate and set aside. Leave the batter to rest, refrigerated, for 2 hours.

3. After the rest period, re-blend the mixture once more with a few whisks or pulses, then check for the appropriate thickness. Adjust if necessary with up to 2 Tbsp. of flour or soy milk.

# Traditional Savory Crepe Batters

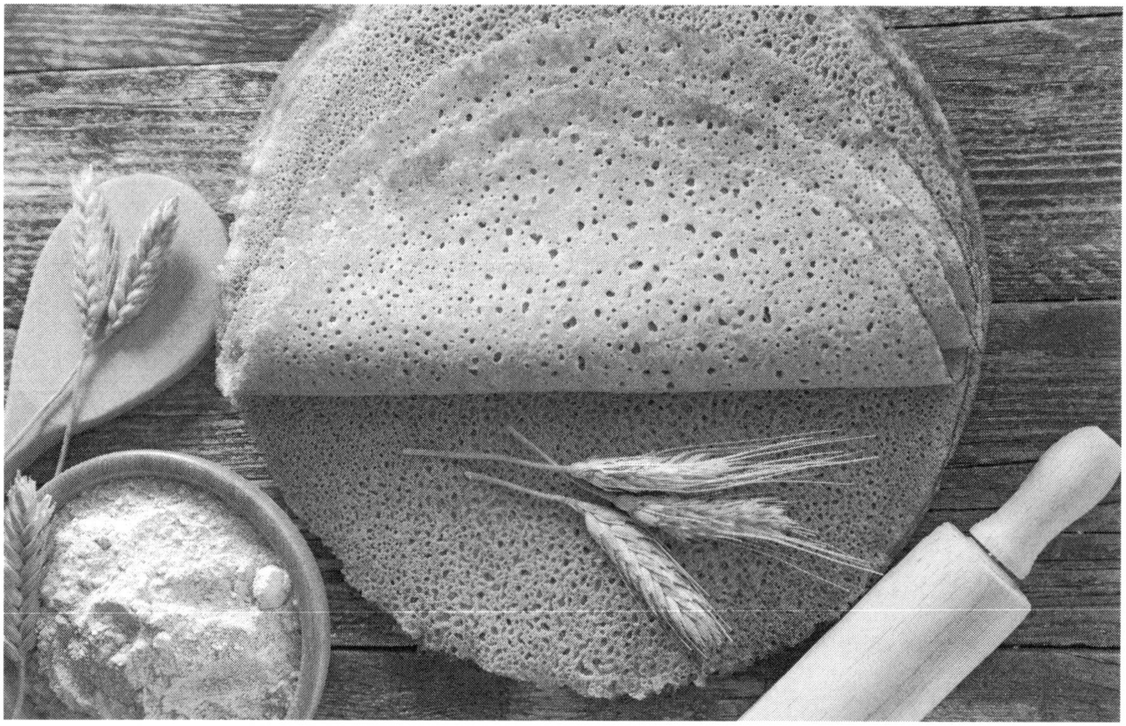

# TRADITIONAL FRENCH "GALETTE"

*This is a traditional galette recipe in the truest sense: there's no wheat flour added. That makes it gluten-free as well. Enjoy these crepes with any savory filling. The buckwheat adds just enough flavor to complement other ingredients and it gives the crepes a touch more strength to hold a dinner-sized dose of filling.*

---

## INGREDIENTS:

*3/4 cup milk*

*3 large eggs*

*1/4 cup melted salted butter*

*1 1/4 cups (or more) water*

*1 1/4 cups buckwheat flour*

### Servings:

*Servings: About 12 crepes*

*Prep time: 5 minutes plus 1 hour of inactive time*

*Cooking time: 30 minutes*

### Nutritional Info:

*Calories: 101, Sodium: 54 mg, Dietary Fiber: 1.3 g, Total Fat: 5.8 g, Total Carbs: 9.7 g, Protein: 3.7 g.*

## DIRECTIONS:

1. In a bowl or blender, mix milk, butter, eggs and water. Add the buckwheat flour a little at a time, in three or four scoops, blending well between each spoonful.

2. Cover with a dishcloth or plate and set aside. Leave the batter to rest at room temperature undisturbed for one hour if possible, or at least 30 minutes.
3. After the rest period, re-blend the mixture once more with a few whisks or pulses, then check for the appropriate thickness. Adjust if necessary with up to 2 Tbsp. of buckwheat flour or milk.

## Quinoa

*This basic recipe can be adapted to either sweet or savory dishes. If making something other than a dessert crepe, omit the sugar and substitute 1 tsp. of a dried herb or spice.*

---

### Ingredients:

*3/4 cup milk (may use nonfat)*

*2 eggs*

*1 1/2 Tbsp. melted salted butter*

*1/2 cup quinoa flour*

*1 1/2 tsp. granulated sugar*

*1/4 cup cooked quinoa*

### *Servings:*

*Servings: 6 crepes*

*Prep time: 5 minutes plus 1 hour of inactive time*

*Cooking time: 30 minutes*

### *Nutritional Info:*

*Calories: 128, Sodium: 56 mg, Dietary Fiber: 0.5 g, Total Fat: 6.4 g, Total Carbs: 9.5 g, Protein: 7.2 g.*

### Directions:

1. Combine all the ingredients except the cooked quinoa. The mixture's texture will be a little bubblier than traditional batters.
2. Cover with a dishcloth or plate and set aside. Leave the batter to rest at room temperature undisturbed for one hour if possible, or at least 30 minutes.
3. After the rest period, re-blend the mixture once more with a few whisks or pulses, then check for the appropriate thickness. Adjust if necessary with up to 2 Tbsp. of quinoa flour or milk.
4. Just before cooking, stir in the cooked quinoa, mixing well.

# Chickpea Vegan

*This is an incredibly simple, infinitely customizable recipe that is vegan, gluten-free, and low fat. Experiment with different flavorings like onion powder, curry mixes or chopped scallions.*

---

## INGREDIENTS:

*1 cup warm water*

*1 cup chickpea flour*

*1/4 tsp. salt*

### *Servings:*

*Servings: 6 crepes*

*Prep time: 5 minutes plus 2 hours of inactive time*

*Cooking time: 30 minutes*

### *Nutritional Info:*

*Calories: 121, Sodium: 106 mg, Dietary Fiber: 5.8 g, Total Fat: 2 g, Total Carbs: 20.2 g, Protein: 6.4 g.*

## DIRECTIONS:

1. Combine all the ingredients and set aside at room temperature for 2 hours before cooking as directed.

# Chickpea Vegan Socca

*Chickpea flour serves up healthy portions of protein, minerals and B vitamins. These savory chickpea crepes are vegan, gluten-free, and sparked with sunny rosemary for a Mediterranean flare. Note the extra wait time.*

---

## INGREDIENTS:

*1 cup water*

*1/2 cup olive oil*

*1 cup chickpea flour*

*1 1/2 tsp. minced fresh rosemary*

*1/2 tsp. cumin*

*1/2 tsp. black pepper*

*1/2 tsp. salt*

### *Servings:*

*Servings: 6 crepes*

*Prep time: 5 minutes plus 2 hours of inactive time*

*Cooking time: 30 minutes*

### *Nutritional Info:*

*Calories: 268, Sodium: 204 mg, Dietary Fiber: 6 g, Total Fat: 18.9 g, Total Carbs: 20.6 g, Protein: 6.5 g.*

## DIRECTIONS:

1. Combine all the ingredients and set aside at room temperature for 2 hours before cooking as directed.

# Buckwheat Vegan and Gluten-free

*These savory crepes have a slightly nutty flavor that blends well with strong spices like curry mixes. Use these crepes as a substitute for tortillas in fajitas, enchiladas, soft tacos, or wraps.*

---

## INGREDIENTS:

*1 1/4 cups unsweetened coconut milk (can substitute unflavored soy or almond milk)*

*1 Tbsp. coconut oil, warmed to liquify*

*1/2 cup buckwheat flour*

*1/2 cup rice flour*

*2 tsp. arrowroot or tapioca starch*

*1/8 tsp. salt*

### *Servings:*

*Servings: 6*

*Prep time: 5 minutes plus 1 hour of inactive time*

*Cooking time: 30 minutes*

### *Nutritional Info:*

*Calories: 217, Sodium: 57 mg, Dietary Fiber: 2.4 g, Total Fat: 14.7 g, Total Carbs: 20.5 g, Protein: 3.2 g.*

## DIRECTIONS:

1. Blend coconut milk and warmed oil. Combine the dry ingredients thoroughly and add them a little at a time, in three or four scoops, blending well between each spoonful.
2. Cover with a dishcloth or plate and set aside. Leave the batter to rest at room temperature undisturbed for one hour if possible, or at least 30 minutes.

3. After the rest period, re-blend the mixture once more with a few whisks or pulses, then check for the appropriate thickness. Adjust if necessary with up to 2 Tbsp. of either flour or with water.

## Ethiopian Crepe

*Real injera is fermented, sometimes over several days. This recipe is a good substitute when you're not thinking that far ahead. The lemon juice adds the tart flavor you'd normally get from fermenting, while the club soda adds the bubbles.*

---

### Ingredients:

*2 - 2 1/2 cups club soda*

*Juice of 2 lemons*

*1 1/2 cups flour*

*1/2 whole wheat flour*

*1 Tbsp. baking powder*

*1/2 tsp. salt*

### *Servings:*

*Servings: 8 crepes*

*Prep time: 10 minutes plus*

*at least 30 minutes of resting time*

*Cooking time: 20 minutes*

### *Nutritional Info:*

*Calories: 119, Sodium: 179 mg,*

*Dietary Fiber: 0.9 g, Total Fat: 0.4 g,*

*Total Carbs: 25.8 g, Protein: 3.3 g.*

### Directions:

1. In a large bowl, combine the club soda and lemon juice. Blend together the dry ingredients and add them to the club soda mixture a little at a time, in three or four scoops, blending well between each spoonful. Watch out for foaming overflow caused by the club soda's carbonation.
2. Cover with a dishcloth or plate and set aside. Leave the batter to rest at room temperature undisturbed for one hour if possible, or at least 30 minutes.

3. After the rest period, re-blend the mixture once more with a few stirs of a spoon, then check for the appropriate thickness. Adjust if necessary with up to 2 Tbsp. of the white flour or with club soda.

# World Crepe Batters

# Beghrir

*These Moroccan crepes are made out of semolina and traditionally served with a spread of honey-butter syrup. They have yeast in them and when cooked, develop little nooks and crannies on their surface, the better to soak up that honey-butter syrup.*

*These crepes are not turned while cooking and if the batter is too thick, the bubbles that create the crepes' unique texture won't form. You may have to experiment a little to get it just right.*

---

## Ingredients:

*1 Tbsp. yeast*

*1 tsp. sugar*

*1 cup + 2 Tbsp. warm water*

*1 1/2 cups semolina flour*

*3/4 cup flour*

*1 tsp. salt*

*2 tsp. baking powder*

## *Servings:*

*Servings: 15 crepes*

*Prep time: 20 minutes for yeast to proof, 5 minutes preparation, plus 1 hour of inactive time*

*Cooking time: 30 minutes*

## *Nutritional Info:*

*Calories: 87, Sodium: 157 mg, Dietary Fiber: 1 g, Total Fat: 0.3 g, Total Carbs: 17.8 g, Protein: 3.1 g.*

## DIRECTIONS:

1. Blend yeast, sugar and water in a medium bowl and set aside to proof for 20 minutes.
2. Mix the dry ingredients together and then add to the yeast/water and blend thoroughly, until the batter is very smooth and thin.
3. Cook as for crepes but do not turn them over. They are done when the bubbles have all popped on the side facing up. This will take about three minutes.
4. To make the honey butter syrup: Combine equal parts butter and honey in a small saucepan and cook until bubbly. Dip the rolled crepes in the hot syrup and serve immediately, or pour the syrup over the rolled crepes in a serving dish.

# Cornmeal Crepes

*These crepes are fantastic with Mexican meals, especially as the base for quesadillas and enchiladas. As is, these are not gluten-free, but if you substitute 100 percent buckwheat flour for the all-purpose flour in the recipe, they will be.*

## Ingredients

*1 1/4 cups milk*

*2 eggs*

*2 Tbsp. melted salted butter*

*1/2 cup + 2 Tbsp. flour*

*1/4 cup + 2 Tbsp. cornmeal*

*1/4 tsp. salt*

### Servings:

*Servings: About 12 crepes*

*Prep time: 5 minutes plus 1 hour of inactive time*

*Cooking time: 30 minutes*

### Nutritional Info:

*Calories: 137, Sodium: 171 mg, Dietary Fiber: 0.7 g, Total Fat: 6.6 g, Total Carbs: 14.5 g, Protein: 5.0 g.*

## Directions:

1. In a bowl or blender, mix milk, butter and eggs. Combine the flour, cornmeal and salt and add it to the liquid mixture a little at a time, in three or four scoops, blending well between each spoonful.
2. Cover with a dishcloth or plate and set aside. Leave the batter to rest at room temperature undisturbed for one hour if possible, or at least 30 minutes.

3. After the rest period, re-blend the mixture once more with a few whisks or pulses, then check for the appropriate thickness. Adjust if necessary with up to 2 Tbsp. of flour or milk.

# SAVORY LENTIL CREPES

*This recipe is most like the Indian street-food wrapper, dosa. Lentils and rice combine for a walloping dose of protein and fiber, so you could consider this crepe a meal in itself, if it wasn't so doggone good with a variety of sauces and fillings. And is if that weren't enough, they're gluten-free and low fat.*

---

## INGREDIENTS:

- *1/4 cup yellow lentils, rinsed and drained*
- *3/4 cup water*
- *1/4 cup rice flour*
- *1 tsp. powdered ginger*
- *1/2 tsp. cumin*
- *1/4 tsp. turmeric*
- *1/2 tsp. black pepper*
- *1/4 tsp. garlic powder*
- *1/4 tsp. sugar*
- *1/8 tsp. salt*
- *1-2 tsp. melted coconut oil*

### *Servings:*

*Servings: About 10 crepes*

*Prep time: 15 minutes plus 1 hour of inactive time*

*Cooking time: 30 minutes*

### *Nutritional Info:*

*Calories: 41, Sodium: 30 mg, Dietary Fiber: 1.6 g, Total Fat: 1.1 g, Total Carbs: 6.5 g, Protein: 1.5 g.*

## DIRECTIONS:

1. Grind the lentils into a paste with the water. Add to the other ingredients and blend well.
2. Set batter aside for one hour.

*Note: This recipe works best with a food processor or grinder; do not use a mortar and pestle. If you do not have a food processor or heavy-duty blender, you can soak the lentils first overnight. If doing that, you may find the recommended 3/4 cup of water is too much. Add water a 1/4 cup at a time until you achieve the right consistency.*

# BANH XEO

## INGREDIENTS:

*1 cup rice flour*

*1/2 tsp. ground turmeric*

*1/2 tsp. sea salt*

*1 1/2 cups water*

## *Servings:*

*Servings: 4 crepes*

*Prep time: 5 minutes*

*Cooking time: 5 minutes*

## *Nutritional Info:*

*Calories: 146, Sodium: 237 mg,*

*Dietary Fiber: 1 g, Total Fat: 0.6 g,*

*Total Carbs: 31.8 g, Protein: 2.4 g.*

## DIRECTIONS:

1. Whisk together rice flour, turmeric, salt, and water in a large bowl until smooth. Cover and let sit at room temperature 1 hour before cooking.

# 8

## TRADITIONAL FRENCH CREPES

### *Traditional French Sweet Crepes*

# :: Beurre-Sucre ::

## (Butter & Sugar)

*Crepes are born in butter — melted butter smoothes their batter and sizzling butter crisps their edges. Bathe them in butter one last time with a sprinkling of plain white sugar. Any white sugar will do, but caster sugar has just the right delicate crunch.*

---

### Ingredients:

*8 Tbsp. salted butter, not too cold*

*8 tsp. caster sugar*

### *Servings:*

*Serve with 8 Sweet Crepes*

*(your preference of batter)*

*Servings: 8 filled crepes*

*Prep time: 5 minutes*

### *Nutritional Info:*

*Calories: 117, Sodium: 82 mg,*

*Dietary Fiber: 0 g, Total Fat: 11.5 g,*

*Total Carbs: 2.6 g, Protein: 0.1 g.*

### Directions:

1. Spread each open, warm crepe down its center with butter. Sprinkle half a tsp. sugar along the butter. Fold the crepe in half, then fold again to make a triangle. Stack at angles.

# : Au Confiture ::

## (Jam)

*Crepes with jam. No big deal, right? A couple of tiny tricks make them extra special. Don't scrimp on the butter. To quote James Beard, "A gourmet who thinks of calories is like a tart who looks at her watch."*

### Ingredients:

*1/2 to 1 cup jam*

*8 Tbsp. salted butter*

### Servings:

*Serve with 8 Sweet Crepes*

*(your preference of batter)*

*Servings: 8 filled crepes*

*Prep time: 5 minutes*

*Cooking time: 5 minutes*

### Nutritional Info:

*Calories: 157, Sodium: 88 mg,*

*Dietary Fiber: 0.2 g, Total Fat: 11.5 g,*

*Total Carbs: 13.8 g, Protein: 0.2 g.*

### Directions:

1. Spread each open crepe down its center with the jam mixture. Fold the crepe in half, then fold again to make a triangle. Stack at angles.

# :: La Vergeoise ::

## (Fig or Raspberry Jam, Whipped Cream)

*Vergeoise is a dark French sugar made from beets. Vergeoise does not pour like white sugar, so you have to be extra sure to blend it thoroughly with other ingredients. To make these crepes, substitute vergeosie (or, if you can't get it, dark brown sugar) for the white sugar in your sweet crepe recipe. Save a tsp. or two to sprinkle on each crepe.*

---

### INGREDIENTS:

*3/4 cup fig or raspberry preserves*

*1/4 cup vergeoise*

### *Servings:*

*Serve with 8 Sweet Crepes*

*Servings: 8 filled crepes*

*Prep time: 10 minutes*

### *Nutritional Info:*

*Calories: 101, Sodium: 11 mg,*

*Dietary Fiber: 0.3 g, Total Fat: 0 g,*

*Total Carbs: 25.1 g, Protein: 0.1 g.*

### DIRECTIONS:

1. Prepare crepes. While they're still warm, spread each open crepe with a Tbsp. or two of preserves. Fold in half, then fold again to make a triangle. Sprinkle each folded crepe with vergeoise, and stack at angles.:

## : La Sauvage ::

### (Wild Berries, Honey, Whipped Cream, Sugar)

*De-civilize the urbane crepe with the wildest, freshest berries you can find, gently warmed and softened in honey. This treat has perfect versatility— serve it for a romantic dessert for two, or for breakfast to sneak a little fresh fruit into younger diets.*

---

### Ingredients:

*1 1/2 cup blackberries, raspberries, or other seeded berry*

*1/4 cup honey*

*1/4 cup orange juice*

*1 cup whipped cream*

### *Servings:*

*Serve with 8 Sweet Crepes*

*(your preference of batter)*

*Servings: 8 filled crepes*

*Prep time: 5 minutes*

*Cooking time: 10 minutes*

### *Nutritional Info:*

*Calories: 91, Sodium: 6 mg,*

*Dietary Fiber: 1.5 g, Total Fat: 4.8 g,*

*Total Carbs: 12.6 g, Protein: 0.8 g.*

## Directions:

1. Cook berries, honey, and orange juice on medium high heat for about 3 minutes, stirring occasionally.
2. Spread each open crepe down the middle with a Tbsp. of whipped cream. Spoon a generous Tbsp. of berry sauce over the whipped cream. Roll the crepes and serve them seam side down, topped with whipped cream.

# :: LA RUCHE ::

## (Honey Whipped Cream)

*Ruche is French for "beehive." Enjoy the rich and lavish flavor of honey in this lighter-than-air combo. The darker the honey, the more earthy and exotic the flavor.*

---

### INGREDIENTS:

*1 cup heavy cream*

*2 tbsp of honey, plus extra for drizzling*

### *Servings:*

*Serve with 8 Sweet Crepes*

*(your preference of batter)*

*Servings: 8 filled crepes*

*Prep time: 15 minutes*

### *Nutritional Info:*

*Calories: 68, Sodium: 6 mg,*

*Dietary Fiber: 0 g, Total Fat: 5.6 g,*

*Total Carbs: 4.8 g, Protein: 0.3 g.*

### DIRECTIONS:

1. In a medium sized bowl whisk cream until it begins to stiffen. Add honey (it will pour more easily if you've heated it just a few seconds in the microwave) and continue whisking until peaks form.
2. Spread each open crepe with about a quarter cup of whipped cream. Fold in half, then fold again to make a triangle. Stack at angles, allowing the

whipped cream to squeeze out of the crepes. Drizzle slightly warmed honey over the stack.

# :: La Châtaigne ::

## (Chestnut Whipped Cream)

*Rich, creamy chestnuts are a luxurious treat. You can make your own chestnut puree, if you're willing to shell the nuts and remove the bitter inner peel. But many delicious prepared purees are available.*

---

### Ingredients:

*1/2 cup heavy cream*

*3/4 cup chestnut puree*

### *Servings:*

*Serve with 8 Sweet Crepes*

*(your preference of batter)*

*Servings: 8 filled crepes*

*Prep time: 5 minutes*

*Cooking time: 5 minutes*

### *Nutritional Info:*

*Calories: 28, Sodium: 3 mg,*

*Dietary Fiber: 0 g, Total Fat: 2.8 g,*

*Total Carbs: 0.7 g, Protein: 0.2 g.*

### Directions:

1. In a medium sized bowl, whisk the cream until peaks form, using a hand whisk or electric mixer on low. Fold in the chestnut puree.

2. Spread each open crepe with chestnut whipped cream. Fold in half, then fold again to make a triangle. Stack at angles, allowing the cream to ooze out of the crepes. Top the stack with the last of the whipped cream.

# :: NUTELLA BANANE ::

## (Nutella, Banana, Whipped Cream)

*Chocolate-hazelnut plus bananas seems like the simplest of crepes— and it is! Try some of the recently available bananas like lady fingers or red bananas for an alluring twist. You might not use the entire 13 ounces of Nutella, but some days you just need that much chocolate.*

---

### INGREDIENTS:

*1 13 ounce jar of Nutella*

*4 bananas*

*2 cups whipped cream*

### *Servings:*

*Serve with 8 Sweet Crepes*

*(your preference of batter)*

*Servings: 8 filled crepes*

*Prep time: 15 minutes*

### *Nutritional Info:*

*Calories: 389, Sodium: 30 mg,*

*Dietary Fiber: 4 g, Total Fat: 23.2 g,*

*Total Carbs: 43 g, Protein: 3.8 g.*

### DIRECTIONS:

1. Prepare crepes. While they're still warm, spread each open crepe down the center with a Tbsp. or two of Nutella.
2. Slice the bananas and place them down the ribbon of Nutella, overlapping each slice slightly.

3. Roll the crepes and serve them seam side down, topped with whipped cream.

# :: VALENTINE ::

## (Nutella, Fresh Strawberries, Bananas, Whipped Cream)

*What says Valentine's Day better than chocolate? And hazelnuts. And strawberries. Also bananas, just in case things weren't sweet enough. And whipped cream. Uh, nothing?*

---

### INGREDIENTS:

*1 13 ounce jar of Nutella*

*3 cups strawberries*

*4 bananas*

*1 cup whipped cream*

### *Servings:*

*Serve with 8 Sweet Crepes*

*(your preference of batter)*

*Servings: 8 filled crepes*

*Prep time: 15 minutes*

### *Nutritional Info:*

*Calories: 363, Sodium: 25 mg,*

*Dietary Fiber: 5.1 g, Total Fat: 18.7 g,*

*Total Carbs: 46.7 g, Protein: 3.8 g.*

### DIRECTIONS:

1. Hull the strawberries and slice them vertically (the larger slices should look like little hearts). Slice the bananas.

2. Spread each open crepe down the middle with Nutella. Arrange alternating banana and strawberry slices. Roll the crepes and serve them seam side down, topped with whipped cream.

## :: Coco-Caramel ::

### (Caramel Creme, Coconut, Walnut, Banana)

*Sweet smooth crepes with sweet creamy fillings are all well and good. Okay, they're one of the most perfect creations on earth. That said, sometimes you want a little crunch and texture to go with you perfection. Here it is in the form of chopped walnuts and a sprinkling of coconut.*

---

### Ingredients:

*3/4 cups sugar*
*2 Tbsp. water*
*1 cup heavy cream*
*3 Tbsp. creme fraiche or sour cream*
*1/4 tsp. vanilla extract*
*Pinch of salt*
*3/4 cup chopped walnuts*
*1/2 cup shredded coconut*

### *Servings:*

*Serve with 8 Sweet Crepes*
*(your preference of batter)*
*Servings: 8 crepes*
*Prep time: 15 minutes*
*Cook time: 15 minutes*

### *Nutritional Info:*

*Calories: 222, Sodium: 29 mg,*
*Dietary Fiber: 1.3 g, Total Fat: 15.1 g,*
*Total Carbs: 21.3 g, Protein: 3.4 g.*

### Directions:

1. To make the caramel cream: Set a medium sized bowl in a baking dish half filled with ice water— this is where you'll place the caramel when you remove it from the heat, so it will stop cooking immediately.

2. Combine sugar and water in a medium saucepan and bring to a boil over medium-high heat. Prevent sugar crystals from forming on the sides of the pan.
3. Reduce the heat to medium, and cook about 5 minutes, until sugar darkens to amber. Immediately remove from the heat, and whisk in 1/2 cup of the cream. Return this mixture to medium heat, and bring it to a boil again.
4. Remove the caramel from the heat and pour it into the bowl set in ice-water. Let caramel cool, stirring often, for 10 minutes. Stir in creme fraiche, vanilla, and salt. Just before using, beat the remaining 1/2 cup cream until stiff peaks form. Fold it into the caramel with a rubber spatula, and whisk until blended.
5. Using a rubber spatula, spread each crepe with caramel cream sauce down the middle, slice bananas in a line down the center of each crepe, overlapping the slices just slightly. Sprinkle with ground walnuts. Roll crepes and serve seam side down, sprinkled with shredded coconut.

Variation: Prepare as above, sprinkling rolled crepes with cinnamon along with the coconut, and top with chocolate ice cream.

# :: Frangipane Maison ::

## (Almond Cream)

*Frangipane is a creamy almond paste which is common to French and Italian desserts. This particular recipe is inspired by a creperie in St. Malo, an ancient seaside fortified village in Bretagne. The heavenly flavor of creamy, sweet almonds served on a hot crepe is beyond words. Try at your own risk!*

---

### Ingredients:

*1 cup almond powder (almond meal)*

*3/4 cup powdered sugar*

*2 whole eggs*

*1/2 cup butter (salted is ok)*

*1 Tbsp. rum or 1 tsp. vanilla extract*

### *Servings:*

*Serve with 4 Sweet Crepes*

*(your preference of batter)*

*Servings: 4*

*Prep time: 10 minutes*

*Cooking time: 1 minute*

### *Nutritional Info:*

*Calories: 468, Sodium: 195 mg,*

*Dietary Fiber: 3.0 g, Total Fat: 37.1 g,*

*Total Carbs: 27.7 g, Protein: 8 g.*

## DIRECTIONS:

1. In a large mixing bowl, using a whisk, mix together all ingredients. Start with the eggs, add sugar, then almond meal, then warmed butter, and finally the vanilla extract (or rum).
2. When the mixture is creamy, it is ready. It can be stored in the refrigerator for up to one week.
3. To use, warm in microwave for 30 seconds before spooning onto a warm crepe.

# :: LA TATIN ::

## (Caramelized Apples, Cinnamon, Whipped Cream)

*The renowned tarte tatin is basically French upside-down cake made with apples. It originated in Hotel Tatin, south of Paris. In this recipe, crepe batter is poured over the cooking apples so that they're cooked into the crepe itself. Leave the peels on for rustic texture.*

---

### INGREDIENTS:

*30 (1/8-inch thick) Fuji apple slices (3 or 4 apples, depending on their size)*

*2 tsp. lemon juice*

*4 eggs*

*1 cup flour*

*1 tbsp sugar*

*1 tsp vanilla*

*2 Tbsp. triple sec*

*2 Tbsp. melted salted butter*

*1-1/2 cups milk*

*1/2 cup vegetable oil*

*1/2 cup sugar*

### *Servings:*

*Serve with 8 Sweet Crepes*

*(your preference of batter)*

*Servings: 8 crepes*

*Prep time: 15 minutes plus*

*1 hour waiting time*

*Cooking time: 20 minutes*

### *Nutritional Info:*

*Calories: 362, Sodium: 360 mg,*

*Dietary Fiber: 2.6 g, Total Fat: 19.6 g,*

*Total Carbs: 40.3 g, Protein: 5.7 g.*

## DIRECTIONS:

1. Put the apple slices in a bowl of cold water with lemon juice to keep them from turning brown.
2. In a large mixing bowl, blend eggs, flour, sugar, vanilla and triple sec until very smooth.
3. Add butter and milk and continue to blend until the mixture is as smooth as heavy cream.
4. Let the batter rest for at least an hour.
5. Place your crêpe pan over medium-high heat. Add 2 Tbsp. of the vegetable oil.
6. Use about 4 apple slices per crepe. Sauce apple slices for about a minute. Ladle enough batter over the cooking apples to cover them. Slowly tilt the pan in a circular motion to spread the batter. Cook until outer edge crisps and curls up from the pan. Flip and cook another minute. Add a slice of butter and 2 tsp. sugar on top of the crêpe. Flip again and allow the sugar and butter to caramelize, about a minute, maybe two. Flip onto a plate and serve warm.

## :: POMMES CANNELLE ::

### (Apples & Cinnamon)

*This recipe slices the apples so thin that they just barely hold their shape, with strands of peel keeping the texture from venturing toward soggy. Use tart apples like Pink Lady or Granny Smith.*

---

### INGREDIENTS:

*1/2 tsp. ground cinnamon*
*4 apples*
*1/2 cup white sugar*
*2 tsp. cinnamon*
*1/4 cup water*
*2 Tbsp. cornstarch*

### *Servings:*

*Serve with 8 Sweet Crepes*
*(your preference of batter)*
*Servings: 8 filled crepes*
*Prep time: 5 minutes*
*Cooking time: 10 minutes*

### *Nutritional Info:*

*Calories: 104, Sodium: 1 mg,*
*Dietary Fiber: 2.6 g, Total Fat: 0.2 g,*
*Total Carbs: 27.5 g, Protein: 0.3 g.*

### DIRECTIONS:

1. Quarter and core the apples, then slice them thin enough to be transparent. Combine with sugar, cinnamon, cornstarch and water, and heat over low heat until just a few apple slices break when you stir.

2. Spoon apple mixture down each crepe's center. Roll the crepes and serve them seam side down.

# :: GERMAIN ::

## (Caramelized Apples, Vanilla Ice Cream)

*Think of this autumnal recipe as apple pie for adults. The lemon cuts the sweetness just enough that you can serve this with an apple eau de vie or calvados. It also makes an excellent brunch crepe sans ice cream.*

---

### INGREDIENTS:

*5 Tbsp. unsalted butter*

*3 pounds medium apples (Golden Delicious caramelize well)*

*3/4 cup (packed) golden brown sugar*

*1/2 cup apple juice or cider*

*2 Tbsp. lemon juice*

*1 tsp. lemon zest*

*1 tsp. ground cinnamon*

*3 Tbsp. dark rum*

*Vanilla ice cream*

### *Servings:*

*Serve with 8 Sweet Crepes*

*(your preference of batter)*

*Servings: 8 filled crepes*

*Prep time: 30 minutes*

*Cooking time: 10 minutes*

### *Nutritional Info:*

*Calories: 243, Sodium: 65 mg,*

*Dietary Fiber: 4.4 g, Total Fat: 8.6 g,*

*Total Carbs: 41.1 g, Protein: 0.9 g.*

### DIRECTIONS:

1. Preheat oven to 350.
2. Peel, quarter, and core the apples, cutting each quarter cut into 3 chunky pieces.

3. Melt butter in large skillet over medium low heat. Saute the apples about 15 minutes, stirring often. Add sugar, apple juice, lemon juice, zest, and cinnamon. Simmer up to 5 minutes, stirring regularly, until juices thicken and apples are very tender. Remove from heat.
4. Butter a 9"x13"" baking dish. Using a slotted spoon, place apples into center of crepes. Fold 1 side of crepes over filling; roll up, enclosing filling. Arrange on platter, seam side down. Stir rum into sauce in skillet. Bring to boil, stirring, until you can smell the alcohol burning off. Spoon sauce over crepes and bake until warm, about 10 minutes.

## :: Beurre-Citron ::

### (Butter, Lemon Juice, Sugar, Lemon Whipped Cream)

*It's hard to beat this fresh tasting, scrumptious combination. There's just something perfect about how the powdered sugar dissolves in the lemon juice just enough to make an instant lemon sauce. Serve the lemon whipped cream on the side so you can dip in and out of it at will. Or, if you prefer, with abandon.*

---

### Ingredients:

*8 Tbsp. salted butter*

*Juice of 1 lemon*

*1/4 cup powdered sugar*

### Lemon Whipped Cream

*1 cup chilled heavy whipping cream*

*2 Tbsp. sugar*

*1 Tbsp. lemon zest*

*2 tsp. lemon juice*

### *Servings:*

*Serve with 8 Sweet Crepes*
*(your preference of batter)*

*Servings: 8 filled crepes*

*Prep time: 10 minutes*

*Cooking time: 0*

### *Nutritional Info:*

*Calories: 175, Sodium: 90 mg, Dietary Fiber: 0.1 g, Total Fat: 16.3 g, Total Carbs: 7.6 g, Protein: 0.6 g.*

### Directions:

1. Combine butter, lemon juice and powdered sugar and set aside.

2. Combine all ingredients in medium bowl and beat to stiff peaks.
3. Spread each warm crepe down its center with a Tbsp. of butter. Sprinkle with lemon juice and powdered sugar. Fold the crepe, then fold again to make triangle. Stack at angles and top with whipped cream.

# :: CARAMEL-CITRON ::

## (Caramelized Lemon Sauce)

*This recipe takes the sweet and sour love triangle of crepes, lemons, and butter to the next level. Time and heat bring out lemon's darker, more mellow flavors. Serve aside a flourish of thinly sliced lemon pieces.*

---

### INGREDIENTS:

*1/4 cup of water*

*1 cup sugar*

*3 Tbsp. fresh lemon juice*

*2 Tbsp. unsalted butter, cut into small pieces*

*2 Tbsp. water*

### *Servings:*

*Serve with 8 Sweet Crepes*

*(your preference of batter)*

*Servings: 8 filled crepes*

*Prep time: 5 minutes*

*Cook time: 15 minutes*

### *Nutritional Info:*

*Calories: 121, Sodium: 22 mg,*

*Dietary Fiber: 0 g, Total Fat: 2.9 g,*

*Total Carbs: 25.1 g, Protein: 0.8 g.*

### DIRECTIONS:

1. Over medium-high heat, cook the sugar and 1/4 cup water, stirring occasionally, until sugar has dissolved and syrup is clear. Bring the

mixture to a boil, without stirring and without letting sugar crystals form on the side of the pot. Continue to let it boil until it turns a dark amber.

2. Remove from heat and whisk in lemon juice, butter, and 2 Tbsp. water. Serve over folded crepes.

# :: CARAMEL SALÉ ::

## (Salted Caramel Sauce)

*Salted caramels started trending about 10 years ago, but salt has always been the secret ingredient in caramels' complex yumminess. If this recipe isn't quite sweet enough for you, serve it up with whipped cream or vanilla ice cream.*

---

### INGREDIENTS:

*3/4 cup salted butter*

*3/4 cup heavy cream*

*1 1/4 cup granulated sugar*

*3/4 cup water*

*1/8 tsp. sea or other coarse salt*

### *Servings:*

*Servings: 6 filled crepes*

*Prep time: 10 minutes*

*Cook time: 25 minutes*

### *Nutritional Info:*

*Calories: 412, Sodium: 209 mg,*

*Dietary Fiber: 0 g, Total Fat: 28.6 g,*

*Total Carbs: 42.1 g, Protein: 0.6 g.*

### DIRECTIONS:

1. Melt the butter in the heavy cream in a saucepan set over medium-low heat. Remove the pan from the heat as soon as the butter has melted. In a separate pan over medium low, mix sugar and water, allowing the sugar to dissolve. Avoid stirring it— it sticks too much to the spoon. Instead, swirl the pan.

2. When the caramel colors a rich gold, take the pan off the heat and slowly pour in the hot cream and melted butter in a thin stream, watching that the foaming mixture doesn't come over the lip of the pan. Return the mixture to low heat, whisking constantly, for two minutes. Remove from the heat and add salt, stirring till dissolves.
3. Spread each open crepe with caramel cream. Fold in half, then fold again to make a triangle. Stack at angles, allowing the cream to ooze out of the crepes. Drizzle the last of the cream over the stack.

## :: BEURRE AMARETTO ::

### (Amaretto and Butter)

*Amaretto smells like almonds and tastes like love. These crepes are perfectly romantic. Prepare them for a first date— or a twentieth anniversary dinner.*

---

### INGREDIENTS:

*1 stick (4 ounces) salted butter, cut into pieces*

*1 cup confectioners' sugar*

*3 Tbsp. amaretto*

*2 egg yolks*

*1/4 cup of sliced, toasted almonds.*

### *Servings:*

*Serve with 8 Sweet Crepes*

*(your preference of batter)*

*Servings: 8 filled crepes*

*Prep time: 5 minutes*

*Cooking time: 10 minutes*

### *Nutritional Info:*

*Calories: 208, Sodium: 523 mg,*

*Dietary Fiber: 0.4 g, Total Fat: 14.1 g,*

*Total Carbs: 15.7 g, Protein: 1.4 g*

### DIRECTIONS:

1. Melt the butter in a double boiler. Slowly whisk in the sugar until it dissolves. Continue to whisk as you add the amaretto and then the egg yolks, one at a time. Cook for another 3-5 minutes, whisking constantly.

2. Spoon sauce down each crepe's center. Roll the crepes and serve them seam side down, sprinkled with toasted almonds.

# :: La Suzette ::

## (Sugar, Lemon Juice, Whipped Cream)

*La Suzette, c'est magnifique! This most classic of French sweet crepes is perfect for every occasion, whether you're making a quick dessert for the family, or impressing new in-laws. Like many great foods, Suzette has an origin myth: supposedly, a young kitchen assistant burnt the liqueurs while rushing a crepe for the Prince of Wales. This is exactly the crepe to serve the next time royalty drops by.*

---

### Ingredients:

*6 Tbsp. unsalted butter, softened, plus more for buttering*

*1/2 cup sugar*

*2 Tbsp. cognac*

*1/4 cup Grand Marnier*

*1 Tbsp. orange zest*

*1/3 cup orange juice*

### *Servings:*

*Serve with 8 Sweet Crepes*

*(your preference of batter)*

*Servings: 8 filled crepes*

*Prep time: 15 minutes*

*Cooking time: Just a few minutes under the broiler*

### *Nutritional Info:*

*Calories: 159, Sodium: 647 mg,*

*Dietary Fiber: 0.1 g, Total Fat: 8.7 g,*

*Total Carbs: 13.8 g, Protein: 0.2 g.*

## DIRECTIONS:

1. Preheat oven on broil.
2. Blend 6 Tbsp. of butter with 1/4 cup of the sugar and the orange zest. Gradually add the orange juice until incorporated.
3. Butter a large, rimmed baking sheet and sprinkle it with sugar. Spread 2 generous tsp. of the orange butter in the center of each crêpe. Fold the crêpes in half and in half again. Arrange them on the baking sheet overlapping slightly. Sprinkle with the remaining sugar and broil on the middle shelf of the oven until they are caramelized, about 2 minutes.
4. While the crepes are in the oven, heat the Grand Marnier and cognac. Light it carefully with a long-handled match or lighter, and drizzle the flaming mixture over the crêpes. Serve immediately.

## :: La Suzette Reprise ::

### (Orange Marmalade, Grand Marnier, Butter, Sugar)

*This is a twist on crepes suzette. Chunky marmalade gives extra character, while the cayenne provides kick.*

---

## Ingredients :

*3/4 cup orange marmalade*

*3/4 cup water*

*3 tsp. white granulated sugar*

*Pinch cayenne*

*3/4 cup Grand Marnier® or other orange liqueur*

### *Servings :*

*Serve with 8 Sweet Crepes*

*(your preference of batter)*

*Servings: 8 filled crepes*

*Prep time: 5 minutes*

*Cooking time: 10 minutes*

### *Nutritional Info:*

*Calories: 179, Sodium: 23 mg,*

*Dietary Fiber: 0.2 g, Total Fat: 5.6 g,*

*Total Carbs: 22.3 g, Protein: 0.4 g.*

## Directions :

1. Combine orange marmalade, water, sugar and cayenne in a small saucepan over low heat. Simmer until reduced to a thin syrup and drizzle over the crepes.

2. In another small saucepan, heat the Grand Marnier® until it just barely begins to simmer. Ignite it with a long-handled lighter or fireplace match and pour it over the crepes at the table.

## Whipped Cream

*1 cup heavy cream*

*2 Tbsp. confectioners' sugar*

## Directions:

1. In a medium sized bowl, blend cream and sugar. Whisk until peaks form, using a hand whisk or electric mixer on low.

# :: Poire Chocolat ::

## (Red Wine-Poached Pear, Roasted Almonds, Nutella Whipped Cream)

*A blend of flavors exotic and homey. Make the Nutella whipped cream ahead, up until the step when you chill it, then blend it for the last time right before you serve.*

---

### Ingredients:

*Nutella whipped cream*

*2 cups heavy cream*

*1 cup Nutella*

### Poached Pears:

*4 Bosc pears*

*2 1/2 cups Pinot Noir or other light, fruity red wine*

*1/2 cup sugar*

*1 strip of lemon peel, about 2 inches long and 3/4 inch wide*

*1/2 a vanilla bean*

*1 1/2 cups water*

### Servings:

*Serve with 8 Sweet Crepes*

*(your preference of batter)*

*Servings: 8 filled crepes*

*Prep time: 10 minutes*

*Cooking time: 15 minutes*

### Nutritional Info:

*Calories: 404, Sodium: 28 mg,*

*Dietary Fiber: 4.8 g, Total Fat: 19.7 g,*

*Total Carbs: 48.2 g, Protein: 2.5 g.*

## Directions:

1. Bring heavy cream to a boil over medium-high heat. Remove from heat and whisk in Nutella until smooth. Transfer mixture to a bowl and refrigerate until chilled. Thoroughly beat the chilled mixture with electric beaters until creamy and smooth and use immediately.

## Poached Pears:

1. Peel the pears, but leave the stems on. Place pears in a saucepan large enough to hold them lying down. Add the wine, sugar, lemon peel, vanilla bean and water, and stir to distribute evenly. Bring to a boil over medium high heat, then reduce the heat to low.
2. Simmer gently for about half an hour. To keep the pears submerged in the liquid, set a heatproof plate or pan lid on top of them. Remove the plate covering the pears and let them and the liquid cool.
3. Lift the pears from the liquid with a slotted spoon. You can put each pear in its own bowl or set all four together. Boil the cooking liquid over high heat until it is reduced by half, about 10 minutes. Pour the liquid over the pears.
4. When pears and liquid have cooled, remove the lemon peel and vanilla bean and discard.
5. Prepare crepes and set aside.
6. Balancing poached pears on the wide end, slice vertically into slices of about half an inch.
7. Using a rubber spatula, spread each crepe down its center with Nutella whipped cream. Arrange pear slices down the center of the crepe so they overlap just a bit. Roll crepes and serve seam side down, sprinkled with toasted almonds.

# Traditional French Savory Crepes

Here are 20 savory crepe recipes sure to make your mouth water. Enjoy them for dinner or lunch.

Each of these can be made with savory crepes, but you can try them with a sweet crepe recipe too, if you leave out the added sugar from the batter.

Except in the case where you're cooking the ingredients in the still-cooking crepe, cooking times in these recipes are only for how long it takes to prepare the filling ingredients, and, if necessary, bake the final product.

In most cases, we've left salt and pepper additions up to you.

# :: JAMBON-FROMAGE ::

## (Ham & Cheese)

*Any ham and cheese will do for this simply savory combo. If you choose Black Forest and brie, serve a few very fresh slices of a tart apple, like Granny Smith or Pink Lady, at the side.*

---

### INGREDIENTS:

*8 slices Black Forest ham*

*8 slices brie, each about 4 inches long*

### *Servings:*

*Serve with 8 Savory Crepes (your preference of batter)*

*Servings: 8 filled crepes*

*Prep time: 5 minutes*

*Cooking time: 12 minutes*

### *Nutritional Info:*

*Calories: 273, Sodium: 793 mg, Dietary Fiber: 0.4 g, Total Fat: 21.2 g, Total Carbs: 1.4 g, Protein: 18.8 g.*

### DIRECTIONS:

1. This crepe needs to be heated, either on a crepe pan at medium heat or in an oven at 400.
2. Place ham first, then cheese, along the center of each crepe. Fold once, then again to make triangles. Arranged the folded crepes in the baking

dish and heat about 12 minutes, until you can see cheese oozing out the sides, and the crepes are toasted brown.

# :: La Parisienne ::

## (Ham, Swiss Cheese, Tomatoes, Basil)

*A classist Parisian street lunch or light dinner. Here the homey taste of ham and swiss gets bright touches with tomatoes and summer's favorite, basil.*

---

### Ingredients:

*1 cup chopped ham*

*1 1/2 cups shredded Swiss cheese*

*About 3 large tomatoes (enough for 8 slices)*

*8 basil leaves*

### *Servings:*

*Serve with 8 Savory Crepes (your preference of batter)*

*Servings: 8 filled crepes*

*Prep time: 10 minutes*

*Cooking time: 10 minutes*

### *Nutritional Info:*

*Calories: 117, Sodium: 262 mg, Dietary Fiber: 1.1 g, Total Fat: 7.2 g, Total Carbs: 4.4 g, Protein: 8.9 g.*

### Directions:

1. This crepe needs to be heated, either on a crepe pan at medium heat or in an oven at 400.
2. Slice tomatoes and lay the slices on a paper towel to absorb extra moisture.

3. Combine ham and cheese in a medium bowl. Evenly divide the mixture between the 8 crepes, placing a mound right in the center of each crepe. Fold in each side of the crepe so the center mound is all that's exposed (**Chapter 5: How To Fold Your Crepes**); place one slice of tomato and a leaf of basil on top of each mound.
4. Heat for 10 minutes, until the cheese has melted and the crepes are golden brown.

# :: PETIT DEJUNER ::

## (Egg, Ham, Swiss Cheese)

*Brunch is served! Here's your Sunday morning favorite, wrapped up in a delicious, homemade crepe. Get these scrambled eggs extra fluffy by whisking thoroughly then cooking over low heat.*

---

### INGREDIENTS:

*8 eggs*

*Pinch salt*

*1 Tbsp. butter*

*8 slices Black Forest ham, cut into halves*

*8 slices Swiss cheese, cut into halves*

### *Servings:*

*Serve with 8 Savory Crepes (your preference of batter)*

*Servings: 8 filled crepes*

*Prep time: 15 minutes*

*Cooking time: 10 minutes*

### *Nutritional Info:*

*Calories: 228, Sodium: 510 mg, Dietary Fiber: 0.4 g, Total Fat: 16 g, Total Carbs: 2.9 g, Protein: 17.7 g.*

### DIRECTIONS:

1. The filling in this crepe needs to be cooked, either on a crepe pan at medium heat or in an oven at 400.

2. Whisk the eggs and salt thoroughly in a medium bowl. When you think you've whisked enough, give them an extra two minutes of whisking.
3. Place ham along the center of each crepe. Spoon whisked eggs on top of the ham and top the eggs with the halved Swiss cheese slice, end-to-end.
4. Roll the crepes and place them in the baking dish, seam side down. Heat about 10 minutes.

# :: La Bretonne ::

## (Eggs, Ham, Swiss, Tomatoes)

*Prepare this recipe as you cook each crepe, cracking the egg right on top of the crepe as it cooks. Have all your ingredients prepare and at the ready so you don't have to pause as you fill the crepes.*

---

### Ingredients:

*8 eggs*

*8 slices of Swiss cheese, cut into halves*

*8 slices of Black Forest ham, cut into halves*

*3 large tomatoes (enough for 8 slices)*

### *Servings:*

*Serve with 8 Savory Crepes (your preference of batter)*

*Servings: 8 filled crepes*

*Prep time: 10 minutes*

*Cooking time: 10 minutes*

### *Nutritional Info:*

*Calories: 227, Sodium: 484 mg, Dietary Fiber: 1.2 g, Total Fat: 14.7 g, Total Carbs: 5.6 g, Protein: 18.3 g.*

### Directions:

1. Slice tomatoes into thin circles, then crescents. Place them on a paper towel to absorb extra moisture.

2. Start by pouring the crepe batter as you normally would, flipping when ready. As soon as you've flipped the crepe, crack an egg in its center. Gently scramble the egg as it rests on the crepe by piercing the yolk with a fork and spreading the egg to the edges of the crepe.
3. When the egg has become firm, top it with slices of tomato, ham, and cheese, adding these slices only on one half of the crepe. When you can see the cheese melting, fold over the other half of the crepe.
4. Feed your fellow diners one at a time, as each filled crepe is finished, or keep the filled crepes in a baking dish in a 200 degree oven until you're ready to serve them all at once.

## :: ALSACE ::

### (Ham, Mushrooms, Swiss Cheese, Bechamel)

*The five "mother sauces," béchamel, veloute, espangnole, Hollandaise, and tomate, are the basics on which all French sauces are built. They can transform even the most humble ingredients into a meal to be remembered. Béchamel is the simplest and most adaptable.*

---

## INGREDIENTS:

### BECHAMEL SAUCE

*2 cups whole milk*

*1/2 cup salted butter, cut into pieces*

*2 1/4 Tbsp. flour*

*1/8 tsp. salt*

*Pinch of nutmeg*

### CREPE FILLING

*1 1/2 cups mushrooms*

*1 small yellow onion*

*2 Tbsp. olive oil*

*2 tsp. fresh thyme*

*1/4 tsp. salt*

### *Servings:*

*Serve with 8 Savory Crepes*

*(your preference of batter)*

*Servings: 8 filled crepes*

*Prep time: 15 minutes*

*Cooking time: 40 minutes*

### *Nutritional Info:*

*Calories: 288, Sodium: 475 mg,*

*Dietary Fiber: 0.7 g, Total Fat: 24.2 g,*

*Total Carbs: 7.6 g, Protein: 11.1 g.*

*1 cup chopped ham*

*1 1/2 cups shredded Swiss cheese*

## DIRECTIONS: BECHAMEL SAUCE

1. Place 2/3 cup milk and butter In a medium saucepan melt the butter in 2/3 cup of milk over medium-low.
2. Meanwhile, whisk together the remaining milk, the flour and salt, in a medium bowl.
3. Add about half the warmed milk mixture to the cold, and combine them, then pour all the bowl's contents into the saucepan.
4. Continuing to whisk, cook over medium-low heat until thickened. If you'd like to test with a thermometer, the temperature will be around 180 degrees. Remove from heat and stir in nutmeg.

## DIRECTIONS: CREPE FILLING

1. Preheat oven to 400 degrees. Butter a large baking dish; oil a cookie sheet.
2. Slice the mushrooms and chop the onion. In a large bowl, toss them together with olive oil, thyme and salt. Spread on the cookie sheet and bake for 10 minutes, stirring once with a spatula.
3. Distribute ham and mushrooms down the center of each opened crepe. Sprinkle with cheese. Roll the crepes, and place them seam side down in the baking dish. Top with béchamel. Bake for 10 minutes.

# :: FRANCILIENNE ::

## (Sautéed Chicken, Onion and Mushrooms in Onion-Infused Bechamel)

*To make onion-infused béchamel, just peel and quarter a small yellow onion and allow it to simmer in the milk and butter mixture. Discard it when you're ready to make the sauce.*

---

### INGREDIENTS:

*2 pounds skinless, boneless chicken breast, cut into strips*

*Salt and pepper to taste*

*1/2 cup olive oil*

*2 cup assorted sliced mushrooms (such as crimini and oyster)*

*1 yellow onion*

*4 garlic cloves, minced*

*1 Tbsp. fresh rosemary*

*2 cups low-salt chicken broth*

*1/4 cup sherry or dry white wine*

*1/4 cup salted butter*

### *Servings:*

*Serve with 8 Savory Crepes (your preference of batter)*

*Servings: 8 filled crepes*

*Prep time: 10 minutes*

*Cooking time: 30 minutes*

### *Nutritional Info:*

*Calories: 322, Sodium: 118 mg, Dietary Fiber: 0.7 g, Total Fat: 22.5 g, Total Carbs: 2.7 g, Protein: 26.4 g.*

## DIRECTIONS:

1. Season chicken with salt and pepper. Heat about half the olive oil in a medium nonstick skillet over medium heat. Sauté chicken until golden and almost cooked through. Transfer to a plate.
2. Heat the remaining oil in the same skillet; add mushrooms, garlic, and rosemary and cook, stirring frequently, until mushrooms are golden brown. Stir in chicken broth, sherry and chicken strips; simmer another 5 minutes. Stir in butter and allow it to melt before removing from heat.
3. Distribute chicken and mushrooms down the center of each opened crepe. Roll the crepes, and place them seam side down in the baking dish. Top with béchamel. Bake for 10 minutes.

# :: JURA ::

## (Bacon, Swiss Cheese, Tomato, light Garlic)

*This savory lunch or brunch crepe combines flavors you might think of as heavy, but with a light touch. Draining the tomatoes keeps the crepe from becoming soggy. Enjoy this crepe with a crisp salad in a white wine vinaigrette.*

---

### INGREDIENTS:

*1/2 pound bacon*

*4 tomatoes*

*4 cloves garlic, minced or crushed*

*3 cups grated Gruyere cheese*

### *Servings:*

*Serve with 8 Savory Crepes*

*(your preference of batter)*

*Servings: 8 filled crepes*

*Prep time: 10 minutes*

*Cooking time: 25 minutes*

### *Nutritional Info:*

*Calories: 334, Sodium: 794 mg,*

*Dietary Fiber: 0.8 g, Total Fat: 25.1 g,*

*Total Carbs: 3.4 g, Protein: 23.2 g.*

## DIRECTIONS:

1. This crepe needs to be heated, either on a crepe pan at medium heat or in an oven at 400.
2. Chop tomatoes and let them rest in a colander over the sink.
3. Cut the bacon slices in half and cook until crispy. Remove them from the pan. Sauté garlic in the bacon fat for about a minute; add tomatoes and cook, stirring, for five minutes, then remove from heat.
4. Place a layer of bacon strips at the center of each crepe. Top with cheese, then tomatoes, then finish with more cheese. Fold in each side of the crepe so the center mound is all that's exposed. Heat for about 10 minutes, until cheese melts.

# :: MARSEILLE ::

## (Chicken, Ratatouille)

*This recipe is redolent of the flavors of France's Mediterranean coast. Named for the city that brought us tomato-y bouillabaisse and garlic-rich aioli, the Marseille crepe soaks up the tangy, rustic flavors of fresh vegetable ratatouille.*

---

### INGREDIENTS:

*2 small eggplants, peeled and cut into 1-inch cubes*

*Salt*

*2 Tbsp. olive oil*

*8 medium boneless, skinless chicken breast halves*

*4 zucchini unpeeled and thinly sliced*

*2 yellow onions, thinly sliced*

*2 green bell peppers, cut into 1-inch pieces*

*1 pounds mushrooms, sliced*

*32 ounce can of diced tomatoes, drained*

*4 cloves of garlic, minced*

*1 1/2 Tbsp. fresh basil*

### *Servings:*

*Serve with 8 Savory Crepes*

*(your preference of batter)*

*Servings: 8 filled crepes*

*Prep time: 15 minutes*

*Cooking time: 30 minutes*

### *Nutritional Info:*

*Calories: 418, Sodium: 242 mg,*

*Dietary Fiber: 9.1 g, Total Fat: 10.6 g,*

*Total Carbs: 22.5 g, Protein: 61.3 g.*

## Directions:

1. Place the eggplant cubes in a colander over the sink and salt liberally, tossing to be sure all pieces are salted. Let them drain for five minutes, then rinse and place in one layer on paper towels.
2. Heat oil in large skillet over medium heat. Add chicken and sauté until lightly browned, 3-5 minutes. Add zucchini, eggplant, onion, green pepper, and mushrooms, and let them cook for about 15 minutes, stirring occasionally. Add tomatoes, garlic, and green bell pepper. Let simmer for about 15 minutes. Stir in basil.
3. Distribute ratatouille down the center of each opened crepe. Roll the crepes, and serve them seam side down.

# :: TOULOUSE ::

## (Ground Beef, Ratatouille)

*Here's a hearty variation on a theme— France's favorite vegetable stew, made richly dense with ground beef. All the ingredients are simple, but together they create a fine dining experience. Serve for guests or just when you want to make your loved ones feel special.*

---

### INGREDIENTS:

- *2 small eggplants peeled and cut into 1-inch cubes*
- *Salt*
- *1 pound ground beef*
- *2 yellow onions, thinly sliced*
- *6 cloves garlic, minced*
- *2 zucchini unpeeled and thinly sliced*
- *2 yellow squash*
- *1 green bell pepper, cut into 1-inch pieces*
- *1 yellow bell pepper, cut into 1 inch pieces*
- *3 tomatoes, diced*
- *2 Tbsp. fresh basil*

### *Servings:*

*Serve with 8 Savory Crepes*

*(your preference of batter)*

*Servings: 8 filled crepes*

*Prep time: 15 minutes*

*Cooking time: 30 minutes*

### *Nutritional Info:*

*Calories: 187, Sodium: 74 mg,*

*Dietary Fiber: 7.7 g, Total Fat: 4.2 g,*

*Total Carbs: 18.3 g, Protein: 20.9 g.*

## DIRECTIONS:

1. Place the eggplant cubes in a colander over the sink and salt liberally, tossing to be sure all pieces are salted. Let them drain for five minutes, then rinse and place in one layer on paper towels.
2. Sauté the ground beef over medium heat, breaking it up into small pieces. Remove to a plate with a slotted spoon.
3. Sauté the onion and garlic in the beef fat. Return the beef to the skillet and add zucchini, squash, eggplant, green and yellow peppers, and let them cook for about 15 minutes, stirring occasionally. Add tomatoes. Let simmer for about 15 minutes. Stir in basil.
4. Distribute ratatouille down the center of each opened crepe. Roll the crepes, and serve them seam side down.

## :: SAVOYARD ::

### (Sausage, Sautéed Apples, Swiss Cheese)

*This droolingly good combination works best with Gruyere cheese. Try it for brunch or for a hearty midday meal on a wintry day. To dress it up for dinner, use a chicken apple sausage or a fine pork sausage flavored with fennel.*

---

### INGREDIENTS:

*2 12-ounce packages frozen breakfast sausage links*

*2 cups apple cider*

*4 apples, such as Jonathan or Johnny Gold*

*1 Tbsp. salted butter*

*16 ounces Swiss cheese, grated*

### *Servings:*

*Serve with 8 Savory Crepes*

*(your preference of batter)*

*Servings: 8 filled crepes*

*Prep time: 10 minutes*

*Cooking time: 15 minutes*

### *Nutritional Info:*

*Calories: 413, Sodium: 864 mg,*

*Dietary Fiber: 2.3 g, Total Fat: 22.1 g,*

*Total Carbs: 27.5 g, Protein: 27.9 g.*

## DIRECTIONS:

1. In a saucepan over medium heat, sauté the sausages until they're browned on all sides. Add apple cider and increase heat to medium-high. Simmer the sausages until cider becomes a sticky glaze. Remove from heat.
2. Slice the apples into twelve slices each. Over medium low, sauté them in the butter just until the peels begin to pull away from the flesh.
3. Distribute sausage and apples down the center of each opened crepe. Top with the grated cheese. Roll the crepes, and serve them seam side down.

# :: La Jardiniere ::

## (Mozzarella, Tomatoes, Artichoke Hearts, Bell Peppers)

*Here's a crepe like one of your favorite pizzas. Mellow mozzarella and sweet bell peppers balance the tangy, salty flavors of artichoke and tomato. Serve these crepes as an upgrade to pizza— it comes together faster than Friday night delivery!*

---

### INGREDIENTS:

*1 Tbsp. olive oil*

*1 yellow onion*

*2-3 bell peppers*

*1 cup sliced artichoke hearts (not marinated)*

*2-3 tomatoes*

*1 tsp. dried oregano*

*16 ounces Mozzarella, grated*

### *Servings:*

*Serve with 8 Savory Crepes*

*(your preference of batter)*

*Servings: 8 filled crepes*

*Prep time: 15 minutes*

*Cooking time: 10 minutes*

### *Nutritional Info:*

*Calories: 211, Sodium: 374 mg,*

*Dietary Fiber: 2.9 g, Total Fat: 12.1 g,*

*Total Carbs: 9.4 g, Protein: 17.9 g.*

## DIRECTIONS:

1. This crepe needs to be heated, either on a crepe pan at medium heat or in an oven at 400.
2. Slice onion and dice the other fresh vegetables. Sauté the onion in olive oil for about five minutes, then add bell peppers, artichoke hearts, tomatoes and oregano. Sauté about five minutes more.
3. Distribute the sautéed vegetables down the center of each opened crepe. Top with the half the grated cheese. Roll the crepes, and place them seam side down in the baking dish. Top with the rest of the cheese and heat for about 10 minutes.

## :: LA NORMANDE ::

### (Turkey, Swiss Cheese, Tomatoes, Basil, Parsley)

*This super easy recipe is one small degree more difficult than making a sandwich, and ten times more impressive.*

---

### INGREDIENTS:

*8 slices of turkey sandwich meat*

*8 slices Swiss cheese*

*About 3 tomatoes (enough for 8 slices)*

*8 basil leaves*

### *Servings:*

*Serve with 8 Savory Crepes*

*(your preference of batter)*

*Servings: 8 filled crepes*

*Prep time: 10 minutes*

*Cooking time: 10 minutes*

### *Nutritional Info:*

*Calories: 133, Sodium: 194 mg,*

*Dietary Fiber: 0.6 g, Total Fat: 8.9 g,*

*Total Carbs: 3.7 g, Protein: 9.8 g.*

### DIRECTIONS:

1. This crepe needs to be heated, either on a crepe pan at medium heat or in an oven at 400.
2. Slice tomatoes and lay the slices on a paper towel to absorb extra moisture.

3. In the center of each crepe, place a slice of turkey topped with a slice of cheese. Fold in each side of the crepe so the center mound is all that's exposed; place one slice of tomato and a leaf of basil on top of each mound.
4. Heat for 10 minutes, until the cheese has melted and the crepes are golden brown.

# :: La Biquette ::

## (Bell peppers, Tomatoes, Basil, Goat Cheese)

*"La biquette" is an endearment for a lady goat, in this case, the dear nanny who supplies the creamy cheese topping. This summery crepe is ripe for a dinner at sunset.*

---

### Ingredients:

*1 Tbsp. olive oil*

*2-3 bell peppers*

*2-3 tomatoes*

*8 basil leaves*

*8 ounces crumbly goat cheese*

### *Servings:*

*Serve with 8 Savory Crepes*

*(your preference of batter)*

*Servings: 8 filled crepes*

*Prep time: 10 minutes*

*Cooking time: 10 minutes*

### *Nutritional Info:*

*Calories: 111, Sodium: 84 mg,*

*Dietary Fiber: 1 g, Total Fat: 8 g,*

*Total Carbs: 6 g, Protein: 5.6 g.*

### Directions:

1. This crepe needs to be heated, either on a crepe pan at medium heat or in an oven at 400.
2. Slice onion and dice the bell peppers and tomatoes and sauté them in olive oil for about five minutes.

3. Using a slotted spoon, place some of the bell pepper and tomato mixture in the center of each crepe. Fold in each side of the crepe so the center mound is all that's exposed. Sprinkle with goat cheese and place a leaf of basil on top of each mound.
4. Heat for 10 minutes, until the cheese is browning and the crepes are golden brown.

# :: La Fromagerie ::

## (Goat Cheese, Swiss Cheese, Mozzarella, Basil, Parsley)

*Enough with the vegetables, sometimes you just want cheese. Prepare these as you cook each crepe, grating the cheeses on top of each crepe as it cooks. Have all your ingredients ready so you don't have to pause as you fill the crepes.*

---

### Ingredients

*Crepe batter for 8 crepes*

*1 1/2 cups Swiss cheese, grated*

*1 1/2 cups Mozzarella cheese, grated*

*1/2 cup goat cheese*

*1/ 4 cup minced fresh basil*

*1/4 cup minced fresh parsley*

### *Servings:*

*Serve with 8 Savory Crepes*

*(your preference of batter)*

*Servings: 8 filled crepes*

*Prep time: 10 minutes*

*Cooking time: 10 minutes*

### *Nutritional Info:*

*Calories: 170, Sodium: 192 mg,*

*Dietary Fiber: 0.1 g, Total Fat: 11.9 g,*

*Total Carbs: 2.1 g, Protein: 13.7 g.*

### Directions:

1. Start by pouring the crepe batter as you normally would, flipping when ready. As soon as you've flipped the crepe, sprinkle one half of it with the Swiss and mozzarella cheeses. Continue cooking the crepe as the cheese

melts, watching the crepe edges for browning. Fold over the other half of the crepe and remove from the pan.

2. Keep filled crepes in a 200 degree oven until they're all prepared. Once you've plated them, sprinkle each folded crepe with goat cheese, basil and parsley.

# :: Jambon Pesto ::

## (Ham, Emmental Cheese, Pesto)

*This rough-cut basil gives the crepes a rustic look. If you prefer a smooth pesto, spread it on the sliced cheese before you fold the crepes, then grate some extra cheese to sprinkle over the folded crepes.*

---

### Ingredients:

*1/2 cup pesto*

*8 slices Black Forest ham*

*8 slices Emmental cheese*

### Pesto (makes 1/2 cup)

*1 cup coarsely chopped basil*

*1 Tbsp. olive oil*

*1 tsp. minced garlic*

*1/2 tsp. lemon juice*

*Salt and freshly ground black pepper*

### *Servings:*

*Serve with 8 Savory Crepes*
*(your preference of batter)*

*Servings: 8 filled crepes*

*Prep time: 15 minutes*

*Cooking time: 10 minutes*

### *Nutritional Info:*

*Calories: 226, Sodium: 461 mg, Dietary Fiber: 0.7 g, Total Fat: 18.1 g, Total Carbs: 2.3 g, Protein: 13.9 g.*

### Directions:

1. Combine all the pesto ingredients and mash together with a wooden spoon, or even your hands.

2. This crepe needs to be heated, either on a crepe pan at medium heat or in an oven at 400.
3. In the center of each crepe, place a slice of ham topped with a slice of cheese. Fold in each side of the crepe so the center mound is all that's exposed; place a serving of pesto on top of each mound. Heat until you can see the cheese melting, watching to be sure the pesto doesn't crisp.

# :: FLORENTINE ::

## (Eggs, Spinach, Feta)

*Crepes cross the border to Italy in this recipe, calling up the rich flavors of Tuscany. The real border dispute comes down to what wine to enjoy with these crepes. Chianti would suit nicely for those who tend toward Italian reds, while a buttery Chardonnay would stand up nicely if you favor white wines.*

---

### INGREDIENTS:

*4 cups creamed spinach*

*4 hard-cooked eggs, chopped*

*2 cups crumbled feta cheese*

*Salt and freshly ground pepper, to taste*

*Freshly grated nutmeg, to taste*

### *Servings:*

*Serve with 8 Savory Crepes*

*(your preference of batter)*

*Servings: 8 filled crepes*

*Prep time: 5 minutes*

*Cooking time: 10 minutes*

### *Nutritional Info:*

*Calories: 219, Sodium: 651 mg,*

*Dietary Fiber: 1 g, Total Fat: 16.2 g,*

*Total Carbs: 7 g, Protein: 9.8 g.*

## Directions:

1. This crepe needs to be heated, either on a crepe pan at medium heat or in an oven at 400.
2. Combine the creamed spinach, eggs, 1 cup of the cheese, salt, pepper and nutmeg. Spread 1/4 cup of the filling over each opened crepe and fold into quarters. Transfer to the prepared baking sheet. Sprinkle the crepes with the remaining cheese. Heat about 10 minutes, until the cheese is browning.

# :: VEGETARIAN ::

## (Sauteed Mushrooms, Tomato, Zucchini, Onion and Garlic)

*Just the lightest sautéing will bring out the flavors of vegetables in this recipe without making them wilt. The mushrooms take on the role of meat, providing a dense texture and mellow backdrop to zesty tomatoes and garlic.*

---

### INGREDIENTS:

*2 Tbsp. olive oil*

*4 zucchini unpeeled and thinly sliced*

*2 yellow onions, thinly sliced*

*1 pounds mushrooms, sliced*

*32 ounce can of diced tomatoes, drained*

*4 cloves of garlic, minced*

*1 1/2 Tbsp. fresh basil*

*1 tsp. dried oregano*

### *Servings:*

*Serve with 8 Savory Crepes*

*(your preference of batter)*

*Servings: 8 filled crepes*

*Prep time: 15 minutes*

*Cooking time: 20 minutes*

### *Nutritional Info:*

*Calories: 92, Sodium: 197 mg,*

*Dietary Fiber: 3.2 g, Total Fat: 3.9 g,*

*Total Carbs: 12.4 g, Protein: 4.2 g.*

### DIRECTIONS:

1. Heat oil in large skillet over medium heat. Add zucchini, onion, and mushrooms, and let them cook for about 15 minutes, stirring

occasionally. Add tomatoes, garlic, and oregano. Cook for about 15 minutes, then stir in basil.

2. Using a slotted spoon, distribute the cooked vegetables down the center of each opened crepe. Roll the crepes, and serve them seam side down.

# :: LA CREVETTE ::

## (Garlic Sauteed Shrimp & Arugula)

*You've enjoyed arugula raw in salads and sandwiches, why not try it lightly sauteed? Here it soaks up garlicky goodness and provides a deep green counterpoint to pink shrimp.*

---

### INGREDIENTS:

*2 Tbsp. butter*

*4 cloves garlic, minced*

*2 pounds shrimp, peeled and deveined*

*1 Tbsp. lemon juice*

*1 pinch cayenne pepper*

*1 cup arugula*

### *Servings:*

*Serve with 8 Savory Crepes*

*(your preference of batter)*

*Servings: 8 filled crepes*

*Prep time: 20 minutes*

*Cooking time: 15 minutes*

### *Nutritional Info:*

*Calories: 164, Sodium: 299 mg,*

*Dietary Fiber: 0.1 g, Total Fat: 4.9 g,*

*Total Carbs: 2.4 g, Protein: 26 g.*

### DIRECTIONS:

1. Sauté the garlic in butter over low heat. Add shrimp, stir, cover the pan and cook until about 5 minutes, until the shrimp are pink. Add lemon juice and cayenne pepper and cook about 5 minutes more with the pan partly covered.

2. Add the arugula, stir a few times, and remove pan from heat.
3. Divide the shrimp and arugula between the crepes, spooning the mixture into one half of the crepe, then folding the other half over. Serve immediately or keep all the filled crepes in a 200 degree oven and serve as soon as all are ready.

# :: RATATOUILLE ::

## (Eggplant, Zucchini, Mushroom)

*Simply satisfying ratatouille comes to us from the Provence region of France, the same fruitful locale that brings us world-class cuisine like salade Nicoise and the bean-rich soupe au pistou. All ratatouille's vegetable ingredients are at their best in the summer, but in the global produce economy you can find quite acceptable versions year round.*

---

### INGREDIENTS:

*2 small eggplants, peeled and cut into 1-inch cubes*

*Salt*

*2 Tbsp. olive oil*

*4 zucchini unpeeled and thinly sliced*

*2 yellow onions, thinly sliced*

*1 pounds mushrooms, sliced*

*2 green bell peppers, cut into 1-inch pieces*

*32 ounce can of diced tomatoes, drained*

*4 cloves of garlic, minced*

*1 1/2 Tbsp. fresh basil*

### *Servings:*

*Serve with 8 Savory Crepes*

*(your preference of batter)*

*Servings: 8 filled crepes*

*Prep time: 15 minutes*

*Cooking time: 20 minutes*

### *Nutritional Info:*

*Calories: 135, Sodium: 315 mg,*

*Dietary Fiber: 9.1 g, Total Fat: 4.4 g,*

*Total Carbs: 22.5 g, Protein: 6 g.*

*1-2 tsp. salt*

## Directions:

1. Place the eggplant cubes in a colander over the sink and salt liberally, tossing to be sure all pieces are salted. Let them drain for five minutes, then rinse and place in one layer on paper towels.
2. Heat oil in large skillet over medium heat. Add zucchini, eggplant, onion, and mushrooms, and let them cook for about 15 minutes, stirring occasionally. Add tomatoes, garlic, and green bell pepper. Salt with 1 tsp. of salt and taste; adjust if necessary. Simmer for about 15 minutes. Stir in basil.
3. Distribute ratatouille down the center of each opened crepe. Roll the crepes, and serve them seam side down.

# :: CAMPAGNE ::

## (Sausage, Sour Cream And Cheddar)

*This hearty dish makes a satisfying dinner. You can almost endlessly match and re-match sausage and cheese combinations. Swiss cheeses are great with fennel-flavored sausages.*

---

### INGREDIENTS:

*1 pound bulk pork sausage*

*1 yellow onion, chopped*

*1/4 tsp. dried marjoram*

*1 package (3 ounces) cream cheese, cut into cubes (cut it while it's cold)*

*1/2 cup shredded cheddar cheese*

*1/2 cup sour cream*

*1/4 cup butter, softened*

*Minced fresh parsley*

### *Servings:*

*Serve with 8 Savory Crepes*

*(your preference of batter)*

*Servings: 8 filled crepes*

*Prep time: 20 minutes*

*Cooking time: 30 minutes*

### *Nutritional Info:*

*Calories: 345, Sodium: 549 mg,*

*Dietary Fiber: 0.3 g, Total Fat: 30.9 g,*

*Total Carbs: 2.3 g, Protein: 14.3 g.*

### DIRECTIONS:

1. Preheat oven to 375 degrees. Butter a large baking dish.
2. Sauté the sausage in a large skillet, breaking it up with a fork. When it's cooked, remove it from the pan, leaving half the fat behind (discard the

rest). Sauté the onion and marjoram in the fat. Return the sausage to the pan. Add cheeses stir until they melt.

3. Spoon the sausage mixture down the center of each spread crepe. Roll the crepes and place them seam side down in the baking dish.
4. Cover and bake about 25 minutes. Combine sour cream and butter and spoon over the rolled crepes. Bake, uncovered, another 5 minutes. Sprinkle with parsley and serve.

# 9

## AMERICAN CREPE ADVENTURES

# *American Sweet Crepes*

## HAWAIIAN

*This sweet concoction created with tropical flavors will make you feel like you're vacationing on a Hawaiian island. A hit with kids — let them prepare their own.*

---

### INGREDIENTS:

*1 Banana*

*2 Tbsp. Nutella*

*1 Tbsp. chocolate sauce*

*Fresh mango slices or cubes (1/4 cup)*

*1 Tbsp. shredded coconut*

### *Servings:*

*Serve with 1 Sweet Crepe*

*(your preference of batter)*

*Servings: 1*

*Prep time: 5 minutes*

*Cooking time: 5 minutes*

### *Nutritional Info:*

*Calories: 467, Sodium: 17 mg,*

*Dietary Fiber: 6.5 g, Total Fat: 16.4 g,*

*Total Carbs: 78.8 g, Protein: 4.3 g.*

### DIRECTIONS:

1. Prepare a sweet crepe and lay it flat on your plate. Spread ½ with Nutella or chocolate sauce, then layer area with banana slices. Fold in half twice, creating a triangle shape. Over top, lay remaining banana slices, add mango cubes, then drizzle with chocolate sauce and shredded coconut. Serve warm. Vanilla ice cream optional, but pretty doggone yummy.

# Caramel Crazy

*Caramel cooks down deliciousness to its basic elements: warmed cream and sugar. You could just stop right there. But these crepes are topped with an extra layer of crunchy with crushed toffee.*

---

## Ingredients:

*1/4 cup warmed caramel sauce*

*1 scoop vanilla ice cream*

*1 crushed almond toffee candy like Brown & Haley's Almond Roca*

### *Servings:*

*Serve with 1 Sweet Crepe*

*(your preference of batter)*

*Servings: 1 filled crepe*

*Prep time: 5 minutes*

*Cooking time: 5 minutes*

### *Nutritional Info:*

*Calories: 370, Sodium: 363 mg,*

*Dietary Fiber: 1.4 g, Total Fat: 10.4 g,*

*Total Carbs: 71.1 g, Protein: 3.6 g.*

## Directions:

1. Prepare a sweet crepe and lay it flat on your plate. Drizzle interior with half the warm caramel sauce. Fold into a triangle shape. Place scoop of vanilla ice cream on top, drizzle leftover caramel sauce, and sprinkle the crushed candy.

## MOCHA WHIPPED CREAM

*This decadent filling pairs beautifully with chocolate crepes so don't be put off by the processed ingredients. Let the cream rest at room temperature for 20 minutes so the grains of sugar are thoroughly dissolved, then stir again before using.*

---

### INGREDIENTS:

*1 cup heavy cream*

*1 Tbsp. granulated sugar*

*4 Tbsp. mocha-flavored instant coffee powder*

### *Servings:*

*Serve with 2 Sweet Crepes*

*(your preference of batter)*

*Yield: 2/3 cup whipped cream*

*Servings: 2*

*Prep time: 10 minutes*

*Cooking time: 0*

### *Nutritional Info:*

*Calories: 388, Sodium: 132 mg,*

*Dietary Fiber: 0.7 g, Total Fat: 27.7 g,*

*Total Carbs: 33.2 g, Protein: 3.1 g.*

### DIRECTIONS:

1. Combine all the ingredients and mix until the cream forms soft peaks. Fill the crepes and drizzle with a little chocolate sauce to make the dish even more divine.

## APPLE CREPE STACK

*This decidedly rich, autumnal dessert makes an impressive presentation. The sugary cooked apples ooze their way from between the crepes and create a pool of near-caramelized apple sauce on the cake plate.*

---

## INGREDIENTS:

*1 pound dried apple slices*

*1 cup light brown sugar, packed*

*1 1/2 tsp. cinnamon*

*1/2 tsp. ground allspice*

*1/4 tsp. cloves*

### *Servings:*

*Serve with 20 Sweet Crepes*

*(your preference of batter)*

*Servings: 1 crepe cake (16 servings)*

*Prep time: 20 minutes*

*Cooking time: 20 minutes*

### *Nutritional Info:*

*Calories: 145, Sodium: 163 mg,*

*Dietary Fiber: 2.1 g, Total Fat: 0 g,*

*Total Carbs: 35.1 g, Protein: 0 g.*

## DIRECTIONS:

1. Place the dried apple slices in a medium saucepan with enough water to cover them. Cook over medium heat until they're soft. Strain off excess liquid and mash the apples with a fork before adding the sugar and spices. Continue to cook until the sugar has dissolved.
2. Assemble the stack by beginning with a crepe, then layering the apple filling.

3. Top with whipped cream if desired. Chill in the refrigerator for 20 minutes, until set.

Note: You can vary the spice palette by adding a little ginger in place of the cinnamon. This recipe would be outstanding using gingerbread crepes. This recipe is easily adapted to both gluten-free and vegan diets.

## PRALINE PECAN

*This filling is based on the sinfully rich, heavenly tasting pecan pie so beloved in the South. The pecans soak up the sugary filling to become extra gooey.*

---

### INGREDIENTS:

*1 1/2 sticks unsalted butter*

*3/4 cup light brown sugar, packed*

*1/2 cup heavy cream*

*2 cups toasted, unsalted pecans, chopped*

*1/8 tsp. salt*

### *Servings:*

*Serve with 3 Sweet Crepes*

*(your preference of batter)*

*Yield: 1 cup sauce*

*Servings: 2-3*

*Prep time: 10 minutes*

*Cooking time: 30 minutes*

### *Nutritional Info:*

*Calories: 1172, Sodium: 440 mg,*

*Dietary Fiber: 5.3 g, Total Fat: 109.2 g,*

*Total Carbs: 46.8 g, Protein: 8.9 g.*

### DIRECTIONS:

1. In a heavy saucepan, combine the butter, salt, and brown sugar. Cook over medium heat until the butter and sugar have combined in a smooth mixture.
2. Stir in the cream and bring the mixture to a boil.

3. Continue to cook for 3-5 minutes, stirring constantly, until the mixture begins to thicken.
4. Let the caramel cool slightly, then add the chopped pecans.
5. Stir to combine.
6. Ladle sauce over crepes and serve immediately.

## CREPE CUPS WITH CHOCOLATE PUDDING

*You've probably had desserts that were served in cookie containers. These delicate-looking crepe cups are easy to make fill with ice cream, fruit, or pudding.*

---

### INGREDIENTS:

*Aluminum foil*

### *Servings:*

*Serve with 8 Sweet Crepes*
*(your preference of batter)*
*Yield: 8 crepe cups*
*Prep time: 5 minutes*
*Cooking time: 10 minutes*

### DIRECTIONS:

1. Preheat oven to 350 degrees.
2. Prepare a muffin pan with cooking spray.
3. Fit each crepe into an indentation in the muffin pan.
4. Put a ball of foil into each crepe to create the "cup."
5. Bake for five minutes.
6. Remove the foil and return the crepe cups to the oven.
7. Bake for two more minutes until the cups are golden brown and a bit crisp.
8. Let cool before filling.

## Chocolate Pudding for Crepe Cups

### Ingredients:

*1/4 cup salted butter*

*1 cup semisweet or bittersweet chocolate chips, finely chopped*

*4 1/2 cups whole milk*

*1 1/2 cups granulated sugar, divided*

*1/3 cup Dutch-process cocoa powder*

*1/4 cup cornstarch*

*4 large eggs + 1 large egg yolk*

*1/3 cup heavy cream*

*1 1/2 tsp. pure vanilla extract*

### *Servings: 8*

*Prep time: 10 minutes*

*Cooking time: 15 minutes plus*

*2 hours to chill*

### *Nutritional Info:*

*Calories: 501, Sodium: 158 mg,*

*Dietary Fiber: 2.2 g, Total Fat: 23.8 g,*

*Total Carbs: 67.2 g, Protein: 8.1 g.*

### Directions:

1. Melt the butter and chocolate chips in a double boiler.
2. Over low heat, blend the milk and 1/2 cup sugar until the milk steams. Meanwhile, whisk remaining 1 cup sugar, cocoa, cornstarch, and a pinch of salt in a medium heatproof bowl.
3. Add eggs, including the extra yolk, and cream; whisk thoroughly. Gradually whisk in half of the hot milk mixture.
4. Add the cocoa mixture to saucepan with remaining milk and bring to a boil over medium heat, whisking often. Remove from heat less than a minute after it begins to boil.
5. Whisk in melted chocolate mixture and vanilla.

6. Pour into a large bowl and cover with plastic wrap, pressing the plastic wrap onto the surface of the warm pudding. Refrigerate at least 2 hours before serving in crepe cups.

## PINEAPPLE UPSIDE-DOWN CREPE

*Brown sugar, pineapple, and the sweet accent of maraschino cherries make this a spectacularly delicious dessert. Your guests will want to lick their plates.*

---

### INGREDIENTS:

*Sweet crepes*

*20-oz can unsweetened pineapple chunks*

*1 small jar of maraschino cherries, drained*

*1 cup light brown sugar*

*1/2 cup butter*

*1/2 cup walnut halves (optional)*

### *Servings:*

*Serve with 6 Sweet Crepes*

*(your preference of batter)*

*Yield: Approximately 3 cups of sauce*

*Servings: 6*

*Prep time: 5 minutes*

*Cooking time: 10 minutes*

### *Nutritional Info:*

*Calories: 374, Sodium: 118 mg,*

*Dietary Fiber: 2.7 g, Total Fat: 21.7 g,*

*Total Carbs: 46.1 g, Protein: 3.5 g.*

### DIRECTIONS:

1. Combine all ingredients in a medium saucepan and cook over medium-high heat until the brown sugar and butter have melted and the mixture is syrupy.
2. Pour the fruit sauce over the warm crepes and serve immediately.
3. Pour the warm sauce over the crepes and serve at once.

Note: Buckwheat crepes, with their assertive flavor, do very well in this recipe, and make it Gluten-Free.

# BOSTON CREAM PIE CREPE

*This childhood favorite still pleases long after childhood's end. If you find the heavy layer of chocolate glaze in the traditional Boston cream pie a bit much, you'll like this recipe — it allows you to control just how much chocolate you indulge in.*

## INGREDIENTS:

*1/4 cup salted butter*

*4 1/2 cups whole milk*

*1 1/2 cups granulated sugar, divided*

*1/4 cup cornstarch*

*4 large eggs + 1 large egg yolk*

*1/3 cup heavy cream*

*1 1/2 tsp. pure vanilla extract*

*1 cup chocolate sauce*

### *Servings:*

*Serve with 8 Sweet Crepes*

*(your preference of batter)*

*Servings: 8 filled crepes*

*Prep time: 5 minutes*

*Cooking time: 15 minutes*

### *Nutritional Info:*

*Calories: 451, Sodium: 149 mg,*

*Dietary Fiber: 1.1 g, Total Fat: 15.6 g,*

*Total Carbs: 72.9 g, Protein: 9.1 g.*

## DIRECTIONS:

1. Over low heat, blend the butter, milk and 1/2 cup sugar until the milk steams.
2. Meanwhile, whisk remaining 1 cup sugar, cornstarch, and a pinch of salt in a medium heatproof bowl. Add eggs, including the extra yolk, and cream; whisk thoroughly. Gradually whisk this mixture into the hot milk

and bring just barely to a boil before removing it from the heat. Stir in the vanilla.

3. Spread the Boston cream over crepes. Roll the crepes and serve them seam side down, drizzled with chocolate sauce.

# Apple Pie Crepe

*As French as a crepe and as American as apple pie. This recipe uses dark rum to intensify the apples' mellow undertones. Serve each crepe with a dollop of ice cream, or a slather of freshly made whipped cream and a sprinkling of ground nutmeg.*

---

## Ingredients:

*5 Tbsp. unsalted butter*

*3 pounds medium apples (the tarter the better)*

*3/4 cup (packed) brown sugar*

*1/2 cup apple juice*

*2 Tbsp. lemon juice*

*1 tsp. ground cinnamon*

*3 Tbsp. dark rum*

### *Servings:*

*Serve with 8 Sweet Crepes*

*(your preference of batter)*

*Servings: 8 filled crepes*

*Prep time: 30 minutes*

*Cooking time: 10 minutes*

### *Nutritional Info:*

*Calories: 225, Sodium: 58 mg,*

*Dietary Fiber: 4.3 g, Total Fat: 7.6 g,*

*Total Carbs: 39 g, Protein: 0.6 g.*

## Directions:

1. Preheat oven to 350.
2. Peel, quarter, and core the apples, cutting each quarter cut into 3 chunky pieces.
3. Melt butter in large skillet over medium low heat. Sauté the apples about 15 minutes, stirring often. Add sugar, apple juice, lemon juice and

cinnamon. Simmer up to 5 minutes, stirring regularly, until juices thicken and apples are very tender. Remove from heat.

4. Butter a 9"x13" baking dish. Using a slotted spoon, place apples into center of crepes. Fold 1 side of crepes over filling; roll up, enclosing filling. Arrange on platter, seam side down. Stir rum into sauce in skillet. Bring to boil, stirring, until you can smell the alcohol burning off. Spoon sauce over crepes and bake until warm, about 10 minutes.

# GEORGIA PEACH CREPE

*Gold and blushing, peaches promise summer. Use the freshest peaches you can find for this easy recipe. If you absolutely have to use frozen peaches, cook them with an extra squeeze of lemon.*

---

## INGREDIENTS:

*3 Tbs unsalted butter*

*1/4 cup brown sugar*

*1 tsp cinnamon*

*1/8 tsp nutmeg*

*pinch of salt*

*11/2 tsp vanilla extract*

*6 ripe peaches and/or nectarines, sliced*

*Powdered sugar for dusting*

## *Servings:*

*Serve with 8 Sweet Crepes*

*(your preference of batter)*

*Servings: 8 filled crepes*

*Prep time: 30 minutes*

*Cooking time: 10 minutes*

## *Nutritional Info:*

*Calories: 89, Sodium: 51 mg,*

*Dietary Fiber: 1.3 g, Total Fat: 4.5 g,*

*Total Carbs: 12.2 g, Protein: 0.7 g.*

## DIRECTIONS:

1. Using a skillet over medium heat, melt the butter. When it's almost melted stir in the brown sugar, cinnamon, nutmeg and pinch of salt. When the sugar is almost melted add the peaches, and cook for 5-10 minutes, but don't let them get mushy. Stir in vanilla.

## PHILLY CHEESECAKE CREPE

*This is the classic cheesecake rolled up in a tender, buttery crepe, just much easier and quicker to make. You may never go back to the original. If you really miss the traditional crust, sprinkle the rolled crepes with crumbled Graham crackers.*

### INGREDIENTS:

*2 (8 ounce) packages cream cheese, softened*

*1 cup confectioners' sugar*

*1 cup fresh blueberries*

*2 Tbsp. confectioners' sugar, or as needed*

### *Servings:*

*Serve with 8 Sweet Crepes*

*(your preference of batter)*

*Servings: 8 filled crepe*

*Prep time: 10 minutes*

*Cooking time: 0*

### *Nutritional Info:*

*Calories: 274, Sodium: 168 mg,*

*Dietary Fiber: 0.4 g, Total Fat: 19.9 g,*

*Total Carbs: 21.1 g, Protein: 4.4 g.*

### DIRECTIONS:

1. Blend the cream cheese with 1 cup confectioners' sugar until creamy. Stir in the berries. Some will break and tint the cream cheese. Spread this mixture over open crepes. Roll the crepes and serve them seam side down.

# KEY LIME PIE CREPE

*Welcome to the Florida Keys in a forkful. This is a dessert many of us remember from childhood— the sharp, summery bite of limes offset by rich custard and whipped cream. If you can get real Key limes, all the better, but any will do. For a variation, substitute Meyer lemons in season.*

## INGREDIENTS:

*1 tsp. unflavored gelatin*

*1 Tbsp. water*

*4 large eggs plus 6 large yolks*

*1 cup sugar*

*1 Tbsp. plus 2 tsp. finely grated lime zest (from 2 limes), plus 3/4 cup lime juice (from 5 to 6 limes)*

*6 Tbsp. cold butter, cut into small pieces*

*1 cup heavy cream, whipped*

### *Servings:*

*Serve with 8 Sweet Crepes*

*(your preference of batter)*

*Servings: 8 filled crepes*

*Prep time: 20 minutes*

*Cooking time: 20 minutes*

### *Nutritional Info:*

*Calories: 306, Sodium: 110 mg,*

*Dietary Fiber: 0.2 g, Total Fat: 20.1 g,*

*Total Carbs: 28.1 g, Protein: 6.2 g.*

## DIRECTIONS:

1. Sprinkle gelatin over water and let it stand about 5 minutes.
2. Whisk together eggs and yolks. In a saucepan over medium-low heat, whisk in sugar, lime zest, and lime juice. Cook, stirring, about 10 minutes, until mixture is thick enough to coat the back of a wooden spoon. Remove from heat.

3. Add the gelatin mixture, stirring constantly. Cut in the butter a few pieces at a time.
4. Strain the recipe through a sieve into a bowl or deep, round baking dish. Cover it closely with plastic wrap and refrigerate until set, at least two hours. Fold in whipped cream and refrigerate until ready to use.
5. Spread the key lime filling over spread crepes. Roll the crepes and serve them seam side down.

# Pumpkin Pie Crepe

*This recipe is easy as . . . well, you know! Try it as a variation at special holiday meals. Diners who are accustomed to seeing regular ol' pie will be surprised!*

---

## Ingredients:

*1 1/2 cups pumpkin puree*

*2/3 cup brown sugar*

*1⁄2 tsp. ground cinnamon*

*1⁄2 tsp. pumpkin spice*

*1⁄4 tsp. ground ginger*

*1/2 cup evaporated milk*

## Servings:

*Serve with 8 Sweet Crepes*

*(your preference of batter)*

*Servings: 8 filled crepes*

*Prep time: 5 minutes*

*Cooking time: 15 minutes*

## Nutritional Info:

*Calories: 84, Sodium: 23 mg,*

*Dietary Fiber: 1.4 g, Total Fat: 1.3 g,*

*Total Carbs: 17.4 g, Protein: 1.6 g.*

## Directions:

1. Combine all ingredients in a saucepan over medium heat. Cook while stirring regularly until the mixture has heated through, 5-10 minutes.
2. Spread each open crepe with pumpkin filling. Fold in half, then fold again to make a triangle. Stack at angles, allowing the filling to ooze out of the crepes. You can serve these at room temperature or chilled.

# The Elvis

## (Peanut Butter And Banana)

*The King's favorite sandwich filling goes up-market. This peanut sauce gives you the best of sweet-and-salty peanut butter without the roof-of-the-mouth stickiness.*

---

### Ingredients:

#### Peanut butter sauce

*1 cup smooth peanut butter*
*3/4 cup heavy cream*
*1/3 cup sugar*
*1/4 cup light corn syrup*

#### Caramelized bananas

*6 Tbsp. unsalted butter*
*6 bananas*
*6 Tbsp. brown sugar*
*1/4 tsp. ground cinnamon*
*Powdered sugar*

### *Servings:*

*Serve with 8 Sweet Crepes*
*(your preference of batter)*
*Servings: 8 filled crepes*
*Prep time: 5 minutes*
*Cooking time: 15 minutes*

### *Nutritional Info:*

*Calories: 469, Sodium: 74 mg,*
*Dietary Fiber: 4.3 g, Total Fat: 29.4 g,*
*Total Carbs: 49.5 g, Protein: 9.4 g.*

## DIRECTIONS:

## FOR THE SAUCE:

1. In a small sauce pan, combine the peanut butter, cream, sugar, and corn syrup over medium-low. Stir continually until all ingredients are combined and melted. Remove from heat and cool.
2. For the bananas:
3. Sauté the bananas in the butter over medium heat for just a minute before adding the brown sugar. Cook, stirring regularly, until sugar is melted. Add cinnamon.
4. Spread warm sauce and bananas over opened crepes. Roll the crepes up and serve them seam side down, topped with the last of the sauce.

# Snickerdoodle Crepes

## (Butter & Cinnamon)

*Snickerdoodles are America's simplest cookie romance: cookie meets cinnamon sugar and falls in love. Added here, to keep things romantically sweet, is a vanilla cream sauce as lush and decadent as hot melted ice cream.*

---

### Ingredients:

- *3 Tbsp. sugar*
- *1 Tbsp. cornstarch*
- *1 1/4 cups heavy cream*
- *1 Tbsp. butter*
- *1 tsp. vanilla*
- *2-3 tsp. cinnamon*

### *Servings:*

*Serve with 8 Sweet Crepes*
*(your preference of batter)*
*Servings: 8 filled crepes*
*Prep time: 5 minutes*
*Cooking time: 10 minutes*

### *Nutritional Info:*

*Calories: 101, Sodium: 18 mg,*
*Dietary Fiber: 0.3 g, Total Fat: 8.4 g,*
*Total Carbs: 6.5 g, Protein: 0.4 g.*

## DIRECTIONS:

1. Heat the cream and butter in a saucepan over medium heat. Whisk in sugar and cornstarch. Bring to a simmer and cook for 2 minutes, gently whisking. Stir in vanilla. Keep warm.
2. Spoon some of the sauce down the center of each crepe. Sprinkle with cinnamon. Fold the crepe in half, then fold again to make a triangle. Stack at angles, allowing the sauce to ooze out of the crepes. Sprinkle with cinnamon.

# Maple Syrup Crepe Stack

*Timberrrrrrrrr! Here comes a crepe stack made for a lumberjack. Choose this recipe to warm up a winter brunch or a special weekend breakfast.*

---

## Ingredients:

*2 cups whipping cream*

*1/2 cup pure maple syrup*

*20 crepes*

*Maple whipped cream*

*1/4 cup maple syrup*

### *Servings:*

*Serve with 8 Sweet Crepes*

*(your preference of batter)*

*Servings: 8 filled crepes*

*Prep time: 15 minutes plus*

*an hour to set*

*Cooking time: 0*

### *Nutritional Info:*

*Calories: 280, Sodium: 89 mg,*

*Dietary Fiber: 2 g, Total Fat: 16.3 g,*

*Total Carbs: 34.6 g, Protein: 2.6 g.*

## Directions:

1. Using an electric mixer, blend the maple syrup with the whipped cream, beating until peaks form.
2. Place 1 crepe on a flat serving dish or cake plate. Spreading a little less than 1/4 cup of the maple whipped cream on each crepe, stack the crepes, ending with a crepe on top. Refrigerate about an hour, until firm. Top mille crepe with maple syrup.

# S'mores Crepe

*Here's everything you love about camping, rollup in a sophisticated crepe.*

## Ingredients:

*8 ounces bittersweet chocolate, broken into small pieces or chopped*

*1/2 cup heavy cream*

*2 cups marshmallow cream*

*1 Tbsp. warm water*

*1 cup crushed Graham crackers*

## Servings:

*Serve with 8 Sweet Crepes*

*(your preference of batter)*

*Servings: 8 filled crepes*

*Prep time: 5 minutes*

*Cooking time: 10 minutes*

## Nutritional Info:

*Calories: 405, Sodium: 134 mg,*

*Dietary Fiber: 1.3 g, Total Fat: 12.4 g,*

*Total Carbs: 69.9 g, Protein: 3.5 g.*

## Directions:

1. Melt chocolate and cream over medium-low heat, stirring regularly, until smooth.
2. Whisk together marshmallow spread and 1 tsp. of water at a time until the mixture is easily spreadable.
3. Spread each open crepe with marshmallow cream, then spoon chocolate down the center. Roll the crepes up and top with Graham cracker crumbs.

# GONE BANANAS

*Historic New Orleans' favorite dessert — tropically sweet bananas set aflame with dark rum. Tens of thousands of bananas are set on fire every year at Brennan's, the restaurant where this dense and elegant treat originated.*

## INGREDIENTS:

*3/4 of a stick of butter (6 Tbsp.)*
*1 cup dark-brown sugar*
*4 ripe bananas, cut in rounds*
*1/4 tsp. ground cinnamon*
*Pinch of freshly grated nutmeg*
*2 tsp. pure vanilla extract*
*1/2 cup dark rum*

## *Servings:*

*Serve with 8 Sweet Crepes*
*(your preference of batter)*
*Servings: 8 filled crepes*
*Prep time: 5 minutes*
*Cooking time: 10 minutes*

## *Nutritional Info:*

*Calories: 254, Sodium: 62 mg,*
*Dietary Fiber: 1.6 g, Total Fat: 8.9 g,*
*Total Carbs: 37.7 g, Protein: 0.7 g.*

## DIRECTIONS:

1. In a sauté pan over medium heat warm butter and sugar until butter melts. Add bananas, cinnamon, nutmeg, and vanilla, and cook, stirring, for 1 to 2 minutes. Take the pan off the burner, swirl it to blend ingredients, then add rum and ignite. Keep cooking until flames go out about 1 minute.

2. Divide the banana mixture among opened crepes, reserving sauce in pan. Roll the crepes and serve them seam side down, drizzled with sauce.

## Chocolate-Peanut Butter

*Sure, you can just spread your crepes with chocolate (maybe Nutella) and peanut butter. The secret extra (baby) steps here mellow out the heavy flavor of peanut butter and add a bit of chewy texture with chocolate chips.*

---

### Ingredients:

*1 cup of peanut butter*

*1 8 oz. package of cream cheese, softened*

*1 cup sugar*

*1 tsp. vanilla*

*1 cup semi-sweet chocolate morsels, divided*

*1 cup warmed chocolate sauce*

### Servings:

*Serve with 8 Sweet Crepes*

*(your preference of batter)*

*Servings: 8 filled crepes*

*Prep time: 10 minutes*

*Cooking time: 0*

### Nutritional Info:

*Calories: 529, Sodium: 242 mg,*

*Dietary Fiber: 3.7 g, Total Fat: 34.2 g,*

*Total Carbs: 51.4 g, Protein: 10.5 g.*

### Directions:

1. Using an electric mixer, blend together the first four ingredients, adding a Tbsp. of hot water if you find it too thick. Once that's smooth, add half the chocolate chips.
2. Spread each opened crepe with about a quarter cup of the peanut creme, and sprinkle with half the chocolate chips. Roll each crepe and serve

seam side down, topped with the rest of the chocolate chips and drizzled with chocolate sauce.

## Strawberry-Rhubarb

*Rhubarb is so American you can find it growing on roadsides, but a lot of cooks avoid it because of its fibrous and tart reputation. That's nothing a little extra cooking and some other sweet additions, like strawberries, won't cure.*

### Ingredients:

*3 cups chopped rhubarb*

*1 1/2 cups water*

*1 1/2 cups sugar*

*3 cups quartered hulled strawberries*

*1/2 tsp. anise*

*1 tsp. cinnamon*

*1/2 ground cloves*

*1/3 cup Grand Marnier or other orange-flavored liqueur*

### Servings:

*Serve with 8 Sweet Crepes (your preference of batter)*

*Servings: 8 filled crepes*

*Prep time: 15 minutes*

*Cooking time: 20 minutes*

### Nutritional Info:

*Calories: 202, Sodium: 786 mg, Dietary Fiber: 2.4 g, Total Fat: 0.5 g, Total Carbs: 44.6 g, Protein: 0.9 g.*

### Directions:

1. Bring rhubarb, water and sugar to a boil in a large saucepan. Reduce heat to low and simmer for about 10 minutes, until rhubarb is very tender. Add strawberries and spices. Remove from heat; let stand 5 minutes. Allow the mixture to strain and set aside the thicker filling. Heat the liquid over medium and stir in Grand Marnier; keep this sauce warm while you prepare the crepes.

2. Divide the filling among opened crepes. Roll the crepes and serve them seam side down, drizzled with sauce.

## Rainier Cherry Crepe

*Here's a twist on tradition, using what's arguably America's best cherry — the blushing, golden Rainier. These hybrid cherries from the Pacific Northwest are larger than Bing cherries, and definitely sweeter than pie cherries. The extra lemon juice in this recipe adds a touch of tart character.*

---

### Ingredients:

*4 1/2 cups fresh Rainier cherries, pitted and halved*

*1 1/2 Tbsp. lemon juice*

*3/4 cup sugar*

*3 tsp. cornstarch*

*3 Tbsp. warm water*

*1/4 cup toasted, slivered almonds*

### *Servings:*

*Serve with 8 Sweet Crepes*

*(your preference of batter)*

*Servings: 8 filled crepes*

*Prep time: 20 minutes*

*Cooking time: 10*

### *Nutritional Info:*

*Calories: 143, Sodium: 1 mg,*

*Dietary Fiber: 2.1 g, Total Fat: 1.5 g,*

*Total Carbs: 32.7 g, Protein: 1.8 g.*

### Directions:

1. Stir together cherries, lemon juice and sugar until the sugar has dissolved. In a separate small bowl, mix the cornstarch and water, whisking to remove lumps.

2. Bring the fruit mixture to a boil in a heavy saucepan over medium high, then reduce heat and simmer. Add the cornstarch mixture and simmer for about five minutes.
3. Divide the filling among opened crepes. Roll the crepes and serve them seam side down, sprinkled with almonds.

# WHOOPIE PIE

## (Chocolate-Flavored Crepe With Marshmallow Cream)

*Cream sandwiched between two chocolate cookies is about as easy as a dessert can get. Use warm crepes to make the marshmallow cream even gooey-er, or put filled crepes under the broiler for a minute or two.*

---

### INGREDIENTS:

*8 chocolate crepes*

*2 cups marshmallow spread*

*1/2 cup chocolate sauce*

### *Servings:*

*Serve with 8 Sweet Crepes*

*(your preference of batter)*

*Servings: 8 filled crepes*

*Prep time: 5 minutes*

*Cooking time: 0*

### *Nutritional Info:*

*Calories: 186, Sodium: 51 mg,*

*Dietary Fiber: 0.2 g, Total Fat: 0.2 g,*

*Total Carbs: 45.5 g, Protein: 0.6 g.*

## DIRECTIONS:

1. Spread each open crepe with marshmallow cream. Fold in half, then fold again to make a triangle. Stack at angles, allowing the marshmallow cream to ooze out of the crepes. Drizzle the stack with chocolate sauce.

# Crepe Cup Quiche

*Instead of making quiche in pie crusts, make individual ones using the "crepe cup" recipe and savory crepes. These cook so quickly you can make up a batch of breakfast quiches from scratch in the time it takes your family to shower.*

---

## Ingredients:

*6 savory crepes*

*4 eggs*

*1 cup of milk*

*1 cup grated cheese*

### *Servings:*

*Serve with 6 Savory Crepes*

*(your preference of batter)*

*Servings: 6 filled crepe cups*

*Prep time: 10 minutes*

*Cooking time: 20 minutes*

### *Nutritional Info:*

*Calories: 138, Sodium: 177 mg,*

*Dietary Fiber: 0 g, Total Fat: 10 g,*

*Total Carbs: 2.5 g, Protein: 9.7 g.*

## Directions:

1. Preheat the oven to 350 degrees.
2. Prepare the savory crepe cups.
3. In a mixing bowl, beat the eggs, whisk in the milk, then add the grated cheese.
4. Divide the quiche mixture among the six crepe cups.
5. Bake at 350 for 20 minutes, or until the custardy quiche has set.

6. Let stand for five minutes before serving.

# SEAFOOD CREPE STACKS

*This uniquely American recipe draws from maritime cultures for the seafood and the desert Southwest for the spice of peppers and the tang of tomatillo and cilantro.*

---

## INGREDIENTS:

*1 small bunch cilantro*

*2 tomatillos, husked and quartered*

*3 Poblano chiles, roasted, peeled, and seeded*

*1/2 cup low-salt chicken stock*

*1 large garlic clove*

*Juice of one lime*

*1 tsp. salt*

*1 tsp. black pepper*

*2 cups cooked lobster or crab, shredded*

*2 cups Asiago cheese, grated*

*1/2 cup toasted pine nuts (may substitute chopped almonds)*

*1/2 cup sour cream*

### *Servings:*

*Serve with 4 Savory Crepes*

*(your preference of batter)*

*Servings: 4 filled crepes*

*Prep time: 20 minutes*

*Cooking time: 15 minutes*

### *Nutritional Info:*

*Calories: 711, Sodium: 8945 mg,*

*Dietary Fiber: 1.4 g, Total Fat: 52.7 g,*

*Total Carbs: 13.2 g, Protein: 48.1 g.*

## DIRECTIONS:

1. Preheat the oven to 350 degrees.
2. Combine tomatillo and cilantro in a blender or food process and chop.
3. Add the chiles, chicken stock, lime juice, garlic, salt, and pepper and process until smooth.
4. Add the sour cream and blend.
5. Begin with a crepe, topping with the seafood, then adding grated cheese. Sprinkle with pine nuts and repeat. End with a crepe. Pour the poblano/cream mixture over all the stacks and bake at 350 degrees for 15 minutes. Serve immediately garnished with lime wedges and cilantro.

*Note: Cornmeal crepes are delicious in this recipe, which is an easy and elegant gluten-free entrée.*

# Lobster With Garlic Lemon Aioli

*Lobster is the ultimate luxury food. Dense and meaty with a flavor like butter, how could it miss? This recipe is simplified to two diners. Because you know how romantic lobster is, too.*

---

## Ingredients:

### Lemon Garlic Aioli

*4 cloves of garlic*

*2 egg yolks*

*1/4 tsp. salt*

*1/4 tsp. lemon zest*

*1 Tbsp. lemon juice*

*Black pepper (to taste)*

*1 cup olive oil*

### *Servings:*

*Serve with 2 Savory Crepes*

*(your preference of batter)*

*Serves 2*

*Prep time: 20*

*Cooking time: 25 minutes*

### *Nutritional Info:*

*Calories: 929, Sodium: 302 mg,*

*Dietary Fiber: 0 g, Total Fat: 105.4 g,*

*Total Carbs: 2.9 g, Protein: 3.2 g.*

## Directions:

1. Mince the garlic fine in a food processor. Add all ingredients up to the oil and process thoroughly. Continuing to process, add the oil in a stream and blend until well combined. Remove from processor to a dish and chill until ready to use.

# Lobster Crepes

*Lobster is the ultimate luxury food. Dense and meaty with a flavor like butter, how could it miss? This recipe is simplified to serve just two diners. Because you know how romantic lobster is, too.*

---

## Ingredients:

*2 lobster tails*

*1 egg*

*3/4 cup milk*

*1/2 cup flour*

*1 Tbsp. melted butter (plus more for the pan)*

*1 pinch salt*

*2 Tbsp. chopped chives or parsley, for garnish*

### Servings:

*Serve with 8 Savory Crepes*

*(your preference of batter)*

*Prep time: 20*

*Cooking time: 25 minutes*

### Nutritional Info:

*Calories: 93, Sodium: 225 mg,*

*Dietary Fiber: 0.2 g, Total Fat: 2.8 g,*

*Total Carbs: 7.2 g, Protein: 9.2 g.*

## Directions:

1. Pre-heat oven to broil. Broil the lobster tails for 1 minute per ounce. Remove from the oven and allow to cool a bit before removing the shells.
2. Place some (about 1/4 of a tail) lobster meat in the center of an open crepe, drizzle aioli on top, and sprinkled with chives. Roll the crepe and serve it seam side down with remaining aioli on the side.

## TUNA & CHEESE MELT

*America's classic late-night meal without all that silly toasted bread getting in the way. This would also pass as a fantastic brunch meal: top with béchamel and another sprinkling of cheese and place under the broiler for 5 minutes.*

---

### INGREDIENTS:

- *1 cup shredded mozzarella*
- *2 (5.6-oz.) cans tuna*
- *2 Tbsp. butter*
- *1 cup sour cream*
- *2 tsp. thyme*

### *Servings:*

*Serve with 8 Savory Crepes (your preference of batter)*

*Servings: 8 filled crepes*

*Prep time: 10 minutes*

*Cooking time: 10 minutes*

### *Nutritional Info:*

*Calories: 202, Sodium: 141 mg, Dietary Fiber: 0.1 g, Total Fat: 14.6 g, Total Carbs: 1.9 g, Protein: 15.5 g.*

### DIRECTIONS:

1. Place a spoonful of cheese in the center of each crepe. Top with a spoonful of tuna followed with a sprinkling of cheese. Fold the left side of each crepe over the filling. Fold in the top and bottom, then roll the whole thing to the right to make a pillow shape. Melt the butter in a skillet and transfer crepes to the pan. Heat the crepes in the butter over medium-low

heat for 3-4 minutes on each side. Serve garnished with a dollop of sour cream and a dash of thyme.

## Slow-Cooked Pork

*This recipe calls for using an oven to prepare the pork. You could make it that way on a day when you're home and can keep an eye on the oven, or use a crockpot and smaller portion of pork if you're out of the house for the day. Either way, home will smell like a mouthwatering summer barbecue by dinnertime, and you'll have a line of eager diners at your door.*

---

### Ingredients:

#### Maple syrup pulled pork

*2 Tbsp. sea salt*

*2 pounds pork shoulder*

*1/3 cup maple syrup*

#### Plum sauce

*3 Tbsp. sugar*

*2 Tbsp. maple syrup*

*1 tsp. Chinese five-spice*

*2 Tbsp. soy sauce*

*8 plums, pitted and cut into quarters*

*Orange zest*

*1/2 cup chopped spring onion*

*Maple syrup pulled pork*

### *Servings:*

*Serve with 8 Savory Crepes*

*(your preference of batter)*

*Servings: 8 filled crepes*

*Prep time: 15 minutes*

*Cooking time: 15 minutes plus 6 hours unattended for the pork*

### *Nutritional Info:*

*Calories: 430, Sodium: 1709 mg, Dietary Fiber: 1.3 g, Total Fat: 24.5 g, Total Carbs: 25.1 g, Protein: 27.3 g.*

## Directions:

1. Pre-heat oven to 275
2. Rub the pork shoulder thoroughly with salt and place in a roasting pan. Roast for 6 hours at 275 degrees. Remove from the oven, drizzle with maple syrup and cook another hour. The safe internal temperature is 190 degrees. Remove from the oven, cover with foil and allow to cool enough to handle, then shred into bite sized pieces.

## Plum Sauce

1. Heat the sugar, maple syrup and soy sauce over medium high until the sugar dissolves. Add the spice and orange zest and cook, stirring for 3-5 minutes. Add the plums and cook until soft. Remove from the heat. You can process in a blender or food processor until the sauce is smooth or leave it chunky if you prefer.
2. Spoon the plum sauce down the center of open crepes and top with a serving of pulled pork. Roll the crepes and serve them seam side down, sprinkled with chopped spring onion.

## CALIFORNIAN – AVOCADO AND SMOKED SALMON

*California's culinary tradition focuses on nature's bounty, minimally prepared. Here, the creamy but contrasting flavors of avocado and salmon are brightened with zesty horseradish. This makes a great summer brunch dish.*

---

### INGREDIENTS:

- *10 ounces smoked salmon, cut into bite sized pieces*
- *3 Tbsp. sour cream*
- *1 small onion, finely chopped*
- *1 Tbsp. chopped capers*
- *2 small avocados*
- *2 tsp. lemon juice*

### FOR LEMONY HORSE RADISH SAUCE:

- *3/4 cup sour cream*
- *1/2 cup mayonnaise*
- *1/4 cup lemon juice*
- *2 Tbsp. chopped dill*
- *2 Tbsp. prepared horseradish (not horseradish sauce)*

### *Servings:*

*Serve with 8 Savory Crepes*

*(your preference of batter)*

*Servings: 8 filled crepes*

*Prep time: 15 minutes*

*Cooking time: 0*

### *Nutritional Info:*

*Calories: 267, Sodium: 877 mg,*

*Dietary Fiber: 3.9 g, Total Fat: 21.9 g,*

*Total Carbs: 10.9 g, Protein: 8.8 g.*

## DIRECTIONS:

1. Combine smoked salmon, sour cream, onion and capers in bowl and mix well. Slice avocados and sprinkle with lemon juice. Combine all sauce ingredients in bowl and mix well. This will keep in the refrigerator for at least a couple of days, and the longer you wait, the better it tastes.
2. Spread each open crepe down the center with salmon mixture and top with a few slices of avocado. Roll the crepes and serve seam side down, topped with a dollop of sauce.

## Black-Eyed Peas & Collard Greens

*This recipe combines the best of old and new South: traditionally cooked peas wrapped in barely steamed collards. What's the secret to truly Southern black-eyed peas? A full head of parsley chopped fine and cooked to the point of disappearing.*

### Ingredients:

*One Andouille or kielbasa sausage cut into rounds*

*1 large yellow onion, chopped*

*1/2 tsp. salt*

*1/4 tsp. cayenne*

*4 cloves garlic, minced*

*5 sprigs fresh thyme*

*4 bay leaves*

*1 full bunch fresh parsley*

*8 cups chicken stock*

*1 pound frozen black-eyed peas*

*1 bunch of collards*

*1 Tbsp. lemon juice*

### *Servings:*

*Serve with 8 Savory Crepes*

*(your preference of batter)*

*Servings: 8 filled crepes*

*Prep time: 15 minutes*

*Cooking time: 45 minutes*

### *Nutritional Info:*

*Calories: 108, Sodium: 1050 mg,*

*Dietary Fiber: 3.5 g, Total Fat: 4.2 g,*

*Total Carbs: 13.3 g, Protein: 61.6 g.*

### Directions:

1. In a large sauce pan over medium heat, brown the sausage. Add the next ingredients, up to the chicken stock, and sauté about 10 minutes. Add the

stock and peas. Bring to a low boil, then reduce the heat and simmer, uncovered, until the peas are tender, about 20 minutes. Remove the bay leaves before serving.

2. Wash collards thoroughly and remove lower stems. Place the leaves in a basket steamer and steam until they turn bright green. Sprinkle with lemon juice.
3. Lay 1 or 2 collard leaves over an opened crepe. Spoon black-eyed peas down the center of the leaf. Roll the crepe and serve seam side down.

# NEW MEXICAN GREEN CHILE CHICKEN

*Green chile is a New Mexico obsession. Fall brings the pungent scent of roasting chilies from every backyard and street corner. They're found in virtually every food in the state – from pizza to ice cream. Green chilis vary widely in heat, so this dish doesn't have to be spicy if you choose mild chiles.*

---

## INGREDIENTS:

*2 Tbsp. olive oil*

*1 tsp. cumin*

*1 medium onion, finely chopped*

*4 large cloves garlic, minced*

*2 Tbsp. flour*

*2 cups chicken stock*

*2 cups roasted, peeled, deseeded, and chopped green chiles*

*1 tsp. dried oregano*

*1/2 tsp. salt or to taste*

*2 pounds sautéed chicken breast meat*

*1 cup Monterey Jack cheese, shredded*

### *Servings:*

*Serve with 8 Savory Crepes*
*(your preference of batter)*

*Servings: 8 filled crepes*

*Prep time: 15 minutes*

*Cooking time: 25 minutes*

### *Nutritional Info:*

*Calories: 334, Sodium: 743 mg,*
*Dietary Fiber: 0.5 g, Total Fat: 13.4 g,*
*Total Carbs: 8.4 g, Protein: 42.1 g.*

## Directions :

1. Heat the oil over medium-low heat and sauté the cumin until it scents. Add the onion and the garlic and cook, stirring occasionally, until the onion softens. Add the flour and stir thoroughly so no lumps remain. Stir in chicken broth. Add the chile, oregano, and salt to taste. Bring to a boil then reduce heat for a low simmer for about 15 minutes. Add the chicken pieces and let them heat through.
2. Spoon the green chile chicken down the center of open crepes. Roll them and serve them seam side down, sprinkled with cheese.

## PASTRAMI AND SWISS

*A classic New York diner sandwich perfect for lunch or light dinner. Hot pastrami sandwiches are traditionally served so heavily burdened with meat that you can barely hold them together. This recipe mimics that groaning-board effect, almost turning the crepes into overstuffed pillows.*

---

### INGREDIENTS:

*3 pounds thinly sliced pastrami*

*2 cups sauerkraut*

*2 cups shredded Swiss cheese*

*1/2 cup Dijon mustard*

### *Servings:*

*Serve with 8 Savory Crepes*

*Servings: 8 filled crepes*

*Prep time: 10 minutes*

*Cooking time: 10 minutes*

### *Nutritional Info:*

*Calories: 370, Sodium: 1969 mg,*

*Dietary Fiber: 1.6 g, Total Fat: 18.1 g,*

*Total Carbs: 4.4 g, Protein: 45.4 g.*

### DIRECTIONS :

1. Preheat oven to 400 degrees. Butter a large baking dish.
2. Evenly divide pastrami and sauerkraut between the 8 crepes, placing a mound right in the center of each crepe. Fold in each side of the crepe so the center mound is all that's exposed; sprinkle each crepe with cheese.
3. Bake for 10 minutes, until the cheese has melted and the crepes are golden brow

# Dungeness Crab With Lemon Cream Sauce

*What's so special about Dungeness crab? Its short season, and sweet and tender meat make it the king of Pacific Northwest seafood. This recipe features sauce on the side, keeping additions spare so palates are concentrated on the crab's fresh flavor.*

---

## Ingredients:

*2 cups whole milk*

*1/2 cup salted butter, cut into pieces*

*2 1/4 Tbsp. flour*

*1/8 tsp. salt*

*1 Tbsp. lemon juice*

*2 cups warmed Dungeness crab meat*

*1/2 cup fresh dill, minced*

### *Servings:*

*Serve with 8 Savory Crepes*

*(your preference of batter)*

*Servings: 8 filled crepes*

*Prep time: 10 minutes*

*Cooking time: 15 minutes*

### *Nutritional Info:*

*Calories: 170, Sodium: 229 mg,*

*Dietary Fiber: 0.5 g, Total Fat: 13.9 g,*

*Total Carbs: 6.3 g, Protein: 5.9 g.*

## Directions :

1. Place 2/3 cup milk and butter In a medium saucepan melt the butter in 2/3 cup of milk over medium-low.
2. Meanwhile, whisk together the remaining milk, the flour and salt, in a medium bowl.
3. Add about half the warmed milk mixture to the cold, and combine them, then pour all the bowl's contents into the saucepan.

4. Continuing to whisk, cook over medium-low heat until thickened. If you'd like to test with a thermometer, the temperature will be around 180 degrees. Remove from heat and stir in lemon juice.
5. Spoon the crab down the center of open crepes. Roll them and serve them seam side down, sprinkled with dill, with sauce at the side.

# 10

## WORLD CREPES

### *World Sweet Crepes*

# LEMON RICOTTA CREPES

*This recipe is a variation on the Italian Crespelle, light but luscious crepes that are full of flavor. If you can find Meyer's Lemons, which are naturally sweeter, use those.*

---

## INGREDIENTS:

*8-oz. container ricotta cheese*

*2-4 Tbsp. milk*

*1/4 cup granulated sugar*

*Zest of one lemon*

### *Servings:*

*Serve with 2 Sweet Crepes*

*(your preference of batter)*

*Yield: 1 cup filling*

*Servings: 2*

*Prep time: 10 minutes*

*Cooking time: n/a*

### *Nutritional Info*

*Calories: 267, Sodium: 150 mg,*

*Dietary Fiber: 0.8 g, Total Fat: 9.4 g,*

*Total Carbs: 34.3 g, Protein: 13.8 g.*

## DIRECTIONS:

1. Combine all the ingredients in a blender or food processor and mix until smooth.
2. Spread each crepe down its center with the ricotta-lemon mixture. Roll the crepes and serve them seam side down.

*Note: If you substitute low-fat dairy products and low-fat crepes for the full-fat ingredients, this is a flavorful and satisfying dessert suitable for weight-loss diets.*

## SWEDISH CREPES WITH LINGONBERRY SAUCE

*These traditional sweet crepes are made regional by the addition of a Lingonberry sauce. Lingonberries are a stable of Scandinavian cuisine. Their jam is widely available but if you have access to fresh lingonberries, try making it yourself. It's just like making fresh cranberry sauce.*

---

### INGREDIENTS:

*1 quart lingonberries*
*1 cup granulated sugar*
*1/4 cup water*

### *Servings:*

*Serve with 6 Sweet Crepes*
*(your preference of batter)*
*Yield: 3 cups lingonberry sauce*
*Servings: 6*
*Prep time: 5 minutes*
*Cooking time: 10 minutes*

### *Nutritional Info:*

*Calories: 165, Sodium: 0 mg,*
*Dietary Fiber: 2.7 g, Total Fat: 0 g,*
*Total Carbs: 40 g, Protein: 0 g.*

### Directions:

1. Combine the berries, sugar, and water in a heavy saucepan. Cook over medium heat until the berries begin to "pop" and break down into a sweet, thick fruit mixture. Remove from heat and let cool slightly before ladling over open crepes and serving.

# Japanese Crepe

## (Rolled Like A Cone) With Green Tea Ice Cream

*Crepes are huge in Japan! Perhaps it's their ease and informality. The Japanese especially seem to like them filled with sweets, rolled into a handheld cone, and eaten on-the-go.*

---

### Ingredients:

*1 pint green tea ice cream*

### Servings:

*Serve with 4 Sweet Crepes (your preference of batter)*

*Servings: 4*

*Prep time: 5 minutes*

*Cooking time: 0*

### Nutritional Info:

*Calories: 260, Sodium: 40 mg, Dietary Fiber: 0 g, Total Fat: 21 g, Total Carbs: 24 g, Protein: 3 g.*

### Directions:

1. Place one scoop of ice cream at the top edge of the crepe. Fold the crepe in half, with the dollop of ice cream on the fold line. Next, roll the crepe, starting from the filled part, pivoting on the centre point until you have created a cone.

# TIRAMISU CREPE

*The Italian dessert favorite tiramisu implies layers of pastry (traditionally, lady finger cookies) sodden with something alcoholic and laced with rich mascarpone cheese, espresso and chocolate flavors. Here, mille crepe (not literally mille, which would be a thousand, but a large stack) soak up coffee liqueur and get a fragrant dusting of chocolate from cocoa powder.*

---

## INGREDIENTS:

*1 1/4 cups confectioners' sugar*

*4 cups (32 ounces) mascarpone cheese*

*1/2 cup coffee liqueur*

*Cocoa powder and instant espresso for sprinkling on top*

## *Servings:*

*Serve with 10-20 Sweet Crepes*

*(your preference of batter)*

*Servings: 1 "mille crepe" cake*

*Prep time: 20 minutes plus an hour to chill*

*Cooking time: 0*

## *Nutritional Info:*

*Calories: 2776, Sodium: 847 mg,*

*Dietary Fiber: 1.6 g, Total Fat: 130 g,*

*Total Carbs: 247.7 g, Protein: 112.8 g.*

## DIRECTIONS:

1. Beat mascarpone and sugar with a hand or electric mixer in a large bowl. Add coffee liqueur as you mix. Beat together until smooth.
2. Assemble cake by spreading about 1/4 cup of filling between each crepe layer. Finish with a crepe on top and dust with cocoa and espresso. Chill to set, at least an hour before serving.

# STRAWBERRY VODKA SAUCE FLAMBE

*Strawberries are a delicacy in the short Russian spring. Enjoy them here with a more year-round Russian staple, vodka. This dish could be interpreted as a Russian version of crepes Suzette.*

---

## INGREDIENTS:

*3 cups strawberries, hulled and sliced*

*1 Tbsp. orange zest*

*2 Tbsp. butter*

*1/2 cup powdered sugar*

*1/2 cup vodka*

*1/4 cup Grand Marnier*

### *Servings:*

*Serve with 8 Sweet Crepes*

*(your preference of batter)*

*Servings: 8 filled crepes*

*Prep time: 15 minutes*

*Cooking time: 10 minutes*

### *Nutritional Info:*

*Calories: 127, Sodium: 606 mg,*

*Dietary Fiber: 1.2 g, Total Fat: 3.1 g,*

*Total Carbs: 11.8 g, Protein: 0.4 g.*

## DIRECTIONS:

1. In a double boiler, melt the butter. Add the strawberries, zest, and sugar and stir to combine. Cook until the strawberries begin to lose their shape.
2. Add the vodka and Grand Marnier. Remove the pan from the heat. Using a long-handled match, light the alcohol and stir the flames until they subside. Top each open crepe with a portion of the strawberry mixture. Roll and serve seam side down.

## MEXICAN CHOCOLATE AND BANANA

*What's so special about Mexican chocolate? Those competing, slightly spicy flavors of chili and cinnamon are what make it different. Here, bananas offer a mellow, sweet counterpoint.*

---

### INGREDIENTS:

*2 bananas, chopped into chunks*

*4 Tbsp. melted butter*

*2 tablets Mexican chocolate, grated or finely chopped*

*1 1/2 cups evaporated milk, undiluted*

### *Servings:*

*Serve with 8 Sweet Crepes*

*(your preference of batter)*

*Servings: 8 filled crepes*

*Prep time: 5 minutes*

*Cooking time: 10 minutes*

### *Nutritional Info:*

*Calories: 178, Sodium: 136 mg,*

*Dietary Fiber: 1 g, Total Fat: 10.2 g,*

*Total Carbs: 18.7 g, Protein: 4.1 g.*

### DIRECTIONS:

1. Sauté the chopped bananas in the butter until golden brown. Add the chocolate and milk, stirring until the chocolate has melted.
2. Spread a little banana filling on each crepe and roll up. Serve seam side down.

# Dulce De Leche

*This simple "sweet of milk" tastes like caramel cream. It's very popular in Latin American countries. There are other methods for making dulce de leche, but this is the cleanest. Keep the water at a low boil and maintain the water level at all times. (Caution: there is a risk the can may explode if the water level is low or the heat too high). And yes, it will take a while for the can to cool. Consider cooking the dulce de leche the day before you need it and letting the can cool over night.*

---

## Ingredients:

*1 can sweetened, condensed milk*

## *Servings:*

*Serve with 4 Sweet Crepes (your preference of batter)*

*Servings: 4*

*Prep time: 1 minute*

*Cooking time: 3 hours*

*Cooling time: overnight*

## *Nutritional Info:*

*Calories: 246, Sodium: 97 mg, Dietary Fiber: 0 g, Total Fat: 6.7 g, Total Carbs: 41.6 g, Protein: 6.1 g.*

## DIRECTIONS:

1. Bring a large pan of water to a boil. Take the label off the can and carefully submerge the can in the boiling water with tongs or a slotted spoon. Place the can on its side.
2. Cook the can for 3 hours, keeping the can covered with water at all times.
3. Remove the can from the water and place it onto a heatproof surface to cool.
4. Spread open crepes with dulce de leche and roll up. Heat some of the remaining dulce de leche to liquify it a bit and drizzle over rolled crepes.

## PATISHAPTA — COCONUT CARDAMOM

*Patishapta is a popular dessert from Eastern India. Traditionally made with nothing more than cardamom-scented coconut and jaggery (crystalized beet and cane sugar), this recipe adds raisins and almonds.*

---

### INGREDIENTS:

*The black seeds of 3 small green cardamom*

*2 1/2 cups grated coconut*

*2 Tbsp. raisins*

*1/2 cup milk or half and half*

*1/3 cup brown sugar*

*Lightly toasted almonds, flakes or slivers, for garnish*

### *Servings:*

*Serve with 8 Sweet Crepes*

*(your preference of batter)*

*Servings: 8 filled crepes*

*Prep time: 10 minutes*

*Cook time: 15 minutes*

### *Nutritional Info:*

*Calories: 127, Sodium: 14 mg,*

*Dietary Fiber: 2.4 g, Total Fat: 8.7 g,*

*Total Carbs: 12.4 g, Protein: 1.5 g.*

## Directions:

1. Crush the cardamom seeds between two sturdy spoons or in a mortar.
2. Heat the milk until it steams in a medium saucepan. Add sugar and simmer until it is dissolved. Add the coconut, raisins and crushed cardamom seeds and cook on medium-low till the entire mix starts to

thicken to the texture of yogurt. Spoon into a bowl immediately and let it cool.

3. Spread each open crepe with the coconut cream, roll the crepes and serve seam side down, sprinkled with almonds.

## Italian Dessert Crepes With Lemon, Chocolate, And Raisins

*Here's an unlikely combination of sweets— intense dark chocolate, tart citrus, and densely sweet raisins. What makes it work is the creamy ricotta and the crepe, holding the flavors together literally.*

---

### Ingredients:

- *1 cup ricotta cheese*
- *1/4 cup sugar*
- *1 tsp. vanilla*
- *1 tsp. lemon zest*
- *1/2 tsp. salt*
- *1 cup heavy cream, whipped*
- *1/4 cup raisins*
- *1/4 cup semi sweet chocolate chips*
- *1/8 cup powdered sugar*

### *Servings:*

*Serve with 4 Sweet Crepes*

*(your preference of batter)*

*Servings: 4*

*Prep time: 10 minutes*

*Cooking time: n/a*

### *Nutritional Info:*

*Calories: 301, Sodium: 383 mg,*

*Dietary Fiber: 0.6 g, Total Fat: 17.1 g,*

*Total Carbs: 30.2 g, Protein: 8.2 g.*

### Directions:

1. Whip the cream. Combine all ingredients and spread a portion down the center of each open crepe. Roll crepes and serve them seam side down, dusted with powdered sugar.

# Blintzes With Stewed Apples

*Blintzes, or blini, are Russian crepes, filled and baked or fried. Traditional recipes vary and can include the addition of yeast or grated potatoes to the batter. You can make and fill these, then freeze them until your ready to fry them and serve.*

---

## Ingredients:

*5 Tbsp. unsalted butter, divided*

*3 pounds medium apples*

*3/4 cup (packed) golden brown sugar*

*1/2 cup water*

*2 Tbsp. lemon juice*

*1 tsp. lemon zest*

*1 tsp. ground cinnamon*

### *Servings:*

*Serve with 8 Sweet Crepes*

*(your preference of batter)*

*Servings: 8 filled crepes*

*Prep time: 30 minutes*

*Cooking time: 10 minutes*

### *Nutritional Info:*

*Calories: 206, Sodium: 58 mg,*

*Dietary Fiber: 4.3 g, Total Fat: 7.5 g,*

*Total Carbs: 37.2 g, Protein: 0.6 g.*

## Directions:

1. Peel, quarter, and core the apples, cutting each quarter cut into 3 chunky pieces.
2. Melt 2 Tbsp. of the butter in large skillet over medium low heat. Saute the apples about 15 minutes, stirring often. Add sugar, water, lemon juice, zest, and cinnamon. Simmer up to 5 minutes, stirring regularly, until juices thicken and apples are very tender. Remove from heat.

3. Using a slotted spoon, place apples into center of crepes. Fold 1 side of crepes over filling; roll up, enclosing filling.
4. Heat the remaining butter in a frying pan. Fry the blintzes until each side is brown.

# *World Savory Crepes*

# Crepe Black Bean Corn Enchiladas

*In this recipe, you can use savory crepes made from flour or let cornmeal crepes stand in for tortillas. Either kind of crepe is just a little softer than corn tortillas, so you can skip the traditional step of heating the tortillas in hot water or oil before using.*

## Ingredients:

*3 medium-sized cans black beans, rinsed and drained*

*1 8-oz package frozen corn, defrosted and drained*

*1 cup cooked rice, white or brown*

*1 small container salsa*

*1 brown onion, chopped and sautéed*

*1 large can ranchero sauce or red chile sauce*

*2 cups grated cheese (preferably "Mexican blend")*

### Servings:

*Serve with 6 Savory Crepes*

*(your preference of batter)*

*Servings: 6 filled crepes*

*Prep time: 10 minutes*

*Cooking time: 15 minutes*

### Nutritional Info:

*Calories: 646, Sodium: 525 mg,*

*Dietary Fiber: 16.9 g, Total Fat: 14.4 g,*

*Total Carbs: 97.5 g, Protein: 34.2 g.*

## Directions:

1. Preheat oven to 350 degrees. Butter a large baking pan.
2. In a large bowl, mix together the black beans, corn, salsa, rice, and onion.
3. Pour a layer of ranchero sauce into the bottom of baking pan.
4. Brush each crepe with ranchero sauce, then spoon on a layer of the rice/beans/corn mixture.

5. Top with grated cheese and roll up. Lay the rolled crepes seam side down in the baking pan.
6. Pour the remaining ranchero sauce over the enchilada crepes and sprinkle with the remaining cheese.
7. Bake at 350 until the crepes are heated through and the cheese is melted.
8. Note: You can fill your enchiladas with any number of ingredients, from leftover shredded meat to just plain cheese.

## CREPE SPANAKOPITA

*Feta cheese, spinach, and phyllo pastry are the traditional ingredients of this Greek appetizer/main dish. Crepes are much easier to work with than finicky phyllo dough. Don't bother with the little triangles, this works very well as a casserole.*

---

### INGREDIENTS:

*2 pounds spinach (frozen or fresh)*

*1 large brown onion, chopped fine*

*1 Tbsp. olive oil*

*8-oz. package of feta cheese*

*3 eggs*

*1 tsp. oregano*

*Pinch salt*

*Pinch black pepper*

*Additional olive oil as needed*

### *Servings:*

*Serve with 6 Savory Crepes*

*(your preference of batter)*

*Servings: 6*

*Prep time: 15 minutes*

*Cooking time: 20 minutes*

### *Nutritional Info:*

*Calories: 197, Sodium: 599 mg,*

*Dietary Fiber: 4 g, Total Fat: 13.2 g,*

*Total Carbs: 9.7 g, Protein: 12.8 g.*

### DIRECTIONS:

1. Preheat the oven to 350 degrees. Oil a 9-inch springform pan.
2. Chop the drained spinach and put it in a large mixing bowl. Heat the olive oil in a medium skillet and add the onion, sautéing until the onion is translucent and golden. Add the onion and the crumbled feta to the spinach. Beat the three eggs in a separate bowl and add them to the spinach along with the oregano, salt and pepper. Blend the ingredients thoroughly.

3. Cut the crepes into 2" strips, then fit into the springform pan until the bottom is covered.
4. Brush the crepes with more olive oil and repeat, laying down several layers of crepe.
5. Smooth the spinach/cheese filling over the crepes, then cover that with more layers of crepes, brushing each layer with olive oil. Bake until the crepes are golden brown and the filling is set.
6. Let cool for 10 minutes before removing the side-ring of the pan. Cut into wedges and serve immediately like a frittata.

# CROQUETTA

*These fried cabbage crepes are a Polish delicacy, and no wonder— how can anything deep fried that contains bacon ever be bad? Enjoy these croquettes with a spinach salad in a warm bacon vinaigrette.*

---

## INGREDIENTS:

*1 small head of white cabbage, sliced and parboiled*

*1 small brown onion, chopped.*

*8 strips of bacon*

*1/4 tsp. black pepper*

*1/8 tsp. salt*

*1 egg, beaten*

*Bread crumbs for dipping*

*Vegetable oil for frying*

## *Servings:*

*Serve with 4 Savory Crepes*

*(your preference of batter)*

*Servings: 4 filled crepes*

*Prep time: 10 minutes*

*Cooking time: 20 minutes*

## *Nutritional Info:*

*Calories: 388, Sodium: 919 mg,*

*Dietary Fiber: 6.3 g, Total Fat: 21.9 g,*

*Total Carbs: 32.5 g, Protein: 15.6 g.*

## DIRECTIONS:

1. In a large skillet, fry the bacon until crisp, reserving 2-3 Tbsp. of the bacon fat. Crumble the bacon strips and set aside.
2. Sauté the cabbage and the onion in the remaining bacon fat until they begin to brown.
3. Add the crumbled bacon and salt and pepper to taste.
4. Spread the cabbage filling down the center of each open crepe. Roll the crepe, dip it in egg, then dredge it in bread crumbs.

5. Fill a skillet with 1 inch of fresh oil and fry the bread-crumb dipped cabbage crepes until they are golden brown.

# FAJITA CREPES

*Fajitas are traditionally served with warm flour tortillas (or lettuce wraps for the low-carb crowd). Here the spiced meat and vegetable mixture is rolled in crepes. Nobody likes soggy fajita filling— cook the vegetables very lightly.*

---

## INGREDIENTS:

*1 Tbsp. olive oil*

*2 large yellow onions, sliced thinly*

*3 garlic cloves, minced*

*3 bell peppers, seeded and cut into strips*

*2 boneless, skinless chicken breasts, cut into strips*

*1 Tbsp. lime juice*

*1/4 cup tequila or white wine*

*½ cup chicken broth*

*3 Tbsp. chili powder (or to taste)*

*1 tsp. paprika*

*1 tsp. cumin*

*½ tsp. black pepper*

*½ tsp. dried red chili flakes*

## *Servings:*

*Serve with 4 Savory Crepes (your preference of batter)*

*Servings: 4*

*Prep time: 15 minutes*

*Cooking time: 20 minutes*

## *Nutritional Info:*

*Calories: 292, Sodium: 224 mg, Dietary Fiber: 5.8 g, Total Fat: 10.6 g, Total Carbs: 17.4 g, Protein: 24.5 g.*

## DIRECTIONS:

1. In a large skillet over medium heat, sauté the onion, garlic and bell pepper in the oil until the onions are fragrant and translucent. Remove from the pan and set aside. Put the chicken in the pan (adding extra oil if necessary) and poach it in the lime juice, tequila or wine, and chicken broth.
2. When the chicken turns white and is almost cooked through, return the vegetables to the pan.
3. Combine the spices in a Ziploc bag and give them a thorough shake. Add the spice mix to the chicken and vegetables and cook until the chicken is done.
4. Divide the meat/vegetable mixture among the crepes, fold over and serve with sides of sour cream, salsa, and guacamole.

# LASAGNA CREPES

*Lasagna should be a family-night meal, but in these busy times preparing lasagna noodles can add time you just don't have. Make this version with crepes you've prepared beforehand and kept wrapped in plastic either at room temperature or refrigerated.*

## INGREDIENTS:

*4 cups prepared tomato sauce*

*4 Tbsp. extra-virgin olive oil, divided*

*2 cloves garlic, minced*

*1 pound mixed fresh mushrooms, coarsely chopped*

*1/2 cup dry white wine*

*1 Tbsp. minced fresh flat-leaf parsley*

*10 ounces frozen spinach, defrosted and squeezed to remove excess liquid*

*12 to 16 ounces fresh mozzarella cheese, grated*

*1 cup Parmigiano-Reggiano cheese, grated*

## *Servings:*

*Serve with 15 Savory Crepes*

*(your preference of batter)*

*Servings: About 10*

*Prep time: 30 minutes*

*Cooking time: 30 minutes*

## *Nutritional Info:*

*Calories: 205, Sodium: 772 mg,*

*Dietary Fiber: 2.6 g, Total Fat: 12.7 g,*

*Total Carbs: 9.7 g, Protein: 14.2 g.*

## DIRECTIONS:

1. Preheat the oven to 375. Grease a large baking dish with olive oil.
2. Sauté the garlic in olive oil in a large skillet over medium-low. Add the mushrooms and cook, stirring regularly, for 15 minutes, until the mushrooms are soft. Add more oil if necessary.

3. Increase the heat to medium-high, add the spinach and wine, and let it come to a simmer. Reduce the heat to medium-low and cook for 5 minutes, until the liquid has evaporated. Remove from the heat and stir in the parsley.
4. Spoon a thin layer of sauce into the baking dish. Arrange 5 or 6 crepes, overlapping, in the bottom of the dish. Spread one-fourth of the mushrooms and spinach and one-fourth of the mozzarella over the crepes. Sprinkle about 1 Tbsp. of the Parmigiano-Reggiano cheese over the mozzarella. Repeat with two more layers of crepes, covering the top layer with tomato sauce and Parmigiano-Reggiano cheese.
5. Bake for 25 to 30 minutes.

# LATVIAN BACON CREPES

*This is an extremely hearty dish and not for those who have to watch their weight. Or their cholesterol. Or their blood pressure. But it sure is satisfying for hearty appetites.*

---

## INGREDIENTS:

*1 pound bacon*

*1 16-oz. container sour cream*

### *Servings:*

*Serve with 10 Savory Crepes*
*(your preference of batter)*
*Yield: 10 crepes*
*Prep time: 5 minutes*
*Cooking time: 20 minutes*

### *Nutritional Info:*

*Calories: 343, Sodium: 1,072 mg,*
*Dietary Fiber: 0 g, Total Fat: 28.5 g,*
*Total Carbs: 2.6 g, Protein: 18.2 g.*

## DIRECTIONS:

1. Fry the bacon, then thoroughly crumble it. Cool the bacon grease slightly, then add the sour cream, mixing well. Spread the sour cream/bacon grease mixture over opened crepes. Roll them up and serve seam side down, sprinkled with crumbled bacon.

# Mahjouba

*This popular Algerian street snack is traditionally served in a semolina flatbread rolled out in a rectangle. Here, we've substituted savory crepes.*

## Ingredients:

*4 large yellow onions, coarsely chopped*

*3 jalapenos, seeded and chopped*

*2 medium carrots, scraped and chopped*

*1 cup cilantro, finely chopped*

*3 Tbsp. tomato paste*

*2 Tbsp. salt*

*1 tsp.. black pepper*

*1/4 cup olive oil + more for frying*

### *Servings:*

*Serve with 8 Savory Crepes*

*(your preference of batter)*

*Yield: 8 servings*

*Prep time: 5 minutes*

*Cooking time: 10 minutes*

### *Nutritional Info:*

*Calories: 98, Sodium: 1765 mg,*

*Dietary Fiber: 2.5 g, Total Fat: 6.5 g,*

*Total Carbs: 10.2 g, Protein: 1.4 g.*

## Directions:

1. Combine the onions, chilies, and carrots in a food processor and blend until finely chopped.
2. Sauté the vegetables in a skillet with olive oil over medium-low until they begin to caramelize.
3. Add the tomato paste and continue cooking for another few minutes. Add the salt and pepper, remove from heat then add cilantro.

4. Spread each open crepe with a portion of the vegetable mix. Fold the left side of each crepe over the filling. Fold in the top and bottom, then roll the whole thing to the right to make a pillow shape. Heat the filled crepes in oil over medium-low heat for 3-4 minutes on each side.

# SIMPLE BANH XEO FILLING

*Asian crepes are often gluten-free, like the Vietnamese street food favorite banh xeo. These are meant to be crisp, and become soggy quickly, so get the filling ingredients ready, cook your crepes, and eat them immediately.*

## INGREDIENTS:

*3 cups bean sprouts, steamed*

*1 medium brown onion, thinly sliced*

*1/2 pound cooked pork roast, thinly sliced*

*1/2 pound cooked shrimp*

*1/2 tsp. fish sauce*

*1/2 tsp. granulated sugar*

*1/2 tsp. salt*

### *Servings:*

*Serve with 4 Savory Crepes (your preference of batter)*

*Servings: 4 filled crepes*

*Prep time: 10 minutes*

*Cooking time: 5 minutes*

### *Nutritional Info:*

*Calories: 238, Sodium: 528 mg, Dietary Fiber: 0.6 g, Total Fat: 7 g, Total Carbs: 9.6 g, Protein: 35.2 g.*

## DIRECTIONS:

1. Combine the filling ingredients. As soon as you have flipped the crepe to cook the second side, fill half the crepe with the filling and fold over.

## MEXICAN LASAGNA WITH CREPES

*This south-of-the-border variation on a theme is held together with layers of crepe strips instead of corn tortillas. It's a popular potluck dish or expand it to make a great dinner for a crowd.*

---

### INGREDIENTS:

*4 cups cooked chicken, shredded*

*1 14-oz can fire-roasted tomatoes with juice*

*2 Tbsp. olive oil*

*2 Tbsp. chili powder*

*2 tsp. cumin*

*1 large can black beans, rinsed and drained*

*2 cups Pepper Jack cheese, shredded*

*1/4 cup cheddar cheese, shredded*

### *Servings:*

*Serve with 6 Savory Crepes*

*(your preference of batter)*

*Servings: 6*

*Prep time: 15 minutes*

*Cooking time: 45 minutes*

### *Nutritional Info:*

*Calories: 374, Sodium: 364 mg,*

*Dietary Fiber: 6.4 g, Total Fat: 13.1 g,*

*Total Carbs: 25.3 g, Protein: 38.6 g.*

### DIRECTIONS:

1. Preheat oven to 350 degrees. Butter a large baking dish.
2. Sauté the onion and garlic in the olive oil. Add the chili powder and cumin and mix well. Add the chicken and the tomatoes, mixing well.
3. Cut the crepes into 3" strips. Begin layering the crepe strips in a 9 x 13 baking pan, starting with the meat/tomato sauce. Add a layer of black

beans, then a layer of crepe strips. Top with cheese and add another layer. Finish with a layer of cheese on top.

4. Cover with foil and bake for 30 minutes; remove foil and continue baking until cheese is bubbling and browned.

# INJERA CREPE WITH DORO WOT

*Doro wot is practically Ethiopia's national dish: slow-cooked chicken and hardboiled eggs flavored with berbere (Ethiopia's unique spice mix of chili, garlic, and fenugreek) eaten by hand with injera, a fermented flatbread. Use our quick injera recipe,which relies on lemon juice and club soda for tartness and fluffy texture. Can't find berbere? A good chili powder or even curry powder with a tsp. of ground red chili works just fine.*

---

## INGREDIENTS:

*6 Tbsp. Ethiopian spiced butter (called nit'r qibe), ghee, or melted butter*

*2 1/2 Tbsp. minced ginger*

*5 small red onions, finely chopped*

*5 cloves garlic, minced*

*3 Tbsp. Ethiopian spice mix (called Berbere)*

*1 plum tomato, chopped*

*1 quart chicken broth*

*3⁄4 tsp. ground cardamom*

*8 chicken drumsticks*

*Kosher salt and freshly ground black pepper, to taste*

*4 hard-boiled eggs*

## *Servings:*

*Serve with 8 Savory Crepes*

*(your preference of batter)*

*Servings: 8*

*Prep time: 10 minutes*

*Cooking time: 1 1/2 to 2 hours*

## *Nutritional Info:*

*Calories: 241, Sodium: 977 mg,*

*Dietary Fiber: 1.4 g, Total Fat: 14.3 g,*

*Total Carbs: 8.8 g, Protein: 19.1 g.*

## DIRECTIONS:

1. Heat butter in a large saucepan over low heat. Add ginger, onions, and garlic and saute until they're limp, 20-30 minutes. Add berbere and tomato and cook another 15 minutes. Add chicken broth, cardamom, and chicken, salt and pepper and bring to a boil. Reduce heat to medium-low, and simmer, covered, for about 1 hour. Remove chicken and continue cooking sauce until reduced, about 15 minutes. Add eggs and give them a few minutes to warm through. Pour reduced sauce over chicken, and serve with injera crepes.

# 11

## CREPE PANTRY

Crepes are easy to make! If you're sticking to traditional crepe recipes, here's a good start:

*Fresh Eggs*

*Fresh Milk (whole works best)*

*Butter (real butter, it's better for you!)*

*Wheat Flour (for sweet crepes)*

*Buckwheat Flour (for savory crepes)*

*Sea Salt*

*Sugar*

*Grand Marnier or a flavored brandy*

*Oranges or Lemons (to grate the peel)*

## Common Fillings and Toppings:

*Jam (any flavor)*

*Nutella (or any other chocolate-hazelnut sauce)*

*Whipped Cream*

*Fresh Fruit*

# NEXT STEPS...

## DID YOU ENJOY THIS BOOK?

*IF SO, THEN LET ME KNOW BY LEAVING AN AMAZON REVIEW!* Reviews are the lifeblood of independent authors. I would appreciate even a few words and rating if that's all you have time for.

*IF YOU DID NOT LIKE THIS BOOK, THEN PLEASE TELL ME!* Email me at feedback@HHFpress.com and let me know what you didn't like! Perhaps I can change it. In today's world a book doesn't have to be stagnant, it can improve with time and feedback from readers like you. You can impact this book, and I welcome your feedback. Help make this book better for everyone!

# ABOUT THE AUTHOR

Isabelle Dauphin, known to her friends as "Isa", is a master chef and culinary adventurer who lives a bi-coastal life between Bretagne and California. She trained at Le Cordon Bleu and L'ateliers des Chefs before starting her consulting chef practice which specializes in developing French menus for restaurants located in USA.

Many of Isa's recipes are influenced by her life in France, in a household which lives around gourmet meals made at home with fresh ingredients from the garden or local markets. Her collection also includes family recipes which have been passed down for generations like heirlooms.

Isa lives and travels with her husband, who loves everything Isa cooks except escargot.

## DON'T FORGET TO REGISTER FOR FREE BOOKS...

Every month we release a new book and give it to our readers...absolutely free! This helps us get early feedback before launching a book, and lets you stock your shelf full of interesting and valuable books for free!

Some recent titles include:

1. The Weight Loss Vegetable Spiralizer Cookbook
2. The Cast Iron Recipe Book
3. The Food Dehydrator Handbook

To receive this month's free book, just go to

www.healthyhappyfoodie.org/d1-freebooks

Printed in Great Britain
by Amazon

69497865R00151

# Under the Influence

Charles Spencer

# Under the Influence

This edition published in Great Britain in 2002 by
Allison & Busby Limited
Suite 111, Bon Marche Centre
241-251 Ferndale Road
London SW9 8BJ
*http://www.allisonandbusby.ltd.uk*

First published in 2000



A catalogue record for this book is available from the British Library.

ISBN 0 7490 0532 7

Printed and bound in Spain by
Liberduplex, s.l. Barcelona.

For Nicki and Edward

IN MEMORIAM NG & RS

# 1: Midsummer Night 1982

*That is the land of lost content,*
*I see it shining plain,*
*The happy highways where I went*
*And cannot come again.*

A.E. Housman, *A Shropshire Lad*

I'll never forget that short night's journey into day. It glows across fourteen years. When things got bad last winter, and they got very bad, I would rerun it in my mind like a favourite video.

We began in the garden of the Foley Arms in Claygate, playing a sadistic, addictive card game called Black Bitch. Whoever ended up with the Queen of Spades had to buy the next round, and Henry, the only man I have ever met who looked cool rather than a prat in leather trousers, was returning with the drinks when he sprang the bad news.

"I'm afraid I've got to go, darlings," he said. "Something's come up."

"Oh, Henry," bleated Nicholas, who had caught the New Romantic bug bad, and was wearing a white sailor suit and a dinky little straw boater. "You promised this was going to be a special night. It's only nine o'clock."

"Can't be helped, kid," said Henry. "You know what journalism's like."

Actually we didn't. Not really. Nicholas and I were both in our gap year before going to university and somehow both of us had managed to wangle summer work experience on the *Esher Herald.* Better still, we were being paid what then seemed the princely sum of £30 a week. Nicholas had started a month ago. I'd started the previous week after five months of washing-up seven hours a day in a grim little cafe in Kingston-on-Thames. My hands were still raw and cracked, and just the memory of the filthy kitchen and the stink of fried food made me gag.

Nicholas looked as though he was about to burst into tears as he sipped his Negroni, not a drink for which there was usually much call at the Foley Arms. I felt a bit bereft myself as I took a brave and manly swig of my Ramrod and Bitter. Henry, already the *Herald*'s star reporter after less than a year on the staff, was becoming something of a hero to us both. He was twenty-two, an Oxford graduate, and great things were predicted of him by the paper's benign and snuffling editor, universally known, behind his back at any rate, as Moley.

"How am I going to get home, Henry?" piped up his fifteen-year-old sister, Rose, whose mass of dark curls and shy smile had been bewitching me all evening.

"Don't worry," said slow, solid, kindly Trevor, the sixth and last member of our party. "I'll run you home." Trevor seemed positively middle-aged at twenty-nine and was the paper's chief sub-editor. Like Henry and me, he was bound for further education in the autumn. Unlike us, however, he was going to theological college to train as an Anglican priest. Even Moley now called him Trev the Rev.

Henry kissed us all on the cheek, and Nicholas, to his evident confusion, blushed. When it was Natasha's turn she wrinkled her nose with the air of superior disdain I was going to come to know so well, then suddenly giggled, with a warmth that persuaded you she might not be quite such a stuck-up prig after all.

"See most of you tomorrow," said Henry. "And I very much hope I'll be seeing more of you this summer," he added, with the faintest hint of a leer, to Natasha. Natasha, just down from her first year at Durham University, blushed too, and Nicholas' glow of pleasure seemed to turn into a flush of irritation. I don't think I've ever seen a pinker, or more romantically flustered, pair of siblings.

"Well, I must say I call it a bit thick," said Nicholas, in his most aggrieved and high-pitched voice, once Henry had climbed into his battered Beetle and set off with a series of deafening backfires. "He invites us all out, persuades me against my better judgement to bring along Natasha and then just walks out on us. I needn't have got changed," he added, eyeing his absurd get-up forlornly.

"I'm glad you did, anyway," said Rose. "I think you look really cool." It was my turn to feel a twinge of irritation.

Trev the Rev filled his great log of a pipe with a black, damp-looking flake tobacco, which required much energetic rolling between his palms, tamped it down with the special silver implement he kept in his pocket, applied a match, tamped it down again, applied another match, took two puffs, which he didn't inhale, and laid the absurdly rustic, vile-smelling item down on the table. If he wasn't such a manifestly decent sort, I thought, it would be possible to get very annoyed indeed with Trev the Rev. I had rarely met anyone with such an infuriatingly even temper.

We played another round of Black Bitch and I lost. Rose volunteered to help me with the drinks and I felt a lot better again. Also slightly nervous. Which was absurd. There was I, just turned eighteen with a place waiting for me at St Christopher's College, Oxford. And there was she, still in the fourth form at Surbiton High School. I suspected, however, that Rose probably knew more about boys than I knew about girls. Newly released from a five-year sentence at a public school in which the chaps outnumbered the girls in the sixth form by ten to one, I was still a virgin and bitterly, embarrassedly aware of the fact.

When we got inside the pub, Rose asked me if I'd buy her a brandy and Babycham, with a large brandy if possible. She'd been on bottles of shandy all evening.

"It's Hal," she said, and it took me a moment to realise she must mean her brother, Henry. "He doesn't like me drinking spirits. Promise you won't tell?"

"Promise I won't tell," I said, and ordered the drinks. Rose insisted on drinking hers before we went back to the garden, saying she didn't quite trust Trev the Rev not to spill the beans. A possibly wise precaution, I agreed.

"What do you think of Hal?" she said, taking a greedy swig. "He's really *Gitanes sans filtre*, isn't he?" Her French accent was impeccable but I hadn't got a clue what she was talking about.

"You what?" I said, feeling foolish.

"Sorreee! Silly schoolgirl slang" she giggled. "*Gitanes sans filtre* means really cool because they're the coolest cigarettes. That lovely packet, that gorgeous burn at the back of the throat."

"Hardly cool, but I see what you mean," I said.

"And Embassy Regal means really embarrassingly naff and Rothmans King Size means absolutely vile. I mean, have you ever smoked a Rothmans?"

"I certainly have. They're really, um, Rothmans."

She bummed a cigarette. Apparently, Hal didn't like her smoking either. No stranger to Embassy Regal, I was relieved to find that I was smoking Bensons that night.

"Perfectly respectable, if just a tiny bit unadventurous," she said cheerily. "At least you're not a Silk Cut."

"What's a Silk Cut?"

"A total wimp, of course. Hardly any nicotine or tar. I mean, what's the point of them?"

"None at all," I laughed. I went back to the bar to buy a bottle of shandy to fool Trev, and Rose bolted down the rest of her brandy and Babycham and reluctantly stubbed out her cigarette. Back in the garden Nicholas was waxing indignant about the triumphalism surrounding the Falklands victory and I told him I'd found it all rather exciting, stirring even.

"Boys and toys," said Natasha coldly. "I expect you were a star member of the cadet corps at that public school of yours."

"Not at all," I said, flushing. "In fact, they kicked me out in the end because I kept failing the orienteering test and turning up for parade in my gym shoes."

"What a rebel," she said snidely. "Very *If* . . . , very Malcolm McDowell."

"Hark at the class warrior," said Nicholas, coming unexpectedly to my rescue. "The class warrior who was deputy head girl of Lady Eleanor Holles School for Stuck-Up Young Ladies and who was giving me a lecture only this morning about the merits of Margaret Thatcher. I mean, Margaret Bloody Thatcher . . ."

Natasha stuck her tongue out at him like a petulant child and I found myself warming to her. I was also faintly aroused. There was something sexy about the sight of her wet pink tongue. But I found almost anything arousing in those restless days and nights of sexual frustration. If Mrs Thatcher had offered me a shag, I don't think I'd have turned her down.

We finished our drinks and it looked as though the party was going to break up. It was still only ten o'clock, the dusk deepening, the air velvety and warm. I felt a wrench of disappointment. I wanted to keep drinking, talking, and looking at Rose and Natasha, Natasha and Rose. But Natasha got up to go.

"The evening's not quite over yet," said Trev the Rev. "Henry wasn't being entirely truthful. He's got something planned."

Nicholas's face broke into a great grin and even Natasha smiled.

"You might just want to phone your folks and tell them you're going to be back late," he added. From anyone else, this would have sounded insufferably patronising, but it was impossible to take offence at slow, kindly Trev.

"How late?" asked Natasha.

"Very late," said Trev. "You can tell your mums and dads I'll be *in loco parentis*."

The fussy Latin tag was typical of him, but I was glad I could tell my aunt that a twenty-nine-year-old chief sub-editor on the point of going to theological college was to be in charge. Auntie May tended to worry, and I liked to spare her what anxiety I could. We were very fond of each other and I owed her a good deal.

Henry had already squared things with Rose's folks but she accompanied Nicholas and me back to the pub and requested another large brandy and Babycham, since she wouldn't be getting much more booze on board once her brother came back onto the scene. Feeling like a corrupter of youth, I bought it for her and gave her another cigarette. Nicholas and I had large Jack Daniels on the rocks to keep her company.

"You want to watch dirty old men like him," said Nicholas.

After making our phone calls, we trooped back to the garden, and Trev the Rev led us to his car, one of those half-timbered Morris Travellers that look more like a tiny Elizabethan cottage on wheels than a car. Nicholas climbed into the front passenger seat, to Natasha's evident irritation, and I found myself squashed in the middle in the back, with Rose on one side and Natasha on the other. There isn't much room on the back seat of a Morris Traveller, and although I was ridiculously skinny in those days I still found that I had one thigh pressed against Natasha's expensive-looking black velvet trousers and the other against Rose's thin Indian print summer frock. Both girls felt delightfully warm and cosy and I would have been quite happy if Trev had announced that we were driving up to Scotland.

"Where are we going?" asked Natasha, who I'd just realised was wearing a rather wonderful scent. "Not one of those ghastly discos in Kingston, I hope? If that's the plan, I'm afraid I'd rather go home."

"No disco, I promise," said Trev. "It's not far and you'll find out soon enough."

We drove through Claygate and turned left onto the Leatherhead road. After a few minutes, Trev turned right into Sandy Lane and parked next to Henry's VW in the otherwise empty car park. Oxshott Woods. I'd been coming here all my life. One of the last pictures of my parents was taken here. I'm three, sitting on my mother's lap in a silly sun hat with a melting ice cream, my father, in a rather sinister pair of dark glasses, has his arm round my mother's shoulder and we're all laughing at some long forgotten joke of Auntie May's, who took the picture. The photo's in a frame on the mantelpiece at Auntie May's house in Thames Ditton. A few weeks after it was taken, my parents were killed in a car crash. I look at it often, and still can't remember anything about the vanished strangers to whom I seem so close in the picture, its colour now almost as faded as my memory.

"You're not seriously suggesting a tramp through the woods?" said Natasha.

"A very short walk," said Trev the Rev consolingly. "It's quite dry, and I've got a torch."

"This is a notorious haunt of sex maniacs and perverts," said Nicholas gleefully. "Personally, I can't wait."

The air smelt of pine, and the ground was carpeted with the needles of the twisted, wizened trees, their exposed roots a trap to the unwary. Night had fallen now, but once our eyes became acclimatised, we didn't really need Trev's torch. Wherever you go in suburbia at night, there's that oddly reassuring orange-maroon glow in the sky from the lights along the main roads.

I guessed where we were going. In the middle of the woods, there's an enormous sandpit, a great hollow, 100 yards in diameter, excavated generations ago and now a favourite picnic spot for families. It was there that Auntie May had taken the family photograph fifteen years earlier and I had returned regularly ever since, first with my aunt, latterly on my own on my bike. There were marvellous rides to be had through the paths and trees surrounding the pit, sudden bends and slopes, and usually, with luck, there would be other kids there to race with. There is an instant freemasonry about boys on bikes which, as a largely solitary child, I had greatly welcomed.

As we walked, Rose's hand kept brushing briefly against mine, then speedily withdrawing, like a butterfly. The first time, I thought it was an accident, the second time, I wasn't so sure, and the third time, I realised that she wanted me to hold her hand. There was something so touching – so tentative and brave – about her innocent advances, that I cruelly let her do it a few more times, enjoying the delicious mutual suspense. Finally, I took her nervously questing hand in mine. It was small, warm, wonderfully alive. I gave her hand a squeeze and she squeezed mine back. It felt like a generous promise of unknown intimacies to come.

"*Gitanes sans filtre,*" she whispered happily under her breath.

"Capstan Full Strength," I replied.

Just as we reached the edge of the sandpit, there was the sudden sound of a steam train: near, close, eerie, the aural equivalent of a painting by Magritte. We all jumped, then slowly moved forward. The steam train was overtaken by a wail of feedback, and then an ominous beat kicked in. We stood among the pine trees, looking down into the great hollow. Towards the middle, though not actally in the middle, for that always contained a smelly pool of stagnant water, a small fire was blazing. Four flaming torches were stuck into the sand, and blankets were spread on the ground. Next to the fire, a silhouette was dancing wildly.

"'Station to Station'", said Trev the Rev, with a beatific smile on his face. "One of bloody David Bowie's very best." I'd had him down as an earnest folk music fan and Trev went up several notches in my estimation.

"Race you to the bottom," he said, and we all ran pell-mell down the steep slope of the sandpit, arms outstretched, like five-year-olds pretending to be aeroplanes. I looked behind me. Improbably, miraculously, even Natasha had briefly returned to her childhood.

"Hi, kids," said Henry as we arrived, reducing the volume on the biggest ghetto-blaster I'd ever seen, so that Bowie became agreeable background music rather than a roar. "So glad you could all make it."

As well as the fire, with a sack of neatly chopped logs beside it, which Henry had presumably brought with him rather than hewn in the woods, there was a metal barbecue on spindly legs with sausages and chicken cooking on it, and a cool-box full of drink and bags of ice. While we were all drinking in the pub, Henry must have made several lonely trips through the woods to set this little lot up. I felt a wave of gratitude for him, followed by one of those almost orgasmic spasms of pure happiness you experience quite often in childhood and very rarely afterwards. I could think of nowhere I'd rather be, no one I'd rather be with.

Henry delved into a bag and set out six cut-glass tumblers on the sand before producing a cocktail shaker with a flourish.

"Dry martinis, anyone?" he asked, a forelock of dark hair falling across his brow as he spoke. He looked so cool and beautiful in his black leather trousers and white tee shirt; Nicholas, I noticed, was licking his lips, though not merely, I fancied, at the prospect of a drink.

Henry knelt on the ground to pour the drinks and, to her evident relief, even half filled a glass for his sister.

"To friendship and wild times," he said, passing them round.

"To friendship and wild times," we replied, clinking glasses before taking a swig. The martinis were deliciously cold, all gin with merely a herby shadow of vermouth and a zing of lemon zest.

Henry busied himself with the cooking with that peculiarly proprietorial air that seeems to afflict all men in charge of barbecues and got his sister to lay out the plates, the salad and the French bread. When we'd finished the martinis, Trev poured out glasses of rough red wine that made you shudder violently at first gulp but which seemed quite delicious by the time you were in the middle of your third glass. We sat on the blankets in a companionable huddle by the fire and ate the sausages and the chicken, followed by fillet steaks, deliciously charred and crisp on the outside, bloody and melting within. Natasha, whom I'd marked down as a fastidious eater, proved a surprisingly voracious trencherwoman, and in one of those moments that print themselves in the memory, I looked up to see the blood running down her chin. Instead of looking abashed, she flashed me an animal grin. Just for a second, there was something vampiric about her.

"When did you find time to get all this together?" asked Trev the Rev.

"Nothing that can't be found in Waitrose," said Henry. "I made a quick trip in the lunch hour. I brought the barbecue, the logs and the venerable family cocktail shaker in with me this morning from home." It struck me then that for all his cool, Henry was a twenty-two-year-old who still lived with his mum and dad and had returned to work on his own privileged, familiar turf. Surely he ought to be living in a bedsit and reporting hard news about Thatcher's Britain from some grimy northern city riddled with slums and unemployment? But then, why should discomfort and grittiness be somehow more admirable than pleasure and security? There was also something endearing about such a cool cat living unembarrassedly at home with his folks and being so protective of his kid sister.

It's about this point that my memories start blurring in a benign haze of alcohol. There was, I think, some lemon cheesecake, and scalding coffee from a Thermos, and a shot or two of delicious cognac ("I nicked it from the parents' drinks' cabinet," confided Henry), which turned the blurry glow euphoric. We lay on our backs and looked at the moon and talked about newspapers and university and the brilliance of David Bowie. I was a big Deadhead in those days, but I also knew that Bowie was special. What we didn't know then was that this apparently inexhaustible, constantly startling artist had already recorded his last great album, 'Scary Monsters'. Trev the Rev, Henry and Nicholas were in the middle of an animated debate about whether 'Station to Station', 'Ziggy Stardust' or 'Low' was his greatest work, Rose was gamely insisting that Soft Cell were just as good as Bowie and (to howls of derision) that Marc Almond was dead dishy, while Natasha was entering the unpopular view that she much preferred a Mozart piano concerto herself, when I drifted off to sleep.

I was woken by a trickle of beer on my forehead and jerked up to see Henry grinning and then taking a swig from the bottle.

"We've put the world to rights while you've been crashed out," he said. "Trev the Rev reckons he's even sorted out the problem of suffering."

"God, I'm sorry. How long did I nod off for?"

"An hour or so. It's OK. You're cool." He passed me the beer bottle. "Wake up now though. We're about to draw lots."

"What for?"

"You'll see."

To this day, I don't know if he fixed it, and if he did, how he managed it. Maybe it was just the random blessing of an enchanted midsummer night. He held out six matches with only the heads showing and we all had to pick one. On the first selection Rose and I both picked matches that had been broken in half.

"Right, that's the first team," said Henry, whom I was already thinking of as our leader. He turned his back, fiddled with the matches and held out the remaining four. Nicholas and Trev the Rev drew the broken ones.

"Right, that's team two," said Henry. Trev the Rev slapped Nicholas heartily on the back. "You and me then, sailor boy," he said. Nicholas responded with a smile so wan it was barely visible. "Quite," he said. Whatever we were going to get up to, he had clearly hoped to be paired with Henry.

"Which means," said Trev, laboriously spelling out the obvious, as he did each week in his standfirsts for the *Esher Herald*, "that Henry and Natasha are the last team."

"Yes, but what's the game?" asked Natasha, gazing at Henry and not entirely able to keep an edge of breathy excitement out of her voice.

"Hare and hounds," said Henry. "Only, since it's probably not entirely sensible for you girls to be wandering around in the woods on your own after midnight, there will be two hares on each occasion and a pack of four."

He explained the rules. Each pair of hares would be issued with a torch and given a three-minute start. They would have to draw an arrow in the sand showing the direction in which they were leaving the sandpit, and mark arrows in luminous paint on the trees to show which way they were going. Each arrow should lead clearly to the next, but once a place of concealment had been found, it was permissible to leave no clues within a fifty-yard radius. Whichever pair of hares remained undetected for the longest would win the "fabulous star prize" but if the hunt proved unsuccessful after half an hour, the hares should declare themselves. I couldn't quite believe my luck – the prospect of half an hour alone in the dark with Rose. Perhaps Henry guessed what I was thinking.

"Take care of Rose, Will," he said soberly. "She's only young."

"Oh Henreee!" squawked an embarrassed Rose. "We'll be all right."

Henry handed me a quarter-inch paintbrush and a bottle with a screw-cap. "Right, off you go then," said Henry. "Godspeed." There was a strange formality and tenderness to his last words. Then he turned his back on us, told everyone to close their eyes, and started counting loudly. They joined him, shouting, 'three, four, five, six' . . ., For several seconds, Rose and I stood rooted to the spot and then I drew an arrow in the sand, grabbed her by the hand, and dragged her in the direction it was pointing.

All those visits to Oxshott Woods stood me in good stead and I knew just where we were going. We headed south-west and, when we reached the lip of the circular pit, puffing after the steep scramble up the side, I painted an arrow on a fir tree pointing south. We could hear them shouting below us, "forty-two, forty-three, forty-four," as I found the path I was looking for and led Rose at a jog along it. We came to a small pond and I painted a curvy arrow indicating they should go round it to the other side. And that was all they were going to get. Thirty yards from the pond, and well off the path, was a large clump of rhododendrons, now in luxuriant flower. You could crawl through the shrubbery and inside was a secret bower, entirely hidden from outside view.

I'd been shown it years ago by boys on bikes and it was a favourite resort of underage smokers anxious to avoid being ticked off by the officious middle-aged busybodies who always seemed to be patrolling Oxshott Woods, determined to prevent kids having fun.

"Wow," said Rose, just a deeper blackness in the dark under the dense cover of the rhododendron leaves. "They'll never find us here."

We hadn't needed the torch out in the open, but it was so dark in our hiding place that I turned it on. I'd been half expecting to find old fag packets, used condoms and worse, but the place was clear and clean, just carpeted with last year's crunchy dead leaves. The present generation of underage smokers and illicit lovers clearly hadn't discovered this growing refuge. We knelt on the ground, very still, holding hands and recovering our breath, listening. We could just make out the voices of the others counting in the pit, "140, 141, 142," and a train rattled along in the distance, somehow the most comforting of night-time sounds.

"Shall I leave the torch on, then?" I asked Rose, careful not to shine it into her eyes. "Are you frightened of the dark?"

"Not with you," she said, making one scraggy teenage boy feel like Superman. "Aren't you going to give me a kiss?"

I laid the torch among the leaves on the ground, so there was just a faint glow in our shadowy hiding place, put my arms round her shoulders and kissed her gently on the lips. She opened her mouth and our tongues met in the aching, urgent whirlpool of a good-old teenage snog. I'd had the odd snog before, of course, at parties and even the occasional house dance at school when they'd bus in girls from Priors' Field down the road and the evening would end in an orgy of French kissing and desperate groping to the gorgeous, heartbreaking sound of Harry Nilsson singing

'Without You'. But I always seemed to end up with sulky, lumpen girls I didn't remotely fancy, and on one occasion found my tongue exploring a mouth filled with a hideous armoury of orthodontic metal which contained disgusting fragments of my unlovely partner's supper. A particularly stringy Irish stew, I fancied.

Rose, in contrast, tasted of the peppermint she must have sucked as we set off, and it was she, rather than me, who whispered, "Let's lie down." We lay on our sides, and she wriggled deliciously against me. I fumbled awkwardly with the buttons at the top of her Monsoon dress, and Rose suddenly sat up and I feared that she thought, in the phrase so dreaded by teenage boys, that we were 'going too far'. Instead, she unbuttoned the dress herself and let it fall to her waist. In the vestigial light, I could just make out her small, pale breasts. I gently touched one of them, leant forward to kiss a hard nipple, then gently sucked. I felt as though I had come home to something I'd been missing all my life as Rose moaned in my ear and pulled me down on top of her in our bed of brittle leaves.

It couldn't last, of course. Within what seemed like seconds, we heard the voices of the others as they pounded towards us from the pond. Rose was at that very moment, miraculously as it seemed to me, inserting her hand inside my jeans. She withdrew it as if stung and cursed.

"Oh shit, I'm sorry, Will," she whispered, pulling up her dress and doing up the buttons. "I can't let Hal find us like this." The idea seemed to cause her real distress and I kissed her gently on the cheek as I pulled the zip over my erection.

"It's OK, Rose," I said. "I understand. And it was lovely."

She gave me a hard, fierce kiss on the lips and we sat side by side, holding hands. She gripped mine so tight it almost hurt, and there was something frightening, atavistic, about hearing our pursuers rustling through the undergrowth, getting ever nearer. I turned off the torch, though I was sure it couldn't be seen outside the thick rhododendrons, and realised my heart was pounding and there were butterflies in my stomach. We didn't have to wait long. There was a violent rustle in the branches of the shrub and a blinding light was shone in our faces.

"I've found the Babes in the Wood," cried Trev the Rev exultantly. "They look like terrified rabbits." Frankly, I could have kicked the bugger.

Rose and I shuffled sheepishly out of our hiding place, and I belatedly realised that since it offered the only remotely feasible cover within the immediate area, it perhaps hadn't been such a brilliant refuge after all.

We made our way back to the sandpit, had another drink, and Henry flashed me an interrogatory look, which I returned with what I imagined to be an enigmatic, man-of-the-worldish smile. Months later, Rose told me that it was the smile of a man looking insufferably smug and I might just as well have told him that I'd recently been sucking his sister's tits. But Rose and I were having a terrible row at the time. That night, the gods were still smiling on us, and Henry gave first me and then his sister a quick supportive hug. It seemed like a brother's blessing.

Nicholas and Trev the Rev set off next, Nicholas grumbling about getting his sailor suit in a mess. We closed our eyes and counted and set off in pursuit. Henry led the pack, running fast, and feeling in high animal spirits myself, I enjoyed the chase. The last arrow was at the edge of a large expanse of waist-high bracken, and as Hal flashed his large hand-held torch over it, it became clear it was going to take some searching.

"Right, we'll link arms, and tackle it methodically," said Henry. "Hold hands everyone."

We ploughed our way through the springy, stinging ferns, stamping down the stalks, then after fifty yards or so, repeated our progress in the opposite direction. The process was just beginning to get tedious when there was a cry of, "ouch!" followed by explosive snorts of laughter about ten yards to our right. We rushed towards it and there were Nicholas and

Trev the Rev sitting surprisingly close together in the bracken. Trev's shirt was unbuttoned to the waist and he looked distinctly sheepish. Nicholas, in contrast to the irritable figure who had set off a few minutes earlier, appeared quite ridiculously pleased with himself, and his blond hair was all messed up.

"What have you two been up to?" asked Natasha, her voice at its most dauntingly imperious.

"Ill met by moonlight, proud Titania," replied her brother, and then we all got the giggles, even Natasha.

"You really can't beat a spot of midsummer madness," said Trev the Rev at last, and as we walked back to the pit, I swear I saw him pinching Nicholas's bum.

Henry and Natasha set off last. They headed off towards the war memorial, overlooking the sloping heath that leads down to the railway station. But once we reached the war memorial (their last arrow was painted on the pavement that surrounds it, pointing right), we could find no trace of them. We searched for fifteen minutes but there was no bracken to hide in, no rhododendrons, just slender saplings, the odd bare pine and one vast, incongruous oak tree, but since it didn't have any branches below ten feet, it seemed inconceivable that they were up there unless they had transformed themselves into monkeys. I pointed my torch up it anyway, but could see nothing but branches and a canopy of leaves.

"They must have cheated," said Nicholas at last, and I think we all secretly felt the same, with a slight pang of disappointment. I shone the torch up the tree again, without any hope, and thought I saw a moving shadow. Then a tiny green acorn bounced beside me at my feet and another and another. I stared up, and one caught me stingingly on the cheek.

"They're only up the bloody tree," I screamed with a mixture of relief, incredulity and delight. Henry was no cheat. He'd played another blinder.

"Time to go, sweetheart," said Henry, and I couldn't believe that Natasha was up there with him; Natasha in her smart black velvet trousers, pristine white silk shirt and more or less permanent expression of superior disapproval.

"There's only one problem," said the still invisible ice queen with a mixture of excitement and fear. "I think I'm stuck."

"Of course you're not stuck," said Henry, still invisible like Natasha. "Put your foot there, and the other one there."

"Right," she said meekly. "I think I'm getting the hang of it now."

Nicholas took the torch from me and shone it up into the tree. Henry's legs appeared first, then his chest and head. He was at least forty feet up.

"I simply don't believe he got her up there," said Nicholas. "To my certain knowledge, she's never climbed a tree in her life."

But she just had. Henry supervised her descent, but she seemed surprisingly competent and unfazed. The two were roped together like mountaineers, and eventually both were sitting on the lowest bough, ten feet up and laughing exultantly and, in Natasha's case, faintly hysterically, at the anxious watchers down below. Natasha's trousers were torn at the knee and there was a large lichen stain on her blouse, which seemed to have lost several buttons. The upper slopes of her full breasts were visibly heaving beneath the plunging décolletage. She looked magnificent.

Henry untied the rope, threw it to the ground, then leapt agilely onto the springy ground below. It was a jump I would have thought twice about and I was sure Natasha wouldn't follow. But without a second's thought, she launched herself towards him and he half-caught her in his arms to break her fall.

"Golly," she said. "That was wonderful. We went so high."

"How on earth did you manage it?" I asked Henry.

"I did quite a lot of mountaineering at university," he replied. "I'm afraid I cheated. I brought the rope with me and put a few crampons in the tree before you came. Once you've got up to the first branch, which is easy with the rope, it's an absolute doddle. Though I must say Natasha has nerves of steel. I thought I'd probably have to haul her up by the rope, but she did almost all the climb herself."

We headed back for the sandpit, and Henry stopped for a canvas bag hidden in the bracken *en route,* which, he showed me, contained a stock of crampons and a hammer. He coiled the rope neatly and stowed it away, throwing the bag over his shoulder.

"I had an unfair advantage over the rest of you," he said. "So you can all have a share of the star prize." No one asked him what it was. By this time, we had learned that Henry liked to retain tight control and an air of secrecy about his night of midsummer madness.

We arrived back at what I'd begun to think of as the base camp. The evening, I realised, was a bit like a night op. with the Combined Cadet Force at school with better food, more drink and an edge of sex. Trev the Rev and I heaped more logs onto the fire, Rose found a Bowie compilation tape and slammed it into the ghetto-blaster and Nicholas and Natasha just sat on the ground and gazed with frank adoration at Henry, who had turned his back on us and was busy with some private little project of his own.

"Right", he said at last, "Who's for a nice invigorating line?"

He carefully placed a silver salver on the sand near the fire, with six lines of white powder neatly arranged on it. One was half the length of the others.

"I bet that titchy one's mine," said Rose mournfully.

"It's quite enough, indeed more than enough, for a little girl of fifteen," said Henry patronisingly and Rose pouted sulkily. "And if you breathe one word about this to the old folks, I'll personally dismember that ridiculous old teddy bear of yours."

"You wouldn't," said Rose. "Not Archie?"

"I would and you know it."

"I promise," she said with sudden anxiety. "Cross my heart and hope to die."

"What is this exactly?" drawled Natasha, gazing at the salver as if inspecting a particularly unsavoury specimen on a fishmonger's slab.

"Amphetamine sulphate," said Henry. "Speed, whiz. I'd dearly love to offer you cocaine but I can't afford it on our derisory wages. So we'll just have to make do with this poor man's substitute instead."

I could hardly wait to get it up my nose. My experience of drugs had been limited to the odd joint at school, usually with distinctly dodgy dope that didn't seem to do anything except make you feel extremely sick. Nicholas looked eager too, and even Trev the Rev had an anticipatory gleam in his eye. I had a hunch, however, that Natasha wasn't going to like this one bit. Indeed, I wouldn't have put it past her to flounce off and phone the cops.

"Is it legal?" she asked.

"No, of course it isn't, you daft bitch," said Nicholas viciously. Natasha merely ignored him.

"And is it safe?"

"In these quantities it's as safe as houses," said Henry reassuringly. "I tried it the other day. It will just give you a nice little buzz. You'll probably feel a bit shagged out tomorrow, that's all."

"In that case," said Natasha. "I'll certainly have an . . . er . . ."

"Line," said Henry kindly and she flashed him the most melting of smiles.

Henry rolled up a five quid note, shoved it up one nostril, blocked the other with his forefinger and knelt by the fire to snort up the speed with a single sharp intake of breath. Natasha followed, then Trev, Nicholas and Rose. As I put the fiver up my nose I felt a terrible urge to sneeze and had visions of the precious white crystals being blown away into the sand. Fortunately, I managed to turn my head away in the nick of time but the fiver shot out of my nostril trailing what seemed like several yards of snot in its wake. I was always a martyr to summer colds.

"Delightful," said Natasha coldly and the others burst into inane laughter. Blushing horribly, I retrieved the fiver, did my best to wipe off the revolting mess of catarrh and sand that now adhered to it, and shoved it back up my nose. The amphetamine crystals stung, and there was no sign of the instant rush I'd been hoping for.

"Is that it then?" I asked, the disappointment sounding in my voice.

"Give it a couple of minutes to kick in," said Henry. We sat there quietly and then Rose went over to the cassette player, turned it up to almost painful volume and began to dance. Natasha joined her, and then the others and I suddenly began to feel a wonderful surge of energy, euphoria and lack of inhibition myself.

"This is just fucking ace," screamed Rose, stamping her little feet and waving her arms dementedly to Bowie's 'Rebel Rebel'. Spontaneously, we put our arms round each other's shoulders and made a circle and wheeled wildly round and round, stamping and singing raucously along to the lyrics. 'Rebel Rebel' gave way to 'Ashes to Ashes' and as Bowie sung "Ashes to ashes, funk to funky," and we all roared back, "We know Major Tom's a junkie!" I felt a thrill of divine decadence. 'Heroes' followed and 'Diamond Dogs' and 'Fame' and, just as I was beginning to think I couldn't keep up the frenetic pace much longer, 'Lady Grinning Soul', perhaps the most yearningly romantic of all Bowie's songs came on, and we paired off instinctively for this slow and lovely number.

Rose put her head against my shoulder and clung to me like a cuddly koala and, as Bowie hymned his Beetle-driving, canasta-playing *femme fatale*, I watched the others in the light of the fire. Henry and Natasha were snogging and appeared to be approaching the climax of a particularly energetic bout of frottage. More remarkably, Trev the Rev and Nicholas were enjoying a passionate embrace too and Nicholas had got his busy fingers deep inside the future vicar's trousers.

I watched Natasha temporarily remove herself from Henry's face and glance at her brother with what looked suspiciously like affectionate approval. She caught my eye and winked and I winked back. I wanted the song to go on for ever and found myself muttering under my breath, "Let it last, let it last," when I saw a light coming down the side of the sandpit.

"There's someone coming," I shouted, but the others didn't seem bothered and kept dancing until the song ended. Only when Bowie had finished did Henry disentangle himself from Natasha and calmly switch off the tape recorder.

"I wonder who it is at three o'clock in the morning?" he said, burying what looked like a small plastic bag in the sand.

I don't suppose the copper, young, acne-scarred and flushed, really said, "Now then, now then, what's going on here?" but that's how I've always remembered it. As usual when confronted by authority, I found myself blushing, and convinced that my crimes were about to find me out. I knew, without a shadow of doubt, that the gauche young copper would know we were all off our heads on speed and that we'd soon be banged up in the cells of Esher nick. I even became paranoiacally convinced that the white sulphate crystals were probably still visible around my nose, and that I might just as well have had a neon sign above my head saying, "This boy has been taking drugs." Trev, Nicholas and even Natasha were looking distinctly shifty, too, but dear little Rose just had a happy smile on her face and Henry, as always, seemed to be in complete command of the situation.

"Can I get you a drink?" he inquired sweetly. "Gosh, if it isn't Officer Whitworth." The cop gave a barely perceptible nod of the head and Henry hurried over to him as if greeting the very man he had been hoping would turn up all evening.

"Henry Sutton," he said. "Chief reporter on the *Esher Herald.* We've met at the police station a couple of times when I've come to go through the crime book with Detective Inspector Miller. We're just having a midsummer night picnic."

A masterly performance, I thought, instantly establishing respectable credentials with just the faintest hint that any out-of-order behaviour on Whitworth's part would get straight back to a superior officer. But Henry's beaming countenance betrayed no sign of a threat.

"You must know you're not allowed to light fires in the woods," said PC Whitworth. "And there have been complaints about noise."

"But we're not actually in the woods," said Henry reasonably. "There's no chance of the fire spreading in the middle of this sandpit and I give my solemn word we'll clear up afterwards. And as for noise, I can't think of any houses within earshot."

"Well, I'm not going to make an issue of it," said the constable. "There's a lonely old insomniac who roams the woods at night with his poor exhausted dog and he quite regularly phones up to complain. Just keep the noise down a bit and don't let the fire get out of hand."

"Absolutely," said Henry. "Now, what about that drink?"

To his great credit, Whitworth didn't come up with any guff about not drinking while on duty, and nodded eagerly. He sat down awkwardly on the sand and gratefully drank a can of Holsten Pils. Henry introduced us all, then started talking about a forthcoming court case involving thefts from local antiques' shops, which Whitworth had helped to crack by catching a couple of teenagers smashing a shop window on his beat one night. Henry managed to make Whitworth's lucky break sound like the kind of coup that might have defeated the combined talents of Sherlock Holmes and Inspector Maigret and the constable basked in the praise, little realising that it came within an ace of outright piss-take. The rest of us struggled to keep straight faces.

As Whitworth launched into an account of the Mysterious Case of the Stolen Bikes at Hersham Station ("I particularly draw your attention to the cycle bell that didn't ring in the night," Trev the Rev murmured subversively under his breath), I feared the constable was going to keep us there till the end of his shift with the highlights of his career but mercifully his radio cackled. Looking somewhat flustered, Whitworth answered the call, and there was a jabber of harsh noise from the other end in which the words 'RTA' and 'A3' were clearly audible.

"Road Traffic Accident on the A3," he announced unnecessarily after a good deal of Tango-one-two and Roger-Bravoing over the radio. "I say, I don't suppose any of you have got a mint have you?" he added endearingly. "I'm going to be in trouble if I start giving breathalysers while breathing beer fumes myself." Rose produced a grubby looking paper bag from her tote bag. "Everton Mints," she said kindly. "You can take a few if you like." He helped himself to a couple, thanked us for our company and set off at an eager trot in the direction of Sandy Lane.

"Phew," said Trev the Rev when he was out of earshot. "For a few minutes, I was worried that next week the *Esher Herald* would be splashing on a drugs bust in Oxshott Woods."

Henry grinned, and dug up his plastic bag. "I think we all need a nice calming joint after that."

He rolled a couple of five skinners with a minimum of fuss and told Rose she could have six hits and that was her lot. It was mild, mellow stuff, and gently parachuted us down from the speed and the recent nervous tension. We lapsed into gently spaced silence, hypnotised by the flames of the fire. A few streaks of pewter grey slowly became visible in the sky.

"Dawn's breaking. We'd better go home soon for a couple of hours kip before work," said Trev.

"I wonder what we'll all be doing ten years from now?" said Rose dreamily.

"I hope I'll have my own parish – and a stronger faith," said Trev the Rev without embarrassment.

"I don't like to be rude," said Nicholas, "But aren't the drugs and the groping rather against the rules of your particular form of superstition?"

*"Da mihi castitatem et continentiam, sed noli modo,"* replied Trev.

"You what?" said Rose.

"Give me chastity and continency – but not yet," smirked Nicholas, who had been in the classical-sixth at Kingston Grammar School. "St Augustine's Confessions. Touché, vicar."

"What about you, Nicholas?" asked Rose.

"I'd like to be an eminent art historian at an agreeable university," he said. "Preferably a university with a great gay scene. What about you?"

"I want to be a doctor," she said. "And discover the cure for cancer. Will?"

"What I'd really like to be is a pop star. But since I can't sing or play an instrument, I suppose I'll have to settle for being an award winning investigative journalist. And you, Henry?"

"Oh, I'll be a legend of some kind," he said.

"A legendary what?" asked Natasha.

"I haven't decided yet," he replied infuriatingly. "You'll have to wait and see. What about you, Natasha?"

"I want to be rich," she said simply. "And happy, of course."

"But how? Doing what?" asked Nicholas sharply.

"Making a good marriage, I expect," said Natasha serenely and I think the rest of us were faintly shocked. I know I was. It was such a safe, smug, dependent kind of ambition. Surely, at nineteen you ought to want to change the world yourself, not be aiming to marry into money? But perhaps Natasha was wiser and more honest than the rest of us. She certainly fulfilled her ambition.

"I'll tell you what," said Rose, taking a quick drag at my cigarette while Henry was busy bashing out the last glowing remains of the fire with a stick. "Let's all meet here on midsummer night ten years from now and see what's happened. Even if we're all still in touch with each other then, which I hope we will be, we won't ever mention it again, we'll just turn up."

"It's a lovely idea," said Natasha, unexpectedly. "I'll bring the food." "I'll bring the drink," I said. "And I," said Henry, "will bring the drugs. Top class cocaine next time, I promise."

"Shake on it," said Rose earnestly, and we all shook hands and promised faithfully that in ten years time we would all meet on midsummer's night in Oxshott Woods, ten p.m. on the dot.

The sky was turning pink at the edges and Henry doused the fire with water from the stagnant pool and put the remains into an empty cardboard box. We packed up the clutter and returned through the woods to the cars amid a crazy chorus of birdsong. Before following Rose down the path, I stopped for a moment to gaze down at our campsite from the lip of the sandpit. In the grey, opalescent light of dawn, it looked as though no one had been there that night, no romances started, no promises made.

Henry and Rose drove back home to Claygate, and Trev the Rev dropped me off at Thames Ditton before taking Natasha and Nicholas to East Molesey and returning to his own small flat in Kingston. Nothing was stirring in the comfortable semi in the quiet street where I'd lived for as long as I could remember. I climbed the stairs and looked in at my Auntie May and she was fast asleep, snoring lightly. I was too excited, too full of thoughts, to go to bed, and I had to leave for work in a couple of hours anyway. So I sat at the kitchen table and listened to the birds in the garden and smoked and drank coffee. I'd found, I realised with a throb of happiness, what I'd always wanted, always missed. A gang.

# 2: Wednesday 18 December 1996

*To move wild laughter in the throat of death?*
*It cannot be; it is impossible.*

*Love's Labour's Lost*

I'd been reduced to drinking on my own that lunchtime. But I wasn't really enjoying my pint of Guinness in the Perseverance and the chilli con carne I'd forced down as a kill-or-cure remedy for yet another throbbing hangover was already causing mutinous murmurings in my guts. For the third time in twenty minutes, I had another desperate search through the amazing squalor of my briefcase. My notebook and contacts' book were still there, for which relief much thanks. So too were the programmes for three shows I'd seen but still hadn't quite got round to reviewing. So was a half-bottle of Famous Grouse with an inch and a half of whisky at the bottom, which was mentally labelled For Emergency Use Only, an improbable number of Mars bars, Love Hearts, Refreshers, Munchies and Fry's Chocolate Cream wrappers, a cheese and pickle sandwich suppurating in its cellophane wrapping and two days past its sell-by date and about forty-five press releases for shows no one could possibly want to see. But the Birthday Bible was nowhere to be found.

The Bible, painstakingly compiled over many years by JB, the at-present absent editor of *Theatre World*, was a list of actors, actresses, producers, agents, comedians, singers, directors, opera singers, ballet dancers, arts administrators and various other forms of showbiz riff-raff carefully arranged from January 1 to December 31st and showing the date and year of each individual's birth. It was the source of the Many Happy Returns feature, sometimes cruelly known in the business as the No Chance of a Comeback column, which appeared each week in the theatrical trade paper. Famous celebrities (or, more usually, their agents) had been known to complain when they were left out and occasional mistakes produced howls of outrage and threats of litigation, particularly when we ran an actress's real age, culled from an ancient, reliable edition of *Who's Who in the Theatre* rather than the age she had subsequently invented for herself in interviews while the plastic surgeons battled with the ravaging years.

There was a strict instruction on the front of the Bible, in J.B.'s famously spidery handwriting, that it was not to be removed from the office. Naturally I had removed it the previous evening, with the firm intention of bashing out the column at home, together with the three late theatre reviews. With Christmas looming, we were going to press a day earlier than usual, and I was determined to show willing in the office. Instead, I had met my neighbour and new best friend, Maxie, and gone on a reckless crawl with him round the pubs of Pimlico. My memory of the later section of the evening was blurred, but I was fairly sure I'd produced the Bible when we got into one of those pointless pub arguments, which seem so vitally important at the time, about the real age of Joan Collins. I'd probably left the file of neatly typed pages of A4 on a beer-drenched table. The trouble was I couldn't remember which pub I'd been in at the time. I was going to be in trouble – again.

I drained my Guinness, selected 'Matchstalkmen and Matchstalk Cats and Dogs' on the juke box just to complement my mood of self-flagellating despair and went up to Larry at the bar.

"Another pint of Guinness please, Larry, and whatever you're having yourself." It turned out that Larry, who usually confined himself to a half of bitter, was celebrating a win in the 1.10 at Wincanton that lunchtime, so he gave me the drink for free as well as providing us both with a large Bells apiece.

"What's up, Will?" he said. "You look like you've just found a tenner and dropped a grand."

I explained about the Bible.

"And our friend Colin isn't going to like that at all," said Larry with a malign grin on his face. I sometimes thought it was only the delightful news of other people's misfortunes that kept Larry in the licensed victualler's trade, but he'd proved himself a good friend over the years. "When's JB getting back?" he added.

"We're not sure he's coming back at all. It turns out his heart attack was much more serious than we thought it was. He's just had a triple by-pass and he's definitely out of action for the next three months. But the word is that the doctors might advise him to retire altogether. He's sixty-four, you know. We all thought he was still in his mid-fifties."

"And I expect Col the Obnoxious is rubbing his hands together with glee at the prospect of becoming editor?"

"He's been rubbing them so hard he's got fucking blisters," I said.

The pity of it all was that with better luck I might now have been acting-editor of *Theatre World* myself. Two years ago, I'd been JB's deputy but had reluctantly left, for pressing financial reasons, to work for a soft porn outfit that provided a much higher salary. Everything had come to grief when I discovered that the soft porn was in fact a cover for the hardest porn imaginable, as well as belatedly realising that my best mate on the sex mags was guilty of killing a prostitute. I'd spent the past eighteen months trying to keep my head above water as a free-lance when I wasn't giving evidence in two long trials down at the Old Bailey. All the accused had gone down, taking the legitimate side of Botticelli Publications with them. My old mate, Brian, copped ten years once the original murder charge had been reduced to manslaughter. Sometimes I woke up in the middle of the night with a start, and remembered the odious smirk he'd given me as they led him away.

The court cases hadn't helped what only the most charitable could describe as my "career". Finally, broke, broken-hearted and desperate, I'd asked JB if there was any chance of returning to *Theatre World*. He'd kindly created a non-existent vacancy for me, but by then Col was firmly in the deputy's chair. I'd been back on *Theatre World*'s notoriously miserly payroll for the past six weeks. And two weeks ago, JB had copped his heart attack, right in the middle of a Domingo performance at Covent Garden. The St John Ambulance Brigade had got him to the hospital just in time.

"What I've never understood is that years ago Col more or less got the sack from *Theatre World,* didn't he?" said Larry, offering me a Rothmans King Size, which I accepted. Bloody Rothmans was about as good as life got these days, I thought self-pityingly. "And yet now there he is, snugly installed as acting-editor."

"Col jumped minutes before he was pushed back in '91," I confirmed. "He filched some hot copy, my copy as it happens, and flogged it to *the News of the Screws,* who promptly offered him a contract. But he was beginning to suffer tabloid burn-out. He moved from the *Screws* to the *Daily Mail* a couple of years ago and after about six months of being the golden boy in the ent's department someone else found favour. His by-line was appearing less and less. Our Col isn't as tough as he seems, he was sick of writing for the spike and he was hankering after a bit of job security. So, when he heard my successor as deputy editor wasn't working out, he got in touch with JB, promised he'd mended his old ways and smooth-talked his way into the job. You know what a soft touch JB is when he hears a hard luck story. I mean, he even took me back."

"And what about Kim?" he asked. "How's she doing at the *Guardian*?"

"Alarmingly well," I said, managing to sound remarkably casual, I thought. "After endless three-month contracts they've finally done the decent thing and given her a staff job as a features' sub. Pension plan, the lot."

"Well done Kim," said Larry, "I miss her. Any chance of you and her getting back . . . ?"

I cut him short. "I'd rather not talk about it, Larry," I said, my throat suddenly constricted. I felt alarmingly close to tears and crying in front of the gnarled old publican would be the final humiliation. I didn't think I could bear to witness his pity. His contempt I could stand.

"Understood," said Larry gruffly, turning his back to refill the whisky glasses at the optics. I'd come out for "the one". I'd be returning with another eight units sloshing their way around the already poisoned bloodstream. Fuck it, I thought, as so often these days. I was beginning to feel a bit better. I paid for the drinks – Larry's generosity never extended very far – and tossed back the Scotch in a couple of gulps.

"I've got to get back," I said. He nodded, and wished me luck. I'd probably need it. Outside, there was a nice freezing drizzle, with the bonus of a blustery wind that gusted the wet into your face. The big office buildings were still boarded up after the IRA Docklands bomb attack, but *Theatre World*'s jerry-built premises had withstood the blast miraculously well compared to the steel and glass towers and had needed only minor repairs. Shame. We might have forsaken this antiseptic brave new world and returned to somewhere more whole-some. Soho would have done nicely.

I managed to get through reception before Martha had a chance of engaging me in conversation and smelling the whisky fumes. The only wonder was she didn't keep a breathalyser behind her desk.

I climbed the stairs like a small boy returning reluctantly, resentfully, to school. Without Kim and now without JB, *Theatre World* was no longer the happy ship I'd once been genuinely proud to serve.

As I entered the newsroom, with its dying rubber plants and yellowing piles of old newspapers and discarded press releases, Colin looked up from his desk, and made a big show of consulting his watch, shaking his head in mock amazement before returning to his computer screen. Only it wasn't his desk, of course, but JB's. To Col's credit, he hadn't moved straight into the editor's chair as soon as we'd heard the news of JB's heart attack. He'd waited, and I'd timed it, all of one hour and twenty-three minutes. There was, of course, no need for him to move desks at all. Ours was an open-plan office, and the editor worked on the editorial floor along with everyone else. Col, however, after a solicitous visit to the proprietor, Mr Torrington, to confirm that he should indeed take over the helm in this sudden emergency, had changed desks without a word. There was no way he could justify this decision on grounds of practicality. Indeed, since JB's drawers were all full of his own things, it was ludicrously inconvenient, as Col had to cross the room whenever he wanted anything from his old desk. But the point had been made. Col was now in charge. Three days later, and doubtless at his own prompting, for *Theatre World* was traditionally informal to the point of chaos, a small notice appeared on the staff notice board confirming that, until JB's return, Col had been appointed acting editor. He'd probably been negotiating a pay rise as JB lay under the surgeon's knife.

I went to my own desk, and kindly Angela gave me a wink, whispered that I stank of booze, and offered me a Cherry Menthol Tune in case Col summoned me over for one of his "little chats". He always seemed to enjoy a little chat when I got back from lunch. But not today. The pre-Christmas issue was bigger than usual, had colour on the cover, and getting it out on time was going to be Col's first real test in his new position.

Kevin, the production editor, came over and said he needed the three reviews I hadn't written by the end of the afternoon. It was good of him not to shout out for them across the floor, alerting Col to another possible lapse on my part, and I promised I'd have them finished by five o'clock, gamely, but I suspect lamely, trying to give the impression that I just wanted to give my jewel-like prose one last loving polish.

It's not usually a good idea to write when you're half pissed but it's a damn sight easier than trying to write when you're in the terrible double grip of hangover and depression. I pitched into an insufferably sentimental clown from Russia first of all, and putting the boot into his ludicrously overpraised act

("Speaks, movingly and beautifully, to the inner child in us all." – *The Times*) cheered me up no end. I followed the demolition job with some modified rapture about a new play at the Royal Court, yet another saga of no-hopers in the big city with more vomit, drugs and buggery in ninety minutes than seemed humanly possible, and ended with a paean of praise for the great Des Barrit playing Dame Trot in panto at Norwich. "What's coq-au-vin?" Simple Simon had inquired. "Sex in the back of a Dormobile," leered the magnificent twenty-two-stone Welshman to the bewilderment of about 900 riotous tinies in the audience. I buzzed the reviews over to the subs' desk by five as promised and received an E-mail from Kevin on my computer screen a few minutes later. "As pissed old farts go, you're not too bad, I suppose," he'd written. It was the nicest thing anyone had said to me for weeks.

Only the Many Happy Returns column remained. I had three options. I could confess to losing, or at least mislaying, the Bible, which had the virtue of honesty but absolutely nothing else to recommend it. I could discreetly wander over to the files of past issues, look up last year's entry for the same week and duplicate it, which was clearly the sensible thing to do, but dull. Or I could make it up. Elated by having finished the reviews, and with just enough alcohol coursing round the system to switch off the caution circuits in the brain, this suddenly seemed an excellent idea. It would give Kevin a laugh, and I secretly hoped that he might just let the column get as far as page-proof stage. JB always read the proofs meticulously, spending many hours of drudgery on the job each week. Col already showed signs that he had bigger fish to fry, like talking endlessly to what he odiously called "the movers and shakers of the entertainment industry" on the phone. The fact that he was now acting editor was invariably dropped into the conversation at an early point and occasionally there was the pleasure of watching him becoming increasingly exasperated as the person at the other end waxed over-eloquent in sympathy or admiration for poor JB. "Oh, yes, great man, lovely man, a legend," Col would say. "We're all absolutely shattered here." All the while he would be writhing in his chair with impatience, and making wanking gestures with his right hand. All of which left little time for proof-reading and a few serious literals had occurred in the previous week's paper. It would be interesting to see just how bad a mistake had to be before Col got round to spotting it. He occasionally betrayed terrifying vistas of ignorance about the arts.

I created a new file and typed 'Many Happy Returns' at the top.

Wednesday Dec. 25. Sir Ian McKellen (35), busy showbiz agent and fiancé of Spice Girl, Mel B.
Thursday Dec. 26 Patricia Routledge, OBE, (28), Page 3 model and star of the doomed nude musical *Voyeurz.*
Friday Dec. 27 Trevor Nunn (69), much loved showbiz hairdresser.
Saturday Dec. 28 Bonnie Langford (47), award winning member of the Royal Shakespeare Company, a stunning Cleopatra last season.
Sunday Dec. 29 Sir John Gielgud (19), hot young actor who made his name in the Royal Court's controversial *Smegma and Snot.*
Monday Dec. 30 Melvyn Bragg (31), genial host and commentator on Live TV's Topless Darts show.
Tuesday Dec. 31 Max Hastings (32), gay rights campaigner and *EastEnders* actor.

It was 5.30 by the time I'd finished. I sent the copy over to the subs before I had a chance to have second thoughts, and raised an imaginary glass in an interrogatory way at Kevin across the newsroom. He grinned eagerly and logged off before he'd had a chance to read the piece. With a bit of luck, it would cheer him up tomorrow morning.

Mirza, the chief reporter who was every bit as unhappy about Col's return to *Theatre World* as I was, joined us, as did

Kevin's beautiful twenty-two-year-old deputy, Felicity, who looked like a bimbo with her big hair and tiny leather skirt but was actually intimidatingly bright. I had the serious hots for Felicity but she always made a very thorough job of letting me know I was way out of her class, treating me like a vaguely disreputable uncle whose name she couldn't quite remember. The tragedy was that she seemed to have a genuine crush on Kevin who was a celibate gay Catholic.

As Mirza got in the drinks at the Perseverance, Kevin asked me if I'd heard anything from Kim recently.

"No, nothing recently," I said as non-committally as I could.

"It's silly this, you know," he said gently.

"It's also none of your business," I said savagely, and immediately regretted it. "I'm sorry, Kevin."

"It's OK," he said, though he looked hurt and flushed. "I'm sorry to have intruded."

Felicity was obviously agog with curiosity. She'd joined the paper six months earlier and had never met Kim, though I couldn't believe Kevin, her former deputy, had never mentioned her. Apart from anything else, it was Kim who had written *Theatre World*'s style guide which was consulted almost daily on the subs' desk. I felt I owed Felicity an explanation but couldn't bring myself to offer it. Fortunately, at that moment, Mirza brought the drinks over, and a couple of minutes after that, Angela, who'd been finishing a story when we left, came in and told me someone had phoned the office and wanted me to call back urgently.

"Did he give his name?" I asked.

"Gray," she said, "Nicholas Gray". My hand started trembling and I had to put my drink down before I spilled it.

"You look as though you've just seen a ghost," said Felicity.

"I sort of have," I said. "A name from the past anyway."

"I'll just look up his number," said Angela, reaching for her notebook.

"It isn't 01 978 0126, is it?" I said, the number springing at once from some deep recess in the memory.

"Yeah," she said. "Only the code's 0181 now, of course."

I went over to the payphone and dialled the number, feeling breathless, anxious and excited all at once. It was, I calculated, ten years since I'd seen Nicholas and I'd never forgotten the circumstances of our last meeting. Would he still be talking in the ridiculous camp cockney accent he'd started using all those years ago?

"Nicholas Gray," he said crisply, his familiar nasal middle-class voice mercifully returned to normality.

"Nicholas, it's Will. How lovely to hear from you. But what's so urgent after all these years?"

"We need to talk," he said. "Can you come round? Tonight?"

"I've got to go to the theatre," I said.

"Well, after the theatre. I could put you up here for the night."

"I've got to come back to work in the morning. I haven't got a car at the . . ."

"Yes, yes, yes," he said, with a flash of his old, oddly endearing impatience. "They run trains into London most mornings these days, you know. People called 'commuters' use them every day."

"Back into the knife drawer, Miss Sharp," I said, the old phrase, like his old phone number, leaping back across the years. "You don't want to resume our last quarrel, I take it?"

"No. And I'm sorry about it. That's one of the reasons why I'd like to see you. How's your wife, er, Kim, wasn't it?"

I'd sent him an invitation to our wedding, proffering the olive branch after years of mutual silence, and had been hurt to have received no reply.

"She's fine," I said. If anyone else asked me how Kim was today I was going to scream.

"I gather from the number you're back in Molesey. How are your parents?"

"Er . . . dead," he said, and I felt a stab of grief. I'd liked his mum and dad a lot.

"I'm so sorry."

"It's been a few years now," he said, though there was an edge of pain in his voice. "Look, there's no point in talking now. I'll see you later." He gave me a few train times and I said that, show permitting, I'd get the 10.26 from Waterloo and be round at his place not long after eleven.

"Great," he said. "Lots of love till then."

"Friendship and wild times," I said, and as I put the phone down I realised I felt happier than I had for months.

"Everything OK?" asked Angela as I returned to our table.

"Yeah, fine," I said. I bought a round of drinks and went over to the juke box. Larry had finally given up on his old 45's machine when a drunken punter, driven to the point of certifiable insanity by the fact that the *Theatre World* staff had played Rolf Harris's 'Two Little Boys' six times in a row, had laid about the trusty Wurlitzer with a pool cue. He'd done a remarkable amount of damage by the time he was dragged off and the police were called. The great night had passed into legend, known as Rolf's Triumph, the anniversary marked each year by a giant piss-up. Fortunately, *the Theatre World* staff had been able to reassemble many of the worst moments in the history of pop on CD by diligent perusal of the discounted bins of 60's, 70's and 80's greatest hits' compilations, usually selling for £1.99 a time in service stations. Larry had kindly agreed to include them in his new state-of-the-art machine, along with some perfectly decent CDs supplied by the firm that hired it to him. It seemed like a night for old favourites. Benny Hill's 'Ernie', natch. Cliff Richard's 'Congratulations'. Carl Palmer's 'Mistletoe and Wine'. But I put on Bowie's 'Heroes' as well, in honour of Nicholas and the rest of the gang.

By the time the selection had played itself out, and Mirza had delivered a passionate, perceptive, and extremely welcome ten-minute monologue on the various shortcomings, professional, personal and physical, of Col the Obnoxious, I was in serious danger of being late for the theatre. But the

Docklands Light Railway, much improved in recent years, provided a train to Bank as soon as I arrived on the platform and I was able to take my seat at the Apollo, Shaftesbury Avenue, with five minutes to spare. You might well wonder whether the West End really needed yet another pop nostalgia show, and it has to be said that the story of Freddie and the Dreamers is not one overburdened with dramatic interest, or indeed hits. But there was a load of other Sixties' golden oldies thrown in, and as I walked back across Hungerford Bridge humming 'You Were Made For Me' and practising my dinky Freddie back-kicks, even the icy drizzle couldn't extinguish my high spirits. I was just going down the staircase on the south side of the Thames when I saw them, emerging from the Festival Hall.

It was like a sudden, vicious punch below the belt, and I gasped out loud. They were among the first out of the concert and as soon as I saw them, I was convinced they were hurrying home to bed. Whose home? Col was in evening dress beneath his regrettable Loders overcoat, Kim was wearing the black astrakhan jacket I'd given her a couple of birthdays ago and a preposterous floppy green velvet hat I didn't recognise. As I stood at the top of the steps, mouth dry, heart pounding, Col put his arm proprietorially round her shoulder and she snuggled comfortably into his embrace like a sleepy cat. The concert-goers were streaming out of the hall now, and I realised that if I didn't move fast I would lose them.

I leapt down the steps, told the beggar at the bottom to fuck off when he asked for some change, hating myself as I did so, and joined the throng wending its way to Waterloo. They were all in evening dress, a gala night obviously, and then I remembered that a couple of days ago Col had been boasting about his free tickets to a rare recital by Pollini and a big champagne reception. A fundraiser for the latest millennium plan for the South Bank if I remembered rightly. I stayed a few yards behind the lovebirds, forcing my mind to go blank and pulling desperately on the providential stub of a half-smoked roll-up I'd found in the bottom of my pocket. The couple, and they looked so like a couple, walked under the railway viaduct into York Road, heading for the steps that led up to the elevated walkway into Waterloo. Kim still lived in the flat we'd once shared in Vauxhall. Col lived in St Katherine's Dock in an "enviable duplex" as he rarely failed to describe it, with views of the Thames and Tower Bridge. Neither needed a train, so perhaps they were making their way to the Waterloo cab rank. I could at least satisfy my feverish curiosity. Would they take one cab or two? If it was two cabs, things were better than I feared. If it was one, I'd rush to the front of the queue, making whatever scene was necessary, and follow it. Tough buns on Nicholas, but this was an emergency. What I didn't expect was that at 10p.m. in a pedestrian-clogged York Road, they'd manage to pick up a cab off the street. But a taxi, yellow light cheerfully shining, suddenly came into view from a side-street, Col stepped authoritatively out onto the road to hail it, and I watched, impotent and furious, as the pair of them climbed inside and the taxi performed a nifty U-turn. Heading towards Vauxhall, I realised, with a sickening lurch of the stomach.

Needless to say, there was no other cab in which to follow, and I stood dejectedly in the middle of the pavement until a hurrying pedestrian bumped into me and told me to get the fuck out of his space. Nice. I made my way up the staircase, walked across the walkway like a somnambulist and entered Bonaparte's Bar, that grim little dive that so tactfully greets patriotic Frenchmen arriving off the Eurostar at a station named after their greatest military disaster. It might just as well be called Screw You, Froggie.

As always, it took an age to get served as the staff had far more important things to do, like chatting amongst themselves. Eventually a bolshie, acne-infested teenage foreigner (French?) came and stood in front of me with a scowl on his erupting face. I ordered a pint of Bass and a large Grouse and, realising I was sweating profusely, took them out to one of the tables on the chilly concourse. I had two options. I could have these drinks, get a cab, and knock on the door at Rita Road to find out what the hell was going on. Or I could try to put the whole horror out of my mind and catch the 10.26 to see Nicholas. Miserably, I remembered that I'd had another attack of rancid jealousy about Kim and Colin, shortly before she and I started going out together. On that occasion, my jealousy had been fully justified, which was no comfort at all.

The confrontation plan seemed attractive, as the initial shock gave way to cold anger. But then I imagined Col undressing Kim and Kim undressing Col, the two of them clutching, kissing, laughing, unable to keep their hands off each other until at last they fell gratefully on to the bed. Our bed. I began to tremble, and realised I must put this scenario right out of my mind, even if it was happening, now, just a mile down the road. The thought of catching them *in flagrante* was intolerable. I drained the Scotch and went and got another. Perhaps Col was just gallantly dropping Kim off before taking the cab back to the duplex. Perhaps I should go and wait there and have it out with him when he got back. He might, wildly optimistic though it seemed, be back by the time I arrived. I could always invent some story about wanting to see him about something to do with work, improbable though it would undoubtedly seem to us both.

But as I drank the second Scotch at a fractionally less frantic pace, I realised that I didn't really want to find out what was happening at all. Uncertainty was undoubtedly horrible, but it was a great deal less horrible than knowing beyond all doubt that Colin was screwing my wife. Even if I arrived at St Katherine's Dock to find him at home, the kernel of doubt would remain – the more I thought about the way she had buried her head in his shoulder, the more I wanted to scream out loud in protest. It was such an intimate, unguarded moment, suggesting bodies that had grown familiar and comfortable with each other, bodies that fitted together snugly after long practice. I tried to remember the last time Kim had snuggled up to me like that, and was distressed to find that I couldn't. I'd sleep on it, I decided, draining my Bass; perhaps even talk to Nicholas about it.

I walked towards the Hampton Court platform, briefly considered stopping off for a quarter-bottle of Grouse at the station off-licence to anaesthetise the pain on the train, then concluded that, after so long a rift, I owed Nicholas the courtesy of turning up more or less sober. I bought a cup of tea instead, discovered that South West Trains didn't run to smoking compartments any more, and found a seat among bleary commuters and a party of voluble Scandinavian au pairs on their way back to the suburbs after seeing *The Phantom of the Opera.*

Whenever images of Kim and Col flickered into my head; Col humping dementedly away, Kim moaning in her most abandoned manner, I tried to block them out with memories of that summer of 1982. It worked, or at least it worked some of the time, but the stopping train was infuriatingly slow and past happiness kept giving way to present anguish. Eventually, after what felt like several weeks, the train ground to a halt at Hampton Court, the terminus of the suburban line. The cold air, the chance to move freely, were both a huge relief, and before making my way to Nicholas's house, I walked to the middle of Hampton Court Bridge and gazed at the massive yet intricate silhouette of the palace against the maroon sky. Unexpectedly, I experienced a sudden sense of detachment from all the throbbing turmoil in my head. I was less than a mile from my childhood home. I was going to see Nicholas. It felt like old times.

There is a cheerfully raffish, resort-like atmosphere to the environs of Hampton Court Palace. Three times a year, on bank-holiday weekends, a huge travelling funfair pitches up on the green, glory days of my childhood from the age of four when Auntie May took me there for the first time. You can take pleasure-boats up and down the Thames, eat in several excellent restaurants and drink in a delightful riverside pub. On summer afternoons, there's an attractive, cosmopolitan bustle. Tonight, it was quiet, almost deserted, and bitingly cold. I shivered, retraced my steps and crossed the road into the quiet backwaters of East Molesey. Nicholas' and Natasha's parents had lived in a handsome, three-storeyed Victorian house with a monkey puzzle tree in the front garden, which always made it easy to find. Or had done. I walked well beyond the point where I thought Nicholas' house was, and realised that the monkey puzzle must have been felled. I retraced my steps, wishing I'd asked Nicholas for his street number, peering disconsolately at front doors and houses that all looked much the same. Then I remembered that Nicholas' house had a stained-glass half-moon window above the front door. Several other houses had them too, but the designs were all different and I remembered that Nicholas' had been of a particularly lurid sunset over a bilious green sea. There it was, at last. I walked to the front door, noticed the rotting stump of the monkey puzzle in the front garden and felt a pang of regret. There had been something engaging about that once fashionable suburban status symbol. I rang the bell and Nicholas opened the door. He looked like death. No, it was worse than that. He looked as though he was dying. And, of course, he was.

"Don't look so shocked," he said, a shadow of his familiar mocking smile momentarily illuminating his blotchy, haggard face. "It was you, after all, who rightly warned that it would all end in tears." I found tears stinging in my own eyes and hugged him close to me, partly to hide my embarrassment, partly because all my old affection for him had come flooding, unbearably, back, now that it was too late, or almost too late. His upper body felt like a frail skeleton in my clumsy embrace.

"It's good to see you, Nicholas," I said over his shoulder, unable to keep a sob out of my voice. "I can't tell you how much I've missed you."

He said, "And I love you too," in a voice that combined his usual mocking irony with a hint of real tenderness then gently disengaged himself, led me into the sitting room, and took a long disconcerting look at me through glasses that seemed to be made of bottle glass.

"Christ, Will, you've got fat," he said. "And you look," he paused, as he always had done when searching for the lethal *mot juste* "unhappily dissipated."

"That just about sums it up," I replied. "And while we're trading offensive personal remarks, I have to say that I've seen you looking better yourself." There was a tense second's silence between us and then we both broke into the laughter that had so often united our differences in the past. The gay and the straight. The art historian and the piss artist. The polished, promiscuous bright young thing and the scruffy, usually monogamous hack. Nicholas began to wheeze alarmingly and sat down on the sofa to get his breath. The sofa he'd once tried to seduce me on.

"Who do you have to fuck to get a drink around here?" I asked.

"Sorry," said Nicholas, still wheezing. "Do you mind getting it yourself. There's a bottle of the usual in the fridge."

I went out to the kitchen at the back, unchanged and as impeccably clean as when I'd last seen it. The stripped pine units were burnished into a golden glow, the real-marble work surfaces gleamed. One newly rinsed mug on the draining board and a couple of medicine bottles on the window sill was all there was in the way of clutter. Except in the small matter of the exchange of bodily fluids, Nicholas had always been as fastidious as his poor dead mum.

I found the stone bottle of Dutch gin in the fridge, went instinctively to the glasses' cupboard and found a couple of tumblers, and put all three on the exquisite Chinese lacquer tray that had always been one of Nicholas's pride and joys.

"Nice to see the good old Genever again," I said. "I haven't had it for years."

"Just a small one for me," said Nicholas. "Drink doesn't agree with me any more. Fortunately, these do. In fact, they're a positive life-saver at times." He opened a small wooden box on the glass coffee table and produced a neatly-rolled joint.

"One for you?" he asked, reaching for another. "You won't want to share mine," he added neutrally.

"I don't go in for dope much these days," I said, feeling thoroughly suburban. "I'll stick to the booze."

"Marijuana does you much less harm," he said.

"I know," I replied, pouring a small measure for Nicholas and sloshing out a quadruple for myself. I handed him his glass.

"Bottoms up," I heard myself saying before I could stop myself.

"No longer, unfortunately," he replied. "Dear old Will. Still afflicted by foot-in-mouth disease."

The cold, oily, aromatic gin brought memories flooding back. It must have been at the end of my first week on the *Esher Herald*, a few days before midsummer night, that Nicholas had brought me back here and chased me round the sitting room while Soft Cell's *Non-Stop Erotic Cabaret* played on the hi-fi. His parents had been out at the theatre, Natasha was still up at university and Nicholas had given me far more to drink than I was used to and then moved uncomfortably close to me on the sofa. I got up, and pretended to be hugely interested in an all-white painting on the wall and he came and stood next to me. I went over to another picture, white with a smidgen of pink in the corner this time, and he followed me there. I began examining the bookshelves and there was Nicholas yet again. I could feel his breath on my cheek. The sexual tension was like static electricity flashing between us and eventually, realising this couldn't go on all night, I went back to the sofa, and Nicholas came and sat next to me and put his arm round me.

"Are you trying to seduce me, Mrs Robinson?" I'd giggled because the gin was kicking in nicely by now.

"That's the general idea," he said.

He'd leaned forward, put his tongue in my mouth. I tried to enjoy it but couldn't, and to his great credit, Nicholas instantly recognised the fact and didn't press his advantage.

"You don't fancy me then?" he'd asked with a rueful grin.

"I'd like to, Nicholas, I'd really like to. It's just that men, boys, do nothing for me. I've often wished they did. Life at boarding school would have been a lot more fun."

"Not even the teensiest, weensiest bit?" he asked.

"'Fraid not."

"Fair enough," he said, and we'd then got so ecstatically sloshed that his dad had to drive me back home when he and his wife got back from the theatre.

I smiled at the memory and Nicholas asked me what I was thinking about. I told him.

"Never such innocence again," he said sadly.

"Tell me about your parents. If it's not too painful," I said.

"Roger died suddenly of a heart attack in 1992," he said. As a teenager I'd always been tremendously impressed by the easy way in which Nicholas and Natasha called their parents by their Christian names. "Jennifer went into a sharp depressive decline and six months later was found to be riddled with cancer. I'm sure it was the grief that did it. Theirs was one of the only truly happy marriages I've ever come across. God, they were great. You know my father shaved my pubic hair the first time I came home with crabs. Greater love hath no father than that."

"Did they know about . . . ?" I couldn't bring myself to say the A-word.

"They knew I was HIV positive. Luckily, I didn't start getting sick until after their deaths. I've had a good run really. It's only been the full blown beastliness for the past 18 months."

"When were you diagnosed?"

"In 1987," he said. "A year after our, er, falling out."

"Jesus, Nicholas, for most of your adult life you've known . . ." Again, I couldn't get the words out.

"That I was under sentence of death. Yes," he said simply. "It's strange, most of the time you can come to terms with it. You were quite right about my New York adventures, of course. It's almost certain that's when I became infected."

I thought back to the autumn of 1986. I'd been on the *Bridport Chronicle* for a year by then, and was sharing a scruffy flat above a shop in the High Street with my girlfriend, Cathy. Nicholas, who'd been awarded a starred first in History of Art at Cambridge, was about to start his second year of postgraduate research and had come to visit for a couple of days before returning to his college. Only he didn't stay that long. He'd reinvented himself that summer. He'd adopted that absurd cockney accent for a start, like a parody of a rent boy, and shaved his hair to within a few millimetres of his skull. My camp, sophisticated friend who had always hated being called Nick now insisted on it, and his wit had given way to militant gay pride of the separatist kind. Within a few minutes of his arrival, I wondered why he had come at all. It was clear that he deeply disapproved of my cosy domestic set-up with Cathy and he sneered at her as though he found the very presence of a woman objectionable. We'd gone to the Riverside Cafe, a terrific if ruinously expensive fish restaurant in West Bay, and he'd regaled us, loudly in order to cause maximum embarrassment to neighbouring tables, about his erotic exploits in the bath-houses and gay clubs of Manhattan that summer, a few of which still flourished, recklessly, dementedly, in the face of the "gay plague". Part of me found the idea of so much casual anonymous sex exciting, part of me was appalled. Cathy just sat there and blushed miserably.

"But there's a terrible risk, Nicholas, you must know that better than me. It's like dancing on board the *Titanic*."

Nicholas didn't want to listen. "The very best thing to do on the fucking *Titanic*. What I do with my body is my affair," he insisted sullenly.

"No one's saying it isn't," I replied. "It's just that I care about you. I don't want to be turning up to your funeral in a few years' time."

"I wouldn't want you there," he'd said viciously. "Sanctimonious, tight-arsed bourgeois straights."

Cathy and I sat in stunned silence, staring miserably at the glorious plate of *fruits de mer* in front of us. It had cost about half a week's wages. How on earth were we going to get through the meal together now?

"Let me tell you about fist-fucking," said Nicholas, almost screaming now, his face set in a rictus grin of antagonism. "You really ought to try it, you know."

It was too much for Arthur, the usually genial proprietor.

"One more disgusting squeak out of you, sonny, and you're out," he said with magnificent, unexpected menace. "How dare you speak like that when there are women and children present?" Several people at neighbouring tables broke into spontaneous applause at this. Nick flushed dangerously and rose to his feet. "I wouldn't eat this shit if you paid me," he said, and turning on the heel of his elegantly tooled cowboy boot, he flounced out. Cathy, just turned nineteen and the previous year's Miss Bridport in the summer carnival, was, I noticed for the first time, crying quietly into a tiny pocket handkerchief. I patted her ineffectually on the shoulder, apologised for my friend to Arthur and made my way outside. Nicholas, Nick, whatever the bastard was calling himself these days, was lurking by the harbour slipway. I felt like smashing him on the nose.

"What was all that about?" I said.

"Just a display of entirely justified contempt for you and everyone like you," he said. "I'm off."

"But you've left all your stuff at our place. And you haven't got a car," I bleated. Cathy and I had picked him up that morning at Crewkerne station.

"Just fuck off back to Miss Prissy," he said. So I did. Arthur had cheered Cathy up and she tucked voraciously into her seafood. Nicholas was just a temporary embarrassment to her, and I wished I could feel the same. In fact, I was suffering from a mixture of rage, resentment and loss, and couldn't eat a thing. Even the Chablis, excellent at first sip, now tasted acid in my mouth. The wine has always reminded me of soured friendship on the rare occasions I've drunk it since. I sent Nicholas's bag by rail to Cambridge station and dropped him a line to tell him it would be waiting for him there. I'd never heard from him again. Until today.

Nicholas seemed to have been eavesdropping on my thoughts. "I'm so sorry about that lunch, Will," he said.

"I've always wondered how you got back."

"Picked up a lift at the Bridport roundabout with a friendly lorry driver. Very friendly indeed as it turned out."

"You didn't have it off with him?"

"I did. We stopped in a layby on the A35. He must have had a good time. He went out of his way to drop me just outside Hampton Court Palace."

"You weren't that upset then?" I said, still vaguely hurt after a decade.

"Not then. Just angry, which made the sex better. But I did feel remorse later."

"Why were you so angry, why had you changed so much?"

"Well, I still fancied you for a start. I hoped I'd grown out of that little crush but it turned out I hadn't and seeing you with that prim little girlfriend didn't exactly cheer me up."

"She's actually very nice," I said "We're still in touch."

"Right, sorry. Well, that was part of it. There was also a terrific gay backlash going on at the time. All those gay plague stories; talk about isolating AIDS patients in what sounded not much different from concentration camps. It felt like us against the world. And then there was the bitterness that having fully discovered my sexuality, become confident with it, the whole thing was suddenly tainted by fear, disease and death."

"It didn't stop you in New York. Or with that lorry driver."

"I wasn't as wild as I let on. I was pretty wild but I did practice safe sex. Most of the time. The trouble is that in the heat of the moment, with the coke, the poppers, the beer and the music, you're sometimes not quite as sensible as you ought to be. Which proved to be my undoing."

"How do you cope with the knowledge . . ." There was no tactful way of putting this. "With the knowledge that you've literally fucked yourself to death?"

"What would you feel if you were diagnosed as having lung cancer?" he said, indicating the roll-up between my fingers.

"Guilt. Anger. Indignant surprise that it should have happened to me. Fear."

"That about sums it up," said Nicholas. "Life's a series of risks, some of them avoidable. We make our own calculations and we have to face the consequences if it turns out we got it wrong. Sometimes, life just deals you a lousy hand anyway, like my father. That's harder to bear in a way."

We sat in silence. It was hard to recall the beautiful young Nicholas in the face of the stricken, emaciated man who sat opposite me. But he'd acquired courage, even grace, as his body withered around him.

"I'm going blind, you know. Something horrible called a cytomegalovirus is eating away my eyes."

"God, I'm sorry," I said. For an art historian, for a man who had always delighted in the visual, from great masterpieces to muscle-bound hunks in gay porn mags, this must be the bitterest of all pills.

"I miss the reading more than anything. I can only manage about half an hour before I feel dizzy. I'm not bothered about the pictures, oddly enough. They're all there in my head. And I've got the radio, talking books, music. A world of pleasure in this room."

"I've followed your career a little," I said. "You wrote a piece years ago in the *Literary Review*, demolishing the academic vacuity of some hugely expensive art book and it said in the contributors' notes that you were reader in History of Art at East Anglia. And then I met someone from the university at a bash for the Norwich Theatre Royal a couple of years ago and asked about you. He said you were a brilliant teacher. He sounded a bit sad, I didn't realise why then."

"Sounds like my head of department, David Totton," said Nicholas. "He's chairman of the Theatre Royal board and a bit of a fan of mine. I wasn't a brilliant teacher, but I enjoyed it, which is more than can be said for most academics, and I miss it badly. I, um, retired in the summer. With AIDS you sometimes get very sick, very quickly, and it often means a few weeks in hospital. The university authorities were very good about it, but I was missing so many lectures and seminars it wasn't fair on the other members of the faculty or my students. I left this June. Luckily, I was well enough in my last term to get the third years properly prepared for their finals.

"And then you came home?"

"Yeah, after my parents died, Natasha and I rented this place to a couple of Americans, but I gave them six months notice last Christmas. I've been here ever since."

"But don't you miss all your friends in Norwich? Don't you need some kind of support?"

"Yes, in a way, I suppose. But the expressions of sympathy become hard to bear after a while. The look of anxiety, even panic on the faces of other HIV victims who know that they're going to look like you, too, before long. The whole of Norwich had become so shadowed with death for me. My partner, Robert, died just over a year ago. We'd been together for seven years. We were both HIV when we met, but luckily we were allowed that time together. He went very fast at the end."

He turned away from me for a moment, and I went and sat beside him on the sofa, and put my arm round his scrawny shoulder. I found myself half-wishing I'd surrendered to his advances all those years ago. It would have been a memory of life amid all this death.

There was a catch in his voice as he turned back to look at me. "What about you, Will? What kind of hand has life dealt you?"

"OK," I said, and burst into tears. It was pathetic. Here was a bereaved and dying man and it was me that was blubbing like a child. I cried and cried, and eventually I cried myself out.

"Do you want to talk about it?" he said.

I did but I couldn't. The great absence that had grown between Kim and I as we repeatedly tried and failed to have a child, the terrible rows, my sullen retreat into booze . . . I ought to have told Nicholas all those things. But then I remembered Kim burying her head into Colin's shoulder and the pain and jealousy were too intense to describe.

"I'm sorry, Nicholas," I said. "Kim and I are going through a bit of a rough patch at the moment and I'd rather not talk about it." It was a betrayal of friendship, particularly after Nicholas' frankness with me. But I couldn't admit to my failure, to the fact that, for the past three months, Kim and I had been living apart and hardly ever spoke, even on the phone. If he was hurt, he didn't show it.

"It's all right, Will. I know how you feel. The AIDS counsellors were always on at me to talk, bring all my feelings of fear and confusion out into the open. And in the end I think you have to. But only when you're ready. Despite all the psychobabble I think there's sometimes a place for good old fashioned British repression, the stiff upper lip. Dignity, endurance, self-sufficiency – unfashionable qualities but they're not to be mocked."

He took my pudgy hand in his skeletal one and gave it a squeeze. "It's an odious phrase but I'll always be here for you," he said, then gave a wry grin that gave a glimpse of his tremendous heart. "Well, not always, obviously. Try not to leave it too long till your next visit, Will."

"I won't," I said, "and thank you." I poured myself another slosh of Dutch gin so that he wouldn't see how moved I was (why was I so scared of revealing my feelings? I wondered bleakly) and Nicholas relit his joint from which he'd only taken a couple of puffs. He took down a couple of lungfuls, relaxed back in his chair, and I took the joint from him and put it to my own lips. If I couldn't find the words to acknowledge our friendship, at least I could offer this small gesture of solidarity.

"That was kind . . . and brave," said Nicholas. "You'll be relieved to learn that saliva isn't generally reckoned to be a factor in spreading the virus. You'd need a couple of bucketfuls of spit to be at any kind of risk." It was such a revolting image that I suddenly found myself laughing uncontrollably, and Nicholas joined me with his wheezy death rattle.

"How's Natasha?" I asked. "She's certainly done what she said she'd do. I don't know if she's happy, but by Christ she must be rich."

"Lady Natasha Gilbert-Smith is much the same as she ever was. Uptight and snobbish on the outside, but with glimpses of a much nicer person underneath. She's been a tower of strength recently."

"Did you go to the wedding? I'm ashamed to admit it but I bought *Hello!* magazine the week she was featured on the cover."

"Yes, Robert and I were invited."

"It looked amazing. That baronial castle in Scotland, the massed band of pipers. Fergie was there, wasn't she, wearing a ridiculous tartan dress with those poor little princesses in matching outfits? And Mick Jagger, Michael Heseltine, Bryan Ferry, Bruce Forsyth . . ."

"Yeah, they were all there. All 600 of us," he said, "but the most interesting guest wasn't in any of the pictures."

"Who was that?"

"Henry."

"Blimey, wasn't that a bit awkward. I mean after you and Natasha and him . . ."

"It was particularly odd since he hadn't been invited. Security was amazingly tight and I've no idea how he got in. Anyway, he was quite shameless. Robert and I had already offered our congratulations to the lovely couple and were happily star-spotting and bitching on the other side of the room. And then suddenly, standing just behind Sir Cliff in the line-up, I saw Henry. He kissed Natasha on the cheek and shook Sir Dominic warmly by the hand. Natasha looked as though she'd seen a ghost. I don't think she ever forgave him, you know. It's only in the last few months, since Robert died and I've been really ill that she's finally forgiven me. Even though it all happened so long ago."

It had indeed all been a long time ago, but it still seemed amazingly vivid to me. It had been in late September, at the end of that marvellous summer, and the old gang was on the point of breaking up. For the start of new terms as we thought. For ever as it turned out. The six of us had booked tickets on one of the disco boats that plied up and down the Thames, lights blazing, music throbbing to the huge annoyance of anyone who lives near the bank. As well as us, there'd been a big office party on board that night, too, and an air of bacchanalian frenzy prevailed on the dance floor. Suddenly, the Stones had given way to ABC's 'The Look of Love' and I'd gathered Rose gratefully into my arms for a slow number. She'd buried her head in my chest, just like . . . no, I really mustn't think about that . . . and I'd gazed over her shoulder at the rest of the dance floor. Among the entwined couples, Trev the Rev and Natasha had been dancing rather formally, bodies well apart, like a middle-aged couple taking a trip down memory lane on the floor at the Tower Ballroom in Blackpool. And then I'd seen Nicholas and Henry. To the evident amazement of several boozed up secretaries and gawping junior accountants, they were openly snogging.

And then Natasha spotted them too, and I saw her mouth form a cry of distress drowned out by ABC in all their overblown, criminally underrated glory. Henry and Nicholas must have seen her watching them, for a second later they had disappeared from the dance floor like fleeting shadows. Natasha stormed over to Rose and me, tapped Rose peremptorily on the shoulder, and Rose unsnuggled herself, looking like a sleepy squirrel woken from hibernation.

"Did you see what that brother of yours and Nicholas were up to?" she asked.

"No," said Rose, sullenly or it might just have been sleepily.

"They were . . ." For once, Natasha seemed lost for words, then found some, though they seemed more appropriate to a pre-war governess than a nineteen-year-old English Lit. student, "making the most disgraceful exhibition of themselves on the dance floor."

Rose gazed round at the couples swaying together on the beer sticky floor. "But everyone's making a disgraceful exhibition of themselves . . ." she said mildly. At that moment, as if to prove her thesis, one of the raucous males of the party threw up down the back of his partner's dress, to cruel cheers and jeers from his colleagues.

"But with Nicholas," said Natasha, ignoring the incident and speaking on a rising note of disbelief that would have done justice to Lady Bracknell.

"I'm not my brother's keeper," said Rose, unusually sharply for her. "And nor will you be if you've got any sense."

Natasha suddenly looked exhausted and terribly unhappy. I couldn't blame her. She and Henry had been very much an item since midsummer night, though I didn't know if they were actually going out together when the rest of us weren't. Henry, who so enlivened both the office and our social lives, could be infuriatingly discreet at times. Natasha gazed bleakly round the deck, but there was no sign of Nicholas and Henry.

"We've got to find them," she said firmly.

"I wouldn't do that if I were you," said Trev the Rev mildly, "it was probably only a bit of fun."

"A bit of fun," she said, almost spitting. "Bloody fine vicar you're going to make."

To my horror, Natasha took me by the arm. "Come on, Will, I know you'll help me," she said, her voice, one part flattery to two parts bullying, eerily reminiscent of Margaret Thatcher's.

"I say, do you think that's a good idea?" I said, but Natasha had my arm in a vice-like grip and was already leading me downstairs to the bar. There were a lot of noisy accountants down there, and a few more pools of sick, but no sign of Nicholas and Henry.

We went up another companionway, as I believe sea-dogs call them, and found ourselves on a deck on the starboard side of the boat. Just in front of us, sealing off the front end, sorry, bow, was a chain with a notice saying "no passengers beyond this point". A small thing like that wasn't going to stop Natasha. She climbed nimbly over it before I had time to stop her, let out a gasp, stumbled back over the chain and began to heave her guts out over the side of the boat. To judge by the amount of protein spill on and around the Disco Boat Diana anyone would think the craft was crossing the Bay of Biscay in a severe gale rather than cruising the Thames on a mild autumn night. I stepped over the chain myself. There, in the shadows beneath the wheelhouse and out of the line of vision of whoever was steering the boat immediately above, were Henry and Nicholas. Henry had a happy grin on his face, his head tilted back to gaze at the night sky. Nicholas was kneeling in front of him, head busily working. Henry must have sensed my arrival, for he turned round, his smile broader than ever, and flicked me an amiable V-sign while putting a finger to his mouth. From his relaxed demeanour, I could only conclude that he was either a very cool customer indeed or that he had been so transported by the pleasures of the flesh that he had missed Natasha's earlier arrival on the carnal scene. I stumbled back and put my arm round Natasha as she retched her heart out. Silently, that was the alarming thing about it. As if she didn't want to disturb Nicholas and Henry. Eventually she shuddered for the last time, wiped her mouth with a hankie, and stumbled a few paces down the deck. I hurried after her, and again she grabbed me by the arm.

"You've got to get me off this wretched boat," she said. It seemed a tall order. No stops were scheduled on the round trip from Hampton Court to the Tower of London and back. But I could see the lights of Hammersmith Bridge approaching and guessed their might be a landing stage nearby. With unusual command of a tricky situation, I walked up the companionway that led to the wheelhouse, knocked on the door, and confronted an ancient mariner with a nicotine stained white beard and a greasy cap. He looked as though he ought to be safely banged up in an old folk's home, not steering a clapped-out craft by night with a hundred drunken revellers on board.

"Is there any chance of stopping? There's a very sick passenger out there," I said.

"Tell me another," he said wearily. "To judge by the mess at the end of these cruises you'd think most people had come on board with the express intention of throwing up."

"Not just sick. Distressed," I said. He looked unimpressed. I'd have to raise my game. "She's pregnant and her waters have just broken. I think she's going into labour." This did the trick.

"Right," he said. "Take her round to the side and someone will help you off." He pressed a button and spoke into an old microphone. "Try and look pregnant," I said as I walked Natasha through the couples on the dance floor, now raving dementedly to something horrible by Spandau Ballet. She gave me a look of infinite contempt. Trev the Rev, with Rose in tow, came over, looking concerned. "Anything I can do?" he asked.

"Natasha's been taken ill," I said. "I'm taking her home. Can you look after Rose?"

"Yes, of course," he said. Rose wrinkled her nose at the idea of needing to be looked after, and I kissed her on its snub tip and told her to take care.

"Rothmans," she murmured mutinously.

Another old lighterman in a greasy nautical jumper came over and eyed Natasha suspiciously. "If you're in labour, I'm Michael bleeding Foot," he said to his own bronchial amusement, and Natasha favoured him with one of her especially thin smiles. The boat slowed down, and the sailor threw a rope over a bollard and brought us to the side of the jetty. He wheeled out the gangplank and we tottered down it, and as the boat sailed away I saw the silhouettes of Nicholas and

Henry up on the prow, waving cheerfully. I put my arm round Natasha's shoulder and we walked along the towpath, past a couple of pubs and up Crisp Road towards the Hammersmith flyover. It had begun to rain and it took twenty minutes to find a cab, which gave Natasha all the excuse she needed for venting her hurt and her spleen on me. Oddly enough, I didn't mind a bit . . .

I jerked myself back into the present.

"Natasha went back to university soon after that fatal night, didn't she?" I asked Nicholas.

"The very next day, in the afternoon. Ten days earlier than she needed to. She didn't emerge from her bedroom until after I'd left for the *Esher Herald* the following morning and I didn't see or hear from her again till the Christmas holidays. A very frigid Christmas too as it turned out."

"But you carried on seeing Henry for a while, I remember. Those last couple of weeks at the paper you only had eyes for each other, and I was left on my own with only Trev the Rev for company."

"It was a *coup de foudre,* but it didn't last long after I went up to Cambridge. He came and saw me at the end of my second week . . ."

"And told you he'd got that job on the Hong Kong *Morning Post.* I remember. Mine was the shoulder you cried on at the end of our third week. You caught the bus to Oxford, remember?"

"Henry and I corresponded for a while, but it soon petered out. I hadn't seen him for almost twelve years when he turned up at Natasha's wedding."

"And what did he say?" I asked, agog for news of our lost leader.

"Nothing at all. Or hardly anything at all. After he'd congratulated Natasha and her new husband he sauntered over to us, said, "Hi" as though we'd last seen each other a fortnight earlier, and announced he was dying for a pee and he'd be back straight away for a proper chat. And that was the last we saw of him. He just disappeared and never came back. I searched for him for at least an hour, I could write a guide book to that fucking castle, but he'd just gone."

I remembered how he and Nicholas had simply melted away from the dance floor, the way he'd eluded us up the tree in Oxshott Woods.

"He had a knack for vanishing," I said.

"Yes," said Nicholas, a half-smile on his face. "He did it again last night."

"Last night?" I asked incredulously. It was strange how just the mention of Henry still gave me a thrill.

"Yes, he turned up out of the blue about ten o'clock. Just rang the bell, holding a suitcase. He didn't seem remotely surprised by my changed appearance, just gave me a kiss and asked if I'd got a can of beer in the fridge, which I hadn't. He said never mind, he'd have anything, so I went and got the gin. And when I came back to the sitting room with the drinks, he'd got a little surprise for me. It was lying on this coffee table and it was spectacular even by Henry's standards."

"What was it?"

"An exceptionally beautiful painting by Vermeer. It's called *Pregnant Lady with a Bible.* It was stolen many years ago."

"Jesus," I gasped.

"I'm worried about Henry," said Nicholas, in a parody of Mrs Dale. "And callous though it may sound, I'm even more worried about that Vermeer."

# 3: Thursday 19th December 1996

*Let me tell you about the very rich. They are different from you and me.*
F. Scott Fitzgerald, *All the Sad Young Men*

I was up early and amazingly bright the next morning considering Nicholas and I had stayed up till two, planning what to do next. As soon as he'd sprung the news about Henry, I'd found it surprisingly easy to stop drinking. More amazingly still, I'd actually enjoyed my Lapsang Souchong and mineral water and going to bed with a clear head. Nicholas had looked utterly exhausted by the time we decided to call it a night, and I'd helped him up the stairs to his bedroom. It hadn't changed much since the days I'd first known him, and I was touched to see the big poster of Bowie in his Aladdin Sain incarnation still pinned to the door. I slept in his parents' double bed next door, and, though my mind started racing round one of those terrible repetitive loops of despair, jealousy and feverish hope about Kim and Colin, a few pages from the book about Vermeer Nicholas had lent me quickly dispatched me into a deep, untroubled sleep.

I woke at six, and wrote a note to Nicholas, thanking him for his hospitality and promising to keep him posted. I left it on his bedside table. His breathing was laboured and his brow was drenched in sweat. I went to the bathroom for a flannel and wiped his forehead. He stirred slightly and a ghost of a smile appeared on his face, as if he were enjoying his dream.

"Sleep on, old friend," I whispered under my breath, "God bless."

The 6.30 train was crowded with city types, desperate to be at their desks before their colleagues, and I felt out of place with my grubby hack's mac and unshaven face. The heating wasn't working, and not for the last time I cursed the fact that I'd left my overcoat in a restaurant the previous week – needless to say, I'd never got round to going back for it. I'd just about thawed out by the time we reached Waterloo, and once I'd downed a double espresso (three sugars) a doughnut and the first blissful roll-up of the day in Costa Coffee, I felt more or less ready for whatever the world might throw at me. The first hurdle looked like being by far the worst.

There was a surprisingly short queue at the cab rank – for once I would have welcomed a long one – and I pitched up outside my old home in Rita Road before 7.30am. The curtains of our ground floor sitting room were drawn. What was it to be? The unannounced dawn raid, letting myself in with my own key? Or ringing the bell which would give Kim a chance to establish who it was and Col an opportunity to hide or even escape over the garden wall? Even I could appreciate the Feydeau-like possibilities of this. The thought of Col in very few clothes, or indeed no clothes at all, fleeing through the still-dark streets of Vauxhall on a freezing cold morning almost brought a smile to my face. On the other hand, I couldn't face the idea of Kim deploying delaying tactics on the doorstep to give him a chance of a getaway.

I opened the door as quietly as I could and entered my own house like a thief. I switched on the light in the sitting room and saw an almost full bottle of Talisker, a jug of water and two glasses, one still unfinished, on the coffee table. Shit. On the other hand the room wasn't strewn with abandoned clothes. I went to the kitchen next. Unusually clean and tidy (as if she had been expecting guests, I thought miserably) and with two plates in the draining board sideboard. Also two wine glasses, and the remains of a leek and pheasant casserole, my particular favourite, on the stove. I looked into the spare room, and then the bathroom. Just one toothbrush in the jug, but that didn't mean a thing. Which left the bedroom. I must have stood stock still in the hall for three minutes, listening intently and feeling sick with apprehension. Eventually, I found the courage to open the door, silently. She was alone, curled up in a ball under the duvet with just the top of her head showing. I wanted to climb in next to her, hold her tight, tell her I was sorry, but there was one more thing I had to do. I crept round to the other side of the bed in the dim light from the lamp in the hall and stared at the other pillow on my side of the bed. It didn't look as if it had been slept on. I knelt down and sniffed it, disgusted with myself yet consumed with terrible fascination, like someone picking at a scab. As far as I could tell, it smelled only of Persil and Kim. Even that wasn't enough for me. I picked it up with the intention of carrying it out to the hall to conduct a forensic examination for stray hairs, but instead I stubbed my foot on the convector heater and yelled out loud in pain.

Kim screamed and sat bolt upright in her bed. "Who's that?" she said, scared and urgent, as she fumbled for the bedside light.

"It's only me, Kim," I said. "Will. Your husband. Remember?"

"What the fuck are you doing creeping round here in the middle of the night and scaring me half to death?" She'd turned on the light now. She was wearing her faded Dennis the Menace tee-shirt and her short dark hair was tousled. She looked irresistibly sleepy and cross.

"I'm sorry," I said. "I was trying not to disturb you. There's something I need urgently from my desk." Luckily, because our flat was so small, my desk was indeed in the bedroom, so I didn't seem too much like a private detective who had come to examine the bed linen. I'd managed to chuck the pillow onto the floor before she'd turned the light on.

"The arrangement was you'd ring if you wanted to come round," she said coldly. Did she look guilty as well?

"I know. But I've just come back after spending the night with an old friend in East Molesey and it seemed too early to ring."

"Well make sure you bloody do next time." There was a flicker of malice in her eyes. "I might have had somebody here," she said, twisting the dagger in my heart.

When the rows and the silences had become intolerable and we'd agreed on the six-month trial separation, nothing had been said about how we were going to conduct our separate lives. Needless to say, I'd been living like a monk, an alcoholic monk to be sure, but a celibate monk. I'd sort of assumed that Kim would be leading a nun-like existence too. During the traumas of IVF treatment, we'd both gone off sex anyway. Watching her sitting up in bed, her breasts pushing against the thin cotton of the tee shirt, all my old desire for her came flooding back. Accompanied by a great wave of jealous despair.

I came within an ace of saying, "Yeah, your old flame Colin, I suppose?" but bit my tongue just in time. As far as I knew, Kim had never lied to me, and in her present angry mood, she was unlikely to start now. The idea that she might coolly reply in the affirmative was more than I could bear.

I turned my back on her to cover my distress, switched on the desk lamp and started going through the drawers. It was a jumble of old bills, old photographs, old cuttings, not to mention the impressive collection of porn mags which, one way or another, had been such a feature of the test tube baby experience. Eventually, I found what I was looking for, my first address book covered in adolescent graffiti. The words Captain Trips, Janis Lives and Steve J is a Wanker were prominently etched in biro on the grubby cover. I couldn't for the life of me remember who Steve J was.

"What are you looking for?" asked Kim, sounding more friendly.

"None of your business," I replied savagely, images of Colin and Kim sharing whisky and a great deal more on our sofa playing like a slide show in my head. I was bitterly to regret that reply a few days later.

"Well, if you want to be like that . . ."

"Yeah, I want to be like that," I said. I ought to have made her a cup of tea and brought it to her in bed like the old days. I could have sat on the edge next to her, feeling her warmth, her shape, through the duvet, and told her all about my meeting with Nicholas. Instead I walked out, slamming the front door angrily behind me as the self-righteous, self-pitying tears streamed down my face.

Returning to my squalid Pimlico flat was too desolate to contemplate, so I gave the idea of a bath and a change of clothes a miss and instead caught a cab I couldn't afford to the office. Thanks to the rush hour traffic, I arrived at the office £20 lighter and fifteen minutes later than if I'd taken public transport. It was still only 8.30, ludicrously early by *Theatre World*'s standards, but, surprisingly, the door was unlocked and the lights were on inside. No sign of Martha, unfortunately. The shock of seeing me so early might have killed her.

Needless to say, Colin was the earlybird, huddled over his terminal and typing dementedly.

"Hi, Col," I said jauntily. "How's tricks?" He almost jumped out of his chair at the sound of my voice, but quickly recovered himself.

"To what," he said, voice loaded with irritating irony, "do we owe the privilege of this dawn visitation?"

"I've just been to see Kim actually," I replied, voice casual, eyes glued to his face. He blushed, he definitely blushed.

"Oh yes, and how was she?"

"Sleepy." Was it my imagination, or was there the merest hint of a supercilious smile on his face, the complacent look of a man thinking, "Well, she would be, after the night we spent together?"

I toyed with the idea of asking him whether he'd been to any good concerts lately, or if he'd enjoyed his pheasant casserole, but, once again, the idea of full confirmation of my worst fears seemed intolerable. The fact that he hadn't mentioned being with Kim himself the previous evening was suspicious enough.

"Well, I'd better get on, deadlines loom, paper to bring out and all that you know," he blustered as the tension grew oppressive between us.

"Yes, you do that, Col," I said, sitting down at my own desk and feeling wretched. The Forthcoming Attractions column was the first job of the day, and I reached wearily for the pile of press releases containing that week's announcements of new and mostly doomed productions. Even the information that Sir Cliff Richard was to star in a new musical version of Sophocles's Theban tragedies to be called *Oedipus Rocks* somehow failed to cheer me up. Sir Cliff helpfully explained that after the massive success (*sic*) of *Heathcliff* he felt compelled to continue exploring the darker side of his psyche.

After about ten minutes, Colin announced that he was off for a "damn good shit". I'm usually the least fastidious of people but I've always found something peculiarly revolting about people who feel the need to offer public service announcements about their past and imminent bowel movements. "Good for you, Colin!" I said cheerily.

He was away a very long time and I found myself hoping that the pheasant casserole had brought on a violent stomach upset. In fact, he must have made a silent return to the newsroom, for when he returned it wasn't through the main door that led to the gents, but from the side door that led to the usually empty boardroom. We used it for editorial conferences, interviews and, most importantly of all, phone calls of a personal nature. He must have been checking that Kim hadn't spilled the beans, I thought angrily. If I'd only noticed I could have jammed my ear to the door and eavesdropped. On the other hand, perhaps it was just as well that I hadn't. I almost certainly wouldn't have liked what I heard.

The others drifted in, and I grimly battled away at a "think-piece" about Arts Council funding and the impact of the lottery, which rendered me virtually comatose, never mind the reader. By noon, after half a dozen poisonous coffees from the vending machine and more roll-ups than I cared to contemplate, I'd finally cracked it and discreetly took myself off to the board-room.

It was strangely disturbing seeing the half-forgotten names of my childhood and adolescence in an assortment of colours and hand-writing styles that varied with the years. "Buffy" Bowerman from prep school, Sian Browne, whom I'd worshipped, age twelve, Johnny Myerson, my closest friend at boarding school who'd emigrated with his parents to Canada after O levels.

I tried the number for Henry and Rose Sutton first, at the house I'd come to know so well in Claygate, hoping their parents might still be living there. They'd been in their early sixties when

I'd first met them, so they would be seriously old now if they were alive at all. I let the number ring and ring, gazing at the hearts and flowers I'd doodled round Rose's name in the first flush of our teenage pash, but I'd somehow known there would be no reply from the very first ringing tone.

Trev the Rev was next on the list. Nicholas had kept in touch with him for longer than me, and had given me the number of the house he'd occupied during his first curacy in Bristol. "St Paul's Parish Team," said a brisk woman's voice. "Duty Priest Janis Parsons on call." It was more like phoning the emergency services than a parsonage. In my mind's eye, I saw the Revd. Janis in Paramedic motorbike leathers, ready to race off to an urgent crisis of faith or tricky confirmation class.

"Sorry to trouble you," I said. "I'm trying to track down a priest who used to be at this number years ago."

"Name?" said Janis crisply, apparently too revved up for small talk.

"Trevor Keenlyside," I said.

"Oh Trev. Big Bowie fan, ever so kind?"

"That sounds like the Trev I used to know."

"I used to go to his Christian fellowship classes," said Janis, in a fond tone of reminiscence. "Bloody riot, they were. More Bowie than Bible. In fact, if anyone's to blame, it was Trev that got me started in the Jesus racket."

"Racket?" I said.

"Only my little joke. In this line of work, you take what laughs you can get. Anyway hold on a minute."

She was gone for a couple of minutes but returned triumphant. "Got him out of *Crockford's*," she said. "The Vicarage, Sheep Lane, Royston-in-Arden, Warks. Sounds like he's got himself a nice cushy billet." She gave me the number.

"Give him my love," she said. "Great guy. Great shag."

"You what?"

"You heard," said the Revd. Janis. "I must go. A drunk's just walked in with a knife."

"Christ," I said. "Do you want me to call the police?"

"Joe quite often comes in with a knife. He's fine after a couple of glasses of Communion wine. Still, I'd better go. Come to think of it, I could use a drink myself."

"Right," I said. "God Bless."

"You took the words right out of my mouth," she replied with a very fanciable giggle. If I was ever in Bristol, I decided, I'd make a point of going to one of the Revd. Janis's services.

I replaced the phone and dialled Trev at his rural retreat. His familiar, reassuring and, I suddenly realised, much-missed voice came on the answering machine. "The Vicarage, Royston-in-Arden," he said. "If you have a message for Trevor, Judy, Matilda, Meredith, Huw, Freya, Luke, Charlie or Elinor please speak after the tone." No doubt about it, Trev was no slouch in the shagging department.

I left my name, told him I'd seen Nicholas recently and asked if he could get in touch as soon as possible, family commitments permitting. "It's about Henry and it could be urgent," I added, leaving the numbers of both *Theatre World* and the appalling Pimlico bedsit.

Then I tried the *Esher Herald*. It was unlikely, but Henry just might have maintained contact with the paper. Apart from Henry and Trev, the editorial department had been staffed by three maternal, middle-aged women who wrote stories of dutiful dullness, an engaging, boozed-up old hack on a one-way ticket back from Fleet Street who, in his rare interludes of sobriety, helped Trev with the subbing, and a quiet fortyish chap called Bob Biggs, officially deputy editor but in fact so self-effacing that he would do anything Henry told him to. And Moley, of course, benign, vague and venturing only rarely from his office where he battled at inordinate length each day with *The Times* crossword.

"*Esher Herald*," said a terminally glum Brummie voice. "This is Trish. How can I help yow?" The courteous words were spoken in a manner that suggested that Trish had been interrupted just as she was about to apply the razor blade to her wrists.

"I don't suppose a Mr Bob Biggs still works there?" I asked.

"Never 'oid of 'im," replied Trish.

I racked my memory. "Or a Phyllis Logan, an Ann Dent or a Pam, it was a Pam something – got it – Edwardes?" I said, triumphantly remembering the jolliest and reddest faced of the three cheerful lady reporters, invariably referred to by Trev as the secret, black and midnight hags.

"Never 'oid of them oither. You're not having much luck, are yow?" said Trisha, sounding perceptibly more cheerful herself as my own luck diminished.

"Or a Seamus Price?" I added, the memory of a couple of near-suicidal sessions in the pub with old Seamus rendering the very idea of his survival absurd.

"Now," said Trish.

"Now what?"

"Now, I've never oid of 'im."

I tried the last forlorn shot in my locker. "Last question," I promised. "What about a Mr Ted Johnson. It's not very likely he'd still be around. He must be about eighty by now if he's not dead."

"Owld Mowley, you mean?"

"Christ, he's not still editor, is he?"

"Now, of course he's not but he comes in a couple of times each week to do the Parish Pump section."

"He's not there by any chance today?"

He wasn't, but Trish cheerfully gave me his home number. "'Lovely man, owld Moley," she said. "Quiet loik, but kind."

I dialled the number, remembering the old buffer who had bailed me out of the job in the Kingston caff and given me my first break in journalism. He hadn't actually needed another green-behind-the ears work experience kid that summer but he'd been so appalled as I described life in the Eden Street Buttery that he'd taken me on at once. "I've eaten there a couple of times myself," he'd said feelingly. "Never again."

Moley wasn't at home either. Gathering news at the parish pump presumably. But unusually for an old man, he had an answering machine. I left my name and numbers as well as gently reminding him of who I was.

Which left, of course, Natasha. Though they got on fine these days, according to Nicholas, the one subject they never talked about was Henry. Natasha had been genuinely in love with Henry, apparently, and Nicholas said he'd always felt bad about that blow job. It was Henry who had made all the running that night, Nicholas insisted. I got the impression that Nicholas had told Natasha the same thing and that she hadn't believed him. I wasn't at all sure that I did. Anyway, Nicholas felt it was better that I should break the news of Henry's startling reappearance and the stolen Vermeer rather than him.

"You have reached the residence of Sir Dominic and Lady Gilbert-Smith," said a plummy voice, which I at first mistook for an answering machine. "How may I be of service?" Jesus Christ, it sounded like the butler at Blandings Castle.

"I'd like to speak to Nat . . . er, Lady Gilbert-Smith please."

"Who shall I say is calling?"

"Will Benson." I said. "There's a chance she won't remember who I am. Just mention Oxshott Woods," I said, and then, unable to resist it, "a notorious haunt of perverts and sex maniacs."

"I'm sure that won't be necessary, sir," said the flunky. "I'll just go and see if my lady is free."

I waited for almost five minutes, before Natasha's familiarly disapproving voice came down the line.

"Will Benson?" she said, as if naming a small but revolting species of vermin. "How lovely to hear from you," she added unconvincingly.

I decided not to beat about the bush. "Natasha, I've been to see Nicholas. And he's just been visited by Henry who appears to be in trouble. I wondered if you'd heard anything from Henry at all."

There was a long silence. "I haven't heard anything from Henry for years. And I can't talk now . . . I've got people here."

"Well, could I come and see you sometime?" I said, feeling like Lazarus at the rich man's gate.

"I'd like that," she said unexpectedly. "It would be nice to talk about the old days." Nice was a very Natasha word, I remembered. She liked things to be nice. "Why don't you come to tea? About four o'clock?"

I explained that some of us who weren't married to multi-millionaires had to work most afternoons.

"Where do you work?"

"The Isle of Dogs"

"No, I mean what do you do, silly." I knew quite well what she meant.

"I work for *Theatre World*," I said. "Your husband was taking some interest in us a few months ago."

That was putting it mildly. Sir Dominic had fired off a particularly intimidating writ through his flashy and dauntingly expensive firm of solicitors suing us for a piece suggesting that his recent role as munificent patron of the arts was little more than self-promotion and that several of the projects he was involved in hadn't actually received the lavish largesse he had promised them. It had come from a good source, as we thought, someone from within his own office. What we didn't know was that Sir Dominic had recently sacked our mole and the whole story, with its impressive documentation, was an elaborately fabricated act of spite. More unfortunately still, the story had been brilliantly timed so it arrived only a couple of hours before we went to press. There hadn't been time to check it properly with the organisations involved. We received a flurry of "no comments" from junior press officers, but couldn't get through to the bosses who could quickly have confirmed or denied its veracity. Rather than sitting on the story for a week, and losing a particularly juicy exclusive, JB had bravely decided to take a flyer. I was convinced that the subsequent worry had contributed to his heart attack.

Sir Dominic refused all offers of the most grovelling apology, and there was a real risk that a successful libel action could have put the precariously financed *Theatre World* out of business altogether. Fortunately a few people Sir Dominic was eager to suck up to, including the chairman of the Arts Council, quietly told Sir Dominic that, traduced though he had been, closing down

*Theatre World* would be bad news for the performing arts he professed to love. A couple of newspapers, too, had taken up our case, suggesting that the millionaire was victimising a small but much loved institution which had been in the same family hands for more than a century. Sir Dominic, who disliked nothing so much as bad publicity, had settled for the apology, across six columns on the front page, and JB had been close to tears when he saw our humiliation blazoned for all to see. Only after the famous grovel had appeared did we hear further whispers that Sir Dominic had been anxious to acquire *Theatre World* himself, and believed he could get it at a knockdown price if he brought it to the brink of bankruptcy. The suspicion, the completely libellous, entirely unprovable suspicion, was that he had cleverly planted the whole false story himself.

I reminded Natasha of some, but not all, of this over the phone.

"Not that dreadful little trade paper?" she trilled. "Really, Will, I thought you'd have done better for yourself than that."

"Thank you for those few kind words," I said.

"I'm sorry," she said. "But *Theatre World*, what an absolute hoot." I came within an ace of slamming the phone down, but remembered I was working for Henry and Nicholas and, I suddenly thought, Vermeer. My own sensitivities weren't part of the deal.

"If you can contain your mirth, perhaps we could arrange a meeting?" I said coldly. She suggested dinner that night and I told her I had a show to review.

"Well, couldn't I come too? I thought you critics always got a pair of free tickets."

I thought of the show I was due to review that evening. The idea appealed, it definitely appealed. "Yes, that would be great," I said.

"What's the play?"

"Why don't we let that be a surprise?"

"At least let me know what to wear?"

"Well, it's a first night. You know the sort of thing."

"Oh goody, I've just bought the most divine little suit from Caroline Charles."

"Just the job," I said. We agreed that I'd meet Natasha at 6.30 at her place and she'd supply the transport.

"West End, I take it?"

"Well, not quite. But it's a very beautiful theatre," I said, and rang off before she had a chance to ask any awkward questions.

The prospect of seeing Natasha again was curiously cheering. More cheering still was the news from a contact half an hour later that Andrew Lloyd Webber's *Macbeth the Musical* was coming off after a five-year run. Mysteriously, the recently cast John Inman had failed to set the box office ablaze in the title role. Dani Behr's Lady Macbeth had also come in for a cruel critical pasting. I wrote the show's obituary with barely containable glee.

I was just about to set off for Belgravia – miles out of the way for the venue we were going to but the chance of a glimpse of Natasha's gaff was too good to miss – when Col called me over. For once, he seemed almost civilised, even contrite. He'd accepted an invitation to a trade show in Leicester on Saturday, but something had come up and he was now unable to go. He could cancel, but it wouldn't look good, and he'd be eternally in my debt if I'd take over the task myself. Weekends were always a problem without Kim, and even the prospect of a lot of techies in Birmingham seemed preferable to the Pimlico bedsit. What's more, the idea of Colin owing me a favour was not to be sniffed at. I was safe at *Theatre World* for as long as JB was the notional editor, but if Colin ever took over the helm permanently, my career prospects were zilch. As far as Colin was concerned, I was the competition. So I accepted the chore and Col told me not to stint myself when it came to expenses and even – almost unheard of at *Theatre World* – to book a decent hotel for the night rather than some godforsaken B&B. It was only as I sat on the light railway that I realised that this might all be a Machiavellian plan to get me out of the way for the weekend. I'd already told Colin I couldn't work on Friday night as I had to be in Oxford. With me tied up in Leicester on Saturday too, he would have me safely out of the way until at least Sunday lunchtime. Perhaps he was planning a return visit to Kim at Rita Road, and didn't want to be disturbed by another dawn visitation from her husband. I was starting to go into the familiar routine of jealousy and gnawing doubt when I was mercifully overtaken by a rare fit of lucidity. Did I still love Kim? Yes I did. Did I trust her? Yes, I did. Was worrying about her and Colin going to do any good at all? No, it wasn't. It was time, I belatedly realised, to follow Hamlet's advice. Let be. I turned to the *Evening Standard* with a more or less tranquil heart.

Natasha's house wasn't quite as large as some of the embassies in Belgrave Square, but it was quite large enough. I was met at the door by the butler who informed me that Lady Natasha was swimming.

"Down the road at the Victoria Sports Centre?" I said, just to wind him up.

"No, sir," he said, taking my grubby mac into his care as if he wished he'd got a pair of tongs handy. "The house has its own leisure complex." We were standing in a vast hall, with a marble floor, elaborate cornices and a sweeping, beautifully carved wooden staircase. There was a Warhol on each wall, in the style of the famous Marilyn Monroe portraits, depicting a younger and more handsome Sir Dominic. Shame the artist had died before Natasha met her husband. She'd have looked a lot more fetching.

"I'll take you up to the drawing room, sir."

"I don't suppose there's a chance of seeing the leisure complex first is there?" I replied, in unashamedly gawping tourist mode. "I'm sure Lady Natasha won't mind me seeing her swimming."

"I'll go and ask," he said, disappearing through a concealed door in the white panelling. There was a visitors' book on an occasional table, and I had a quick peep at it. Mr and Mrs Mick Jagger, Mr and Mrs Michael Portillo, Lord Yehudi and Lady Menuhin and David Hockney had been among the recent guests. Feeling like a kid, I got out my own pen. Sir William Benson, Bart., I wrote, c/o *Theatre World*, London E14. I'd always fancied a baronetcy. "Lady Natasha will see you now," said the butler, interrupting me just as I was adding Queen Elizabeth I style squiggles to my signature. "Guests usually wait to be invited to inscribe their names in the visitors' book," he added severely.

"Yeah, but what if I hadn't been invited?" I said nastily. It was pathetic really. Just a glimpse of someone else's wealth had made me feel like a bolshie fifteen-year-old. The butler had been squinting at my florid signature. "This way, Mister Benson," he said.

He led the way down a spiral staircase and into the pool area. The walls were covered in abstract mosaics, retina-bruising explosions of gold and cerulean blue, and there were great terracotta pots of decadent-looking orchids scattered all over the black and white tiled floor. At one end was a vast tank of tropical fish. Natasha was doing a very professional crawl up and down the fifty-foot pool, keeping her head below the surface for an unfeasibly long time before taking a quick gasp of air out of the side of her mouth. The butler was hoveringly promisingly by a table stacked with a lip-smacking variety of drinks. I wandered over. I really wanted a malt whisky, but thought I'd catch him out by asking for a cold lager, since that appeared to be one of the few drinks in the world that wasn't on offer. "Of course, sir," he said, turning round to open another concealed door. It led into a gleaming white fitted kitchen, with one of the biggest fridges I've ever seen. "Becks, Czechoslovakian Budweiser or Michelob?" he asked.

"Budweiser," I said. "And perhaps a largish Talisker with a bit of still mineral water."

Natasha emerged from the pool, and I copped a quick look at her in her revealing one-piece emerald green costume. Her breasts seemed as pneumatic as ever; elsewhere there wasn't an ounce of cellulite in sight. When I'd first known her she'd still been carrying a few pounds of puppy fat.

She wrapped herself up in a fluffy white towelling dressing gown, and came over and gave me a peck on my unshaven cheek.

"Fancy a swim, Will?" she said, surveying me with that familiar trick of wrinkling her nose. "I'm sure we could find you some bathers."

The thought of exposing all my white and wobbly flesh in the presence of her lean and golden body made me choke on my drink. "Er, I think not," I managed to splutter at last. "I like to keep myself covered up these days."

She giggled. "Fair enough. Listen, you go upstairs with Clarence and I'll get changed and join you there." Clarence nodded slightly and Natasha disappeared through yet another concealed door.

"If you'll just follow me, sir," said Clarence, placing my drinks on a silver salver. He led the way past the tropical fish and through an arch that led into a gymnasium equipped with fiendish stainless steel instruments of torture. We passed a sauna cabin next, and a shower room, and then entered a small lift, which stopped on the first floor. He led me into the vast drawing room, with four full-length windows overlooking a walled garden and a mews beyond. There's no point in an oik like me trying to describe the furniture, the Chinese vases filled with flowers, the amazing Persian carpets on the polished wooden floor. Suffice it to say that *le tout ensemble* made the average edition of The Antiques Road Show look like a car-boot sale. Clarence put my drinks down on an inlaid occasional table and retired. I'd hoped he'd retreat backwards, bowing as he went; in fact he turned on his heels sharpish and seemed in almost indecent haste to leave the room. Serving the *hoi polloi* was clearly a deep penance to him.

I sipped at my spectacularly large Talisker and had a gander at the pictures. I'd done a bit of history of art at school, and spotted a couple of Gainsboroughs, a hideous Reynolds portrait of a very fat, very grumpy aristocrat, and a Stubbs. The pictures looked distinctly second division – famous names, crap examples of their work. But there was a tiny skyscape by Constable and a small Sisley landscape that showed real class.

Natasha came into the room, She was wearing an exceptionally chic black suit, a creamy silk blouse, plus gold earrings and a necklace that didn't look as though they had come from Accessorize.

"How's your drink?"

"Large and delicious," I said. "Just the way I like them."

"Good."

"I'm so sorry about Nicholas," I added, "and about your parents."

Her eyes misted over. "Yes, it's been a bad few years," she said. "How did Nicholas seem?"

"Frail but brave. You know we quarrelled. I'm just glad that we had a chance to make it up."

"Nicholas quarrelled with everyone in his militant phase," she said. "It's a terrible thing to say, but I preferred him after the HIV was diagnosed." It was a terrible thing to say, but admirably honest.

She sat down on one of the sofas and invited me to join her.

"So tell me about Henry," she said, and I caught a distant echo of the excitement she'd betrayed when she first met him all those years ago.

"There's not a lot to tell. He turned up at your parents' old house the night before last without warning, got Nicholas to get him a drink and when he returned, there was this Vermeer on the coffee table. Out of its frame, but as far as Nicholas could tell, it was in remarkably good condition."

"And Nicholas was sure it was a Vermeer – not a forgery? Wasn't there a famous Vermeer forger?"

"Van Meegeren, shortly after the Second World War," I said. "I asked Nicholas the same question. In fact, Van Meegeren forged works in Vermeer's earlier historical style, and even those don't seem remotely convincing these days. No, Nicholas said that unless there is a quite exceptional new forger at work, this was the real McCoy. And what makes it all seem more rather than less likely is that the picture was stolen years ago and it hasn't been seen since."

"What's it like?"

"It's generally agreed to be one of the most beautiful he ever painted," I said. "It's a woman in a room, standing next to a window, which as you'll know is a recurring theme in his work. She is heavily pregnant, and she's holding a Bible in her hand, but unlike the rather similar *Woman with a Letter*, she's not actually reading it, and her face isn't in profile. She's turning her head to look out at whoever is looking at the canvas and she has an expression of extraordinarily serene happiness on her face. Vermeer is famous for his sense of stillness and balance but in fact, in a lot of his paintings, there's actually quite a lot of tension just beneath the surface. But not here. Nicholas described it well. It is as though the woman has been blessed by spiritual grace, and the effect of the picture is to confer a measure of that grace on whoever is looking at it."

"But Nicholas is an atheist, or an agnostic at best," said Natasha.

"As he is the first to point out. What he said was that for a few moments, looking at that picture, and despite the somewhat freakish circumstances in which he had come into contact with it, he felt blessed not only by the grace of a great artist, but by the grace of God. A god in whom he doesn't normally believe."

"So what did Henry say? Did he offer any explanation at all of how he'd come into possession of the picture?"

"Not a thing. Nicholas said his first words were, "Christ, where did you get that from?" but Henry just gave one of his enigmatic smiles. Nicholas spent about five minutes looking at the picture, examining it for damage first of all, since, as far as he knew, he was the only art scholar to have seen it since it disappeared, before becoming overwhelmed, his word, not mine, by its sheer beauty and peace. He was, he says, reduced to complete silence."

"Unusual for Nicholas," said Natasha, dryly.

"Very."

"But they can't just have stood there all night, in silent communion," added Natasha.

"No, they didn't. The phone went."

"Nicholas's?"

"No, Henry's mobile. He answered it, listened for about ten seconds, and said something had cropped up and he had to go. Nicholas said he seemed extremely rattled."

"It's hard to imagine Henry rattled."

"Nicholas said panic wouldn't be too strong a word. He put the painting back in his suitcase – it's only about two feet by three – packing it carefully with cotton sheets and padding. And he tried to make Nicholas swear he wouldn't report the matter to the police. He said he'd got to sort it out for himself."

"But if he'd come by the painting legitimately, or even more-or-less legitimately, there would be nothing to sort out. He could just surrender it to the authorities and be the hero of the hour. Perhaps even collect a reward. Exactly the sort of thing Henry would enjoy."

"Quite. Nicholas said much the same thing. Henry said matters were more complicated than that but insisted that he had the painting's best interests at heart. Then he said, and this really concerned Nicholas, that if he discovered the police were on his trail, he might have no option but to get rid of it."

"Get rid of it? Where?"

"Nicholas thought he meant destroy it."

Natasha looked exceedingly gloomy. "That's hardly having the painting's interests at heart," she said. "It suggests at the very least a degree of criminality. Plus a determination to save his own skin, whatever the cost."

"I agree. Anyway, before Nicholas had any further chance to argue the toss, Henry said he had to go. He gave Nicholas one of those very direct stares of his and said, 'I'm trusting you, Nicholas,' before getting to his feet and marching out in some haste. As you must know, Nicholas finds fast movement impossible these days, particularly at night when he's tired. By the time he'd got himself out into the hall, Henry had slammed the front door behind him. And by the time Nicholas got to the front doorstep, there was no sign of him. No one on the pavement with a suitcase, not even the taillights of a car disappearing round the corner.

"Another vanishing act?"

"Yeah."

I looked at my watch. It was seven o'clock and showtime beckoned. "You still on for the theatre?" I asked. "Because if so we ought to be setting off."

She nodded and we descended the carved staircase, wide enough to walk two abreast. I could get used to this, I thought. Clarence helped Natasha on with her full length fur coat but she managed the matching hat herself. I was left to fend for myself with the raincoat. Clarence clearly didn't want to get his hands dirty again.

Waiting on the pavement outside was an elderly though hardly vintage Rolls-Royce Silver Shadow in a particularly startling shade of electric blue. Naff was the word that came to mind, the kind of thing a pop star might buy with his first really big royalty check.

"Don't say it," said Natasha. "It used to belong to Mike Batt."

"Not the man who wrote all those ghastly songs about the Wombles?"

"That's the chap. Dommo claims to be genuinely fond of the damn thing though I notice he always takes the Porsche. My Porsche."

"Life can be so unfair," I said. She grinned.

A chauffeur held the door of the Womble-mobile open for Natasha, and I gave him the address of the theatre as he was closing the door on her. His blank face beneath the obligatory peaked hat didn't flicker as he led me round to the other side.

The back of the vulgarly customised car contained two cream leather armchairs rather than a banquette, and a cupboard between them which looked promisingly like a drinks cabinet. The roof was painted with twinkling stars and a smiling moon while the woven carpet had pictures of the Wombles on it, gathering litter. Built into the screen dividing the front seats from the rear was a stereo system and shelves holding CDs.

The car glided smoothly away as I settled into my seat.

"I suppose we may as well enjoy the facilities of this ridiculous vehicle," said Natasha. My own opinion of Sir Dominic had risen on seeing his oddly endearing toy. You couldn't be entirely devoid of a sense of humour and own a car like this. "What do you fancy?" asked Natasha. "A drink? A sandwich?"

"Both," I said. She opened the cupboard, which turned out to be a fridge and produced plates of smoked salmon and cream cheese sarnies, covered with cellophane. Also a bottle of Krug which she asked me to open. There were, I noticed, special drink holders in the arm of each chair and a built-in bottle-holder behind the fridge.

"They're mounted on gimbals like on a ship," said Natasha. "So the drink doesn't spill."

"Of course they are," I said. "You wouldn't want to mess up this delightful carpet."

I managed to open the champagne with the merest murmur rather than a vulgar pop and half filled the glasses Natasha was holding. I raised mine to her in a toast.

"What shall we drink to?" I asked.

"How about friendship and wild times?" she said, and gave me a smile that contained more than a ghost of sadness.

"So tell me how a nineteen-year-old Eng. Lit. student became the wife of Sir Dominic Gilbert-Smith?" I asked.

"Put a record on," said Natasha, before leaning close and whispering that Hastings was an inveterate eavesdropper. The sound of her hushed voice and the sensation of her breath in my ear sent involuntary shivers down my spine.

I leant forward and surveyed the records. Mainstream classical mostly, some jazz and middle-of-the-road pop like Sade and Simply Red. And, terrifically, The Best of the Wombles. I slammed it in. Dear old Mike assured us that the Wombles of Wimbledon Common were underground, overground and wombling free and I felt an irresistible urge to join in.

"Prat," said Natasha, affectionately, jabbing me in the ribs and I spilled champagne all over my mac.

"Shoot, Lady Natasha," I said, refilling my glass. "Or perhaps that should be Lady Penelope."

"Very well, Parker," she said, in a rather good imitation of the Thunderbird puppet.

Natasha described how she'd joined an advertising firm shortly after graduating and after a few high-flying years had married her boss. Unfortunately, he'd wanted to have a nice little wife and children at home and she'd wanted to continue her career. End of marriage and, as it turned out, end of her upwardly mobile progress at Holmes and Appleyard. But she'd been wanting to set up on her own for some time anyway and had established herself as a PR specialising in product launches. It thrived, and when Sir Dominic wanted to launch his latest convenience food – a particularly virulent range of pot noodles called A Touch of Spice – it was Natasha who had arranged the do. I vaguely remembered seeing press pictures of Sir Dominic, with his smug smile and salt and pepper beard, sitting with a bevy of eastern lovelies, all valiantly trying not to look sick as they dug their spoons into their plastic pots. Within a fortnight of their first meeting, he'd whisked Natasha away to his Caribbean island, and a month after that they were married.

"So you don't work any more?" I said.

"Don't be so patronising" she said, a touch of the familiar ice returning. "I'm a director of HappiSnax and I do a lot of work for Sir Dominic's art foundation."

It was suddenly 'Sir Dominic' I noticed. "Aaah, the famous art foundation. Perhaps we'd better not talk about that for the moment."

"Perhaps we'd better not," she said, and turned to gaze out of the window. "Where the hell are we anyway?"

"The further reaches of Islington, I should think," I said, as the Wombles waxed ecstatic about the many admirable qualities of Uncle Bulgaria.

"Just where are we going?"

"Er, Hackney," I said.

She suddenly relaxed again. "Oh, Will," she said. "You certainly know how to give a girl a good time."

"Tell me about the last time you saw Henry," I said.

"There's not much to tell. After that bloody boat trip I didn't see him again till he turned up at my wedding. Uninvited, I might say."

"How did he know about it?"

"I imagine he saw the rather unctuous piece Nigel Dempster wrote in the *Mail Diary* a couple of days before."

"And what did Henry say?"

"I can't remember."

"Oh come on. Your first love turns up out of the blue at your wedding, you hadn't seen him since a parting that was traumatic by any standards. You must remember what he said."

"Well, it's a bit embarrassing. Pour me some more champagne." I did as she asked.

"Well, he told Dommo he was a lucky man and added, rather mischievously, 'Believe me, I know'."

"*Kind Hearts and Coronets.*"

"Oh, of course. I knew I recognised the line and I simply couldn't place it."

"Go on."

"Well he told me I was looking ridiculously youthful, and he was just on the point of moving on when he leant forward and whispered in my ear, on the pretext of kissing my cheek."

"Yeah, and?"

Natasha leant forward and turned the Wombles up to a volume that would have blasted Oasis off the stage before putting her mouth next to my own ear. It was lovely, but I couldn't hear a thing. So she shouted.

"He said I gave much better head than my brother." Unfortunately, just as she was screaming this piece of information, the Wombles song suddenly stopped in mid-flow as the car hit a bump and the CD skipped. The words "much better head than my brother" rang deafeningly and defiantly out and Hastings swerved so violently he only narrowly avoided an oncoming bus.

To her eternal credit, Natasha, instead of being mortified, got an attack of the giggles instead. And then they suddenly turned to tears and she started sniffing violently into her hankie.

"We've got to find him, Will. I can't bear to think of him being in danger. Or of destroying the picture."

I put my arm round her and gave her a squeeze. "You're still carrying a torch then."

"Oh yes," she said. "There's hardly a day when I don't think about him. What are we going to do?"

I told her about my less than brilliant enquiries so far. "Nicholas suggested we should give it a week," I said. "After that he said he it was our clear moral duty to go to the police. He said, provided they knew there was a risk of the picture being destroyed, they'd act discreetly."

"But if they catch him, he'd go to prison," Natasha wailed. "However he got hold of the picture, the mere possession of it must be illegal. If he destroyed it, he'd go down for years."

"Quite, so we've got to find him."

"And what do we do if we succeed?"

"Persuade him to hand over the picture and give him time to get out of the country if he needs to. Henry being Henry, he'll have some kind of escape route planned."

"I can't believe Henry would do anything so obscene as destroy a great painting," said Natasha.

"But how well do we know him? He dazzled us for a few months in our youth and then disappeared from our lives. So far, we don't know anything about his life since he took up that job in Hong Kong towards the end of 1982."

She nodded, then squeezed my knee with surprising force.

"He'd never do anything mean," she said, but I could hear the doubt in her voice. How much meaner could you get than allowing your girlfriend's brother to give you a public blow-job when there was a strong chance of discovery?

We were in Mare Street now, passing the town hall, and our preposterous car drew up outside the Hackney Empire to the delighted derision of several of the kids waiting outside for admission. Natasha opened the window between us and the driver.

"You can go home now, Hastings," she said. "We'll get a cab back."

I started squawking about how difficult it was to get cabs late at night on the mean streets of Hackney. I was already getting used to the luxury of a chauffeur driven Roller and didn't want to abandon its womb-like security.

"Will, stop bleating," said Natasha. "I have an excellent cab charge card and they are extremely reliable."

We climbed out of the car into a bitter drizzle and I envied Natasha her furs until a couple of terrifying, shaven-headed girls in boiler suits noticed them. "How many innocent animals does it take to clothe one dumb bitch?" one of them yelled at her offensively.

I felt like getting back into the car and going straight home but Natasha walked over to them with a huge and menacing smile and said: "It's fake darling," before sweeping in through the main entrance with all the aplomb of not so minor royalty. I caught up with her in the crowded foyer.

"It's not really fake is it?" I asked.

"Of course it isn't," she said, mightily offended. "You're looking at £20,000 worth of sweet little furry animals." Put like that, I began to see the boiler suits' point of view.

I took Natasha to the bar at the back of the stalls, marvelling as always at the dusty decayed grandeur of this great Frank Matcham auditorium, reclaimed from years of bingo and neglect and still heroically functioning as a variety theatre 100 years after it opened.

They didn't serve champagne at the Hackney Empire, and Marie Lloyd, who often performed there, would probably have been as appalled by this oversight as Natasha. I ordered a pint of Holsten for myself, and a glass of very *ordinaire* white for her and she looked as though she'd been poisoned as she took the first sip from her plastic glass.

"For Christ's sake, Will, get me a gin and tonic to take the taste away," she said. "Even the proles can't object to a G and T can they?" A couple of proles gazed at her with open hostility.

"What's the show tonight?" said Natasha when I returned with the drinks "A load of right-on socialist comedians, I suppose."

"Not quite," I said. "It's a hypnotist."

The bells rang, and we took our seats on an aisle near the front of the stalls. The house lights dimmed, smoke filled the stage and music by the Orb belted out of the theatre's p.a. system. And suddenly, zooming up onto the stage through a trap was Johnny Mesmer, the bad boy of British hypnotism.

He was wearing a white tux and a sequined waistcoat, and as he launched into a far from riveting version of Screaming Jay Hawkins' 'I Put a Spell on You', I feared reports of his excesses might be exaggerated. A few months earlier, *Theatre World* had carried a report on his expulsion from the Federation of Ethical Stage Hypnotists and he had recently been roundly condemned by Virginia Bottomley, almost invariably a good sign, in my opinion.

"Welcome to the X-rated Hypno' show," he leered. "In a moment, I'll be calling for volunteers, but if you're drunk, pregnant, or clinically depressed don't even think about coming on stage. On the other hand, if you don't mind making a complete idiot of yourself, you're more than welcome. Like the three girls I had on stage the other night. I asked them where was the most embarrassing place they'd ever had sex. Tracey said on top of the washing machine. Sue said it was the time she shagged her boyfriend in an aeroplane toilet and the flight steward started knocking on the door. Sharon was the one I fancied though. 'Up the bum,' she said."

I looked at Natasha's face and was relieved to see that she was smiling. When she realised I was looking she reassembled her face into its familiar primness. "Wild horses wouldn't drag me up there," she said.

Wild horses, possibly not. Johnny Mesmer, undoubtedly yes. He called for volunteers and there was a stampede of fearless exhibitionists, but not it seemed quite enough for Johnny. The house lights were switched on and he came down into the stalls, where groups started noisily pushing forward their reluctant mates. It was then I realised that we were sitting alarmingly close to the boiler-suited animal-rights' campaigners. They spotted Natasha at the same moment, pointed at her and shouted to Johnny that he should get the "stuck-up bitch" on stage. He ambled over.

"And what's your name?" he asked pleasantly.

"Natasha," she replied through gritted teeth.

"And you'd like to be hypnotised?" he said .

"No, I damn well wouldn't," she said, sounding ludicrously posh and snooty, twisting in her seat to stare malevolently at the boiler suits. Johnny Mesmer quickly realised she would make an ideal target. Just the sound of those cut-glass vowels was good for a laugh in Hackney.

"Come on, Natasha, darling," he whispered, taking hold of her arm. "You don't want to keep all these nice people waiting, do you?" There was a sense of determination, almost menace, about Johnny at close quarters, and Natasha evidently concluded that it would probably be more embarrassing to make a scene now than to take her place among all the others on stage.

"Oh, very well," she said, getting out of her seat and shooting me a murderous look as she made her way to the stage. Johnny bullied a few more people into 'volunteering' and at last the show proper began. Even watching at close quarters, it was hard to see exactly how Johnny worked his magic. He asked the punters to imagine their hands were locked together, repeating words like tighter and concentrate with much clicking of his fingers. People who clearly weren't responding received a whispered instruction to return to their seats, but others seemed genuinely mystified that their hands seemed to be stuck together and collapsed gently back into

Johnny's arms when he told them to sleep. He laid them gently on the floor where they remained immobile until they were asked to move.

Eventually, there were about eight bodies on stage, Natasha's, astonishingly, among them. If anyone could resist the power of hypnosis, I thought it would be her, but she seemed totally and peacefully out of it. Johnny asked his victims to wake up and they climbed, slightly bemusedly, to their feet. It was all charmingly innocent at first. The hypnotist asked the group to pretend they were children, rushing around in a playground, and then to imagine they were shivering at a bus stop on a cold winter's day. There was always the slight possibility that they were putting on an act to spare his blushes, but I couldn't see Natasha doing that. Knowing her, there would be nothing she'd like more than to expose him as a fake. No doubt remained at all when Johnny gave her a raw onion and told her it was the most delicious apple she'd ever tasted. She ate the whole lot with every appearance of relish, and expressed surprise when she'd finished that there wasn't a core.

Two lads with Essex accents started talking a bizarre guttural nonsense language when they were told they were aliens from outer space, and a dumpy middle-aged woman gave a terrific impersonation of Madonna singing 'Like a Virgin'. Then all eight were told that they were at a teenage party, and started bopping as T.Rex came over the p.a. "It's a slow one now," said Johnny, as Diana Ross's achingly beautiful 'Touch Me in the Morning' started up and they paired off, rather unpredictably. The Essex boys entwined themselves around each other, while Natasha seemed irresistibly attracted to the middle-aged Madonna. "I expect what you really want now is a good snog," said Johnny and they all fell eagerly to the task. After a few minutes, Mesmer told them to sleep and they immediately stopped and stood still.

A gauche, acne-scarred man called Alex who had just been having the time of his life with a feisty twentysomething called June was summoned by Johnny.

"Did you know your dick's getting bigger and bigger," said Mr Mesmer. "I don't think I've ever seen such a whopper."

Alex glanced happily down at his crotch. "Yes, it is big, isn't it?" he said cheerfully.

"Perhaps you'd like to show everybody," said Johnny to hoots of laughter.

"Yes, why not," said Alex, dropping his trousers and his pants. He took hold of his flaccid and not especially impressive dick and started waving it cheerfully at the audience. "Huge isn't it?" he cried to an audience now in uproar. "Absolutely fucking enormous. I bet you wish you'd got one as big as this."

There was something child-like about his delight in his own member, and what might have been offensive seemed strangely touching.

"I think you'd better put it away now, Alex," said Johnny. "There's a policeman coming."

"Oh shit," said Alex, pulling up his trousers in perceptible panic. "Sleep," said Johnny, once Alex had adjusted his dress, and Alex promptly froze.

One of the Essex boys simulated sexual intercourse with a mop in the belief that it was actually Pamela Anderson and, invited to describe her naughtiest moment, the elderly Madonna volunteered the news that she'd gone to bed with the best man on the eve of her wedding.

"I don't suppose you've brought your husband along tonight?" asked Johnny with oleaginous concern.

"Fuck me," she said. "Sorry, Brian."

And then it was Natasha's turn. "I want you to imagine that you're lying on a beautiful grassy bank by a river, Natasha," he said.

"It's Lady Natasha actually," she said pleasantly. "But if you want to call me Natasha I suppose that's all right."

"Well, Lady Natasha," said Johnny, with a leer at the audience that elicited ribald cheers. "It's very hot and the river looks so cool and enticing and there's no one around. So you decide to go for a swim. Do you see that bush over there?" He pointed to the middle of the empty stage.

"Yes, of course."

"Why don't you nip behind it and change out of your things?"

"Great idea."

Natasha went and stood centre stage and, quite unselfconsciously, began to take her clothes off. She hummed a little tune to herself, seeming happy and self-contained, and the audience, previously raucous, sat in hushed silence as she removed her black suit and neatly folded up the skirt and jacket, then unfastened her gold necklace and ear-rings which she put, for safe-keeping presumably, in her shoes. She sat on the floor to take off her black stockings, then slowly unbuttoned her white shirt. The audience seemed to be holding its breath as she stood up again, and removed her white satin bra and cami-knickers, and though it was undoubtedly erotic, her quiet strip had dignity and beauty too, like those Degas drawings of women bathing or washing their hair. Like them, Natasha was unaware of any audience. As she stood there, full-breasted and beautiful, I felt suddenly protective of her, exposed as she was, and unknowing, and wanted to join her on stage, wrap her in a dressing gown and lead her quietly into the privacy of the wings.

Johnny invited her to swim in the river – "It's beautifully cool, Lady Natasha, and you're feeling so hot" – and she dipped her toe into imaginary water, gasped quietly at how cold it was, and then seemed to jump in, miming the crawl I had seen earlier as she walked round the stage, bent forward, arms whirling, breasts hanging pendulously.

"There's someone coming, Natasha," said Johnny, his voice less intrusive, less prurient than usual. He too seemed curiously moved by Natasha's dignified nakedness. "Don't worry, it's someone you like, someone you want to swim with."

"It's Henry," said Natasha "Hi, Henry, come on in, it's lovely." She waved at the invisible Henry across the stage, then suddenly became distressed. "Oh Henry, I'd forgotten. That picture, you've got to give it back, you're in terrible danger."

"What picture?" asked Johnny.

"The most beautiful picture," said Natasha, and there were tears streaming down her face, "of a young pregnant woman. Henry, you've got to give it back. They'll hurt you."

The last three words were screamed in what was clearly acute anguish, and Johnny, perhaps a more decent man than he let on, perhaps only wanting to maintain the basically feel-good nature of his show, quietly told her to sleep. Natasha froze, and Johnny went and whispered in her ear. She smiled, with an expression of sudden radiance, picked up her clothes and ambled off into the wings. Johnny ended the show by getting everyone else on stage to remove all their clothes, but the mood was now openly lecherous and the final naked dance sequence to the Bee Gees 'Stayin' Alive' entirely lacked the disconcerting grace of Natasha's solo turn.

Halfway through this final number, a member of the stage crew escorted a now fully-clothed Natasha through the pass door and back to her seat. She gave me a grin, then gasped when she saw what was happening on stage.

"It's like an orgy up there," she said, looking appalled.

"What about your own performance?" I whispered.

"What performance?" she said, and then like someone blearily waking up and suddenly remembering their dream she grabbed me by the arm and said "I didn't, did I?"

"You did," I said. She flushed, then, surprisingly, sunk her face into my shoulder. "Oh, Will," she murmured, "I must have looked a complete idiot."

"You looked terrific," I said, before adding sadistically, "everyone thought so."

Johnny brought the curtain down with all his volunteers taking beaming bows without a stitch on. Natasha seemed anxious to leave.

"Lets get out of here before anyone comes and congratulates me on my act," she said. We fled with the crowd still cheering for more, out onto a freezing Mare Street where the bitter wind sliced through my mac with contemptuous ease.

"We'll find a pub and I'll phone for a cab," said Natasha. "But not a pub too near the theatre. I don't want people ogling me."

We trudged down the bleak street, Natasha looking warm as toast in her furs, and unaccountably cheerful. When Johnny put his spell on you it appeared to be benign. Nevertheless, she resisted the first two ratty pubs we came to, and found, amazingly for Hackney, a perfectly civilised wine bar.

Natasha made for the phone booth, and I bought a glass of champagne for Natasha and a large Australian red for myself. "Here's looking at you with fresh eyes, kid," I said, as she sat down. She clinked her glass against mine and said, "Well, that's not quite true, is it?" before asking me to describe the show. Her memory of most of it seemed to be hazy. She could remember freezing at the bus stop, eating what she still believed to have been an apple, and had a partial memory of taking off her clothes and swimming. But even after prompting, she said she had no recollection of Henry entering her trance.

"You seemed desperately worried about him," I said, "as if he was in some form of specific danger. That certain people were out to hurt him. You were so distressed, Johnny Mesmer put you back to sleep."

"It's gone," she said. "But I suppose he must be in danger. You can't be in possession of a picture like that without exposing yourself to some degree of risk."

Her calm, rational words were entirely at odds with her earlier anguished urgency. "I can't remember anything between diving into the river and coming to in the wings where a very helpful lady helped me to get dressed," she insisted when I pressed her on the matter. "And listen, Will, if you're going to write this up for that damn paper of yours, I'd be very grateful if you could retain a decent reticence about my identity. I don't want the tabloids cottoning on to the fact that I've done a striptease at the Hackney Empire."

"Fair enough," I said. "Though you did announce that you were Lady Natasha. Someone there might have recognised you and be on to the *Sun* as we speak."

"Oh shit," she said, then laughed. "Well, it can't be helped. What a weird evening. Yet I feel . . ." she paused for a moment, as if the word had eluded her, then found it with a kind of wonderment. "Happy," she said. "Happier than I've been for ages."

The taxi driver arrived and we followed him outside.

"Where to?" he said when we were inside the cab. "Account address?"

"Your place, I think, Will," she said, in a tone that brooked no argument. "The least you can do after submitting me to that ordeal is cook me some supper. And I'd like to see where you live."

I bet you would, I thought viciously. The squalor of my 'studio' flat flashed into my brain and I found myself sweating with embarrassment.

"Won't your husband be expecting you?" I whispered nastily. "And besides, the cupboard's bare at home."

"Dommo's in New York on business for the next couple of days. Just give the nice man the address, Will, and stop whining," she replied.

I was always pathetic when confronted with strong women, and I meekly gave the address in St George's Drive.

"That's my boy," said Natasha, and gave my upper thigh a very suggestive squeeze. Wonders would never cease. The strange thing was that I rather wished they would.

By the time we'd reached Pimlico, Natasha had wormed out most of the details of my separation from Kim. It was fair enough. I'd pumped her hard enough. I still didn't want to let her into my little pit of shame, though.

"Look, Natasha, there's a really nice Tapas bar on the corner that stays open late," I said, "Let's eat there. I've got absolutely nothing at home." Unfortunately, Natasha had spotted the all-night supermarket and stopped the cab telling me to wait with the driver. Ten minutes later, she emerged with two bulging carriers. She climbed back into the cab and moments later we were descending the steps to what were laughably known as the garden flats. I opened the front door with a sense of sick foreboding. Maxie, ears alert as always, had his peroxided head out of the door of his own 'studio' before Natasha was over the threshold.

"How many times have I got to tell you? I won't have no dragging back, I run a nice establishment 'ere," he leered in his screaming queen voice. One of Maxie's little fantasies was that he was the landlady of this benighted basement when in fact he was just another exploited tenant. The other was that he was as bent as a nine-bob note when he was actually aggressively and successfully heterosexual. The ecstatic female sounds that emerged from his flat some nights often left me limp with jealousy and loneliness.

I could see Maxie was agog to be introduced. In the three months I'd been living here, I'd never brought anyone home with me. I thought I might as well give him the full works.

"Maxie, this is Lady Natasha Gilbert-Smith," I said. "She's come for a spot of late supper. And Natasha, this is Maxie Riddel, universally known as Fiddle, window-cleaner and painter and decorator in these parts. He's not quite as bad as he seems."

"Showing me up again," whispered Maxie under his breath, before approaching Natasha with exaggerated courtesy, taking a little bow and shaking her warmly by the hand. "It's an honour to meet your ladyship," he said, "though what you're doing with this scumbag, I can't imagine."

"We're very old friends," said Natasha, giving her impersonation of a talking deep-freeze. "And now if you'll forgive me, I really must get the supper on."

Maxie, needless to say, was entirely unabashed. "Well, if it's a bit of rough you're looking for, and Will here fails to come up to the mark, you know where to find me," he said. He looked at his watch. "I'll expect you in about twenty minutes," he added, disappearing into his own, almost pathologically neat bedsit.

For once, Natasha seemed at a loss for words. She was about to be lost for some more. I opened my door, and felt the familiar depression of homecoming wash over me. "Home is so sad," wrote Philip Larkin, "It stays as it was left." Left in my case like a municipal tip, rank with the smell of old food, old fags, old socks and old despair. Sometimes, I fantasised that some charlady from heaven might have cleaned the whole place up in my absence, but she never had. "I'm afraid it's a bit of a mess," I said over my shoulder as I led Natasha into the room. There were, as always, newspapers, mouldering coffee cups, unwashed laundry and empty beer cans all over the floor. The bed was unmade, the sheets grubby. The tiny sink (the rest of the 'facilities' were communal and hellish) contained yet more unattended washing-up and on a table near the window stood that most poignant symbol of the single, bedsit life, a filthy Baby Belling.

"Oh, Will . . ." she said as she surveyed the overflowing ashtray on the bedside table, and the almost empty bottle of Scotch beneath it.

"Quite," I said. "Now why don't we go and eat at that Tapas bar I was telling you about?"

Natasha wouldn't hear of it. "I love tidying things up," she said with a worryingly eager gleam in her eye, "and I so rarely get the chance these days. Where do you keep the bin bags? And the Jif?" I was forced to admit that neither item troubled the weekly housekeeping accounts.

"I'd guessed as much," she said rummaging in one of the bags and producing Jif, washing-up liquid, scourers, bin bags, dusters and even a pair of bright yellow Marigold gloves.

"Now you clear up the rubbish and the dirty laundry, and I'll get on with the washing-up," she said briskly, opening the window to let in a blast of much needed but horribly cold fresh air. I grumbled about freezing to death and Natasha said if I got down to work, I'd soon warm up.

"Yes, Miss," I said meekly. "Have you got a spare pinny?" She grinned and rolled up her sleeves and set to, and I found there was a certain pleasure in clearing up the mess myself. Laundry went into one bin bag, newspapers into another (I'd recycle them I promised myself smugly) and general junk and squalor like half-eaten takeaways, fag ends and cartons of spectacularly decayed milk into a third. I made the bed, Hoovered the now visible carpet and even started tidying the cluttered surface of the old kitchen table that now served me as a desk. I discovered the answering machine under a pile of old press releases. Hardly anyone phoned me here as I hadn't bothered to give many people my new number, and I went for days without checking it. But I belatedly remembered the calls I'd put out that morning.

The flashing light indicated there was at least one message waiting. I pressed the play button and there was Trev the Rev. "Great to hear from you, Will," he said, struggling to make himself heard over a screaming baby in the background. "I'd love to have a chat about old times. I saw Henry a year or so ago and he was in good form. No sign then that there was any kind of trouble. He said Rose was doing OK too. Haven't heard anything from Nicholas or that stuck-up sister of his for years. Do phone back, and if you fancy a night away from the metropolitan fleshpots, there's always a spare bed here. Oh Lord, more trouble, it's sometimes like the Third World War here, Luke, will you stop hitting Freya now! Got to go, Will, sorry, get in touch, God bless." His last words were delivered at amazing, harassed speed and accompanied by the kind of screams you might have heard issuing from the Lubyanka in the days of Stalin. Natasha smiled sadly at me.

"Even vicars seem to think I'm stuck-up," she said.

"Not too stuck up to clean up this slum," I said, feeling a wave of affection for her. "You're all right, Natasha and don't let anyone tell you different."

She flushed and turned her attention to the Baby Belling.

I looked at my watch. It was a quarter to midnight, too late to trouble a harassed vicar with an army of unruly kids. He deserved his sleep. I hauled the bin bags out to the dustbin area, and when I got back, Natasha was frying bacon and eggs in a pan she had somehow managed to liberate of several weeks of unspeakable grease.

"It's like being a student again," she said happily.

"It's not so much fun when you're thirty-three and living like a student all the time," I said self-pityingly and she said 'diddums' and asked me to pour her a drink.

"I've only got this bit of Scotch," I said, holding up the near empty bottle that I used to knock me into unconsciousness most nights. I was getting through about two a week, on top of all the other booze down the pub.

"You'll find some wine in one of the bags," she said, and I shuddered when I remembered the late night supermarket's range of plonk. Somehow, Natasha had managed to find a perfectly decent claret among the Blue Nuns, the Thunderbirds and the British 'sherries', and I opened it with the corkscrew on my Swiss Army penknife and poured generous slurps into glasses that now shined like a picture in *Good Housekeeping.*

Natasha dished up and, since my table was still covered with junk and I'd only got one chair anyway, we sat side-by-side on the bed to eat it.

"Funny how much better food always tastes when someone else has cooked it," I said, chewing the fat off the bacon rind and feeling a rare moment of content. With the room tidy and only the desk lamp on, my horrid little room seemed cosy, almost romantic now that the window was closed and the two-bar electric fire had begin to warm it up again.

"What are we going to do next about Henry?" said Natasha. "It doesn't sound as though Trev's got any particularly fresh info about him either."

"He might have some idea of where he's working, or where he's living. Or perhaps even about Rose. I think I might try to see Trev this weekend. I can also try Henry's parents number again tomorrow, and I'm still waiting to hear from our old editor on the *Esher Herald.* We're bound to get a trace before too long. He can't just have disappeared."

"That's exactly what he could do," said Natasha, putting her plate down on the floor, "as well you know."

It sounded like a typically sharp Natasha remark, so what happened next took me completely by surprise. She suddenly put her arms round my neck, and gently pushed me down onto the bed. She arranged herself on top of me in a purposeful manner and her tongue began to explore my mouth. Odd though this may seem, her amorous assault wasn't entirely welcome. I'd like to say my reluctance to submit was because I was trying to keep myself chaste for the possibly faithless Kim, but at that moment Kim was the last person on my mind. What was on my mind was the overwhelming taste of raw onion. Being French-kissed by Natasha at that moment was like being forced to eat a raw onion yourself. Unfortunately I hadn't been hypnotised. Natasha herself seemed curiously unaware of my lack of response and wriggled her tongue doggedly while fumbling for the buttons on my shirt. I felt like some hapless teenage girl at a party, landed with the boy in the room she least fancies. The only thing for it was to lie back and think, if not of England, then at least of Listerine Mouthwash and Extra Strong Mints. After several minutes even Natasha became aware that I was displaying all the sexual responsiveness of a dead fish.

She beat a tactical retreat from my mouth and propped herself up on one elbow to look at my face.

"What's up, Will? Don't say all that booze has made you impotent?" It was, I suppose, the equivalent of the spotty nerd at the party telling his physically repelled victim that she knew she wanted to really.

"It's not that," I said, "or at least I hope it's not that. The fact is that your breath stinks." It's not a nice thing to say to a girl, and judging by the expression of shock and anger that suddenly tensed her face, I thought she was about to give me a good slap. Then the memory of the onion, or at least me telling her about the onion, came flooding back. "Oh Christ," she giggled, "That fucking hypnotist. I knew there was a funny taste in my mouth when we were having the bacon and eggs, I could hardly taste them at all. I'm sorry, Will."

"Me too," I said. "I'm sure your intentions were entirely dishonourable and I respect them. It's not every day that I get half-raped by the most beautiful stripper in Hackney . . ."

"But I smell," she said with a grin.

"Exactly. By the way, do you do this sort of thing often? I mean, doesn't Sir Dominic mind?"

"I think that's rather my affair, don't you?" she said, sharply.

"Yes, of course it is. Sorry."

"Let's have another drink," she said. "Now I know it's onion, the taste is driving me mad."

I refilled both our glasses and we clinked them ironically. "Friendship and wild times," we said, routinely, as though we'd been saying it all our lives. I found myself thinking of Natasha's naked body and began to regret my earlier squeamishness. Perhaps I could suggest nipping down to the corner shop for some mouthwash. But this time I did think of Kim and changed my mind.

"Will," she said. "Could I come with you to see Trev? I'd like him to know that I'm not a totally stuck-up bitch for one thing."

I explained my unusually full weekend – a college Gaudy the following evening and the Professional Lighting and Sound Association on Saturday. "I thought I'd hire a car in Oxford and see Trev *en route* to Leicester."

Natasha blushed like a teenager. "Well," she said, "would you entirely object if we made a weekend of it? I could supply the transport."

I wrestled glumly with my conscience for a couple of seconds. Making a weekend of it presumably meant making a dirty weekend of it if her recent assault was any indication. But while a surprise, and promptly curtailed snog with Natasha was one thing, turning up in hotels together was another.

"Listen, I'm sorry, Natasha," I said, feeling like a prig. "I'd love the company but . . ."

"Separate rooms," she said, as if reading my mind. "I understand how you feel about your wife, Will."

I was touched. "There's just one other thing," I said. "We're not going in that joke Rolls-Royce with the chauffeur are we?"

"No – we'll go in the Porsche. Leave it all to me. What time does the Gaudy start?"

"Seven for seven-thirty," I said. "And I'm afraid we're not allowed to take guests."

"I realise that, silly. I'll go to the pictures."

"And the technology show's going to be dreadfully dull. And it's in Leicester, than which cities don't come more boring. Perhaps you might want to go home after we've seen Trev?" It was pathetic really. Here was a rich, beautiful woman apparently eager to spend the weekend with a scruffy, overweight, drunken slob like me and I was doing everything in my power to put her off.

"Listen, Will," she said. "I could do with some company too. And I probably know more about lighting boards and sound equipment than you do after all the launches I've been involved in."

"Then consider yourself hired as chauffeur and reservation manager," I said. "And chief interviewer at the trade show."

She smiled. "I'd better get home. I can easily walk from here."

"I'll walk you back. Or we can easily get a cab at the rank in Lupus Street."

"I'd sooner go on my own, Will. To be quite honest, it's been such a strange evening that I'd like the chance to get my hypnotised mind back in some kind of working order."

"It's very late," I said, "I'd feel much happier . . ."

"I'm a big girl now, Will. I can look after myself." She reached into her handbag and produced an aerosol spray. "And I've got this."

"I can't see a can of spray-on deodorant deterring any muggers," I said.

"It's not deodorant, silly. It just says it's deodorant in case of prying customs and policemen. It's Mace. Dommo likes me to have it."

"And I expect you'll be telling me next that the Porsche is equipped with an ejector seat, and transforms itself into a submarine as soon as you drive through a deep puddle?"

"Naturally," she said. "All that comes as standard."

She got up to go, and I helped her on with her fur coat and led her up the area steps.

"I'll pick you up here tomorrow then. About four to beat the worst of the Friday night traffic?"

"Great," I said. "And just remember that I prefer my martinis stirred rather than shaken."

"I'll remember."

I kissed her on the cheek and thanked her for her help and she set off up St George's Drive. The moment I let myself back into the basement, Maxie's head was round the door.

"You didn't fuck it then? I could see she was way out of your class."

"I kicked her out, my old son," I said, giving a not half bad impersonation of Michael Caine as Alfie. "Bad breath. But once she's got her oral hygiene sorted out we're spending the weekend together."

"You're never?"

"You can wave us off tomorrow at four o'clock if you like. We're going in the Porsche, naturally."

"Well fuck me sideways," said Maxie.

"I'd love to, but I'm afraid I've got to catch up on my beauty sleep. I imagine it's going to be a pretty strenuous weekend." That, as it turned out, was the understatement of the year.

# 4: Friday 20th December 1996

*Let's have one other gaudy night; call to me*
*All my sad captains; fill our bowls once more;*
*Let's mock the midnight bell.*

*Antony and Cleopatra*

I walked down St Giles in a state not far short of agony. All week, I'd been niggled by the knowledge that I had some minor task to perform but had been unable to remember what it was. It had belatedly dawned on me while hastily packing my clothes for the trip to Oxford. It wasn't just that my evening dress looked crumpled, food-smeared and, worrying possibility, vomit stained. It was also long past its wear-by date, or my wear-by date anyway. All that beer, all those McDonald's, all those comforting Mars bars and Munchies since my break-up with Kim had done terrible things to my already distended waistline. My stomach now resembled an over-inflated barrage balloon and the trousers had already been worryingly tight when I'd last squeezed myself into them, in a far less gross condition, six months earlier.

Had I had any moral courage at all, I'd have got Natasha to whisk me to Moss Bros in Covent Garden to hire a replacement before heading west to Oxford. I couldn't however face yet another display of my own squalid inefficiency. As it was, I'd kept her waiting for thirty minutes in her fearsome-looking Porsche after a late departure from the office. Col had called me over for a few words about the trade show and, although he knew I had to get away early for the gaudy, had then kept me hanging furiously around while he gossiped on the phone at quite unnecessary length to one of his cronies. It was perfectly clear that the main reason he wanted a chat was to make sure that I had indeed booked a hotel in Leicester on Saturday night and intended to stay in it. I remained tantalisingly opaque on the matter, which didn't please him, but my paranoia about Kim went up several notches on the ratchet. When I'd finally got away from the obnoxious brat, he'd chilled my blood as I crossed the newsroom to freedom by asking me if I'd seen the Birthday Bible recently.

"It's in my desk drawer, Col," I'd called over my shoulder, and then legged it double-quick down the stairs before he had a chance to find out that it wasn't. There was going to be hell to pay on Monday morning.

All of this had left me frazzled, while Natasha was in a state of quietly simmering fury about being kept waiting for so long. Needless to say, we hit a traffic jam getting out of London on the A40 and, needless to say, Natasha wasted little time in pointing out that if I'd been home in time we'd almost certainly have avoided it. I grovelled as best I could and ate a Fry's Chocolate Cream and a king size packet of Love Hearts on the principle that it was far too late to start thinking about losing weight now. I found one that said, 'Sorry' and passed it to Natasha. She looked at it, frowned and threw it out of the window. "Disgusting cheap sweets," was all she said before tuning into Radio 3 which was broadcasting a particularly rebarbative contemporary string quartet recital. It sounded like cats being tortured and it suited our mood perfectly.

As soon as we hit the M40 and the traffic eased, Natasha put her foot down and took the Porsche to over 100 mph. Since we kept hitting knots of congestion, the journey entailed sudden braking as well as acceleration and by the time we reached the Randolph, my nerves were in shreds and I was already late for the gaudy. We were shown up to a rather fabulous suite with bedrooms on either side of a luxuriously furnished sitting room commanding views of the dreaming spires. Neither of us were on speakers by now.

I went into my room to change, and by holding my breath and pulling in my stomach, just about managed to get my trousers on. When I exhaled and relaxed it was as if my guts had been bound with razor wire. I tried to wipe off the worst of the many stains on my evening dress with a damp flannel, becoming particularly exercised by some nasty white smears around the crotch. They had been caused, I dimly recalled, by a spectacular accident with the cream jug at the *Evening Standard* drama awards, but it looked as though someone, possibly me, had ejaculated prolifically on my trousers. By the time I'd finished, it looked as though I'd pissed myself instead.

I went out into the living room and Natasha looked up from her glossy magazine. "Christ, you look a mess," she said before returning to the *Tatler*.

"Thank you, sweetheart. Don't wait up," I said, before making a haughty exit. Unfortunately, I walked straight into Natasha's bedroom, which rather spoiled the effect.

And now I was walking head down through the icy drizzle of St Giles with my midriff already feeling as if it had suffered severe internal injuries. Why had I come? I wondered wretchedly. It took a bit of admitting, even to myself, but I hadn't actually enjoyed Oxford much. Shortly before going up, I'd made the fatal mistake of reading *Brideshead Revisited* and as a result spent much of my time convinced that somewhere there was a glamorous golden Oxford going on from which I'd been excluded. No charming aristocrat was ever sick through my window, ready and willing to introduce me to a life of fine wines, Turkish cigarettes and plovers' eggs; but then I suppose he was hardly likely to since my room was on the second floor. Instead, I'd worked too hard for a very average degree, wasted a lot of time with people I didn't much like, and fretted about my non-existent sex life. Even now, I sometimes pretended to recent acquaintances that I'd had a terrific time at Oxford, all champagne and punts and girls and terrific drugs. In fact, far too many evenings had been spent alone with endless cups of instant coffee, good books that became a chore rather than a pleasure, and a corrosive feeling of social failure.

St Christopher's, just next door to St John's, had been the cruel suggestion of my English master at school. It's Victorian Gothick design suggested a Hammer Horror film set, and in my day it was both famously reactionary (when all the other colleges were discovering the joys of co-education, it still refused to admit women) and alarmingly schizophrenic. On the one hand, there were loud, sporty, and, in many cases, spectacularly dim public school types, who spent their time getting drunk and baying for broken glass when they weren't rowing or playing rugger. On the other, there were earnest, state-educated young men who seemed to regard the very idea of fun and frivolity as a grave error of taste. They minded their books when they weren't canvassing for either the Labour Party or the sweatily evangelical Christian sect of their choice. I didn't fit happily into either category and had been pathetically timid about discovering a world beyond the college walls. I'd become prematurely sad, middle-aged and respectable at St Christopher's and I sometimes felt I'd been making up for the wild student days I'd never had ever since.

I entered the gloomily lit porter's lodge and there was Tom, the head porter, looking as explosively red faced as he had in my undergraduate days. It was a wonder his blood pressure hadn't killed him years ago. I wished it had.

"Evening, Tom," I said with false good cheer. "How's the world been treating you?"

"What's it to you?" he said. "Name?"

"Will Benson."

"I don't remember no Will Benson," he said, gloomily surveying his list. "But it says down here you're expected so I suppose I'd better let you in." He went off to get the key for the college room I'd booked months earlier but I told him I didn't need it.

"I'm staying at the Randolph," I said, realising with horror that my words sounded like a pathetic boast.

"Well, bully for you," said Tom. "They're all getting pissed in the SCR if you're not too grand to join them."

"Right," I said, the permanently cowed feeling of my student years flooding back with sickening familiarity. "Well, I'll be on my way then."

As always, I half expected bats to be flying round the cavernously gloomy front quad, while the sight of several hundred men in dinner jackets through the window of the Senior Common Room made an evening *á deux* with Natasha, even in her present filthy mood, seem infinitely appealing. I entered the room feeling like a gate-crasher, and tried to look nonchalant as I gradually realised there didn't seem to be a soul there I knew. The gaudy covered six years worth of St Christopher's undergraduates. Those that I'd known had clearly decided, more sensibly than me, that this was likely to be a night of purgatory rather than pleasure and stayed away. A waiter wafted by with a drinks tray, and I was relieved to see that it contained a sizeable tumbler of Scotch as well as the inevitable flutes of gaseous champagne which would play havoc with my cramped innards. I helped myself to it, and was told that at gaudies only the Master and the fellows were allowed to drink spirits before dinner, the kind of obscure and ludicrous rule (no croquet on Wednesdays, academic gowns to be worn at breakfast during Lent) that added that cruel extra layer of irritation to life at St Kit's, as it was known by those who pretended to like the place. I should have told the waiter to fuck off but instead I meekly handed back the Scotch and took the champagne. It was, of course, warm.

I wandered miserably around, trying to find a friendly, or at least not actively hostile face, and caught fleeting fragments of conversation. "Expecting a two hundred grand bonus this year" . . . "I tell you, the school fees at Charterhouse are just a joke" . . . "We're all looking forward to the Phil Collins concert next month" . . . "Just bought a wonderful old wreck of a farmhouse in Tuscany" . . . "So you still play with the Old Kitonians?" . . . "Personally, I've got a great deal of time for Peter Mandelson" and "Have you ever thought of inviting Christ into your life?" among them.

I was unhappily aware that everyone seemed thinner than me, almost certainly richer too, and I was reasonably certain that not one of them was wearing evening dress that caused them extreme physical distress. By the time I'd completed my circuit of the room, I'd drunk four glasses of champagne from passing trays and the old bubbling acid was building up menacingly below. It was then that I had my brainwave. Why not simply do a runner? I could tell Natasha that I'd been taken ill, which was in any case beginning to look increasingly likely, and spend the evening in bed with a non-stop supply of medicinal malts from room service. I was just edging out through the door when I heard a familiar whiney voice.

"Not leaving us already, Will?"

Oh shit. It was Graeme Cook, my particular *bête noire* whom I'd somehow missed on my trawl through the room. Graeme had the unusual knack of being both extremely clever and extremely boring. Needless to say, he'd got a first in English, thanks to painstaking slog and, ghastly though it was to admit it, the occasional original insight. But he turned everything he talked about into a desert of balls-aching tedium. I'd spent more hours than I cared to remember in his company, drinking pints to his halves (needless to say he was a member of Camra, but one who never got more than cautiously pissed), listening to his plans about becoming a Labour MP and enduring his enthusiasm for Delius and Vaughan Williams. What made Graeme an even bitterer pill to swallow was that in the middle of our first term he had somehow persuaded a remarkably beautiful, vivaciously good humoured girl from Somerville to let him fuck her. On the many occasions when we went out as a threesome, she seemed almost as bored with Graeme as I was, and one of my secret fantasies was that one day she'd ditch Gray, as she so aptly called him, and take up with me instead. Unfortunately, she never did, and I'd attended their wedding a couple of months after we all graduated, before losing contact with them as I hoped for ever. When life got really miserable, I'd occasionally console myself with the thought that at least I'd never again have to sit in a pub with Graeme, listening to him bang on about Labour's urgent need to scrap Clause Four.

"I was just going for a slash actually," I said, nursing the fleeting hope that escape might still be possible. "See you in a minute, Graeme."

"No need to go skulking out into the night," he said. "The fellows have their own facilities, you know, and on a night like this we're allowed to use them."

How like Graeme to use the word 'facilities'. How like him to have checked the college rule about their permitted use. As if half guessing that I had been planning a bunk, he escorted me to the facilities personally and loitered embarrassingly close to me as I stood at the urinal. I felt as though I was being solicited in a cruisers' cottage and the thought of sexual contact with Graeme, combined with the tight trousers, meant that I only managed the most half-hearted piss. There was also a terrible problem doing up the zip afterwards and for a ghastly moment Graeme seemed to be on the point of asking if he could lend a hand.

"My word, you've put on a lot of weight," said Graeme cheerily as I tried to pull the zip over the blubber. "And lost quite a lot of hair too."

"Thanks, Gray," I said, my foot itching for his groin, my fist yearning to smash him in the repellently smug kisser. "You're looking much the same as ever." As indeed he did. Prolific brown hair, skinny body, too large a head and a complexion of almost albino pallor. He was curiously unmarked by the passing years. I had the sudden nightmarish idea that perhaps he shed his skin each year like a snake and grew a new one.

"Not much of a turn out from our set," said Gray as we rejoined the throng in the SCR, its occupants now leaving through the other door to cross the quad to the cavernous dining room, or hall, as I vaguely remembered it was called. "Jerry Logan's come, and Mark Alexander." He named two of my former fellow undergraduates; Jerry, I remembered, was a terrific enthusiast for immensely long and boring sub-titled films and had gone into the civil service. Mark had been a frighteningly intelligent mathematician who lived across the landing from me and who spent his leisure hours composing almost unplayable, and certainly totally unlistenable, pieces for the piano. I'd never had anything in common with either of them and found that I could hardly remember what they looked like. The idea that we had once constituted a set, or part of a set, was absurd.

We joined the throng heading for Hall, Graeme having checked the placement with characteristic thoroughness. "We're sitting next to each other," he said with heroic good cheer. "And Jerry and Mark are sitting opposite us."

"We should be in for a great evening then," I said, and Graeme, hearing the faintest edge of snide in my voice, flashed me an anxious look. The fiction of happy memories and firm friendship had to be maintained on an occasion like this. Otherwise it was all going to seem as desperately sad as it really was.

"I thought you'd be a Labour MP by now," I said, and instead of looking crestfallen as I'd naturally hoped, he looked smug. "Just a few months to go," he said. "I'm fighting a marginal near Birmingham. But we only need a three per cent swing and with the polls looking the way they are, there shouldn't be any problem. I hope to keep my practice going for a few years, but naturally the long term plan is to get into government."

"What practice's that?" I asked.

"At the Bar," he said. "I was taken on as a pupil at Lincoln's Inn a couple of years after going down. Management consultancy didn't suit me. I specialise in restraint of trade."

"I do quite a lot of practice at the bar myself," I said. It was a pathetic joke, and one I instantly regretted making. Especially when Graeme didn't get it and I had to explain it to him.

"Oh, a joke, ha ha, jolly good," he said, as if he had just been informed of some deviant new form of human behaviour. "And what do you do for a living?"

"I work for *Theatre World*," I said, before adding with a shudder of self-loathing, "I'm deputy editor." Christ, I was lying now, trying to make myself sound fractionally more significant. It was at that point I realised how far I'd sunk in the last few months. I wanted to go home, not to the Pimlico bedsit but to Kim, to apologise for all my moody behaviour and to be forgiven, hugged and comforted. And that brought Colin's eager little face to mind and I felt like bursting into tears. There was no help for it. I was going to have to get heroically pissed tonight to blot out the pain, the failure, the insidious lack of confidence.

"I can't say I go to the theatre much these days," said Graeme. "Any chance of the editorship?"

"Shouldn't be too long now," I said. "The editor's just had a nasty heart attack." Somewhere in the quad, a cock should have crowed.

We entered Hall, with its lingering smell of the vile breakfast kedgeree unchanged after more than a decade. So were the hard wooden benches and the gloomy portraits of incredibly bewhiskered St Kit's *alumni.* We found our places and there were Mark and Jerry. A good deal of bogus bonhomie ensued, much of it centring on my weight. With typical St Kit's parsimony, I noticed, the wine glasses were actually the size of sherry glasses. Even the quest for alcoholic oblivion seemed doomed.

The college parson intoned a Latin grace that didn't seem to last all that much longer than an episode of *The Archers* and our glasses were filled with a disgustingly acidic and – it appeared to be yet another college custom – warm white wine. The always sullen college servants in their grubby white mess jackets then plonked down the starters, which consisted of a grey/green lump of chicken liver paté floating in a sea of what looked, and incredibly proved to be, heated up Golden Shred marmalade. I drank down my glass of wine, took a taste of the paté that I instantly regretted, and settled in grimly for the duration. The only plus point was that I was able to undo my trousers under cover of the table. Another came when Graeme, with elaborate fake concern for my empty glass and "legendary thirst", passed me over his wine since he was a "firm teetotaller" these days. "The thing about booze is that it gives you a headache the next morning," he said, as if this were some amazing insight no one else had previously been vouchsafed.

Jerry, it transpired, was now a permanent under-secretary at the Ministry of Agriculture and I noticed that he, like me, gave the paté a wide berth. Presumably he knew what was happening to the country's chickens. Anyway, he was too busy, telling us about the new print of a rare Fellini film he'd just seen, to eat.

Mark was now something big in British Nuclear Fuels, but said he still composed at weekends, and launched into a long account of how Radio 3 had commissioned a piano sonata from him, recorded it with a pianist even I thought I might have heard of, and then unaccountably decided not to broadcast it. I raised a glass to the Controller of Radio 3. The man couldn't be all bad. Though when you thought about the kind of stuff his station seemed perfectly happy to put out, that string quartet on the way to Oxford, for instance, the awfulness of Mark's piece began to assume truly monumental proportions.

"That's the trouble with life today," said Mark, gamely attacking his leathery hunk of venison, which appeared to come not in its own *jus*, or indeed any kind of *jus* at all, but the congealing granulated gravy which had always been such a feature of the St Kit's cuisine. "No one's interested in danger, risk any more." I thought about interjecting that working for BNF showed an appetite for risk which went beyond the call of duty but Mark was not to be stopped. "We live in a timid play-safe culture. I mean, look at the Labour Party, Gray, borrowed Tory clothes. Where's the radicalism, the sense of adventure?"

This was all the excuse Graeme needed for a twenty-minute party political broadcast on behalf of New Labour, and I half expected to see Peter Mandelson hovering in the background, disguised as a waiter, making sure he adhered to the party line.

When he'd finally run out of steam, Jerry took over, with another set-piece speech on the failings of Hollywood. Mercifully, it now turned out that Jerry drank very little too, and in return for looking interested and nodding my head occasionally, he passed me over his glass of red, and continued to do so each time our glasses were refilled, which turned out to be surprisingly often. With the further supplies from Graeme on my right, the evening was beginning to lose its more intolerable edges, which was just as well, because during the long wait for pudding the family photos came out, and there was much talk of nappy changing, breast-feeding, cute childhood sayings and the ruinous price of private education. I tried to look interested in Gray's blob of a baby, held by his wife, whose name I could no longer recall; she still looked unfairly fanciable. Then there were Jerry's twin boys, five years old and looking impossibly sweet in their blazers and caps, and Mark's three girls, whose pained expressions suggested that Mark had just treated them to his latest piano composition.

"What about you, Will, you entered the fatherhood stakes yet?" one of the insufferably smug trio asked.

"No," I replied sullenly. I suppose I could have treated them to an account of IVF treatment, I was after all the only member of our "set" who hadn't yet delivered a public speech of major cultural or sociological importance, but a simple no was all I was capable of.

"Wise fellow," said Jerry with the forced affability of a man who believes exactly the opposite. "Mind you, to judge by the amount you're drinking, you wouldn't be much use when it came to the night feeds." This was greeted by patronising little smirks all round, and I thought quite seriously about seeing how many of them I could take out with my Swiss Army Penknife but mercifully at this moment the Master, new since my time, rose to give a speech.

The words flowed blandly on . . . "Improved position in the Norrington Table" . . . "Generous bequest to the Library" . . . "Marvellous to see so many old members" . . . "St Kit's enviable reputation for academic rigour and good fellowship" . . . "Cheques gratefully appreciated." At last, the old fart sat down, and some creep from our generation stood up to make a speech about what fond memories we all had of the good old days, retelling various anecdotes about "legendary incidents and characters" in college life, none of which rang any bells with me at all.

The pudding – the chef had really pushed the boat out with Angel Delight and synthetic cream – was followed by cheese and port. Realising that I had eaten no more than three exploratory half-mouthfuls all evening, I made amends with the cheese. There wasn't much even this chef could do to spoil mature English cheddar and a decent stilton, and there were Bath Oliver biscuits and celery as well. It seemed I'd come all the way to Oxford for a ploughman's lunch, but the quantities of port were prodigious. Inspection of the room and the subdued nature of the whole proceedings – I'd been looking forward to watching the bread rolls fly – indicated that the college's boozy hoorays had decided to stay away *en masse.* Perhaps they'd all succumbed to cirrhosis or good sense. Anyway, there was no doubt that this was a night for the college's always substantial contingent of nerds, whose idea of a gaudy time made the average WI meeting seem like an orgy of self-indulgence. As a result, the decanters circled the table with almost indecent haste, each old Kitonian passing it nervously on as if it contained class A drugs. Recklessly, I filled my boots. Eventually, the padre got up for another interminable grace, and we were invited to return to the SCR for coffee and "for those who require it, further alcoholic refreshment."

Getting up from the table posed several hazards. First, there was the problem of doing up the zip and button of my trousers, now, it transpired, a complete impossibility. With what seemed to me amazing ingenuity, however, I buttoned up my jacket to cover the shame below. Why I hadn't thought of this before I couldn't imagine. I tripped climbing out of the bench, always a tricky procedure even when sober, though Graeme managed to prevent my falling headlong onto the floor.

"Bed for you, I think, Will," he said. "Which staircase are you on?"

"Bed?" I said, expansively, "bed? This is supposed to be a gaudy night for Christ's sake. We're meant to get pissed. Indeed," I continued, with the appalling fervour of the seriously drunk, "we've got a bounden duty to get pissed. 'Let's have one other gaudy night'. There was Mark Antony, up against it with the Romans and with what might prove to be his last ever chance to shag Cleopatra. And did he go to bed? No, of course, he didn't. He got fucking pissed. Like the hero he was."

Graeme who, for all his faults, was a man devoid of malice, helped me down the steps rather than giving me the hearty shove I deserved.

Swaying slightly and with only the need of occasional physical support from Graeme, I made my way back to the SCR. It was an attractive room, panelled with fumed oak and with a fire burning at one end. There was also a table stocked with a variety and quantity of drink which made Natasha's poolside bar seem miserly. You could see the way the St Kit's authorities were thinking. Knowing its own graduates, or at least those who turned up for dire nights like this, it could safely order vast quantities of booze knowing they would be left more or less untouched. Leaving, of course, a terrific surplus for the fellows already paid for out of gaudy funds.

"Large kümmel with ice," I slurred at the waiter, determined that at least someone should make inroads into the dons' stash. "And I expect Octavius Caesar here could probably do with a Diet Coke," I added, gesturing to where I thought Graeme was. Only Graeme had gone. Abandoned his old mate and left him to swim or sink in a sea of booze. I could hardly blame him.

Something was missing from my sudden euphoria and I realised I was dying for a fag. Foolishly, I'd forgotten to bring some proper cigarettes with me and the waiter confirmed there was no fag machine. I looked around to bum one, and discovered, with no real surprise, that no one else seemed to be smoking. Intelligent people don't smoke, as I tell myself most mornings when I wake up and hawk my guts out. Unfortunately, I always have to have a cigarette immediately afterwards to calm me down after this distressing early morning trauma.

I'd got the usual packet of Old Disgusting in my pocket but there was no way I was going to be able to roll one in my present state with a glass of kümmel in my hand. I lurched round the room and found a sofa in a dimly lit corner. There was an old man, apparently asleep at one end, so I settled down quietly at the other and began the tricky task of rolling a gasper. My hands now seemed stubbornly incapable of a simple routine they performed automatically some thirty times a day. Tobacco kept falling into my lap and onto the floor, but almost none would stay in the paper. Eventually, I produced a pathetically loose packed and shapeless cigarette that would have disgraced a fourth-former behind the bike sheds, and when I lit it, half of it burnt away in a single whoosh.

"Perhaps you'd care to try one of mine," said the old don, proffering a packet of untippped Gitanes.

"You're a saint," I said, taking the fag and managing to light it all by myself on only the third attempt.

"It's Will Benson, isn't it?" he asked.

I thought there had been something familiar about him. His once longish brown hair was still longish but now white. He'd also added a small goatee beard, almost always a mistake, and so it proved here. With his spec's and benign smile he looked a dead ringer for Colonel Sanders of Kentucky Fried Chicken fame. Nevertheless, I belatedly recognised him, the taste of Gitane acting like Proust's madeleine. I'd been farmed out to him for tutorials at Magdelen for a couple of terms in my final year while my own tutor took a less than well-earned sabbatical. They were, in retrospect, the only two terms at

Oxford I'd really enjoyed. He'd told me, frankly, while dishing out the Gitanes and pouring a bone-dry sherry, that, while I was a perfectly competent student, there was no way I was going to get a first, and – apparently glimpsing something of my confined and unhappy existence – tactfully suggested I might like to broaden my horizons a little. As a result, I'd written some articles for *Isis*, stayed up all night on several occasions preparing the magazine for press, and stage managed a couple of plays. In those two terms I'd glimpsed the Oxford that had always eluded me, and actually enjoyed myself. But it was too little too late. The last term was spent cramming for finals with my own tedious Marxist of a tutor, and by the time I went down, it was with a feeling that I'd squandered a golden opportunity. Still, at least I'd had a taste of what Oxford might have been like if only I'd approached it with less caution. All this flashed through my mind in the time it took to take a drag on the cigarette.

"It's Dr Maxwell, isn't it? But what on earth are you doing at St Christopher's?"

"Pure vanity on my part, I'm ashamed to say. They've got a professorship for more or less clapped-out old English dons here, very much not a major chair, but I couldn't resist the chance of becoming a prof in my old age."

"Congratulations," I said.

"Commiserations, you mean. St Christopher's, as you must know all too well, is neither a fashionable nor an enjoyable address."

"But at least it's got girls now."

"It is amazing how they manage to choose young women, as we must learn to call them, who are every bit as earnest – and physically unattractive – as their male counterparts."

He signalled a waiter who brought over a couple of large strong coffees, much needed in my case, then earned several million brownie points by saying he was a subscriber to *Theatre World*, and enjoyed my reviews. I could have kissed him, goatee beard and all.

"You disappeared from its pages for a year or so . . ." he said neutrally.

I told him about my stint on the porn mags, and my troubles with Kim, and he laughed and commiserated in all the right places and I realised how much I missed having a father figure now JB was lying in hospital. The professor was just getting up to go, having promised his wife he'd be home sober by midnight, when I belatedly remembered that Maxwell had also been Henry's tutor when he was up at Magdalen. I'd mentioned Henry at my first tutorial with him, and his reply, as I now belatedly recalled, had been somewhat ambiguous. "Very bright and very devious" were the words I remembered him using.

"By the way," I said. "I don't suppose you've kept in touch with Henry Sutton? I'm trying to run him to earth."

"We used to exchange Christmas cards but I've heard nothing for several years now. Let me think. The last I'd heard, he'd given up his job at the *Hong Kong Morning Post* and had gone to Scotland to run one of those outward bound courses for middle-ranking executives. If Henry remained true to character, I expect the execs found some of the exercises contained a nasty sting in the tail."

"How do you mean? I remember you had mixed feelings about him when I was an undergraduate."

"Mixed feelings is exactly right. I liked him enormously. He could charm the birds from the trees as you must have discovered yourself, and he was extremely intelligent. Not that he did much work of course. He was too busy with his extracurricular activities. Girls. Mountaineering. And technical work on stage shows, of course."

I knew about the mountaineering and could guess about the girls but his theatrical interests were new to me.

"He had terrific flair for it," said Maxwell. "There was a terrible production of *King Lear* he worked on, with the unforgivable gimmick of having Lear played by a woman."

"You're joking?"

"I'm afraid I'm not. It was even more unendurable than you can imagine but the storm sequence was fantastic. Among the best sound and lighting effects I've ever seen in a theatre. He also did the lighting for the college ball. Naturally, being a middle-aged and respectably married don, I shouldn't have attended, but Henry was keen for me to see what he'd done and smuggled me in. It was like entering a world of light, with different effects in every marquee, one dark and sinister, another pink and welcoming, a third like being underwater in a vast aquarium. He lit the pop groups too. I could only stand the racket for about ten minutes, but even I, eardrums bleeding, could see he'd done a marvellous job. He told me afterwards that the Stranglers had offered to take him on full time."

"You mean he turned down a life of sex and drugs and rock 'n' roll?" I said incredulously.

"Yes. Remarkably, in his final year, he really got down to work. He got an extremely good first."

"So why the mixed feelings?"

"You remember the 8,000 word mini-thesis option?" I nodded. I could still remember the squirm-inducing title of mine: 'Time and the Sense of Isolation in the Poetry of Thomas Hardy.' It was, nevertheless, the one thing I'd achieved at Oxford of which I was proud.

"Well, Henry chose to compare Chaucer's *Troilus and Criseyde* with Shakespeare's *Troilus and Cressida,*" continued Maxwell. "It was a superb analysis of the differences between those two works, the one warm and humane, the other cynical and despairing, but it was rather more than that. Everyone knows that Shakespeare must have read Chaucer, but Henry showed, far more clearly than I'd ever seen before, that Shakespeare took specific themes and motifs from Chaucer and deliberately subverted them, juxtaposing images of growth in Chaucer with images of disease for instance. He also argued that the peculiar atmosphere of corrosive despair and moral sickness in the play, more nihilistic than anything elsewhere in the canon, might well have been the result of his contracting venereal disease. Pure speculation but intriguing speculation, particularly since the symptoms of syphilis usually seem to disappear for several years before returning with a vengeance. That could explain the sense of hard-won peace and reconciliation in the late romances, and his sudden decision to return to Stratford and write no more for the theatre when he seemed to be at the very height of his powers. The syphilis had returned.

"You remember at the end of *The Tempest*, which I don't believe is sentimental to regard as Shakespeare's valediction to his art, Prospero says of Caliban, "This thing of darkness I must acknowledge mine." It's a moment when Shakespeare himself seems to recognise that ultimately it is impossible for an artist of even his powers to change the human condition; more than that he seems to accept that he is corrupt himself, that darkness is part of his nature too. Anyway, Henry argued, with a good deal of persuasive if far from conclusive evidence, that Prospero could well be referring specifically to venereal disease."

"It sounds brilliant, " I said.

"It was brilliant. Unfortunately, it wasn't original. Naturally, I didn't mark the thesis being Henry's tutor, and I didn't read it until after the degrees had been awarded. And when I read it, I realised it was ringing a distant bell. I was sure I hadn't read it anywhere else, I'd have remembered it if I had, but I knew I'd heard some of it before.

"And then I remembered. When I was an undergraduate back in the dawn of time, one of my contemporaries had delivered a halting and not nearly so persuasive account of the same theory in a tutorial. I usually dozed through his contributions, but this one had made me sit up and though it was badly written and totally devoid of the textual analysis Henry supplied, it struck me as an ingenious theory. So, after the tutorial I congratulated him on a fascinating essay and he blushed in his endearing way and said he'd pinched the whole thing from a recently published periodical he'd found in the Bodleian. Since at the time I was courting the woman who eventually became my wife, I never went and looked up the article myself. And then, shamefully, I simply forgot all about it.

"Anyway after reading Henry's thesis, I realised that after thirty years, I couldn't rest easy until I had finally tracked the article down. As you probably remember, you're required to put a bibliography at the end, and Henry had duly obliged. He referred to a lot of the standard works, and a variety of articles in periodicals relating to Chaucer and Shakespeare, most of which I was familiar with. It was a long list running to two pages, and knowing Henry, he probably hadn't read half the works cited and was just listing them to impress the examiner and, perhaps, blind him with sheer quantity. But two-thirds of the way through the list there was a mention of an essay in a journal I'd never even heard of, with the unpromising title of the *Proceedings of the University of Winnipeg Shakespeare Appreciation Society*. Winnipeg, as far as I know, has never exactly been a hot-bed of Shakespearean research, and I'd certainly never heard of the journal. What also aroused my suspicion was that while all the other references to learned journals listed dates and volume numbers as well as the title of the particular essay referred to, all Henry had listed on this occasion was the title of the publication itself.

"So, I went to the Bodleian and sure enough the Winnipeg Proceedings turned up in the index. Bodley had only three issues, published annually from 1948 to 1950. 1950, I realised, was the year when my friend had given his startling essay. Needless to say, such an elderly, obscure and apparently short-lived journal was no longer on the open shelves, and so I asked the librarian to get all three up from the stacks. And when I went back the following morning, I got my nasty surprise."

"The journal had gone conveniently missing?" I guessed.

"Nastier than that. I examined the list of contents, and sure enough in the first volume there was an essay called 'Love,

Lust and Disgust: A comparison of Chaucer's *Troilus and Criseyde* and Shakespeare's *Troilus and Cressida*' by the superbly monickered, Dr Sylvanus Forrest, not a name in Shakespeare studies I had previously encountered. It turned out he was also co-editor of the magazine. It looked as though I had Henry bang to rights, as you might say, and I turned eagerly to the essay. Only to discover that it had been neatly removed by what must have been a razor blade or a Stanley knife."

"But that's about the worst crime you can commit in a library."

"Quite," said Maxwell. "And adding insult to injury there was a small, neatly typed note on a piece of blank A5 paper where the essay used to be."

"What did it say?"

"NICE WORK BUT YOU CAN'T PROVE A THING."

Maxwell beckoned to a waiter, and ordered a new malt for himself and asked me what my poison was, but I didn't want to lose this story in alcoholic oblivion and ordered another black coffee. The don nodded approvingly. He must have seen that I was more than half pissed but was far too polite to mention the fact. He offered me another Gitane when the drinks arrived and we smoked and drank in silence for a couple of minutes.

"So did you leave it there?" I asked, guessing that he hadn't.

"No. I tried the English faculty library next, but they'd never had the journal there. Then I contacted a friend in Cambridge and asked if he would mind checking there. He dropped me a line two days later, together with a sheet of A5 paper, containing the words 'FOILED AGAIN'.

"The British Library was obviously the next place to try, and since I didn't want to get Henry into serious trouble by confronting librarians with evidence of his vandalism I decided to make the trip personally. It took them twenty-four hours to unearth the Winnipeg Journal and once again Henry had been there before me."

"Another note?

"Yes. 'TOO LATE' was the laconic inscription this time."

"So what next?"

"Well, I'd run out of British copyright libraries now, and it seemed unlikely that there would be a wide circulation for such an obscure journal in many other British institutions. The obvious answer was the University of Winnipeg. So I wrote to the librarian, said the article had been recommended to me and appeared to be unobtainable in Britain, and asked if he could send me a photocopy."

"Henry surely hadn't made a special trip to Winnipeg?"

"But he had. The librarian wrote back reporting that the article had been neatly removed and enclosed a photocopy of the note."

"Which said?"

"'ADMIT IT, YOU'VE MET YOUR MATCH'. Only I hadn't, or rather my librarian hadn't. In his covering letter he said Dr Forrest had been a much loved member of the English faculty who retired in 1968 and died in the mid-seventies. He'd published very little because he preferred teaching to writing and had been, apparently, an inspiration to his students. Particularly to one of them, whom he'd married in his early sixties shortly after she graduated with a phenomenal first. She still lived in Winnipeg, and the librarian explained the problem to her. She had naturally kept all her husband's papers, including several copies of the journals he'd edited and contributed to. So she sent a replacement copy of the vandalised journal to the library, and the librarian sent a photocopy of his article to me."

"And?" I said, on tenterhooks, though part of me didn't want to think of Henry as a plagiarist. It somehow seemed a meaner, more morally squalid crime than running around with a hot Vermeer.

"Dr Forrest had made every major point in Henry's thesis."

"Oh, Henry," I said, feeling suddenly deflated.

"My own feelings precisely. What was interesting was that Henry had actually improved Forrest's essay without making a single substantial contribution of his own. Reading Forrest, one readily understood why he hadn't published much. The poor man couldn't write and his prose had the laborious, worked-on quality of someone painfully aware of the fact. But Henry had made Forrest's ideas sing. Almost every sentence was completely rewritten and with considerable style. The Canadian academic had finally found the eloquent words his insights deserved."

"So what did you do?"

"It was a piquant moral dilemma. Plagiarism and the mutilation of scholarly journals by a first-class honours student isn't something to be taken lightly. But, as you will recall, the mini-thesis was an entirely voluntary option. Henry would have got his first on the strength of the papers he sat in Schools without it. Secondly, he'd quoted his source in the bibliography, even if he didn't acknowledge the article in the text. And thirdly, and most crucially in my view, he had done Forrest a service, though admittedly for his own ends. As a piece of creative editing, Henry's work was, well, first class. So, possibly wrongly, and largely because I'd always liked him, I decided not to cause a stink." Maxwell paused for a moment and took a largish gulp of malt.

"I was also able to exact a kind of punishment. A year or so later the English Faculty decided to publish some of the most outstanding mini-theses of the past decade. I had a word with the editor and we agreed that Henry's essay should be included but with a prominent note at the beginning drawing attention to an appendix at the back. And the appendix comprised . . ."

"A reprint of Forrest's original article," I said, delightedly.

"Yes, with the date of its publication and gracious acknowledgements to his widow who was delighted by the ruse."

"A brilliantly elegant solution if I may say so," I said. "Forrest's ideas get the wider circulation they deserved and in a more eloquent form than he managed himself. And Henry is exposed as a plagiarist to anyone with enough intellectual curiosity to read the appendix."

"Exactly. Henry himself congratulated me on my resourcefulness when I sent him, without comment, a copy of the anthology. Characteristically, he seemed tickled by the whole thing rather than ashamed. And why not, I suppose? As far as intellectual theft goes he had the style of a latter-day Raffles."

I was about to tell Maxwell about the stolen Vermeer, which I suddenly realised had at least one element in common with the *Troilus* theft. Why turn up at Nicholas' house with the painting if at least a small part of him didn't want to be tracked down? It was like mentioning the Winnipeg journal in his bibliography. Without that clue he would almost certainly have got away with it. But Maxwell forestalled me.

"Henry's been up to something again, hasn't he?" he said, climbing stiffly to his feet. He suddenly looked his age and I was astonished to see that his eyes were misted with tears. "I'd greatly prefer it if you didn't tell me about it. Henry Sutton was one of the most gifted and charming students I ever taught. And," he added fiercely, "he was rotten to the core. There was an arrogance about his action, a knowledge that he was defying the basic principles, the morality if you will, of academic study. And I have never been able to bring myself to forgive him."

I walked with him to the cloakroom and helped him on with his shabby tweed overcoat. "My wife is going to be seriously displeased with me," he said with a wry grin, and I was glad that he seemed to be his old urbane self again. "But if you can't stay up late with an old friend at a gaudy, when can you? It's been good to meet you again, Will," he said, and with that he disappeared into the quad.

I felt tears stinging my own eyes. To be described as an old friend by Maxwell was an honour I did not look to have. It was now, of course, that I should have made my own departure. Indeed, I was just about to ask for my own coat when I was slapped heartily on the back. It was Jack Gilbert, two years my junior, who had played Puck in the half-way decent production of *A Midsummer Night's Dream* I'd stage managed at the

Newman Rooms. He had been entirely without the earnestness of my exact contemporaries, and I'd spent a lot of enjoyable time with him in my last year.

"Don't go," he begged. "You're the first person I've met all evening who I actually want to talk to." He looked as forlorn, and if truth be told, as wretchedly drunk, as I'd been before my encounter with Maxwell.

"If you can't stay up late with an old friend at a gaudy, when can you?" I said, and we made our way to the bar. Large malts were consumed, the malt that wounds in Pinter's fine phrase, followed by more large malts, that wound even worse. Jack feared he was on the point of being made redundant from his advertising agency and I told him about the humiliations I'd suffered recently at *Theatre World*. There are few things that bond men quite as firmly as malt whisky and shared misery.

"This always was a peculiarly horrible college wasn't it?" said Jack loudly, surveying the occupants of the room, and I agreed that it was and helped myself to the bottle of whisky since the waiter seemed to be otherwise engaged, sloshing half a tumblerful into each of our glasses and quite a lot onto the floor.

"And you know absolutely the most horrible thing about it?" said Jack, grinning malevolently, "It was that jerk, that bully, that absolute arsehole who pretended he was teaching us Anglo Saxon."

"A complete jerk, bully, and absolute arsehole. And, moreover, an intellectually dishonest arsehole. He must have known full well that we could never hope to learn fucking Anglo Saxon in eight weeks out of Sweet's God-awful fucking *Primer*, he must have realised we'd learnt the translations of those poxy poems by heart from the crib book . . ."

"The shitty Seafarer, the wanking Wanderer, the bugger that was Beowulf," put in Jack with a relish for alliteration the Anglo Saxon poets might have envied.

"And yet," I continued, "the fiction was maintained that we'd actually learnt the language. That we actually understood the tedious crap . . ."

"And then the bastard would have the temerity to criticise our interpretation of poems we all knew we didn't actually understand. And in the nastiest, most superior and patronising manner."

"I once cried before one of his tutorials," I said, confessing to an ancient, long buried shame. "I had a *crise* with *The Dream of the Rood.*"

"I once cried during one of his sodding tutorials," said Jack. And all might still have been well. Unfortunately, at that moment, I caught sight of the arsehole in question, Carey Kenneth Briggs, balloon of brandy in one hand, large cigar in the other, his abundant hair no less black and no less oily than it had been in our undergraduate days. He was sitting in a deep armchair, surrounded by a coterie of admirers. Graeme, who once confessed that he really did understand Anglo Saxon, was actually kneeling at Briggs's feet, looking for all the world like the faithful page before his liege-lord.

"I think it's time we told him all this, don't you?" I said.

"Actually, Will, I don't think that would be an altogether good idea," said Jack, who I noticed had scarcely touched his last gigantic malt whereas mine had more or less completely disappeared.

"Well, I'm going to." To his credit, Jack laid a firm, restraining hand on my arm, but I shook him roughly off and marched to the edge of Briggs's court of admirers.

He was treating his audience to one of his execrable poems, poems that appeared annually in the college record, rolling the words round his mouth as if they tasted better than the brandy in his glass.

"And in the gloom of an autumn afternoon, great Tom chimes across the mist of the meadows, metallic remembrancer of lost hours and promises betrayed . . ."

"Why don't you shut the fuck up for once?" I said, cutting brutally into his lyrical outpouring. "The fact is that you're a wanker and a bully and intellectually dishonest . . ."

He gazed at me with that well-remembered supercilious smile. As so often before, it stopped me dead in my tracks.

"Wanker, occasionally yes, but who isn't? A bully in only the most deserving cases. But the charge of intellectual dishonesty is a serious one. Your evidence, Mr Benson?"

I gulped a couple of times, but no words came.

"As mentally flabby as your really quite distressing physical appearance," said Briggs. "Now leave us, sot." I stood there, swaying, humiliated, unable to form a coherent sentence. And then something miraculous happened. I realised I was feeling sick. Not disastrously sick. I had all the time in the world to make it to the gents if I so desired. But I didn't. I knew I could be sick, at will, at any time within the next five minutes. And now seemed to be the perfect time. I thought briefly of grey-green paté and Bisto-basted venison, and then voided the contents of my stomach into his lap. There were, I was pleased to note, disgusting bits of half-digested cheese floating around in the mighty spume of wine and whisky and black coffee.

"For Christ's sake, Will," said Graeme after a couple of seconds of appalled silence, his hand ineffectually attempting to sweep away the worst of the vomit from his master's crotch. To my huge pleasure, I found I was still capable of one last heave and aimed it, with stunning accuracy, onto the crown of Graeme's head.

"Goodnight, gentlemen," I said, and though I may be flattering myself, I think my words were crisp and well enunciated. And then I lurched out into the night.

# 5: Saturday 21st December 1996

*A sad tale's best for winter.*
*I have one of sprites and goblins.*

*The Winter's Tale*

I woke with one of those sickening lurches that so often presage the very worst kind of hangover. The room was in complete darkness and for a few seconds I had no idea where I was. Then memories of the gaudy came flooding back, and in particular its spectacular conclusion. I felt a pit opening in my stomach, as it does when you realise you have done something truly unforgivable. And then something peculiar happened. I laughed, and felt much better. Of course I would never be able to go back to St Christopher's again, but would that be such a loss? And hadn't Briggs, and to a lesser extent Graeme, deserved punishment by summary vomiting? I remembered Briggs's for once speechless look of horrified indignation, I remembered Graeme's ineffectual attempts to clear up the mess with his bare hands and I felt a glow of pure, almost righteous happiness. Revenge is a dish best eaten cold. I'd waited more than a decade, and it tasted absolutely delicious. Unlike my mouth, which tasted like an open sewer. Although I discovered I could remember every detail of the gaudy, I couldn't remember much about walking back to the Randolph, apart from the minor embarrassment of my trousers falling down to my knees as I walked through the gate of the porter's lodge. The gallant little zip had finally given way after many hours of extreme pressure, but at least I'd not left the SCR like a figure from a Brian Rix farce. And then I heard a gentle snore and almost jumped out of my skin before lying absolutely rigid and pretending to be asleep. Christ, I was in bed with Natasha.

But I couldn't even work out whether I was in my room or hers. Had I come lurching back, climbed into bed with her and made violent drunken advances? But surely she wouldn't still be in bed with me if I had? And surely I would have some vague memory of thrashing limbs and bitter outrage? Now I thought about it, I could just about remember ringing the Randolph's nightbell so the porter could let me in. It had been 1a.m. and I'd blearily asked him for a quadruple Scotch. He'd disappeared into the interior recesses of the hotel and returned with the welcome beaker within a couple of minutes. He'd been a mournfully moustached and rather kind man, I remembered, and he'd seen me stumble as I headed for the lift and very kindly escorted me back to the suite with a helpful arm on my shoulder. "A rough night, sir?" he'd asked, without any hint of a smirk as I'd collapsed into an armchair in the main room, and I told him it had been a very rough night indeed. He laughed companionably, said that was usually the way with college reunions, put my drink on an occasional table next to my chair and shimmied out like Jeeves. And that really was the last thing I could remember. If past form was anything to go by, I'd simply have crashed out in my chair, drunk, certainly, but chaste.

Although not nearly as hungover as I deserved – the great thing about throwing up at the end of a session is that you get rid of a lot of the booze before it does any real damage – I realised I was desperately thirsty and the vile taste in my mouth was screaming for the toothpaste. The need to put these things right finally outweighed my desire not to wake up Natasha and very quietly I climbed out of bed. My eyes had grown accustomed to the dark and I could just make out the brass doorhandle of the bathroom. I was, I belatedly realised still wearing my dress shirt, my underpants and my socks, another encouraging sign that nothing untoward had taken place the night before. Even I draw the line at having sex in my socks. There was, I recalled, a very noisy fan in the bathroom, so I groped around in the dark, found my sponge bag (so I was at least in my own room after all) and then headed out into the living room of the suite. I stood at the door for a moment, heard Natasha's reassuringly heavy breathing, and closed the door behind me. I turned on the light. The room didn't appear to have been the scene of a drunken barney, and the quadruple whisky was sitting smugly on the table, looking virtuously untouched. I must have stumbled into bed before I'd had a chance to drink it. I rather fancied the hair of the dog, but instead I picked it up, took it to Natasha's bathroom and poured it down the sink before the temptation became too strong. I eyed myself in the mirror. Eyes a bit puffy, skin very pale, tongue distressingly furred. There were a few minor sick stains on my dress shirt, but all in all, it looked as though I'd got off lightly. I looked at my watch. 5.30am, that traditional hour of drunken waking. I cleaned my teeth thoroughly and then drank six tumblers of water and dropped two Neurofen and a valium. I stripped off my remaining clothes and had a shower, with some extremely fragrant gel that really did revitalise the system. I dried myself and put on the complimentary towelling dressing gown. Now what?

I admit I was tempted to return to my own room and see what might transpire with Natasha. She had, after all, made her intentions perfectly clear in Pimlico, and now there she was in my bed despite her foul temper earlier in the evening. I had been celibate for a long time, and hangovers always make me feel randy. But then the little private porn movie of Kim and Col that kept playing in my head suddenly flickered into life again and it was only by an immense effort of will that I was able to suppress its maddeningly graphic images. I was, I realised miserably, becoming more than a little obsessed with the possible size of Colin's penis. It seemed to get bigger every time the movie started playing, a bit like that chap in the hypnotism show. It was more like a sizeable log now than a cock. But since I was still desperately clinging to the notion that Kim might actually remain faithful to her estranged and feckless husband, it seemed absolutely wrong to stray from the path of righteousness. I also had the superstitious suspicion that if I strayed, Kim would somehow know about it, through a kind of telepathy, and adjust her own behaviour accordingly. I imagined her now, with a curious intensity and tenderness, and I suddenly seemed to be standing in our bedroom in Vauxhall, watching her sleep, as I'd done a couple of mornings earlier, only this time she didn't wake up and rebuke me. She was alone and at peace, and I said 'God bless, Kim,' under my breath, and she smiled slightly and turned over. I felt a sudden glow of happiness and for a moment I knew, with crystalline conviction, that eventually everything would be all right between us.

So I returned to the living room and made a cup of coffee and gazed out over the black silhouettes of the dreaming spires against the only slightly less dark sky. A feeling of sleepiness, delicious sleepiness, crept over me as I sat in my armchair, and I got up, turned off the light, and fell into a deep sleep in Natasha's empty bed.

When I awoke, I had a hard on. Not only a hard-on but someone was holding, in fact caressing, my hard-on. "That's nice, Kim," I said sleepily, and rolled over to hug my wife who until our troubles began had always been gratifyingly keen on early morning sex. Natasha immediately removed her hand and sat up, looking hurt. She seemed cross and vulnerable at the same time, and the sight of her breasts intensified my erection.

"Did you say that on purpose, out of spite?" she said, angrily and I promised her it had been a complete mistake.

"Why do you keep running away from me, Will?" she asked in a gentler tone. "Don't you want to?" And of course I suddenly did want to, very much, though another part of me, the better part of me, knew that this was actually the very last thing I wanted. I was hating myself even as I leant forward to kiss her, first on the mouth, and then those breasts that had so transfixed me, in Oxshott Woods, more than fourteen years earlier. They were so much bigger than Rose's. That had been the trouble. I sucked hard like a greedy child, and she groaned with what might have been pleasure, might have been pain, and I didn't care, I just wanted to lose myself in sensation, to obliterate the horrid little voice in my head that kept saying, 'Kim'.

After a few minutes, Natasha wriggled free, and produced a condom from under her pillow. She removed it from the packet with an efficiency that had always eluded me, pulled it on and guided me deep inside her. She had extraordinary internal muscular control and after only a few thrusts I realised I was coming. "Christ, I'm sorry" I said, as I spent myself in rubber, the shame of premature ejaculation now added to my deeper guilt. "Oh Christ, I'm sorry." The second time I said it, I think I really was praying to the Christ in whose forgiveness I only half believed.

"It's all right, Will," she said with what sounded like slightly strained tolerance, as I eased myself out of her and removed the forlorn condom. "Just lie back and relax." She cleaned me, with disagreeable clinical thoroughness, with a wet-wipe she had in a sachet by the bed, and then she went down on me, and slowly, my erection was restored. When I was hard again, she put on another condom and impaled herself on me, using me as if I were some inanimate object. I tried to move with her at first, but she told me, angrily, to keep still, that it only worked for her if I kept absolutely still, so I lay back, and remembered that this was how I'd lost my virginity, joylessly, miserably, when I'd taken Natasha home from that disastrous boat trip. Her parents had been out and she'd taken me grimly up to her bedroom. It had been an act of anger and revenge then, as she got even with her brother and the faithless Henry, and I'd felt like a mere implement of her hate and frustration, just as I felt like a mere implement now. A handy tool. An available cock. Not a person. She came, repeatedly, with noisy gasps, but it had nothing to do with me; her pleasure was self-created, self-absorbed. That was how it had ended last time. I'd come pathetically early, she'd sucked me back to life, and once she'd finished herself off, she'd quickly disengaged herself and told me that I'd better go home as she didn't want her parents to find me there. We didn't even kiss each other good night and the next day she'd returned to university.

It appeared, however, that there was another trick in her repertoire these days. She collapsed on top of me, panting, then rolled me on top of her with a strength that took me by surprise.

"Pretend you're raping me, Will. Fuck the arse off me."

By now, what I really wanted was a nice cup of tea and a quiet spot of Breakfast TV, but she wasn't to be denied. I made a few half-hearted thrusts, but she kept screaming, 'harder, harder.' I was beginning to hate her now, as well as myself, and I suddenly found it worryingly easy to oblige. I rammed myself into her, again and again, hard, joylessly, lovelessly. She began to struggle and whimpered, "stop, stop", and for a terrible moment I thought she was genuinely distressed and immediately froze in mid-thrust.

"Don't stop, you fucking idiot, I like it like this," she said, so I pumped grimly on and she struggled beneath me, and scratched me, hard and painfully, on my arms, chest and back. She was drawing blood, so I grabbed her wrists and pinned them down against the mattress, holding her hard so it would hurt, and a horrid smile of complicity flashed across her face and she breathed, "yes, yes, yes, hurt me, I want you to hurt me." And the terrible, the disgusting thing, was that I wanted to hurt her, and when she said, "spit in my face," I spat in her face, and then I came, and collapsed head down in the pillow and sobbed my heart out. She seemed oblivious of my distress. She quickly climbed out of bed and went to the bathroom and I heard the shower running. I snivelled a bit longer, and thought about Kim, and realised I couldn't face seeing Natasha again without any clothes on and scuttled across to my own room. I was covered in bloody scratches and felt used, abused, degraded. But there was also something else, something much more upsetting than that. Beyond the guilt and what I suddenly realised was not altogether minor physical pain, lurked another sensation. Excitement. It was the worst sex I'd ever had. But a maggot in my brain whispered that it was also.the best.

I had my second shower of the morning, and the water ran pink down the plughole, stained with my own blood. A terrible hypochondriac, I fumbled for the emergency bottle of TCP in my sponge bag, soaked some cotton-wool balls kindly supplied by the management, and, as the antiseptic dug in, discovered that the aftermath of sex with Natasha could be just as painful as the act itself. I didn't have any elastoplast, and just hoped that the gore wouldn't soak all the way through my thick Viyella shirt. I looked at my watch. It was, still, incredibly, only 8.30 in the morning, although I felt I'd been awake for several days and had just been brutally mugged on a street corner in the Bronx.

I returned to the sitting room. Natasha was sitting quietly at the table, reading her complimentary copy of *The Times* and looking impossibly demure in a long dark skirt and a crisp white cotton blouse with a high neck.

"Well that was a shag and a half," I said inanely, trying to make light of an experience that had left me deeply disturbed.

She wrinkled her snub nose in the familiar expression of distaste and put a finger, unsmilingly, to her lips. Apparently, Natasha didn't like being reminded of what went on in the bedroom once the bloody horror was over. I wasn't going to let her off the hook that lightly.

"Do you always have sex like that? I mean does Sir Dominic –"

"Just shut up, Will, OK?" she said with real venom in her voice.

"But –"

"Just shut up."

So I did and the silence was beginning to become oppressive when breakfast arrived. Natasha stood up, gave the waiter the brightest of professional smiles and watched as he arranged the breakfast things on the round mahogany table.

"I ordered you a cooked breakfast, Will. I hope you're up to it after last night."

"Never better," I said, and the truth was I did feel disgustingly hungry. I'd puked up what little I'd eaten the night before and horrid though it was to admit it, the sado-masochistic sex had given me an appetite. The waiter removed the silver covers with a flourish and there were two perfectly cooked English breakfasts. One of the nicer things about Natasha was her appetite. I remembered the steak blood dripping down her chin at the barbecue all those years ago. The waiter lingered unaccountably until Natasha hissed the word tip and I forked out a couple of quid from my pocket. You couldn't take me anywhere. I poured the coffee, as delicious as the food, and wished I was sharing this luxury with Kim. We'd never stayed anywhere half as posh.

"The weather forecast is vile," said Natasha, looking up from her paper. "What time did you arrange to meet Trev?

"Ten o'clock," I said. "And we need to be at the trade show not much later than 12.30. There's an opening ceremony at 1p.m.."

"Right, well we ought to set off in about half an hour." I polished off the last of my black pudding and mushrooms, and poured us both another cup of coffee.

"How was the gaudy?" she asked and I treated her to the full story, starting with the grand climax, which I was relieved to discover made her laugh. I'd been expecting frost and the wrinkled nose. She was extraordinary. Stuck up as hell one moment, friendly the next, and thoroughly depraved in the sack.

"I also learnt quite a lot about Henry," I said describing my conversation with Maxwell. Like me, like the professor, she was disappointed by Henry's dishonesty, impressed by his resourcefulness, intrigued by the fact that he had laid a trail for his own crime.

"He must know that Nicholas would have set some kind of investigation in motion even though he's too ill to undertake it himself," she said. "Henry's instruction about not going to the police and threatening to destroy the painting if he thought they were after him was almost like inviting us to see if we could find him ourselves. I wouldn't be at all surprised if he's guessed that you and me and possibly Trev are on his trail." She paused for a moment, and smiled fondly. "The old gang."

"I think you're probably right," I said. "But remember Henry became seriously alarmed when he took that phone call at Nicholas'. It looks to me as though other people, almost certainly more efficient and nastier people than us, are also on his track, presumably eager to get their hands on the painting and, perhaps, exact reprisals on Henry. And for all we know, they may have got there already. We're not exactly making much progress are we? Perhaps we ought to go to the police. It's pathetic, amateurs like us muddling along like this."

"If we go to the police, Henry will go to prison or the Vermeer might be destroyed, perhaps both," she said. "You don't want that, do you?"

I shook my head gloomily. "Right, well take a brace, then." It was the deputy head girl of Lady Eleanor Holles talking. How she co-existed with the Natasha who went so disconcertingly wild in the bedroom was one of life's more unfathomable mysteries. On balance, I preferred the deputy head girl.

We packed up and checked out, and I nervously asked Natasha if I could have a go at driving the Porsche. I'm not one of those men who takes a fanatical interest in cars, or sees them as an extension of his ego – or his prick. Indeed, I don't actually own one myself and have never understood the basic principles of the internal combustion engine, but the idea of putting my foot down in this aggressively sleek, massively powerful car appealed to my love of scary rides in amusement parks.

"No you bloody well can't," she said. "It's only insured for me and Dommo and you're probably still way over the limit anyway after last night."

"All right, all right, no need to get stroppy."

I struggled into the ridiculously low seat and Natasha handed me a road atlas from the shelf at the back. "You can do something much more useful," she said. "You can navigate."

I've never been good at map-reading, and the speed at which Natasha drove, not to mention the driving rain that started up as we were negotiating the ring road, didn't help. We took wrong turnings twice, Natasha fumed, and eventually drew into a lay-by to look at the map herself. "We are going precisely in the opposite direction to Royston-in-Arden," she said.

"I had a nasty suspicion we might have been doing that, " I said.

"Well, why didn't you say so?"

"Because I didn't want you to tell me off," I said in a pathetic, little boy voice and she grinned.

"You're contemptible, Will Benson," she said, setting off with the thrust of a small space rocket and careering round the bends of a country road so fast that I was unable to prevent my foot from applying an imaginary brake on the passenger's side of the car. We fetched up in Royston-in-Arden bang on time, and cruised round trying to find the vicarage. With its honey-stoned cottages and views over rolling countryside, the place must have been delightful when the sun shone. In freezing rain it seemed depressingly forlorn. It isn't meant to rain in enchanted Arden. The vicarage turned out to be an ugly, red-brick Victorian pile, entirely out of keeping with the early Perpendicular church next door.

We walked up through the scraggy front garden, enclosed by an oppressively high yew hedge. Abandoned toys littered a patch of what might charitably have been described as a lawn but actually looked more like a rugby pitch after heavy rain and a hard-fought match. I couldn't believe the vicar was popular with the Best Kept Village committee. Natasha rang the bell and Trev the Rev opened the door, blinking behind his specs and surrounded by an absurd number of children, ranging in age from about two to ten. He held a baby in his arms, a crying baby, but his warm smile indicated a man at peace with the world even though it raged in chaos around him.

"Will and Natasha," he beamed, "How lovely to see you." We entered the hall somewhat nervously, for it seemed impossible to take a step without treading on a child. While still holding the baby, Trevor somehow contrived to give us both a firm, affectionate hug, and the baby, with impeccable taste, I thought, dribbled copiously on Natasha's fur coat. Trev kept a filthy tea towel over his right shoulder for just such eventualities and vigorously applied it to the affected area. Natasha's effort to smile and pretend there was nothing she liked more than being dribbled on by young babies was a joy to behold and I could see that Trev was tickled too.

"If you don't mind holding him, Natasha, I'll lead the way into the kitchen and make us all some coffee," he said, depositing the howling bundle into Natasha's arms. He strode off down the linoleum covered hall, scattering children behind him, and Natasha and I picked our way carefully through the throng of clamorous tinies.

"This baby stinks," hissed Natasha in my ear, "and worse, still, I think its nappy's leaking."

"Take a brace, for God's sake, Natasha," I said nastily and she shot me a look of murderous fury.

We made it to the kitchen, and once Trev had dealt with the cafetière he relieved Natasha of the baby and changed it, to her evident horror, on the kitchen table, throwing the wipes with variable accuracy into a nappy sack, and finally clearing up a few stray smears of crap on the stripped pine table with the tea towel with which he'd recently given Natasha a rub down. Apparently unaware of the baleful malevolence with which she regarded them, the children, or those that were ambulant, seemed to take a distinct shine to Natasha, and took it in turns to come and stroke her coat. "Nice" . . . "Furry" . . . "Like a big black cat" . . . were just a few of the appreciative comments. "Be careful," I warned a snot-encrusted girl who was next in line for the stroking treatment. "She's also got claws."

Trev grinned cheerfully and poured us all coffees, sat down, realised he'd left the open nappy sack on the table, said, "Oh cripes," got up to transport it to an overflowing rubbish bin, and resumed his seat. He pulled a pipe out of his pocket, apparently unconcerned by the current view that smoking in front of small children is only marginally more acceptable than strangling them with your bare hands. He set fire to whatever was in the bowl – old socks by the smell of it – and great clouds of smoke filled the kitchen, causing exaggeratedly theatrical coughs from all the children who promptly retreated into the hall.

"Never fails," he said with huge self-satisfaction. "The older ones have been indoctrinated about the dangers of passive smoking at school and they've passed it on to the rest." He stared down fondly at the baby, now asleep in his lap and almost completely hidden by clouds of blue smoke.

I'd been conducting a quick head count while the children were in the room. "They can't all be yours? There seemed to be an awful lot of names on your answering machine but I'm sure there weren't eleven of them."

"No, we've only got the seven, though another one's on the way, I gather," he said, as though this astonishing fertility were some kind of accident that had absolutely nothing to do with him. "We're looking after the other four for a couple of weeks while the mother's in hospital. My goodness, you wouldn't believe how much they eat. My wife Judy's on yet another visit to the superstore now. Though I must say it's nice to have a full house."

Natasha's expression indicated that it was her idea of hell, but you could tell Trev was fulfilled in fatherhood, though how he made ends meet on his vicar's stipend with so large a brood defeated me.

"Anyway, tell me about Henry. You said it was urgent," said Trev, taking more massive puffs on his pipe. I told him the tale, with frequent interruptions from Natasha when she wasn't waving the smoke away, and also broke the news of Nicholas's illness.

"It's sometimes hard not to hate God, isn't it?" said Trev. "I'll pray for him, of course." Trev didn't seem aware of any contradiction between these two statements, the mark I thought of a mature and tested faith, the kind of faith in which you could be hurt and bewildered by the suffering in the world yet somehow still believe in a loving God. It was the kind of faith I longed to find myself. I reached into my canvas hold-all and produced the book on Vermeer Nicholas had lent me, and turned to the full-page reproduction of the stolen painting. I'd spent a lot of time gazing at it lately, and its sense of serenity and happiness became more moving each time I looked at it. I showed it to Trevor.

"God, it's beautiful – she's beautiful," said Trev after staring in silence for a full minute. "A kind of secular Madonna."

Natasha wiped a tear from her eye, though whether at the beauty of the painting or Trevor's earlier words about her dying brother I didn't know. Both probably. She suddenly seemed vulnerable, even lovable. "Nicholas said he felt momentarily blessed by God's grace when he saw the painting, and he's always been an atheist," she said. "Even in this reproduction you get a glimmer of what he means."

"And you tell me Nicholas reckons Henry might be prepared to destroy this, if things get too hot for him to handle? It's obscene," said Trev, angrier than I'd ever known him. "There was always a certain ruthlessness behind that famous charm."

"So have you any idea how we might trace him, where he might be living?"

"I'll come to that in a minute. But I'd just like to illustrate his ruthlessness. As you know, Will, I left the *Esher Herald* at the end of that summer to go to theological college. Henry had only been on the paper a year by then, and in those days, the training of journalists was taken rather seriously. You had to sign indentures, committing yourself to what was in effect an apprenticeship under the editor. It all sounds ridiculously quaint now, but to break your indentures was regarded as a serious breach of faith and you might well find it hard getting a job elsewhere. Anyway, Henry, being a graduate, had to sign up for two and a half years rather than three, but then he wangled that job on the *Hong Kong Morning Post.* He went to old Moley and asked permission to break his indentures and Moley very generously agreed to let him go, with a covering letter saying he had done so with permission. But Moley did insist that Henry served out a three-month notice period to give him time to find a replacement. As you will recall, Henry was about the only person in the office with a knack of turning up decent stories, and his loss was going to hit the paper badly. Since Moley could legitimately have kept him there for more than a year, it was exceptionally generous.

"But it wasn't good enough for Henry, though he pretended it was. It was Henry who told me about all this, with a pride I found incomprehensible. He'd informed the *Hong Kong Morning Post* he could start in November, and he fancied a holiday before that . . .

"So he just walked out, realising that a small matter like broken indentures wouldn't mean much in Hong Kong?" said Natasha.

"That would have been mean but just about understandable. In fact, he did something much nastier. He told Moley that he was quite happy with the deal offered, and carried on working. And one of his jobs that week was covering the Walton-on-Thames annual craft show. It was actually one of those jobs where you turn up to show willing, get a couple of quotes from the organiser, arrange a picture of the cutest children present and then run all the results from information supplied by the organisers . . ."

There was, I remembered, nothing Trev liked more than a lecture. I wondered what his sermons were like. "I know," I said impatiently. "I'm actually a journalist myself, about to attend the same kind of function and if you keep banging on like this I'm going to miss it . . ."

"Sorry," said Trev with a grin. "I was just remembering my old inky days with affection. Anyway, Henry turned up, told that hilariously incompetent photographer what pictures to take, and apparently got all the results off the organiser. It took place on a Wednesday, the day before press day, and he returned to the office that evening, wrote up his copy and the results and left it all in the copy basket. And then he buggered off, catching a flight to Hong Kong the following morning without saying goodbye to anyone."

"Dishonourable, but perhaps just about understandable in the circumstances," I said.

"No, it was worse than that. He'd left a nasty little time-bomb behind him. He made up all the results, using entirely fictitious names. And all the people who bought the paper that week to see their names in the paper, the big selling point of stories like this as you'll know, found that they had been left out. The phone didn't stop ringing for two days, and Moley had to run the real results the following week with a grovelling apology, as I discovered when I phoned him up to commiserate after reading Henry's letter from Honkers."

"Yes, nasty," I agreed.

"It gets nastier. As you can imagine, Moley spent some time looking at Henry's parting shot and he realised that the first letters of the surnames of the fictitious winners in each class carried a message."

"Which said?"

"FUCK THE *ESHER HERALD*. BOLLOCKS TO OLD MOLEY."

Natasha giggled and I found it hard to suppress a smile myself. But it wasn't funny really. It was childish and spiteful. Moley had been genuinely fond of Henry and it was a cheap way to repay his kindness. I also thought that Henry might have come up with a wittier and more elegant parting shot.

"Moley was broken-hearted," said Trev. "Particularly when one of the readers spotted what she described as an outrage and phoned up to complain about gross indecency. Anyway I wrote to Henry in Hong Kong and told him I thought what he had done was contemptible. He'd told me about the false names but not the hidden message, and I said Moley was distraught. And I received a genuinely chastened reply, saying he'd been demob happy, was now extremely sorry and was going to write to Moley to apologise. As indeed he did, as well as sending him an extremely expensive camera via someone who was flying back from Honkers."

"So Moley forgave him?" asked Natasha.

"Yes, he was full of grace that man. I'm not entirely sure that I have though."

"But you're a vicar," said Natasha.

"We're none of us perfect," he grinned.

I thought about telling Trev about Henry's trick with the mini-thesis but time was marching on and at this rate I'd be missing the trade show and having to make up a story about that. Also, I didn't want to disillusion him further. It seemed to me that Henry's stunts had a certain style that mitigated their dishonesty. As a vicar, Trev was bound to take a harsher view of his old friend.

"Anyway, tell us about your last meeting with Henry," I said.

"Well, he's in the showbiz game now," replied Trev, and I felt a surge of excitement. Trev made the connection at the same time and slapped his forehead. "And you work at *Theatre World*, don't you, Will, I've just remembered your message on the answering machine. Can't think how you haven't come across him."

God he could be infuriating at times. I explained that Equity had more than 30,000 members, not to mention all the technicians in Bectu, and I was hardly likely to have come across all of them. He gave me one of his rueful grins.

"You're quite right, like expecting me to know every parson in the country," he said. "Anyway, Henry phoned up out of the blue one day, about this time last year. He was working on a children's show which was playing at the Swan at Stratford during the RSC's closed season. It was only there for a couple of matinees and he said he'd been in touch with Moley, knew I lived nearby and had kids and would I like to bring the family as they'd got heaps of spare tickets? So the following day we loaded the kids into the battered Bedford, prayed it would get us there without breaking down and went to see the show.

"It was terrific, a small company performing far-eastern folk tales. There were bits of narrative, oriental dancing, fantastic music from this guy with all these pots and pans and bongos . . . There was one story about a king who was turned into a snake, another about a princess who was sent to live underneath the sea and found a pearl of precious price . . ." I could imagine it, and it sounded perfectly ghastly to me, but Trev wouldn't stop until he'd given us the full glowing review.

"And what was Henry's role in all this?" said Natasha when he'd finally run out of steam. "Don't tell me, the king who was turned into a snake."

"No, he wasn't in it at all. He was just the production manager, which he explained afterwards was just a fancy name for stage manager. But he'd also designed the lighting and the sound, though how you design sound is beyond me, and I must say the lighting was wonderful, the most magical effects. There was one scene showing dawn in the forest, with yellow-green light casting patterns on the floor . . ."

"Yes, yes, yes," said Natasha. "But what was the name of the company?"

"The company, yes I suppose it must have had a name. I can't say I remember . . ."

"Fine journalist you must have been," said Natasha, and poor Trev, so animated when he described the show, looked deflated.

"You're quite right – "who? what? where? when? why?" – the first rule of journalism. I could kick myself."

"I ought to be able to find out the name of the company by looking at the What's on Where column in *Theatre World*," I said, and he cheered up. "And it's interesting that he should have gone into the technical side of the theatre, because I heard from his old tutor at the gaudy last night that he was a brilliant lighting whiz while he was an undergraduate."

Trevor began to look cheerful again. "Actually, it might not be too bad I've forgotten to remember the name of the company. Henry treated the whole family to fish and chips after the show, a really excellent place just opposite the theatre, I can really recommend it, the cod just melted in your mouth . . ."

"Trev . . ." said Natasha dangerously.

"Sorry," said Trev, "well, anyway, with the kids there, it wasn't possible to get a detailed resumé of what he'd been doing in recent years, but I gathered he'd been working in the theatre for quite a few years. He'd started in a small way in Hong Kong, did a stint with the RSC, but now spent a lot of his time abroad on touring productions. Apparently, there's one company that does a lot of tours of the Middle and Far East, old comedies, mostly, but apparently they mostly perform in five star hotels, and the company get to stay in them too, so it's very popular."

"If memory serves, Derek Nimmo set it up," I said. "There's a big audience among the ex-pats."

"All day by the pool and delicious food and drink with only the minor inconvenience of *The Amorous Prawn* in the evening was how Henry put it. He always had a taste for the sybaritic. But he's also done worthier work too" – how typical of dear old Trev was the word 'worthy', I thought – "taking Shakespeare to the subcontinent and so on. I think a lot of that's organised by the British Council. They'd surely have some kind of contact number for one of their regular production managers. The other thing he does, apparently, is lighting for rock shows. Mattie was dying to know if he'd met Boyzone, and Henry said he had, though I think he was only pretending to please her."

"You're a wonder, Trev," I said. "I'll try the British Council on Monday, and if they can't come up with anything, Bectu or Equity ought to be able to help."

"We might even get a trace on him earlier than that," said Natasha. "It's a sound and lighting trade show we're going to, isn't it? If we ask around, someone there might have come across him. You never know, he might even be there himself."

I'd heard some unappealing things about Henry in the last couple of days, yet just the possibility of seeing him brought on a familiar thrill of excitement. Things happened around Henry. You were never bored.

There were screams of laughter and howls of protest from the hall, and the girl I assumed to be Mattie since she was wearing a Boyzone teeshirt came rushing in.

"Daddee, Daddee," she cried with a mixture of disgust and delight. "Huw's just wee'd all over Jackie and she's soaking wet and crying."

"Oh Lord, it's watersports now," said Trev, climbing wearily out of his chair and reaching for his trusty tea towel. He handed me the baby, and I held him in my arms, amazed at how little he weighed and how beautiful he looked in sleep. Trev returned with a glum and sodden child of about three, stripped her off, wiped her down and redressed her after rummaging for clothes of vaguely the right size in what looked suspiciously like the dirty laundry basket. The expression on Natasha's face was a joy to behold. "Off you go, Jackie," he said fondly, and she ran happily out again.

"I just hope she doesn't tell her mother when I take her and her brothers to the hospital this afternoon," said Trev. "Very fastidious, Mrs Hunter."

"She must be thrilled that they're staying here then," said Natasha, gazing round at the scruffy, untidy kitchen. Trev said 'Miaow' and she had the grace to blush. The kitchen was a mess, but it was warmed by a battered Aga, and, I felt, by Trev's large and gentle heart. Normally, I found the presence of children a painful reminder of Kim's and my failure to have them. But there was a happiness about this chaotic household that made jealousy impossible, and I loved holding the baby in my arms. Indeed, it was a real wrench to hand the little blighter over but duty, and Henry, called.

"Trev, I'm really sorry but we're going to have to go," I said. "This wretched trade show . . ."

"But I haven't heard any of your news, and you haven't met Judy. She'll be back soon."

"I was wondering if I could invite myself back?" I said nervously. "And I'd like to bring my wife. We could babysit for you. I don't suppose you manage to get out much?"

Natasha looked daggers at the mention of my wife, and I wondered what Kim would say if I proposed a weekend in the country with the child-minding of seven kids thrown in. But I had a strong feeling that if there was any chance at all of sorting ourselves out, it might well be here, surrounded by children, whom I suddenly realised we had come to regard with a kind of fear because they held such a cargo of pain for us. If we couldn't be parents ourselves, it was time we learnt to enjoy rather than resent other people's. And I knew Kim would like Trev, and that we might find peace in his noisy vicarage.

Trev, I was pleased to notice, was glowing with pleasure at the idea. "That would be terrific," he said. "Judy and I haven't been out on our own for ages. For some strange reason," he grinned, "people find the idea of babysitting seven kids rather alarming. When, as you can see, it's a piece of cake."

He shepherded us to the front door and the kids gathered round to see us off. I promised I'd phone soon to fix a date and we jogged down the path through bucketing rain. Natasha tripped on a rusting abandoned tricycle and I only just managed to prevent her falling flat on her face.

"Fucking kids," she said with feeling.

"Have you never wanted them?" I said, as she gunned her phallic car into action and roared out of the village.

"Not for one second," she said. "And that disgusting house. I don't know how poor Trev stands it and his wife must be the most frightful slut. You must be mad to want to stay there and if Kim's got any sense she'll walk straight out as soon as she sees the place."

"You've made your point," I said calmly, refraining from adding that Trev actually seemed much happier than she was. She seemed to read my thoughts.

"I'm perfectly happy," she almost screamed. "By Christ, you can be a pain at times, Will Benson."

I found the remains of the Love Hearts in my pocket and munched a few until I found one that said "My Pal," which I handed to her. This time she didn't throw it out of the window. She read it, smiled, apologised and ate it. "They're actually rather nice, aren't they?" she said emmoliently. She stopped for petrol and came back with Bowie's *Singles Collection* on CD.

"A peace offering," she said, and the miles sped by to the sounds of 'Changes', 'Ziggy Stardust', 'Life on Mars', 'Diamond Dogs', 'Golden Years' and 'Ashes to Ashes'. Natasha sung along to the tunes quietly, and I thought of the Oxshott Wood sandpit and smiled at the memory. "Never such innocence again," I thought sentimentally, echoing Nicholas, then realised that it hadn't really been innocent at all. Just golden. Golden days, golden weeks. If only we'd had golden years as well, but it had all gone rotten that night on the Thames.

"It's so sad what's happened to Bowie," I said. "I mean Tin Machine, for starters, I ask you, and his recent albums haven't been much better though the critics are always loyally pretending that he's recovered his form. Then there's his wretched wallpaper for Laura Ashley and that description of himself as 'a mid-art populist and post-modernist Buddhist surfing his way through the chaos of the late twentieth century.' It's tragic. He used to be so unassailably cool and now he just seems like a pathetic, more or less amiable wanker who's completely lost the plot."

"Yeah, but think of all the great records he made before he lost his touch." 'Scary Monsters' kicked in as Natasha spoke, as if to prove her point. "I'll always love him, always forgive him."

It was such an uncharacteristic Natasha comment that I turned to look at her and saw a tear running down her cheek. She'd have hated me to notice so I stared straight ahead again.

"But that night at Oxshott, you made a big point of saying how you preferred a nice Mozart piano concerto."

"I still listen to classical music most of the time," she said. "But after that night, Bowie was always special. I've bought all his albums and of course all the new ones have been a terrible disappointment but there's always the hope that one day he'll find his old magic again."

"And perhaps that might help us to find ours," I said. "The thing about Bowie, and hardly anyone recognised it at the time because of all his transformations and weirdness, is that he's actually the most romantic of pop singers. The alien aching for love."

"Aren't we all?" said Natasha, gently, regretfully. She might have been Lady Grinning Soul herself. Except she didn't drive a Beetle car and certainly wouldn't have been seen dead wearing anything as naff as "musky oil".

We hit a traffic jam on the outskirts of Leicester and then had terrible problems finding the hotel. This wasn't altogether surprising as it was implausibly located on the top of a singularly grotty multi-storey car park, as a pedestrian finally told us with a look of infinite pity when he learnt of our intended destination.

"I'm sorry about this," said Natasha, as we whizzed round and round the car park up to the sixth floor. "The only decent hotel in Leicester seems to be the Holiday Inn and it was fully booked."

We parked outside a grubby glass door that announced that this was the Hotel Panoramique and took a juddering lift up to the hotel proper. The reception area and bar offered expansive views over the whole of Leicester, and looking at that dreariest of cityscapes through the drizzle, one very much wished they didn't. The receptionist's first words were that if we wanted any security for the car, we should have parked on the ground floor, as that was the only area with 24 hour CCTV.

"But all the signs said drive up to the sixth floor for the hotel car park," said Natasha with heroic politeness.

"Yes, they do say that, but that was before the security cameras up here got smashed by vandals."

"And when was that?"

"Ooh, before my time, must be two years ago now."

"Mightn't it be a good idea to change the signs?" asked Natasha, a dangerous sweetness in her voice.

"Gosh, what a clever idea," said the receptionist, as though a problem that had been troubling her for a long time had at last been solved. "I'll pass your suggestion on to the manager."

A sullen boy with a boil on the back of his neck led us to our rooms which, bafflingly, seemed to be downstairs rather than up. I had a terrible conviction that we might actually be spending the night camped out in the car park. He paused at a door marked the 'Joe Orton Suite' and opened it with a flourish.

It was a small room, and the orange hessian wall covering was stained. There was a double bed at one end, and a camp bed at the other. Exactly the kind of place in which you might choose to hammer your lover to death.

"I asked for a double suite," said Natasha.

"This is a suite. It says so on the door. And it's got two beds in it so what are you grumbling about?" he asked aggressively.

"Don't worry, Natasha. I'll go back to reception and book another room," I said. I hoped it sounded gallant but in fact I was petrified. I had a terrible fear that after sharing a single room with Natasha all night I'd need skin grafts in the local hospital the following morning.

Natasha evidently cottoned on to the way my mind was working. "No, on second thoughts this room will do fine," she said, rewarding the oik with a ludicrously over-generous fiver. He pocketed it without a word of thanks and slouched out.

"Don't you always find, Will," she said, standing very close to me and scratching me gently on the back of the neck, an alarming foretaste of things to come, "that cheap and sordid hotel rooms like this always make you feel frightfully randy?"

"Yes," I said, and had I been sharing the room with Kim rather than her, it might have been true, "and I can't think of anything I'd like more than a repeat of this morning. Unfortunately," and here I made a great show of looking at my watch, "the trade show starts in half an hour and I'm in grave danger of losing my job if I make a balls of it."

"Shame," she said, then brightened considerably. "Still there's always tonight – and all night too." I don't know if she was consciously echoing Regan in *King Lear*, recommending an extra spell in the stocks for the loyal Kent, but it sent a nasty shiver down my spine. "I'd better go and move the car," she added. "Meet you at the bottom in a few minutes?"

"Great", I said, and great it certainly was. As soon as Natasha had gone, I raced back to reception, and booked another room. Not only another room but a room on a different floor. There was going to be hell to pay when we got back to the hotel that night, but it would be a different kind of hell to the sulphurous pit of the sack.

The receptionist gave me a map, showing me where the conference centre was, and I took the lift down to the ground floor.

"You're looking uncommonly pleased with yourself," said Natasha.

"I'm looking forward to tonight," I said, disgracefully, and she took my hand in hers and scratched it, hard, like a promise. "Goody, goody," she said.

We walked the drab streets of Leicester, and as the rain fell and the east wind blew, I cursed myself for leaving my mac in the car. But, as Natasha had recognised, I was in high spirits. I'd done the right thing, for once in my life. I was going to phone Kim tonight, from my solitary room, and suggest a reconciliation and a visit to Trev's.

The Sensational Sound and Light Explosion, as this rather humdrum trade-fair insisted on calling itself, was housed in a drab Sixties hall and contained more sound-boards, dimmer-boards, spotlights, projectors, speakers, amplifiers, laser equipment and projection devices than even Lord Lloyd-Webber could dream of. I was sure I'd fail to make any kind of journalistic sense of it, but the organiser, who was clearly enraptured by Natasha, gave me a very handy four-page press release, containing news of all the latest developments, a great bundle of dull photographs, and a copy of the speech he would shortly be making. As if all this wasn't reason enough to be grateful, he had a beer gut that made me feel positively anorexic, and immediately suggested "large tinctures and a sarnie or two" at the bar.

He sat us down at a table and returned with a huge Scotch and soda for me, a G and T for Natasha and a pint of Guinness for himself. Also a large pile of rare roast beef sandwiches with just the right amount of horseradish and made with white bread. If he hadn't gone on at such incredible length about dual independent DMX512 Inputs, comprehensive diagnostics, moving pan/tilt parameters and a mysterious creature called the 'gobo', which seemed to exercise him greatly, I'm sure we could all have had a delightful time. But with the press pack safe on my lap, I could just let it all wash over me and nod attentively when the occasion seemed to demand it. When Natasha, purely in a spirit of mischief, but showing far more technical knowledge than I was capable of, asked him to describe the latest developments in WYSIWYG Real Time Lighting Visualisation I thought he was going to have an orgasm where he sat. He placed a large hand on her knee, told her she was a canny lass, and bored on for ten minutes without drawing breath.

Mercifully, this insufferable monologue was interrupted by a minion who came to tell him it was time to make his speech, and he hauled his vast weight to a stage at the end of the hall to deliver it. There was much talk of British theatre being the best in the world and what a huge contribution was made by the boffins and the techies who ensured audiences enjoyed the most spectacular shows ever seen. All true enough, as far as it went, but my own feeling was that the relentless advance of the blockbuster musical was in danger of ruining audience's appetite for intelligent drama on a human scale. I like gawping at special effects as much as the next man, but there were too many people who now felt robbed if a show didn't dazzle their retinas and blast their eardrums. Was *Les Misérables* really a more moving experience than *The Winter's Tale*? Still, this was hardly the time or place to say so. Instead I smiled benignly, and even indulged in the odd hear-hear, while all the time surveying the hall in case Henry turned up.

At last, Vic drew to a close, announced that the bar would be open all day (eliciting the loudest cheers of his whole speech) and wished everyone a successful show. Vic, having made his main contribution to the proceedings, could now look forward to a day of the kind of technical trainspotterish chat that was obviously his keenest pleasure, especially when he could exercise his right arm at the same time. It also looked as though Natasha was going to be his favoured companion, and spotting him lumbering in our direction, she led me off at a tangent to examine, with well-feigned interest, a selection of automated lamps.

"They're fully gobo compatible, I take it?" she asked the eager young man in the shiny suit and he blushed as though she had suggested a dirty weekend. He rabbited on at some length, explaining just how fantastically gobo compatible they were, and his eyes kept straying to her cleavage, before flickering nervously back to her face. The technical side of theatre is still an almost exclusively male preserve, and the only cleavages he was probably used to were those that forced their way out of the jeans of hairy-bottomed lighting riggers. Natasha, I noticed, had undone an extra button on her silk blouse. She clearly enjoyed the disconcerting power of her cold fire sexual allure.

When the last inch of mileage had been extracted from gobo compatibility Natasha casually asked him if he had ever come across a talented lighting designer called Henry Sutton. To his evident distress he hadn't, for here was a chance he might have taken to extend the conversation. And so began the dreary pattern of the afternoon, endless technical chatter at stand after stand followed by an inquiry about Henry that invariably met a blank. Natasha played her part with great patience and good will, and I was amazed at her fund of knowledge.

"How do you know all this, they can't have all that much technical equipment at a product launch?"

"When business was slack I used to help out a guy who organised big awards' ceremonies, and some of them really go to town with the stage presentation. The shows for some of the pop mags were more like full-scale rock concerts and I must admit I got interested in stage lighting. I stayed up all night helping with the get-in quite often. It was fun."

"You're a woman of hidden talents," I said.

"As you're beginning to find out," she said with a smile that could only be described as lascivious. "I'm not such a totally stuck-up prig, am I, Will?"

"Of course you're not". I thanked my lucky stars that I'd booked that second room.

By the time we'd reached five o'clock without success I suggested a drink. Natasha was visibly flagging and I'd entered a transcendental realm of bored incomprehension. Unlike the floor of the show, the bar was absolutely packed, and I belatedly realised we'd been barking up the wrong tree. Most of the people we'd been talking to had been salesmen, and Henry was unlikely to have had much contact with them. The bar, however, was packed with people who actually worked in the technical side of theatre, out for a jolly with the show itself coming a poor second to a good old session with the lads.

I fought my way to the bar, desperate to order a pint of Guinness for myself and a double G and T for Natasha who had certainly earned it. And as I was standing there, suffering the invisible man syndrome that has led to so many wasted hours in crowded bars, I realised I was next to someone, in a similar plight to my own, who I recognised as one of the few lighting designers I'd actually met. He'd been at the same table as me at an awards' ceremony. The trouble was I hadn't a clue what his name was.

Finally, the barman condescended to ask me what I'd like to drink. I ordered the Guinness and the G and T, and turning to my neighbour, who appeared to be in the terminal stages of impotent, thirsty desperation, asked if I could get him a drink too. "We've met but I'm afraid I can't remember your name," I said. "I'm Will Benson of *Theatre World* and we were at the same table at the Oliviers."

"I don't care who you are," he said. "I was just considering giving you a kick because I'm sure I was here before you and instead you've revealed yourself as a gentleman and an angel of mercy." His words were slurry, his brow sweaty. He was a man after my own heart. He asked for a bottle of fearfully strong Belgian beer, which turned out to be an alarming shade of red when he poured it into his glass.

We fought our way back to Natasha, who had found a free table, and my new friend introduced himself as Jake Harris and I remembered he'd lit a magical RSC production of *The Comedy of Errors.* The whole design team had been up for an award. And Henry had once worked for the RSC according to Trev. We settled down, agreed that trade shows were thirsty work, and I asked him if he'd ever heard of Henry Sutton.

"Old Henry, he was my deputy on that terrible Michael Bogdanov production of *The Importance of Being Earnest* a few years back," said Jake. "Great sense of humour, Henry's got, and by Christ, we needed it on that tour. Bodger had only set the bastard on a council housing estate in South Wales."

"You're making this up?" I said.

"Honest to God. He 'improved' quite a lot of the dialogue too. It needed to be more demotic he said, so he banged in a few fucks and cunts. When we were playing Brighton and Lady Bracknell said, "A fucking handbag?" the sound of seats tipping up as people walked out was like a volley of machine gun fire."

"And have you kept in touch with Henry?" said Natasha.

"Nah, 'fraid not. You know what it's like in this business. You become best mates for a few weeks while working on a show, and then it's onto the next."

Natasha and I tried to suppress our disappointment. "But someone did mention him to me today. Now who was it?" Jake scratched the top of his head. I'd never actually seen anyone doing this before when they were thinking. It didn't seem to do much good, so he began excavating his ear with a matchstick. I saw Natasha shudder. The operation went on for a long time and proved disgustingly productive. "Got it," Jake beamed in triumph, depositing an ear-wax loaded matchstick into the ashtray, and for a moment I thought he was talking about the recalcitrant contents of his ear. "Michael Howard."

I feared Jake must have been seriously overdoing the Belgian beer but he spotted my look of bemusement. "No, not that Michael Howard you berk," he said amiably, "the other one."

"Who's the other one?" said Natasha, and the question seemed to come through gritted teeth.

"Michael Howard, the lighting designer of course."

"And is he still here?" asked Natasha, as if coaxing a small child.

"No, he said he was having tea with his mother-in-law. She lives round this way."

"I don't suppose there's the smallest chance that he gave you any idea where Henry was working at the moment?" I asked desperately.

"Let me think," said Jake. "By the way, I don't suppose there's a chance of another beer is there?"

I was beginning to hate Jake, but I smiled, and said of course there was, and went and got us all drinks. And when I came back, Natasha looked like the cat that had got the cream.

"Dear clever Jake has remembered," she said.

"Yeah, Michael Howard asked me if I'd got any dope," said Jake, "and I said no, I wasn't doing spliffs any more. I find they slow me down." The idea of Jake being any slower than he was at that moment seemed frankly incredible. "Anyway, Michael said it was a shame Henry wasn't here, because Henry always had excellent grass, and I agreed. And then Michael said he'd heard Henry was doing this tour with the Metal Motherz."

"The Metal Motherz?" said Natasha.

"Halfway decent band actually," said Jake. "My son's into them. You must have heard their new single, "Bring Out Your Dead, Fred." Sort of Alice Cooperish?"

I confessed that it had escaped me. "But they're touring now as far as you recall?"

"Oh yeah, smallish venues though. The tour was all booked up before they had those two big hits. What d'you want Henry for, anyway? Some dope, I suppose?"

"That's right," I said, and Jake looked at Natasha in a new light. "What sort of dope's he dealing now?" I asked, casually.

"You know Henry," said Jake, and not for the first time in this pilgrimage, I wasn't certain that I did. "Won't do anything but very good grass and hash and uncut Ecstasy. He's dead against anything heavier."

It was the first good news I'd heard about Henry for ages.

"Right, well we'd better be on our way, Natasha."

"Absolutely," she said, in her best Lady Eleanor Holles voice, and to Jake's evident amazement, she kissed him on the cheek.

"You're an absolute treasure," she said, which, considering the earwax, was heroic on her part. Jake seemed too stunned to speak and we left him to his beer.

It was five thirty by now, and Vic was on what, at a conservative guess, was probably his twelfth pint of Guinness of the day. He seemed abject that we were on the point of departure.

"But I hoped you'd be our guests tonight. We're having a slap up dinner for the fifty main exhibitors at the Hotel Panoramique." I tried to give the impression that missing this treat was one of the more cruelly disappointing experiences of my life, but said a family crisis had blown up and I'd got to get back to London tonight. He wouldn't let us go without plying one last drink on us, and poor Natasha had her thigh pawed again while we drank it. Eventually, we escaped the brave new world of theatrical technology, which seemed to be exclusively powered by the brave old world of beer, and made it out onto the street.

It was below freezing and the rain had turned to sleet. "We've got to find a newsagent's before it shuts," I said, and led the way at a trot. I knew from past experience that Leicester was a town that shut up promptly at six. Eventually, we found a John Menzies, and I scanned the shelves. *NME. Mojo. Melody Maker. Kerrang! Q.* Somewhere in that lot we ought to be able to find where the Metal Motherz were playing that night. There was always the possibility they'd be having a night off, but it seemed unlikely on a Saturday. Always provided, of course, that Jake's information was correct.

There was the small unpleasantness of the separate rooms to be faced, and I didn't fancy spending the evening with Natasha in a murderous mood. Then I had a brainwave as we reached the car park. "Why don't I check out of the hotel while you take a look at these and see if you can find out where the Motherz are playing?" I said, handing her the bundle of magazines. Natasha, in the excitement of the chase, seemed happy to abandon the threatened night of bloody pash.

"Right", she said, and reached into her handbag, handing me a couple of hundred in twenties. "I'll pay," I said, half-heartedly, remembering the size of my overdraft but not wanting to appear an entirely kept man.

"It's my treat, remember?" she said. "We agreed. Don't be silly and make a fuss, Will, OK?"

I took the money, escorted Natasha to the car and took the lift to reception. Naturally, the woman behind the counter insisted on the full rate for both rooms, but it wasn't my money, and it turned out that the one thing that could be said in favour of the Hotel Panoramique was that it was cheap. I collected the bags, fretted for the lift that took an unconscionably long time arriving, and rejoined Natasha in the Porsche. She was looking smugly triumphant and showed me a display ad in *Kerrang!* giving details of the Metal Motherz tour. They were playing at the Roxy, Buckley, and it appeared to be the last night of a three-week hike round some of the least fashionable venues on the circuit. Stevenage, Grantham, Skegness, Middlesbrough, Welwyn Garden City, Cumbernauld. The Motherz – and Henry come to that – appeared to be paying their dues. I checked the dates, and saw that the night Henry had first visited Nicholas was one of the band's very few rest days.

"Where the fuck's Buckley?" I asked.

"North Wales," said Natasha. "Just across the border from Chester. It looks quite straightforward. M69, M6, M56." She passed me the map, and it did indeed look manageable, even to a navigator of my incompetence. Nevertheless, the journey was a nightmare, with heavy traffic and sleet that turned into driving snow. I got us lost again once we'd abandoned the motorways and the Roxy itself took a bit of finding once we'd fetched up in Buckley, a grim little redbrick town. The venue turned out to be a converted cinema set in a patch of waste-ground by the supermarket.

It was past nine by now, and the large throng of disconsolate, leather and denim-clad youth hanging around outside seemed to indicate a sell-out. I had a hunch however that this dilapidated venue might appreciate the possibility of a review in *Theatre World* (incorporating *Showbiz Today*). JB had always insisted on covering the whole of the entertainment waterfront, and reviews of up-and-coming rock bands had a monthly page of their own. As far as I knew, the Metal Motherz had still to grace it.

We walked past the prime of Buckley's young manhood and entered through horribly smeared glass doors. The local custom of those without tickets seemed to be to spend the evening gobbing at them. There was a band, a spectacularly monotonous band by the sound of it, playing inside, and the foyer was more or less deserted apart from a burly bouncer who eyed us malevolently.

"We're sold out mate," he said. "Tough titty."

"I'd like a word with the manager, please," I said, flashing my Critics' Circle membership card as if it were a police badge. "Will Benson, *Theatre World*." I ask you, cool or what?

Unfortunately, the bouncer didn't seem over impressed. "Like I told you, we're sold out. Tough titty." It seemed a phrase of which he was inordinately fond. Mercifully, Natasha now intervened. She'd undone yet another button of her blouse and looked impossibly glamorous in these down-at-heel surroundings.

"I'd be eternally grateful if you'd get the manager" she said, her voice much huskier than usual and seeming to hold out the possibility of a blow job at the very least.

"Right you are then," he said, with a sickly smile and toddled off.

"It's absolutely shameless the way you exploit your sexuality," I said.

"I know," she giggled. "I've not had so much fun in ages."

The manager arrived, wearing, I was delighted to see, a ruffled lilac dress shirt under an ancient DJ that was turning green with age. He looked about seventy, and it was hard not to feel sorry for such an old man running a deafening dive like this. There were sad wisps of cotton wool emerging from his ears.

"Can I help you?" he asked.

I explained who I was, and said that I just happened to be in the area, an unlikely possibility in Buckley, had seen the gig advertised and was very anxious to review it since the Metal Motherz had suddenly got so hot.

"Is JB still at *Theatre World*?" he asked fondly. "We had a great night together once at a talent contest in dear old Skeggy." His mournful face lit up at the memory.

"I'm afraid he's just had a triple heart by-pass," I said.

"Trouble on the by-pass?" he said, the mixture of thunderous bass and cotton wool rendering him more or less completely deaf.

"A triple heart by-pass," I yelled. "We're all keeping our fingers crossed that he'll make a full recovery."

He looked sad, and gave me his card.

"Give my love to JB," said Algernon Wiggins sadly. "I hate to think of him in pain."

"I will," I said. "And is there any chance of letting us into the gig?"

"Of course," he said, "though why clearly intelligent people like yourselves should want to put yourself through such hell I've no idea."

"You mean the Metal Motherz?"

"I mean all the arrogant, fornicating, yobbish scum who play here. They all want exterminating." He said this with such intensity that I momentarily shivered. One day, I couldn't help thinking, the apparently meek Mr Wiggins might take a terrible revenge on the monsters of rock who made his life such a misery.

He beckoned to the bouncer, who brought over a rubber stamp and inked the back of our hands with a smudgy Roxy logo. He also suggested that Natasha might like to check in her fur coat. "It'll get soddin' hot in there and though they don't seem to mind damaging each uvver, they've mostly got a thing about animals." He looked entranced as she removed her coat, as if she were his personal lap dancer, and said, with something approaching reverence, that he would take personal care of it.

"I don't suppose you've met the Motherz lighting man Henry Sutton?" I asked Wiggins.

The mournful and possibly murderous manager momentarily brightened. "Yes, he's doing the sound tonight too. Absolutely charming fellow. And actually, as scum goes, the Metal Motherz aren't too bad. Apart from the music, of course."

We thanked him for letting us in and he grimaced and said, "Rather you than me."

"It's just the poxy local support band on at the moment," he said. "If you want a drink in civilised surroundings, feel free to drop into the office," he added, pointing to a door marked 'Private'. "I tend to lurk there as much as I can and only venture out when the staff tell me there's some kind of trouble. Unfortunately, there's some kind of trouble most nights."

He shook our hands and returned to his refuge and we went through the double swing doors to the venue proper. We'd been holding our conversation outside at a shout, and inside the volume hit you like a fist in the gut. I remembered how I used to love the noise of sweaty rock concerts, but this time it made me feel physically sick. I was getting old.

All the cinema seats had been removed, but the floor was far from full considering this was meant to be a sold out-event. The kids on stage seemed about fourteen, playing punk rock covers that had been hits before they were born. The bass drum announced, with what was surely prophetic accuracy, that they were called No Future. The whole of pop music seemed to be cannibalising its past glories, I thought. Only the new dance music seemed to be charting fresh ground, particularly the dance music you couldn't actually dance to, but it was ground I was too old and set in my ways to explore. These days I often found myself tuning, shame-facedly, to Radio 2.

Towards the back of the venue, surrounded by sturdy metal barriers, was a big mixing desk and light board. I pointed it out to Natasha. If Henry was going to be anywhere, he was going to be there. We walked through the sparse crowd and peered hopefully over the railings. There was just one guy in a black tee shirt. But unless Henry had dyed his hair blond and undergone massive cosmetic surgery, it wasn't him. Natasha and I both clocked him and shook our heads, and headed to a door at the side of the auditorium with the word 'Bar' on it. The room was huge and packed to the gunwales with heavy metal fans, predominantly male but with a smattering of rock chicks in tiny crushed velvet frocks, Dr Marten's boots and more body piercing than seemed humanly feasible. One girl had her nose pierced with at least twenty rings and studs. What on earth did she do when she had a nasty cold? I wondered, in concerned grandfatherly fashion. We were, I noticed, attracting some fairly sneering looks from the kids. Natasha looked cool enough in her blouse and tight black trousers, but I must have looked like something from outer space to the metal fans in my battered sports jacket with the leather elbow patches and the olive green corduroy trousers from M&S. I was also beginning to sweat, with a mixture of anxiety and heat.

Wiggins may not have liked pop music, but he certainly knew how to run a venue. I was ready to kill for a pint of lager but looking at the crowded bar, the possibility of being served before the Metal Motherz took to the stage seemed as unlikely as getting my weight down to below twelve stone. I toyed with the idea of taking Wiggins up on his offer, but found I couldn't quite face a long cosy chat about JB and *Theatre World.* I was mourning JB too much myself, and my own position on the paper seemed too frighteningly precarious to discuss. So I took my place despairingly at the bar, only to find that the service was amazingly prompt. One of the of fleet bar-staff, a reassuringly mumsy middle-aged woman, spotted me almost at once and said she could see I was an urgent case. I ordered two pints of Holsten, Natasha's favoured G and T and a couple of bottles of mineral water. Realising I'd never get both pints plus Natasha's drink across the room, I drank the first pint at the bar, stuck a bottle of mineral water in each pocket, and made it back to Natsaha in double-quick time.

"Impressive," she said kindly. "And if you think I missed that sneaky second pint, you're wrong."

"What are we going to say to Henry?" I asked.

"It's him that's got the explaining to do," said Natasha. "We'll just have to play it by ear. You never know what's going to happen with Henry anyway."

I nodded. "You know I can hardly wait to see him," she said. "Whatever he's done, whatever kind of mess he's in, I'm still longing to see him."

The appalling noise next door suddenly came to a stop, and the die-hards who had endured it began to besiege the bar.

"Let's get out of here," I said. "Presumably Henry will have to check everything before the show and we might be able to have a word with him." The hall was now virtually empty, and another bouncer was guarding the fenced-off enclosure of electronic equipment. No sign of our man. I gestured to a dark alcove at the back, and suggested we waited there.

"I think it might be a good idea to give Henry a surprise for once," I said. "If he sees us, he might decide to disappear. Let's wait until he's safely inside the security barriers and then wander over to say hello." Natasha nodded and we lurked in the shadows.

After a few minutes someone appeared on stage, now lit only by the worker lights. He was stocky and bearded, and wearing a Metal Motherz teeshirt. Definitely not Henry. Then the man we'd seen earlier wandered into the sound enclosure. There was a lot of tedious "One-two, One-twoing" from the roadie on stage while the man at the sound board fiddled with the knobs. The sound test brought the fans streaming out of the bar and I began to resign myself to the fact that Henry must have heard about our arrival from either the manager or the bouncer and eluded us yet again. And then suddenly out of the pass door on the side of the stage, he appeared. Natasha and I spotted him at the same time and we both gasped. He was wearing black leather trousers and a white teeshirt, just like that glorious night at Oxshott Woods and from a distance at least he seemed completely unchanged. His long forelock still flopped boyishly over his eyes, and he brushed it away and actually jogged across the floor to his colleague at the mixer desks.

"Jesus, he's like Dorian Gray," said Natasha.

"I just hope he hasn't got a painting in the attic. I'd guess it would be showing signs of wear and tear by now."

We watched him in silence for a couple of minutes, while he conferred with his colleague, and then the unmistakable riff of Deep Purple's 'Smoke on the Water' started pumping out of the p.a. system.

"Now?" said Natasha.

"Or never," I replied. Touchingly, she took my hand and we fought our way through what was now becoming an exceptionally crowded floor to the front of the mixing desks. Henry had his head bowed under a low wattage angle-poise light, consulting the set list.

"Hi, Henry," I yelled absurdly above the enjoyably bombastic racket of Deep Purple. "Nice to see you again after so long."

He looked up, and I studied his face intently. There wasn't a trace of surprise or alarm. Just his familiar dazzling smile that convinced you that, at that moment, you were by some distance the most important person in his life.

"Natasha and Will," he cried, "I was wondering how long it would take you to find me. What kept you?" And then he vaulted youthfully over the barrier and I was sure he was going to sprint towards the exit.

"Stop him," I yelled at the lurking bouncer, who remained as if carved in stone. And then I blushed, for Henry was ambling towards us, arms outstretched, with that marvellous smile. He hugged us both, hard and intensely, like an anxious mother who has just found her errant children, and kissed us both on the lips.

"Do I detect a touch of paranoia, Will?" he grinned when he finally let us go.

It was me who felt guilty, not him, the man with a priceless Vermeer on his hands.

"I'm sorry, Henry," I said. "It's just that it's taken some trouble to find you."

"Well, you're an idiot then. Don't you read your own paper?"

"Most of it."

"But not the Backstage column."

"Not always, no." It was a column compiled by the secretary, Julie, with boring news about the changing personnel in the entertainment industry. The kind of stuff that reported that Mr Joe Bloggs was moving from his post as Chief Carpenter at the Bournemouth International Conference Centre to take up a demanding new role as Administrative Director (Technical Support) at the Embassy Centre, Morecambe. It was printed in seven point at the back of the paper, and no one read it except Julie, a sub (if they'd got the time) and presumably a few of those who were in the process of changing jobs, and liked seeing their name in the paper, albeit in a column with a fair claim to being the most boring in British journalism.

"And I put it there especially for you," said Henry, shaking his head in mock regret.

"How do you mean put it there?" I said, faintly peeved. It was galling to have flogged round the country in search of the elusive Henry, only to find when you'd tracked him down that he'd meant you to come all along. Galling, but absolutely typical of Henry. "You can't put something in that column like an advert. The woman who compiles it just does it at random from a pile of press handouts each week."

"I'd never suggest for a moment that you can buy your way into the editorial columns of *Theatre World*," said Henry. "I merely say I sent a press release about the fact that I was touring with the Motherz, after a long stint as company manager with Shakespeare for Everyone, and it duly appeared after a delay of two weeks under my own headline 'From Romeo to Rock'. And only when it had appeared did I go to Nicholas, in the more or less certain knowledge that he'd tell you all about my fleeting visit, and you would immediately put two and two together, and be hot on my trail."

"Well, I didn't see it," I said sullenly. "Who could expect me to read a boring column like that?" I was, I suddenly realised, sounding like a petulant child who'd dropped his egg in the egg and spoon race and still wanted a prize.

"Sorry, Will. You're quite right. And the fact that you found me without my little clue shows real initiative on your part."

There was, I realised, just the faintest edge of sarcasm to his words. After my earlier outburst it was perhaps no more than I deserved.

"And Natasha," he said. "I didn't expect you to be tagging along with old Will here. What a pleasure." Natasha smirked.

I was beginning to get irritated by Henry's smarm. "It's all very well you laying on the oil," I said. "But what about that fucking picture? It's outrageous you running round with a priceless, exceptionally beautiful painting that ought to be in a public gallery for everyone to enjoy." Having sounded the petulant note just seconds earlier, I was now coming over like an insufferable prig. Henry shook his head and put a finger to his lips but we were hardly likely to be overheard. Black Sabbath's 'Paranoid' was blaring out now and we were conversing with out heads close together, like a trio doing a drugs' deal. It must have been a common enough sight at the Roxy. "Where the hell did you get the painting from anyway?" I hissed in his ear. "It's been missing for years."

"Listen, darlings," he said, giving both our shoulders an affectionate squeeze. "I assure you my intentions are honourable and I'm acting in that beautiful picture's best interests. But I can't talk now. I've got a show to do. I promise you both a full explanation afterwards."

Natasha nodded eagerly, and even I had to admit his proposal sounded fair enough. He went back to the barrier and shouted at his colleague. "Got a couple of passes, Andy?" Andy nodded and handed something to Henry. He peeled off two sticky labels, bearing the legend 'Metal Motherz Bring out the Dead Tour: ACCESS ALL AREAS'. I'd wanted an access all areas pass since I was eleven and began reading tour reports in the *NME.* I was a bone fide rock 'n' roll ligger at last. Henry slapped the badge on the lapel of my sports jacket, bestowing instant hip on that least fashionable item, and affixed it, with what could only be described as tender loving care on Natasha's chest. She didn't seem to mind this liberty at all.

"After the show, nip round to the back of this toilet of a venue," said Henry. "You'll find a staircase leading up to a terrace on the first floor. There'll be a security man at the bottom but he'll let you up if you show him these passes. The band's dressing rooms and the green room give on to the terrace and there'll be what ought to be a fairly sensational party to mark the end of the tour. We'll have a great time, I promise, and I'll tell you everything that's been going on. It's quite a story."

I thought I'd died and gone to heaven. A real rock 'n' roll party. Drugs, groupies, Babylonian excess. I looked down at my Access All Areas pass with the same pride with which I'd once regarded my Blue Peter badge, awarded, aged eight, after the heroic collection of 5,000 silver milk bottle tops.

Henry gathered us both together for another hug. "I can't tell you how good it is to see you both," he said. "Friendship and wild times, eh?"

"Friendship and wild times, Henry," we said, bewitched all over again, and he vaulted back into his enclosure and gave us a camp little wave. "I'd watch from near the back," he shouted. "It's always carnage at the front."

There was a raised platform near the back of the hall, with a small additional bar which had just opened for business.

"What will you have, Natasha?" I asked. She seemed to be glowing with happiness.

"It's got to be champagne," she said. "Wasn't it just great to see him?"

I agreed that it was, and bought the champagne while Natasha paid a quick visit to the ladies. It was thirty quid, and I'd returned the cash left over from the hotel bill, but who gave a toss on a night like this? I found a great spot by the railings that fenced off the bar area. There was even a shelf for our drinks. When Natasha returned, I poured out the fizz, and we repeated the old toast.

"He's not guilty. Not morally anyway, even if he's committed some technical crime," I said. "It's obvious that he wanted us to find him so he could explain. That's why he went to Nicholas in the first place."

"And got that piece to run in *Theatre World*," said Natasha. "Only muggins here missed it."

I was too elated to feel irritated. "You're quite right, sweetheart," I said, refilling our glasses, and kissed her on the lips, with affection, not warped lust.

"There's just one thing," said Natasha. "I know we're feeling dead chuffed now, but we also know that Henry can be a very plausible liar. After the show, I think one of us should keep a discreet eye on him, to make sure he jolly well does turn up at the party. It would be all too easy for us to go round the back only for him to disappear through the front door.

She was right, of course. Henry made you feel wonderful, but that was exactly the kind of trick we knew he was capable of playing.

"You go straight up to the party and set about scoring the cocaine then," I said. "I'll hang around in our convenient alcove and follow him at a discreet distance."

"My hero," she said, and then the band came on with fireworks and smoke canisters exploding all over the stage.

"We're the maddest, baddest band in the land," screamed the bottle blond lead singer sporting preposterous red pvc trousers and an emerald studded codpiece. "Hello, Buckley, are you ready to rock?" He cupped a hand as if straining to hear cheers, which were in fact deafening. "I can't hear you, Buckley, I can't hear you at all, I said, are you ready to ROCK?" The last question was delivered in the falsetto shriek that was to prove such a hallmark of his act. Even I, fat, approaching middle age, a man whose idea of a designer label was the Marks and Spencer's logo, felt that I was indeed ready to rock. "Yeah," I yelled, "Yeah," yelled Natasha, "Yeah," yelled the 800 other fans in the tightly packed venue. There was a roll of drums, a thump of bass, a great grinding of guitars, and our singer let out his own lusty "Yeeeaaaaggghhh!" as if he was enjoying the best orgasm of his life.

No one could accuse the Metal Motherz of subtlety, still less originality. They offered the usual cliché-ridden mixture of apocalyptic and/or diabolic lyrics, most of them mercifully inaudible; numbers that lumbered towards frenzied climaxes with a beat like a pile-driver; and a guitarist whose exhibitionist tendencies would have been obscene if they hadn't been so funny. He tore off flashy, predictable solos with the grimaces of one of the damned, and then, as the notes screamed ever higher up the scale, appeared to be approaching some kind of cosmic nirvana. During the crashing rhythmical passages he held his guitar straight out from his body as though it were some supercharged dick, and in a routine pinched straight from Bowie and Mick Ronson, *circa* 1972, the lead singer got down on his knees and pretended to fellate the Fender Stratocaster. It was crap, but it was hugely enjoyable crap, a giant compendium of rock and roll tat that somehow hit the spot. I discovered that I was cheerfully playing my air guitar through most of the set. Down at the front, the action was more frenzied. The crowd bobbed up and down, relentlessly, unstoppably, a heaving, sweating, terrifying crush of people lost in rhythm. Every so often, some young lad would launch himself onto the shoulders of those in front of him to be passed, horizontally, by dozens of willing hands towards the front of the stage, where he'd be welcomed, almost tenderly, by two implacable bouncers, who'd escort him to the wings.

"This one's called 'Knife Down The Throat'," screamed the singer, lurching into some terrible saga of sexual violence, or, "this one's called 'Nuclear Winter'" as the band lurched into doomy chords signalling global annihilation. Yet there was an inoffensive innocence about the Motherz. It was all cartoon violence, cartoon horror, a gleeful parody of rock and roll menace that was actually about as threatening as the Monkees. Henry's lighting was exuberantly over the top, complete with searchlights tunnelling their way through the smoke, thunder-flash explosions, lasers beaming out over the audience, and almost certainly, though I couldn't put my hand on my heart and swear to this, since I still didn't know what they were, the elaborate use of gobos.

After more than an hour that left me wringing wet and exhilarated, the band returned for their encores, ending with 'Bring Out Your Dead, Fred'. This was the tale of a serial killer, summoned by the police to dump the corpses of his victims on the porch before giving himself up, which featured screeching sirens, flashing blue lights and the lead singer screaming through a megaphone like a latter-day Edith Sitwell. Only our man was much prettier.

"Bring out your dead, Fred, They're under the bed, Fred, How much blood have you shed, Fred?" he yelled, before the audience began the body count, each number followed by a crashing chord. One, crash, two, crash, three, crash . . . we'd reached twenty-four when the singer fired a pistol into the air and the lights suddenly turned the stage blood red. "We've shot you in the head, Fred, you're well and truly dead, Fred, skull shattered by the lead, Fred . . ." You'd have needed a heart of stone not to laugh. The guitarist pulled out one last, ecstatic solo, the singer let out a series of shrieks about the flames of hell, and the band finally ground to a halt with the drummer destroying his kit and the, until now, entirely motionless bass player ramming his guitar through one of the speakers. Black out and mass delirium, but it was clear that the Motherz couldn't possibly top this and after five minutes of stamping and cheering for more, the drab house lights were switched on and the crowd drifted out of the hall, eerily subdued, all passion spent.

Natasha joined the throng heading towards the exit, and I beat a retreat to the alcove. Henry conferred with his colleague for a couple of minutes, then walked out through one of the pass doors. This was the moment I could have lost him. Venues are almost invariably labyrinthine back stage. So as soon as Henry was through the door, I trotted along myself, and when challenged by a bouncer, proudly pointed at my AAA sticker.

"Which way to the party?" I asked, and was told to walk down the corridor, turn right and go up a flight of stairs, which apparently led to the terrace outside the dressing rooms. Once through the magic door, I heard Henry's voice, giving the road crew instructions about the get-out. I hid behind a stage-flat and waited. After a minute or so, he came out into the corridor, and walked confidently along it, whistling, implausibly after all the heavy metal carnage, 'Lara's Theme' from *Doctor Zhivago.* He turned right, as he was meant to do, ignoring the exit sign at the end of the corridor. It looked as though he was going to attend the party as promised rather than do a flit. I stuck my head round the corner and watched him climb up the stairs and disappear through another door. I gave him a thirty-second start, then climbed the steps myself, pushing the security bar to get out. I was no sooner through the door than a hand was placed over my mouth and my arm was wrenched violently behind my back.

"You walked into that one, Will," said Henry, releasing me almost at once. "And you really ought to start trusting me. We're friends, remember?"

"Bastard," I said grinning. I went and stood by the balcony railings and gazed through the swirling snowflakes at a few lights shining in the blackness beneath us.

"In daylight, there's a wonderful view from here towards the hills," said Henry. "Miles and miles of rolling open country."

Down at the bottom of the fire escape leading up to the first floor terrace, the boys were trying to look unconcerned as their girlfriends cajoled and pleaded with the bouncers to let them see their idols upstairs. "It's invitation only," insisted Natasha's burly bouncer. "Tough titty." But two girls simultaneously made a dash for it, and though one was stopped the other slipped between the minders and made it to the top of the stairs.

"Sorry, sweetheart," said Henry, who was making good use of his arm-locks that night, as the girl, who can have been no more than fourteen, thrashed around. He was, I was pleased to see, using a good deal less force on her than he had on me. "Oh please, please, I've just got to see Roderick, I love Roderick."

"Go home and grow up," said Henry, not unkindly, as the bouncer climbed the stairs to collect her. She started struggling again, and without further ado the gorilla put her over his shoulder in a fireman's lift and carried her down the stairs. A grey haired man stepped forward to take her into his custody. "Her dad come to pick her up," grinned Henry. "They're all so young."

He led the way through the front door that gave on to the terrace. "In the days when this was a cinema, the manager used to live here," he explained over his shoulder. With its wonderful views it must have been a lovely little flat once. Now the squalor was indescribable. Grafitti of amazing verbal and graphic obscenity adorned every wall. What had once been a primly suburban sun-burst carpet was covered with the butts of joints and fags and an amazing number and variety of crunched up beer cans. There was a rank smell of sweat, booze and smoke in the air that made you want to gag. It was just like home. Henry led the way into what had once been the sitting room. There were battered old armchairs, and a grubby mattress on the floor. Against one wall stood a trestle table lavishly covered with food and drink. "The rider," said Henry nonchalantly. The room contained about twenty people, most of them looking unexpectedly professional and middle class, and the band themselves had changed out of their ludicrous costumes into mufti, though the lead singer seemed to favour elaborate make-up offstage as well as on.

"There's a lot of suits here for the end of the tour now that the Motherz are breaking into the big league. With a bit of luck, they'll piss off before too long," said Henry. Natasha was standing rather forlornly on her own, a glass of champagne clamped in her hand, with that fixed and desperate smile one wears at parties when one doesn't know anyone and no one's taken the trouble to introduce themselves. It's the smile that says, 'Help, please talk to me, I'm not really a social cripple with bad breath.' It was a smile I had worn myself, too often, at too many showbiz functions and my heart went out to her. I expected Henry to go to her rescue, but he ignored her and headed off towards the suits, so I went and put my arm round her shoulder and led her to the food and drink.

The Motherz' rider was clearly an impressive one, though it hadn't yet reached the *folie de grandeur* of bowls of Smarties with all the dark brown ones carefully removed. In fact, the Motherz appeared to be sybarites of remarkably good taste – or my taste anyway. There were massive salvers of half lobsters, langoustines and oysters on ice, and a not so small mountain of caviar surrounded by chopped onions, crumbled hard boiled egg, sour cream and blinis in a chafing dish. There were warm, fresh baked rolls, big bowls of interesting salads, which even I might have considered eating, and fresh mangoes and pawpaws with lime. Not the sort of food one often got a chance to eat in a one horse town in north Wales. Not the sort of food I got the chance to eat anywhere at all. I loaded my plate – the beef sandwiches at the trade fair seemed to belong to another world – and Natasha was only slightly less greedy than me. There was a small, glass fronted freezer cabinet of the kind you sometimes see in trendy pubs, and it contained half a dozen bottles of Stolichnaya. Natasha said she'd stick to the fizz – there were more bottles of Bolly in ice buckets than I could count – but I poured myself a generous shot of the ice cold vodka and tipped it down the old red lane. It was so delicious I immediately had another, before realising I'd better go a bit easy. It would be a bit silly if having come all this way to find Henry and hear his story I collapsed in a drunken stupor. So, I virtuously poured myself about a quarter of a litre of Pouilly Fuissé instead.

Henry still seemed to be involved with the execs and the band, so Natasha and I sat down on one of the distressingly filthy sofas and ate our meal alone together. It was no hardship. I realised that apart from our time in bed together, which aroused much more complex emotions, I had grown to like Natasha. Looking for Henry wouldn't have been half as much fun without her, despite her occasional sarky moments. I wondered what it was that made her so strange and terrifying in bed, then remembered Nicholas' rampant, self-destructive promiscuity. Perhaps both siblings just liked scary sex. Perhaps I was just impossibly straight.

I slurped out the last of the oysters, and munched reflectively on my blini and caviar.

"You're in seventh heaven, aren't you?" said Natasha, with a note of real affection in her voice.

"Beautiful girl, delicious food, half pissed and ligging with the stars – yeah, I suppose I am."

"It's been fun, Will," she said. "Thank you." There was something faintly valedictory in her tone of voice but I didn't have time to pursue it.

Henry came over. "Come and meet the boys," he said. "They're dying to meet you." This seemed unlikely, since they had no idea who we were and a small review in *Theatre World* was unlikely to have any significant effect on their careers, but Henry made it sound true.

He introduced us to the band – Tubby the drummer who was indeed tubby, Dave the bassist, Andre, the showy lead guitarist and Roderick the singer. What kind of name was 'Roderick' for a singer? What was wrong with 'Rod', apart from the fact that Rod Stewart had got there first? Surely even 'Roddy' would be better than 'Roderick'? The drummer appeared to be braindead, like most of his tribe, while the bassist was a cockney jack-the-lad who was clearly mentally undressing Natasha while engaging her in small talk of stultifying banality. Andre and Roderick were more interesting.

"You're not really reviewing us are you?" asked Roderick. "What did you think?"

"I had a great time," I replied honestly.

"You're joking, it's total shite and you know it."

"Well, I suppose it's not totally original, but as well as being good fun in its own right, there's a nice element of pastiche in there too."

"Ah, he's rumbled us, Andre," said Roderick.

"Can't slip one past *Theatre World*, can you, darling?" said the guitarist. These cock-rockers, I suddenly realised with delight, were actually screaming queens. The lead guitarist indeed sounded remarkably like Julian Clary.

"If we tell you a tragic story, will you promise not to print it?" asked Roderick, "Henry here says you can be trusted." I looked suitably grave and nodded. "Right then. By the way, you must call me Rodders. I absolutely adore Nicholas Lyndhurst and *Only Fools and Horses*."

Rodders looked nervously over his shoulder. "Right, we're fine," he said, apparently satisfied. "All the suits are at the trough." The record company execs were indeed getting well stuck in.

"Well," said Rodders, "we're actually quite serious musicians. Andre here trained at the Royal College of Music in composition and piano and I was going to be an opera singer. I did a bit of irregular chorus work at the Coli but it never went further than that and Andre realised he was never going to become the next Alfred Brendel either. We were broke, living together in a terrible house in Hackney, and signing on every week.

"We were happy though," said Andre wistfully. "You used to love me in those days."

"You know I still love you, babe," said Rodders.

"What about that bit of rough you picked up in Middlesbrough?" put in Andre.

"You can talk, the cruising Queen of the Basingstoke cottages."

They both gave each other affectionate grins. This was, I gathered, not a serious row, but merely the camp patter that provided the froth on a stable partnership.

"Anyway, we shared this flat with a couple of other guys, straight as they come, and one of them was into metal. We became faintly obsessed with it, in the way you do when you're bored and have a lot of time on your hands, and we started the Motherz as a party turn, using backing tapes, just the two of us. It gave us a chance to dress up and wear a lot of slap for one thing."

"And receive the applause we'd always craved," said Andre, self-mocking but also serious, "even if it was playing cheesey old tosh."

"Anyway, the Motherz seemed to be a hit wherever we went, usually in the gay scene, of course. But then we got a weekly residency at a Kilburn pub, and after a couple of weeks real metal fans started to turn up. They took the pastiche perfectly seriously. And when we sent some tapes off to some record companies, just as a joke really, two of them took us seriously too, and a minor bidding war began. Not huge, but enough for us to know that whoever eventually signed us would put a bit of money into promotion. It was A&M in the end, many of whom you see here tonight."

"They're dead chuffed about our first album, which is coming out in February and confidently expected to go platinum. They're determined to market us as proper heavy metal bad boys and get very annoyed when we start camping it up, especially in front of the press."

"So mum's the word," said Rodders, affectionately pinching my cheek.

"But the drummer and the bassist?" I said. "They don't exactly look like . . ."

"Camp ironists?" suggested Rodders. "No, of course they're not, they're the real thing. They used to play in a ghastly outfit called Satan's Revenge. They were terrible the Revenge, truly terrible, and we used to rip them off and send them up shamelessly in the early days. When we got the recording contract, we asked them if they'd like to join us. It was just another little joke on our part."

"And, of course they have a great time, getting drunk, screwing groupies, and trashing hotel rooms, what they've dreamed of all their lives only they were far too thick and incompetent to achieve it. And meanwhile, Andre and I live like monks, because the male metal fans would bottle you if you so much as mentioned a quick blow job, not that you'd want anything to do with the ugly, acne-scarred morons anyway. So, we mourn our lost classical careers and the way we've sold out and drink too much and quarrel." They both looked terminally depressed for a moment.

"There's always the money of course, and the fame and the champagne," I suggested, and they nodded gloomily and said there were indeed minor compensations like that, before bursting into delighted laughter.

At that moment, Tubby the drummer, who was actually nothing like as tubby as me, re-entered the room with a not unfanciable teenage girl in tow. He poured her a glass of champagne, then led her straight off down the corridor, flashing his mates a triumphant thumbs up sign as he went through the door.

"Look what Tubby's dragged back now," said Andre, "Jail-bait again."

Dave, who had been getting precisely nowhere fast with Natasha, detatched himself from our little circle too. Natasha came and stood next to me. "That appalling oik's just offered me the privilege of sucking him off in the back room," she hissed indignantly into my ear. I found it hard to look suitably indignant about this. In fact, I grinned. Natasha wasn't pleased about this either.

Two minutes later Dave was back, with another frighteningly young little girl. She too got the perfunctory glass of champagne before being led down the corridor.

"They just go out there and pick 'em out like fruit from a stall," said Andre. "It's disgusting."

"No worse than many a cottage," said Rodders.

"Yeah, but girls," said Andre in a tone of utter disgust.

Natasha looked miffed at this as well, and they both blushed rather charmingly and told her they naturally didn't mean women like her, she'd got style which was a lot more than could be said for the baby metalettes. Some record execs were beginning to hover, and Rodders announced with a weary sigh that they'd got to talk strategy about the new album. "We should be free in a few minutes, if you fancy a line or two," said Rodders in a stage whisper.

"Cocaine?" I said, like the innocent I was. Almost fifteen years after Henry's promise in Oxshott Woods I still hadn't got within sniffing distance of a line of coke. Show business must have been full of the stuff, but somehow I never seemed to meet anyone who both indulged and was prepared to offer a snort to a straight-looking trade journalist.

"Of course," said Rodders. "Rock and roll sherbert. Another of those little compenastions we were talking about."

I nodded eagerly, and so, surprisingly, did Natasha.

"It's time we spoke to Henry anyway," I said. "See you later – and thanks." The camp couple smiled benignly and greeted the execs with butch slaps on the back. I looked round the room and there was Henry, who I'd always remembered as the life and soul of the party, sitting alone on a sofa looking distinctly forlorn. He had a glass of wine in one hand and a joint in the other and he looked more than a little out of it.

"Confession time, I shuppose?" he said, his words worryingly slow and slurry.

"That's right," I said. "We've waited long enough."

"I need another drink, Natasha," he said, though it looked like the last thing he needed. "Could you bear to go and get it for me, since I'm not sure I'm capable of dragging myself up from this sofa? A large Jack Daniels with just a whisper of dry Martini if you can find it."

"I'll get it," I said, but Henry grabbed hold of my belt and pulled me forcibly down onto the sofa. I was pretty pissed myself now, and ended up falling into his lap, and Natasha, who had had a record five minutes for looking cross, went off to fetch the drink with a bad grace.

Henry seemed to sober up as soon as her back was turned. He shook me violently by the shoulder, fixed me with penetrating blue eyes that were neither drugged nor drunk, and said: "We've got to lose that fucking bitch and soon."

"You what?" I said. "I know she can be a bit of a pain at times but she's all right. More than all right. She still holds a torch for you, you know?"

"Will, this is serious, desperately serious. Has she made any phone calls since you realised I was likely to be here tonight?"

I thought back. "None that I can remember. She's hardly had a chance. Though she did go to the ladies before the band came on. But as far as I know, she hasn't even got a mobile. She certainly hasn't taken or received any calls on one and I've been with her since yesterday evening."

"She'll have a mobile all right," said Henry grimly. He looked at his watch. "They'll have had almost a couple of hours by now, that's if she didn't phone them earlier. Listen, Will, you're going to have to trust me."

"But why, Henry? Who's them? I'm absolutely sure Natasha is on your side and, if you'll forgive me saying so, this all sounds ridiculously melodramatic." But so, I realised, did turning up at an old friend's house with a stolen Vermeer.

"There's no time to talk. When Natasha comes back, I'm going to pretend to feel sick and stagger to the loo. You follow me. She'll be expecting you to keep an eye on me just like you were at the end of the show. I'll get us out of here. If you try to stop me, I'll hit you, Will, I swear it. And if you stay here, you'll be in more trouble than you can possibly imagine."

"But what about Natasha? Won't she be in danger too?"

"She is the danger, Will, or part of it. Trust me, just this once, for Christ's sake."

He had done nothing to earn my trust. Everything I'd heard about him persuaded me not to trust him. And I didn't. On the other hand, if I didn't follow him to the loo, he looked almost certain to give us the slip. My duty was to stick with him. No need to trust, just follow. Natasha could come to little harm on her own with Rodders and Andre around, and was quite grown up enough to look after herself anyway.

She walked over now, told Henry she couldn't find any Martini, and anxiously handed him his drink, a very miserly Jack Daniels.

"Are you sure you really want this, Henry? You don't look at all well."

As indeed he didn't. There was sweat on his brow that hadn't been there a few seconds earlier and he had turned alarmingly white. He gagged violently, repeatedly.

"Jesus," said Natasha.

"Lav," said Henry weakly. "Got to get to the lav."

"Go with him, Will," said Natasha, though whether from genuine concern for his health or fear of losing him I couldn't tell. It was a matter I was to ponder a good deal in the next twenty-four hours.

Henry lurched to his feet, his hand over his mouth, and I followed anxiously in his wake. Henry made a miraculous recovery as soon as he'd got through the door and gave me his most disarmingly boyish grin.

"Well done, Will, mate," he whispered. "Follow me". He led the way down the hall and turned left into what had probably once been the bedroom. And was still being used as a bedroom, though all it now contained were too revoltingly stained mattresses and harsh light from a single 100-watt bulb. Tubby had his head buried between the legs of one of the young girls who was squealing excitedly. Dave was in mid-bonk with the other, his jeans still round his ankles. He had a distressingly spotty bottom and the girl, I noticed, was quietly sobbing. Tubby appeared oblivious to our arrival, but Dave looked up. "'Fraid you'll 'ave to wait your turn, mate," he said, "though it might just give you head if you go up the other end and ask it nicely."

Henry may have been in a hurry, may have been in danger of his life as he claimed. Nevertheless, he found time to drag Dave off the girl, force him upright, and punch him, very hard, in the stomach. Dave crumpled with an agonised howl, Tubby looked up with an expression of incredulity on his smeary face. "Get out now," Henry told the distressed girl who was already climbing into her jeans. "He'll be out of it for a few minutes now, but he can turn nasty. This one," he added, pointing to Tubby, who had already resumed what he had briefly left off, "is more or less harmless and your friend seems to be enjoying herself. Get one of the suits in there to drive you home and threaten to make a fuss to the police if they won't."

The girl, who looked no older than fourteen, her cheeks pathetically stained with mascara, nodded blankly and scurried out into the hall. Dave was still curled up on the floor, groaning. Henry marched over to the window and hauled it open. There was a rickety fire escape outside, and I followed him down it.

I'd just reached the bottom when I heard Natasha's voice calling desperately from the window above. "Will, for Christ's sake, Will." she screamed and for a moment I froze to the spot. "I've got to stay with him," I yelled. "I'll be in touch." Henry grabbed me by the arm. "Run, for God's sake, run," he said, and I hauled my fourteen stone in his wake. We ran past the Roxy's front of house and along Buckley's grim main drag. It can't have been more than 200 yards but it felt like a marathon to me as I stuggled to keep up with Henry who might have been running for England. He turned right down a sidestreet, and as I followed him I glanced over my shoulder and caught a brief glimpse of Natasha standing forlornly outside the Roxy, doubtless realising that she couldn't catch us now. I felt like a traitor and briefly wondered if I'd meet the traitor's usual fate.

Henry had stopped by an old VW camper van, and was climbing into the driving seat. I suddenly realised he might drive off without me so I pounded down the road after him and blocked the sliding door with my foot.

"I admire your persistence, Will, and if you want to climb over me *en route* to the passenger seat, you're more than welcome. But it will be much easier if you get in on the other side like everyone else."

"Give me the ignition keys then," I said stubbornly. He handed them over. "But do hurry, Will. If Natasha gets the number of this van it will be very awkward."

I ran round to the other side, jumped in and slid the door shut beside me. "She was standing outside the Roxy when we turned the corner," I panted, fretting about the terrible pains in my chest. "It would probably be sensible not to drive past it."

"Right," he said. "Give us the keys, Will."

I handed them over and after several coughs, the old van finally got underway.

"Hardly the speediest of getaway vehicles," I said, but in fact the battered state of the van made me more inclined to trust him. Still more did his treatment of the egregious Dave.

"I was glad you did that to that disgusting bass player," I said. "I always thought groupies sounded fun but that was just horrible."

"It's almost always like that," he said. "Impressionable young girls and total shits who'd find it hard to get laid at all if they weren't in a rock band. It stinks, this business."

"The manager was saying exactly the same thing," I said. It was strange. Sitting here with Henry, driving heavens knew where through the snowy night, it was as if the past fifteen years had never happened, and we were merely resuming a conversation that might have begun in the *Esher Herald* newsroom.

"How have you been keeping, Will?" he said. "I enjoy your stuff in *Theatre World.*"

I found myself blushing with pleasure. This was ridiculous. We weren't here for a quiet chat and mutual flattery. I needed answers.

"Spare me the compliments," I said. "What I want to know about is that Vermeer."

"There's something I want to show you before we talk about that. I think it will prove you can trust me."

"Like Professor Maxwell trusted the brilliance of your thesis on the two Troiluses?" I said. "Like old Moley trusted your results from the Walton-on-Thames craft fair?"

"My, my, you have been doing your homework. I'm not particularly proud of either of those exploits. But I think you'll agree that though culpable, neither was vicious."

"Not vicious, but mean," I said. "Unworthy."

"But not without a certain style?"

"That's for me to judge, not you."

"Fair enough," he said, and a silence grew between us and it was I who began to feel guilty and cracked first.

"Isn't it terrible about Nicholas?" I said.

"God, it was awful to see him like that. It was all I could do not to weep in front of him."

"I'm afraid I did weep." I said. "And it was worse than that, I was crying about myself."

"Dear old Will," he said, "What about?"

I mustn't, I really mustn't lay myself open to him, I told myself firmly. "I don't trust you enough to tell you yet," I said. "Ouch," he replied, and asked me how I'd found him. So I told him about the haphazard trail to the Roxy, and by the time I'd finished we'd reached Chester station. He parked the van in the station car park, reached for a hold-all behind him, and led the way across the forecourt, not to the big station hotel but to an unassuming B&B just round the corner. It was snowing heavily again now, and bitterly cold, and I remembered I'd left my raincoat, and indeed all my other things, inside Natasha's Porsche.

Henry had a key, and let me in through the front door, and I followed him up three flights of stairs to a small room under the gables. It was almost as cold inside as out. Henry took his coat off despite the chill, switched on the electric fire, filled the kettle and plugged it in. Then he searched in his hold-all and produced a bottle of Famous Grouse and poured large shots into two tooth mugs. I crouched by the fire, trying to get warm – the camper van hadn't run to a heating system – and took a grateful swig of the Scotch.

"Do you want to have a look at her?" asked Henry.

"At who?" I asked fatuously.

"At the *Pregnant Lady with a Bible*?"

"Jesus, you're not keeping the picture in some cheap B&B?"

"No one's going to think of looking for her here," he said. "I'm not going to have her for long and I want to make the most of her while she's in my care."

He was, I realised, rather absurdly, talking about a living woman rather than a stolen painting, but when Henry produced the picture, carefully stowed away in a suitcase just as Nicholas had described, it didn't seem silly at all.

She was so alive, that anonymous woman in seventeenth century Delft, so happy in her pregnancy. It required an effort of will to remember that the quiet smile, the radiance, the shared joy, weren't for you personally, but for the unseen figure who had clearly just entered the room. It was, of course, a work of art, not necessarily a scene drawn directly from life. But it didn't seem sentimental to imagine that the woman was smiling directly at the man who was painting her, Vermeer. And he had captured her with such tenderness, such harmony, that you knew he loved her too.

"His wife?" asked Henry and I shook my head.

"She's too young. The painting's late. Mrs Vermeer would have been at least forty."

"We'll never know. But my God it makes you feel better about life, doesn't it? That possibility of purity and joy in a fallen, grubby world."

I nodded. There were a few cracks on the canvas, but there were cracks in the canvases of Vermeers that had been safeguarded for generations in museums.

"You're taking care of her?," I said, and Henry nodded solemnly, and tenderly packed her back into the case.

"There's something else you should see before we talk," said Henry. "Have you been to Natasha's house in Belgravia?"

"Yes," I said. "I was patronised by the butler." He unlocked a drawer in the desk and produced an envelope.

"You'll recognise this then."

He passed me a polaroid. It showed one of the end walls of the first floor sitting room. But hanging over the fine marble fireplace, where I had seen an indifferent Gainsborough, was the Vermeer, in an ugly modern frame that didn't suit the painting at all.

"Jesus, where did you get this?"

"I took it myself. There's more." He handed me another polaroid and I gasped out loud. There was the Vermeer again. And standing beside it, her face in profile gazing reverently at the painting was Natasha wearing the very outfit she'd worn to the hypnotism show. "Just one more," said Henry. Natasha appeared again. Only this time she was standing contentedly next to her husband, Sir Dominic. The salt and pepper beard, like some raffish Edwardian admiral. The eyes that seemed to twinkle behind gold rimmed spectacles. The commanding physique and the full head of hair, worn surprisingly, conceitedly, long. The husband Natasha refused to talk about. But then she hadn't talked about having the Vermeer in her own home either. She had pretended that she had never even seen it reproduced in a book. I hated her at that moment. It wasn't just that I'd been duped. It was that to judge by her expression she loved her husband from whom I'd naturally assumed she was estranged. My suspicion had been that Sir Dominic was probably impotent, which would perhaps explain the terrible urgency of her love-making. But she'd been turning tricks in the bedroom with me to create a bond of lust and guilt. She was determined I wouldn't leave her until we'd found Henry.

"But they must have been mad to allow you to take these pictures. They're incredibly incriminating."

"Not really. I helped them put the picture, temporarily, into that rather unsuitable frame. It was the only one around the house that more or less fitted. It was a little rehearsal you see."

"A rehearsal for what?"

"For the press conference they were planning to call the following afternoon. To announce that the long-lost Vermeer had been recovered and that Sir Dominic and his good lady wife were handing it over to a doubtless awed and grateful nation. Unfortunately for them, there wasn't a press conference. Because I stole the painting that night."

"Shit, Henry," I said weakly. "Do you think I could have another drink? I'm all at sea here."

He poured me another Famous Grouse, and a smaller one for himself, then made strong mugs of Nescafe and put a lot of sugar and another slug of Scotch into mine.

"I'd better go back to the beginning," he said, "Or, if not to the very beginning, because we'll never know who the lady was and what she meant to Vermeer and he to her, but to the moment when the lady vanished."

"*Pregnant Lady with a Bible* was one of the last Vermeers in private hands," he continued. "It belonged to a prosperous English family called the Tuckers who had made a fortune in the cotton mills of Lancashire. They sold up just before the stock market crash in 1929 and settled into a fine eighteenth-century country house in rural northern Ireland. The Vermeer had been in the family since early Victorian times. Nobody was remotely interested in Vermeer for more than two and a half centuries after his death when he was rediscovered by a French art historian called Theophile Thoré who published a series of articles on the painter in 1866. And one of the Tucker sons had got his hands on this canvas, one of Vermeer's very finest, before the artist's star rose again, paying just a few hundred guilders for it at an Amsterdam auction house in about 1850. It wasn't even attributed to Vermeer then, but to a minor artist called Van Mieris.

"So it became the chief treasure of the Tucker's fine private collection, and eventually it came to the attention of the IRA who thought stolen paintings might be a nice little earner to run alongside their other scams like drug dealing and protection rackets. What brought it to their attention, because neither the house nor the collection were open to the general public and so weren't widely known, certainly not to thick paddies anyway, was a big feature on the "Hidden Treasures of Northern Ireland" in *Country Life*, which unwisely reported that the paintings at Friel Hall were insured for a total of £20 million, with the Vermeer accounting for about half of that.

"So the Fenians went in. This was in 1980. The Tuckers living there at the time, a brother and sister, were both unmarried and getting on in years. There were no direct descendants and both had made wills bequeathing the collection to the National Gallery in London after their deaths. Friel House had an extremely sophisticated security system, with a direct link to the local nick. But sophistication has its price as the IRA men realised. They'd cased the place thoroughly and also arranged an excellent hiding place for themselves in a ditch across the fields. Then one of them, a teenager, calmly went up to the house, smashed a window, and legged it. The alarms went off, the RUC arrived *en masse*, and once a thorough search of the house revealed nothing was missing and no one seemed to be about, they all went away again. A stone through the window just seemed like a childish act of vandalism, a dare among kids. Now the disadvantage of a sophisticated security system is that once it has gone off it needs to be reset. And the Tuckers were old, and had never learnt how to do it themselves, and the local police weren't fully genned up either. Ridiculously, everyone seems to have decided to wait until the morning before contacting the security firm, presumably on the principle that lightning never strikes twice. Though they did leave a constable on patrol outside.

"The boyos shot him without any trouble and then smashed their way through a window in the certain knowledge that no alarm bells would ring. They woke up the Tuckers, of course, but that didn't matter because they'd already cut the phone line. And when Mr Tucker, brave, foolish Mr Tucker, came down to investigate, they shot him. In the leg, not to kill, which was very decent of them, but he never recovered from the shock and died a month or so later. They helped themselves to seventeen paintings, the Vermeer of course, but also some minor Italian renaissance stuff, and some rather grim, semi-erotic eighteenth century paintings in the style of Boucher. And then the farce began. They'd got a colleague waiting in a van with a walkie-talkie a couple of miles down the road, and they told him to come and pick them and the paintings up. Which he did. But once they'd all got about half a mile away from the house, the van, which had been pinched only that afternoon, broke down. And they were left in the middle of the country, with paintings in heavy gilt frames, and, perhaps surprisingly under the circumstances, not a Stanley knife between them with which to cut out the canvases.

"So what did they do?" I asked.

"Well, they staggered on, junking stuff as they realised they couldn't carry it. They got rid of the second most valuable picture first, because it was the biggest and heaviest, a Salvator Rosa Crucifixion. Then the bad imitations of Boucher went, which was really quite discerning because they were worth very little. Then they dumped a rather good Matisse, presumably because they didn't think it looked either old or realistic enough to be valuable. Which left them with some third division Italian masters and the Vermeer. The police found all the abandoned paintings the following morning, lying in ditches. One of the IRA mob appeared to have put his boot through one of them out of sheer frustration."

"What happened next?"

"The Italian paintings fetched up in a dodgy London antique dealer's about six months later. The police raided his stockroom in connection with something entirely different. He was probably waiting until the heat had died down before disposing of them on the continent. The pictures weren't important enough to create much of a stir, and after a year or two he'd probably have got quite a useful price for them. But the Vermeer completely disappeared, though there have been various rumours about it."

"What I've never understood about the theft of really famous paintings is how anyone actually makes any money out of them," I said, taking a long swig of my deliciously strong, sweet, alcoholic coffee. "Unless of course there really are these mad multi-millionaire collectors who have secret art galleries full of masterpieces or simply get a kick out of knowing they've got some great lost work locked away in their safe."

"I think a lot of art thieves, many of whom are exceptionally thick like our friends in the IRA, hope they will run into a mythical Mr Big like that, prepared to shell out millions for a work he can gloat over in private. But mythical is just what such fanatical private collectors are. I had a long chat once with a very nice former copper who used to work for Scotland Yard's Arts and Antiques Squad. He'd been investigating stolen art for the past twenty years and hadn't only never come across such a collector, he'd never heard rumours that one existed."

"So what do the thieves do with the picture then?"

"What most of them hope, once they've found there's no one prepared to pay a fraction of its value, is that they'll be able to do a deal with the insurance company and claim the reward. Ten per cent of ten million sounds pretty good for a night's work. But in fact the reward on a 'priceless' work of art is a fraction of that – say £100,000. But even this isn't likely to prove realistic. Once word gets around that insurance companies are prepared to buy back stolen works of art, it would start a spate of thefts. The insurance companies might well send in a man pretending to negotiate. They night even get a plain clothes policeman like the chap I met to do it for them. But what they're really interested in is stringing the villains along, establishing identity and criminality and getting an arrest. Insurance companies simply can't be seen to do deals with villains. It's like paying ransoms to kidnappers – it's eventually going to cause far more trouble than it will solve. If someone's going to collect a reward for a stolen painting he's going to have to prove that he came across it legitimately – and that's extremely difficult."

"So what's the point of stealing a priceless or even an easily identifiable work of art at all?" I asked.

"Well, the villains have two main options," said Henry, helping himself to some of my tobacco and rolling himself a particularly emaciated cigarette. "If they can get a disreputable art dealer with fancy writing paper to authenticate it and give some kind of valuation, they might persuade a bank to accept it as security against a loan. Again, they'll only get a fraction of its insurance value, but it's ready cash. It's feared that a lot of great missing paintings are sitting in banks waiting to be reclaimed by criminals who have simply taken the money and run.

"The second is that the painting is used as a form of barter, or if you want to use more sophisticated language, a long bond. It must, after all, have some market value, even if there's no hope of realising the price for which it's insured. So our IRA men will perhaps go to a group of arms dealers and say how many Armalites and rocket launchers, how much Semtex, will you give us for this Vermeer? And they'll come to some kind of deal. Then the arms' dealers may decide they want to set up some kind of money laundering operation in Miami, and instead of buying into some gambling outfit where they can launder their cash, they'll offer the Vermeer instead. And then the man in Miami may decide he wants to start up a sideline as a coke dealer, and instead of paying for the supply, he'll hand over the painting. And so it goes on, round and round. And what's interesting is that this form of barter, which sounds almost medieval, is actually becoming more common. Because of the world-wide 'war' on drugs, which of course no government is going to win, banks have to be a lot more punctilious than they used to be about accepting suitcases full of used notes. They are legally obliged to report dubious cash transactions above a certain value. The great virtue with bartering a Vermeer is there's no money floating through various bank accounts that can be traced back to you. The danger, of course, is that you could be left with a painting you can't find anyone to take in exchange. Sometimes, the painting has travelled so far and gone through so many hands that it might just be possible for whoever is lumbered with it legitimately to claim the reward. But that's always going to be unlikely. Whoever fesses up is always going to be tarnished with criminality. So the more likely scenario is that at this stage the painting is deposited in a bank and is lost to the world for good."

"Understood," I said. "But how an earth does a respectable businessman like Sir Dominic enter the frame, as it were?"

"OK. I'll tell you what he told me, which I foolishly took as Gospel. In fact, it's a good deal murkier, as I subsequently discovered to my cost."

I eyed the Famous Grouse. I knew I didn't need it, I knew I ought to be keeping a clear head, but fascinated as I was by Henry's narrative, I was also stunned by Natasha's treachery. It had also occurred to me that tonight was the night Colin had been particularly anxious I was out of London. Part of me wanted to phone Kim, even though it was now 1a.m., to hear her sleepy voice and to be reassured that she was on her own. The other part of me didn't want to phone her at all. To hear her telling lies, to imagine Colin smirking silently in the background as she told them, would be unbearable. The fact that I actually had betrayed Kim, whereas her betrayal of me was pure hypothesis on my part, naturally didn't make any difference to the gnawing pangs of jealousy. It doesn't work like that. What I needed was another shot of anaesthetic and Henry took the hint.

"Thirsty work, listening, isn't it?" he said, with a barely detectable edge of contempt in his voice. It was the contempt of a man who can cheerfully take or leave a drink confronted with another who needs one desperately. He poured me a whopper, and a standard pub measure for himself. The point was taken. I was a hopeless drunk, he wasn't. And he was right, though that didn't make it any easier to bear. Mercifully, the drink did.

I took a large swig, conjured up images of Natasha and Kim in various states of sexual abandon, then had the double-whammy fantasy of them in various states of sexual abandon with each other. I took another hefty gulp, trying to subdue my rioting imagination into at least a state of armed truce, and told Henry to carry on.

"Well, after my impromptu visit to their wedding, which I'm sure you've heard about, I thought I'd seen the last of Sir Dominic and Natasha. In fact, they asked me round to dinner occasionally" – more lies from Natasha, I thought grimly – "and though I wouldn't say we became firm friends, I found the food, drink and surroundings entertaining, and Sir Dominic himself far from boring. Anyway, one night about three months ago, he took me to one side and said he'd heard I did a bit of dope smuggling. As indeed I do. Cannabis and uncut Ecstasy only, I hasten to add, which I hope we can both agree are more or less harmless, and on a modest rather than a Howard Marks scale. But when you're travelling with a reputable theatre company, with a lot of props baskets and easily devised caches in the sets, you'd be a bit of a fool not to."

"I heard that from the techie we met at the trade show who told us you were working for the Motherz," I said. "He recommended your stuff."

"It doesn't keep me in luxury, but it does keep me a damn sight better than the wages of a company manager with a subsidised touring theatre," he said. "Also, I admit, I enjoy the excitement of criminality while believing that the stuff I deal in is basically benign. Not like that stuff you're making yourself such a pig over, for instance."

"Point taken."

"I was however a bit alarmed that a pillar of the community like Sir Dominic should know about my activities, but it turned out that he'd only heard about it from an actor, a rather distinguished actor, whom I supply. There was no risk of a bust and Sir Dominic claimed to be 'relaxed' about soft drugs. He reminded me that back in the sixties, as well as helping his father run the family food firm, he'd also promoted a few rock festivals. And as a result of that he was asked to sign that famous letter to *The Times* calling for the legislation of cannabis. Daddy wasn't a bit pleased apparently, but Sir Dominic stuck to his guns, and a few years later, daddy died, and lucky Dommo copped the whole of HappiSnax. He said he needed to act straight after that, but insisted, implausibly in my view, that he was still a bit of an old hippie at heart.

"He asked if I'd got any dope on me and I nodded, and he said, 'Let's go into my study and have a reefer then.' It was sweet, no one calls then reefers any more, but it was his way of showing that he wasn't the boring respectable businessman he looked like. So, we sat in his study and shared a mild spliff, and he told me about this friend of his, his oldest friend whom he'd been to Wellington with, who ran a far from thriving antiques business.

"The friend, who moved in more raffish circles than Sir Dominic, had been offered the Vermeer by a drug dealer who had become hopelessly addicted to the stuff he was supposed to be peddling. His stash had been stolen and the Vermeer was his last asset, left over from the days when he was making a good living and not shooting most of it up his own arm. The guy just walked into the antique dealer's shop, and was apparently a pitiable figure to behold. Dominic's friend hadn't seen him for a couple of years and was shattered by his decline from the sophisticated former public schoolboy with plenty of money and a more or less controllable habit to this pathetic wreck. The junkie wanted £30,000 for the painting, which he said would enable him to pay off his debts and re-establish himself as a dealer. Sir Dominic's friend thought it was more likely to kill him with an overdose, but he wasn't over-fussy. He wanted that Vermeer.

"Just thirty grand for a painting like that?"

"I know, it's incredible, isn't it? But it's not so extraordinary when you realise it was in the hands of a junkie doing cold turkey. The trouble was, the antiques' dealer hadn't got anything like thirty grand in liquid assets himself, so he phoned Sir Dominic. And Sir Dominic came straight over, handed over the cash in a back room, and the antiques' dealer paid off the desperate junkie and took over the Vermeer."

"Stop me if I'm wrong," I said. "But it now sounds as though the Vermeer has reached the position where its possessor can duly explain how he came by it and collar the reward. Sir Dominic, or if he was feeling generous, his friend, could simply hand it over to the police and await the thanks of a grateful nation, not to mention a cash bonus."

"Probably yes. There would undoubtedly have been some awkwardness though. The police wouldn't have been pleased about them giving thirty grand in cash to a known drug dealer. They'd have said you should have called us at once so we could have collared him as well as the Vermeer. But the antiques' dealer didn't want to shop a friend, pathetic and almost certainly doomed though that friend was."

"Yes, but if someone of Sir Dominic's stature and gleaming reputation handed it over, and said he didn't want to go into too much detail about how he had acquired it, they would surely have taken his word that he was acting in good faith; that the important thing was that a lost masterpiece had been saved from criminal hands and could at last be seen in a public gallery."

"More or less exactly what I said to Sir Dominic. To which he offered the surprising reply: 'But you, more than anyone, must understand the thrill of a covert operation, of breaking the law and getting away with it.' I said of course I did, but I hadn't got nearly as much to lose as he had.

"'The more you've got to lose, the more exciting it is,' he said, "as any gambler will tell you. I've played straight for forty years now, and I'm on the point of selling up anyway since I haven't got any children to pass the firm onto. For once in my life, I want to have a bit of fun."

Henry said he'd believed him, particularly when Sir Dominic had explained what the "bit of fun" would involve.

"The antiques' dealer had been offered a miscellaneous collection of Indian *objets d'art.* There were miniature paintings, ancient books, some beautiful silverware. It wasn't stolen stuff, the guy who was disposing of them was a wealthy Indian collector who was selling up. But he knew he could get a much better price in Europe, the only problem being that the Indian Government wouldn't grant export licenses on most of the collection.

"The antiques' dealer, realising that Sir Dominic had already put at least a foot into murky waters, suggested that he should loan him the £200,000 needed to buy the collection, with the Vermeer as security, and Sir Dominic liked the idea. In fact, he liked the idea of owning a lot of the treasures for himself. He told me that once he'd sold the firm, he planned to start collecting really seriously.

"'But how are we going to get the stuff out?' Dommo asked his friend, and the friend, who sounded like a complete wally, said he hadn't given it much thought since he had never believed he'd find the money to buy the collection himself. And that's when Dommo thought of me. I'd told him about this tour of Pakistan and India months earlier and he'd promptly offered to sponsor it and put twenty grand in. Then he'd met the actor, at yet another of his artistically philanthropic occasions, and found out about my little sideline.

"Anyway, I hadn't got any smuggling firmly set up for that tour, and the idea of working with Sir Dominic Gilbert-Smith tickled me. And art would make a change from drugs. It was all very straightforward, though it took some time for the details to fall into place. But the end result was that Dominic and his antiques' dealer between them arranged for the stuff to be delivered to the theatre on the last night of the tour, in Bombay, when we'd be striking the set and packing up the props and scenery.

"In fact, it was all exactly as if I'd been taking dope out. I always arrange for the delivery to coincide with the final get-out. I've got a couple of mates who are in on the racket who I always take with me on these tours as ASMs. At two in the morning, there's never anyone in authority around, apart from me, and we usually do the get-out with local labour who can easily be bribed to turn a blind eye if necessary. But, in fact, I usually export such small amounts – 100 kilos max – that it's just a question of placing the stuff in these false-bottomed props' baskets I've had made, plus the old-fashioned dimmer board I take, allegedly as back up in case the more sophisticated one fails, but which is actually completely empty inside apart from a couple of lead weights to give the impression it's a piece of working equipment. You have to make sure that the dope's made smell-proof by wrapping it in silver paper, then dipping it all in molten wax, but I always insist on the suppliers doing that in advance.

"We realised that some of the bulkier items of silverware might have to be left behind but reckoned there would be plenty of space for the miniatures, the books, and some of the smaller silver items as well as some carved jade. It seemed like a perfectly straightforward job.

"So we took a small-scale, undercast and entirely pedestrian production of *Romeo and Juliet* round three cities in Pakistan and another four in India, and on the last night, when I was called to the stage door at 1a.m., everything seemed to be going according to plan. But it wasn't. I'd been expecting a couple of the servants and perhaps the collector himself in one of those marvellous old Indian cars. What I got was a quartet of the meanest looking dacoits you could ever hope to come across."

"Dacoits?" I asked.

"The Indian term for bandits or anyone involved in organised crime. The papers are always full of the exploits of the dacoits. Anyway, my dacoits had arrived in a transit van and it sure as hell didn't contain antiques. It contained about 200 kilos of pure heroin, wrapped in plastic and then rather ineffectually disguised in old rice sacks. Heroin is flooding into India at the moment, over the border from Burma where it's one of the major props of the economy, and more or less tolerated by a corrupt, indeed, vicious regime. But the infection is spreading to India, a country I've always loved. Law and order has more or less broken down in the border town where most of the stuff arrives. Thanks to massive bribery and corruption, there are scarcely any checks on vehicles coming in from Burma. The stuff is incredibly cheap by western standards, and a tragically high percentage of the local population, particularly the younger men, are now addicted. I realised that it must have taken my dacoits a lot of effort – and no small risk – to drive their cargo right across the subcontinent and, when I said there had been a mistake, and I was expecting antiques, they began to get very excited indeed.

"I said there was no way I was taking the stuff and at that point a gun was produced. Needless to say, I had an immediate change of heart.

"'Good,' said the leader, 'very good. The sahib in England said you'd change your mind.' I had an uncomfortable feeling I knew who that sahib was. Anyway, I sent the local labour off on a break, and told my own two to piss off for a while too. I said something unusual had turned up, and I think they guessed it must have been harder drugs and that I didn't want them to get involved in a much more serious and morally dubious crime.

"They were very loyal. They asked if there was anything they could do to help and I mentioned the gun. I added that if there was a bust, I'd be bringing someone big down with me, and then I think they thought I'd planned it all anyway and gave me a terrible look of disappointment as though I'd betrayed them. They'd never grass on me, but I also guessed they wouldn't want to pull any more scams with me in future. They were amiable, harmless potheads and the last thing they wanted to be involved with was a scene involving heroin and guns.

"Anyway, the dacoits and I unloaded the heroin. The stage door man had disappeared as soon as he saw what kind of men they were, and we managed to stash about three quarters of the junk in the props basket and the old dimmer board. They weren't altogether disappointed that we couldn't stash it all.

Presumably, they'd already been paid for the full consignment, and wouldn't have too much trouble in disposing of the rest for an extra profit.

"I made sure everything was neatly hidden and filled in all the bills of loading for the customs men the next day. And then the local crew and my men returned and we got everything loaded into the lorry to go down to the docks. I had to hang around for a couple of days to see it all safely on board and go through the customs' formalities – that was always part of my job – and then I flew home.

"I wasn't afraid of the heroin being discovered. The dope had never been busted. If the paperwork looks correct, and the stuff is going out as part of a bona fide theatrical tour, the customs men aren't exactly going to start smelling rats. I toyed quite seriously with the idea of tipping them off in this case, but realised I was in it up to my ears, and there would probably also be questions about my earlier exploits. Also, I wanted to get Sir Dominic by the short and curlies. Though there was just a faint chance that he too had been double-crossed by his antiques-dealing friend. So when I got home, I phoned him and asked if we could meet, and he said, 'in the office, I don't like to trouble Natasha with my extracurricular activities.'

"So I went to his office in the City and found myself warmly welcomed, indeed congratulated.

"'I gather you coped very well with the um, sudden change of plan,' he said. 'The deal only came together while you were out on tour, and although there wouldn't have been any real problem in telling you of the different nature of the cargo, I thought it better to leave you in innocence until the fatal hour arrived.'

"'In case I objected,' I said. 'You knew I never dealt in hard drugs'."

"'Partly because I thought you might be sentimental about heroin, partly because I wanted to see how you reacted to pressure and the unexpected. You've fully justified all my hopes in you. Thank you, dear boy."'

"I was within an ace of saying, 'don't you dear boy me' and climbing onto my high horse, when I realised I would have a far better chance of getting even and bringing him down if I pretended to be chuffed by his flattery and eager to be employed again.

"'It was a nasty shock,' I said. 'And I'd appreciate it if you kept me fully informed in future. If we're to have a future.'

"'I do so hope we are,' Sir Dominic said. 'By the way, the Indian antiques idea was entirely bona fide, and I think we might think about re-activating it next year. I've paid the collector a substantial sum in advance and he promises he won't try to find another buyer for at least two years. I'm already talking to Trevor about the possibility of a sub-continental tour.'

"'Trevor who?'

"'Nunn, of course. He takes over the National in the summer as you know. I'm sure he could use a good company manager for international touring product."

"Great," I said.

"'Yes, it was a shame my old schoolfriend got so greedy. The thought of waiting another year for all those lovely goodies almost unhinged him. He started getting very hysterical and I thought there was a severe danger of indiscretion."

At this point, said Henry, Sir Dominic handed him a small cutting from a local newspaper. Police were seeking witnesses to the brutal mugging of the sixty-three-year-old antiques' dealer, Angus MacBride, who had been attacked outside his home in Greenwich. He was now in hospital with severe internal injuries. Condition: "Serious but stable," reported the *South London Press.*

'I think he's calmed down a bit now,' Sir Dominic had observed chillingly.

"'I take your point,' Henry had replied.

"This was all a month or so ago," Henry continued. "A few days later, the scenery and the drugs were due to arrive at Southampton on a Saturday night. I saw all the stuff through customs without a hitch and Lucketts, the theatrical transporters, delivered it to the Shakespeare for Everyone scenery and costume store in Clapham on Sunday morning. I asked Sir Dominic what he wanted me to do with the heroin. He said he'd like to see the set-up in Clapham because it might prove useful on future occasions, and he'd bring a couple of his associates along. So we arranged to meet there at two o'clock in the afternoon.

"Sir Dominic turned up with two awesomely tough looking men in their early thirties, whom he introduced as Eric and Ernie. 'Just my little joke, dear boy,' he sniggered. They were clearly his tame thugs employed on the less legitimate side of his business, and they both called him 'sir' as if he was their commanding officer. 'Splendid chaps,' he told me, 'ten years apiece in the SAS. I can't think why my old friend Angus took against them so.' I was being warned that if I ever crossed Sir Dominic, I could look forward to the attentions of Eric and Ernie myself and the thought wasn't a happy one. Especially since I had an associate with me too, installed upstairs with a camera with a telephoto lens."

Henry explained that his covert photographer, Terry, was also the manager of the scenery dock. Naturally, Henry had had to bring him in on his earlier smuggling operations, since he was in charge of unloading sets, props and costumes. When Henry explained the circumstances under which he had been forced to bring in heroin, Terry agreed to take the pictures.

Before Sir Dominic arrived, they took pictures of the heroin, in and out of the rice sacks. They kept a sample of the heroin itself, and a piece of the sacking bearing a distinctive Gujarati logo. And when Eric and Ernie arrived, and started loading the scag into the back of a van in the car park, under the benign supervision of Sir Dominic, Terry hid himself in his dusty first floor office and took photographs of the whole operation.

"Have you got those pictures with you?" I asked. Henry shook his head.

"It doesn't do to keep all your eggs in one basket. Terry's keeping the heroin pictures. If Eric and Ernie were to get me, and the Vermeer and the pictures of the Gilbert-Smiths with the Vermeer, they still haven't got the most damning evidence of Sir Dominic's criminality. Better still, they don't even know it exists. Terry has strict instructions about what to do with the photos if I go missing. Plus a long, signed statement from me telling the whole story."

"But why not just go to the police now?" I asked. "You don't have to tell them about your earlier smuggling exploits, and if Sir Dominic starts accusing you, they're not going to take his word too seriously after the evidence you've got. And how can they prove it anyway?"

"I want to make the bastard suffer. Like those addicts suffer. I want him to be in a nightmare of uncertainty, never sure when his world's going to come crashing down around him. I'm using the Vermeer first. The evidence about the heroin will come later. That's why I went to Nicholas with it. So Sir Dominic would learn that I'd changed sides and was now his active opponent. He knows I've got the Vermeer. He knows I know a lot about him. He can't be certain exactly if or when I'm going to talk."

"You're taking a terrible risk," I said. "If Eric and Ernie find you your victory might prove pyrrhic, even posthumous"

"Exciting though, isn't it?" he said, giving me one of his brightest smiles. "My God, I know I'm living at the moment."

"One thing puzzles me," I said. "How did you steal the Vermeer? I don't know anything about alarm systems but I'd guess the Gilbert-Smiths' place must be like Fort Knox."

"I was hoping it might be possible to repeat the IRA trick. Stone through the window, hang around in Belgrave Square, then in through the back once the alarm had been shut down. But security systems are more sophisticated these days, and easier to reboot, and in that house the windows are made of reinforced glass. It had to be an inside job. So I made a point of getting to know Meadows."

"Meadows?"

"The butler. Not the one you'll have met, if they've got a permanent one at all at the moment."

"They've got one all right," I said, remembering the way I'd been patronised by Clarence. "Supercilious jerk."

"Meadows was all right. I'd got to know him a bit when I went round for dinner, and once I'd decided to pinch the Vermeer, I kept a discreet watch on the place and fell in alongside him when he went shopping one morning. We had a couple of pints together. I told him a little about his employer and I also gave him £50,000 which represented, it transpired, four years' wages to him. The very rich are often very mean. That of course is why they're very rich. It didn't hurt since Sir Dominic had given me £100,000 for the heroin job. At that stage, of course, I had no idea where he was keeping the picture. So I asked Meadows to keep an ear open, and to let me know if he heard anything about it. I also asked him who set the alarm system. Sir Dominic, apparently when he was at home. But Natasha had never got the hang of it and so Meadows was entrusted with the job when Dommo was away. The main thing was, Meadows knew how it worked. We agreed that if the Vermeer came into the house, he'd let me know. The plan was that he'd let me in at an agreed time, and shut down the system. I'd tie him up and walk off with the picture. When the theft and the trussed-up Meadows were discovered, he'd claim he'd answered the front door bell and been ordered to turn off the entire alarm system at gunpoint. They've got infra-red sensors all over the place. We reckoned that if Natasha and Sir Dominic were asleep they wouldn't be certain whether the bell had rung or not. Apparently, Sir Dominic sleeps like the dead and Natasha takes sleeping pills. To make it look more realistic Meadows suggested that I should knock him about a bit. I'd promised him another fifty grand if the theft went off successfully and he seemed to think it was a reasonable price to pay.

"I didn't hear anything for a week, and then Natasha asked me round for dinner on Sunday night. I'd only ever given them my mobile number, and naturally I'd never told them I was doing this job with the Motherz. It had occurred to me that being on the move with a pop band, an area Sir Dominic didn't know I worked in, was as good a way as any of remaining elusive. Natasha mentioned 'a rather special painting'. It was the night we put the Vermeer in its frame, the night before they planned to hold a press conference. I'm still not sure how much Natasha knew about how her husband had acquired the painting, or about any of his other activities. To judge by the little he said at dinner, I'd guess not much. The line for the press conference, and the line I think Natasha believed to be true, was that the painting had been given to him by his old friend the antiques' dealer, MacBride, for safekeeping. Sir Dominic knew that MacBride had come by the painting in suspicious circumstances but nothing more. And he had decided to pay MacBride a 'substantial sum' for it, believing it was important to rescue it for the nation. The subsequent brutal beating of MacBride indicated that hard-core criminal elements were also searching for the Vermeer. Sir Dominic planned to say that he feared he might be at risk himself and it was time that the nation took possession of its lost treasure. It was the sort of story that both the tabloids and the broadsheets would love, and Sir Dominic could hardly contain his glee at all the respectability and favourable publicity it would bring him. Best of all, he knew that MacBride, who must have known who'd had him beaten him up, would keep quiet for fear of a bedside visit from Eric and Ernie.

"Anyway, as I made my farewells that evening, and said how much I was looking forward to reading about the following day's press conference, Meadows came up and helped me on with my coat. I whispered two o'clock and he nodded. It was our last chance. I returned bang on 2a.m., just as Meadows opened the front door. He had the Vermeer, wrapped in brown wrapping paper, and he came out onto the porch with it. He said he'd decided to jump ship. Perhaps he didn't fancy being beaten up when it came to the crunch, perhaps he didn't think his employer would believe his story, and was wondering how he would stand up to interrogation by the police. I was pleased. It would be useful to have someone as resourceful as him around to watch my back and keep an eye on the Vermeer when I was with the Motherz. So I gave him the other £50,000 and asked if he'd like to join me for a while. He instantly agreed.

"We drove up to Middlesbrough that night to rejoin the band, and then last Wednesday I went to see Nicholas, as you know. I realised that Sir Dominic might just think he had a disloyal servant on his hands. I wanted him to know I had the picture, and to raise the stakes a bit."

"Something rattled you, though. You got an urgent phone call and looked panicked," I said.

"Mere subterfuge on my part. I didn't want to go into long explanations with Nicholas, so I'd arranged that Meadows would give me a ring a few minutes after I went in. I didn't think it would do any harm either for Sir Dominic to think things were hot at my end, with the possibility that the police were on my trail, raising the possibility for him of the long conversation I might have with the filth if they arrested me with the painting. So when the phone rang, I feigned panic, hid in a neighbouring front garden and, when Nicholas had gone back inside, walked round the block to where Meadows was waiting for me. And after that we drove back up north to rejoin the Motherz until you enterprisingly caught up with me. As, of course, I hoped you would."

"But what now?" I asked, helping myself to another Grouse I didn't need. "He can't go to the police to report the theft of the Vermeer, because it will lead to all kinds of questions about how he came by it in the first place, and he knows that you possess even more incriminating information about him. By the same token, you can't go to the police without incriminating yourself. It's your word against his, and on balance, it's his word that's likely to be believed, at least initially."

"I've got it all sorted out. On Christmas Eve, Sir Dominic's the host and chief sponsor of some ghastly night of revels at Hampton Court. He was telling me about it at that last dinner. I'm going to offer him a deal, in writing, before then. I'll hand back the Vermeer and all the photographic evidence on condition that he gives me £1 million in cash. It's just a question of exchanging two suitcases which ought to be easily arranged. And because there will be so many people around, Eric and Ernie will find it very hard to intervene. And then I'm going to skip the country. I've had enough of Britain in any case."

I felt a sick sense of disappointment. "But that means you are making a juicy profit from smuggling heroin, and he's going to get away with it unpunished."

"Not at all. It's possible to make copies of photographs, and I'm going to give you a set of both the Vermeer polaroids and the heroin pictures. I'll do the switch early in the evening and get a taxi to Heathrow. Towards the end of the evening, you call the police, give them the photographs, and Sir Dominic gets arrested with a very hot painting no one knows he's got. He can bluster as much as he likes about planning to give it back to the nation, but since he hasn't uttered a public word about it, it's not going to seem very plausible. The drugs' photo's should then sink him good and proper."

"But you're still leaving the country with a million pounds."

"Except I won't be. I'll be dropping it off at a drug rehabilitation centre in Kingston. Where Rose works, as a matter of fact. I'm going to let her distribute the money, bit by bit, as she sees fit. The only proviso being that it must all go to help drug addicts."

"This is beginning to sound like Robin Hood," I said. "When he's arrested, Sir Dominic's bound to say he's given you a million."

"You're missing the point, Will. I won't be there. I've always known that I might have to leave the country in a hurry one day, and I've made my plans accordingly. I've got somewhere to live, and the resources to live there, in a place where I'm most unlikely to be found. And even if I am found, it won't matter because I've naturally chosen a destination without any extradition treaty with the UK."

"Where?"

"I trust you, Will, but I don't trust you that much."

"Why should I trust you, then, about not legging it with the million? If you're planning to disappear for good, it's a hell of a sum to leave behind."

"Listen, Will, there's a very good reason why I've never smuggled hard drugs, and why I'm absolutely determined to screw Sir Dominic good and proper. Rose was an addict for years."

I thought of Rose, sweet, sexy Rose and our first exhilarating minutes under the rhododendrons in Oxshott Woods. I remembered my painful parting from her, and all the old guilt flooded back.

"When?" I asked. "Why?"

"You're not going to like this, Will. Do you really want me to tell you?"

I nodded, blankly, a feeling of sick premonition in my stomach, and had another large Grouse.

"You and she split up at the end of that summer didn't you?" he asked. I nodded glumly.

"She never explained the circumstances. All she said was that you'd betrayed her and her life wasn't worth living any more. She cried, on and off, for a week in her bedroom, and when she finally emerged she was a different girl. Harder. Cynical. Unreachable. My parents thought it would quickly wear off, but it didn't. She'd always been bright at school and happy, but she started bunking off and fell in with what my mother called a 'bad crowd'. She sniffed a lot of glue. She'd stay out all night and didn't give a toss about the worry she was causing my parents. One of the reasons I went to Hong Kong was that I couldn't bear to see what was happening to her. I couldn't help her. I think she hated me because it was me who'd introduced you to her."

"Christ," I said. "I'm sorry."

"I don't think you should blame yourself, Will," he said. "Teenage affairs end. It doesn't usually lead to drug addiction. Hearts get broken. Usually, they heal. But by the time Rose was eighteen she was a junkie. My parents kept sending her to expensive rehab places, and she'd come back clean, and a few weeks or months later, she'd be back on the needle again. That's why I honestly don't think you should blame yourself. The smallest difficulty would knock her off course. She was naturally susceptible. I think the continual heartbreak of it all killed my mother. My father soldiered grimly on, and then he got lung cancer and died very quickly. So I came home, as I should have done years earlier, and took charge of Rose. She was living in a squat, and I got her out and into hospital. And then we lived together for a year and I watched her like a hawk, and she began to live again. She started as a patient at this rehab centre and now she runs it. She's the greatest woman I know. And the sweetest natured."

I remembered the urgency with which Rose had bummed large brandy and Babychams at the Foley Arms. I thought about the way Henry discouraged her from drinking and smoking, had given her the smallest line of speed. She had an addictive personality and he'd known, or guessed it, even then. On our relatively rare outings alone together, we'd almost always got half-pissed. Which had naturally suited me fine. When we'd gone out as a group, she was always sneaking extra drinks when she thought her brother wasn't looking. It had usually been me that bought them. I had been her first supplier.

"I'm sorry, Henry," I said again.

He came over and hugged me. "Listen, Will, like I keep saying, it would have happened anyway. I'm far more to blame for scuttling off to Hong Kong at the first sign of trouble. And she'd never have ended up doing the wonderful work she does now if it hadn't been for the fact that she was once an addict herself. So no guilt trip, eh? There was a kind of pattern to all this, and the negative has finally become positive. And it will become even more positive with an extra million quid."

I nodded but I knew I was going to be haunted by Rose until I'd seen her, spoken to her, received some kind of absolution. If she was prepared to offer it to me.

Henry looked at his watch. "Listen, Will, I've got a lot to sort out. And just in case Eric and Ernie catch up with me, I think it would be an excellent idea if you took charge of the Vermeer."

"You what?"

"I realise I'm asking a lot, and I realise that now Natasha knows you've seen me you could be in some danger yourself. But I think we can minimise that danger and make absolutely sure the painting is kept safe till Christmas Eve."

"How?" I asked bleakly.

"Catch the first train from here tomorrow morning. It leaves at 7.13. When you get to Euston, check the suitcase in at the left luggage office. Then don't go home. Have you anywhere you can stay that Natasha doesn't know about?"

I thought of Auntie May's house, my childhood home, in Thames Ditton. A house now empty because Auntie May was having a month-long Christmas break with her best friend in Tenerife, a break she had taken with considerable reluctance when she realised I would be on my own for Christmas. I'd promised I'd be OK, insisted that she should go. I didn't want my break-up with Kim to start spoiling other lives.

"I've got a place I can go," I said. "But I've got to go into work on Monday and Tuesday." I explained how insecure my job prospects were at *Theatre World*.

"Where are you planning to stay?" he asked. "Don't give me a specific address in case Eric and Ernie are in a position to put any kind of pressure on me. I'm not sure how well I'd stand up to torture."

I shuddered. I knew damn well how I'd stand up to it. I'd start squealing at the first hint of pain.

"It's in the suburbs," I said. "Served by a regular service to one of the main London stations."

"Ideal," he said. "Catch the train to London each morning like a good commuter, and take public transport to the office. No, better still, a taxi that will deliver you to the door. And get a taxi to take you back to the station each evening. Make sure you're not being followed. When you finish on Christmas Eve, get a taxi to Euston, pick up the painting, and then get another to take you all the way to Hampton Court. The revels start at 8p.m. Could you make it to the Mitre next to Hampton Court Bridge by seven?" I nodded.

"I'll see you there then. A double Grouse will be waiting your pleasure."

"Right," I said, and felt weak at the prospect of so much responsibility.

"You'll be fine, Will. Have faith in yourself. Friendship and wild times, remember? We're going to screw the bastard."

He got up to go, handed me the suitcase with the Vermeer in it, then fumbled in his hold-all for an alarm clock. "Just in case you oversleep," he said cheerfully.

"There's just one other thing, Henry," I said. "Either take that bottle of Scotch with you or pour it down the sink. I'm going to need a clear head."

"Good man," he said, and emptied the Grouse bottle into the basin. He gave me one of his big hugs, jabbed my beer-gut playfully, and disappeared through the door. I got up out of my chair and made another cup of coffee with the electric kettle. I was relieved to see there were six sachets of coffee and plenty of sugar. I was going to need them. I longed for sleep but after the amount I'd drunk that night I wasn't confident even the alarm clock would wake me from the forgetful oblivion I craved. It was 1.30 in the morning. I had almost six hours to wait for the train. It felt like the loneliest night I'd ever spent. It was luxury compared to what followed.

# 6: Sunday 22 December; Monday 23 December 1996

*O that 'twere possible*
*After long grief and pain*
*To find the arms of my true love*
*Round me once again!*

*Maud*, Alfred, Lord Tennyson

It was freezing cold on Chester Station and after staying up all night with a skinful of booze, too many cups of coffee and a confused, guilt-tormented mind, I felt close to tears as the wind whipped through my sports jacket and cotton shirt. As so often when you've got really serious things to worry about, my brain kept lurching towards trivial anxieties that momentarily assumed a horrible importance. How was I going to write the story about the tradeshow when my notebook and all the press releases were in Natasha's car? What was Colin going to say when he discovered I'd lost the Birthday Bible? I was going to be lucky if I still had a job by Christmas. But then again, if Sir Dominic and his thugs found me with the Vermeer, I might not be alive by Christmas.

The train finally arrived, and as we pulled out of the station, the senior conductor (has anyone ever clapped eyes on the junior conductor?) announced, with sadistic glee, that there would be no buffet service. I was dehydrated and had a throbbing headache, and opposite a middle-aged couple were pouring cups of tea from their Thermos. I was sure I was going to burst out screaming with sheer misery and fear long before we reached London, but after a night without sleep, and very little the night before, my weary body and over-active mind at last submitted to exhaustion and I fell into a deep, dreamless sleep. I woke up with a start, just as the train was drawing into Euston and for a few delicious seconds, all I was worried about was my hangover. Then all the events of the last few days came flooding back with an intensity that made me feel physically sick.

I picked up the suitcase that I had kept clamped between my legs even as I slept, and tottered out onto the platform. All I had to do now was check in the suitcase at the left-luggage office, purchase and consume a litre of mineral water and three Neurofen, and get myself down to Auntie May's house. It wasn't to be. A few yards short of the concourse two thirtyish men in suits approached me.

"Mr Will Benson?" one of them asked pleasantly enough, and I said, 'Yes.' Except it came out like a squeak.

"Inspector Owen, CID. And this is my colleague, Sergeant Crompton. We'd like to take you to the station for a few questions, if you'd be so kind. It's in connection with a stolen painting."

My first reaction was one of panic, and I seriously contemplated a bolt across the concourse, but both men were clearly fitter and faster than me. My second reaction was a kind of relief. They'd find the Vermeer, of course. They'd ask a lot of awkward questions. I would give the name of Sir Dominic Gilbert-Smith. I'd tell them how I had come by the painting without revealing Henry's identity. Unlike many, I believed that the British police, or most of them, were basically decent. They wouldn't, couldn't, beat it out of me. There were tape recorders in interview rooms these days. The whole ridiculous caper was now in hands more competent than mine. The grown-ups were in charge. It was a relief to be caught.

"OK," I said, and walked with them down to the underground car park.

We stopped by a battered Ford Capri, which ought to have given me pause for thought. It didn't.

Crompton got into the driving seat, and Owen opened the back door and climbed in after me. "Put out your hands," he said, producing a pair of handcuffs.

"There's no need," I said. "I'm coming quietly, as you can see."

"Just put out your hands," he said, so I did. The handcuffs snapped into place. Owen then produced a large roll of white masking tape.

"What the fuck's that for?" I said. I soon found out. Owen got my head in an arm-lock and wound several yards of the stuff round my face, completely covering my mouth. He then punched me in the solar plexus and shoved me roughly to the floor. I was splayed out across the whole width of the car, desperately trying to get air into my lungs through a blocked up nose. Owen had his feet very firmly on the small of my back, and as the car moved off, he gave me a couple of little stamps in the small of my back. They hurt. A lot. "If you even think about struggling, or raising you head, I'll break your spine," he said. And then, very quietly, he began to sing 'Bring Me Sunshine' under his breath. I knew who they were then and as terror got me in its grip, I fouled my trousers.

"Horrible pong in here, Eric," said the driver a couple of minutes later.

"I think he's shit himself, Ernie," said the man with his feet on my back. "They do that sometimes, don't they?" He wound down the window, then jabbed me in the small of the back again, more viciously than ever.

"Thanks to your defective sphincter, we're all going to have to freeze. I won't forget that in a hurry, will I, Ernie?"

"Of course you won't, Eric."

I wanted that car journey to last for ever. I was terrified, shitty, aching, humiliated, but it was probably paradise compared to what was to follow. After thirty minutes or so we appeared to have reached journey's end. The car drew to a halt and both men climbed out. I was told to stay where I was. After a few seconds' silence, Ernie announced that the coast was clear and I was dragged out of the car. I briefly registered a suburban front garden, a high privet hedge blocking the view from the road, a small 1930s house not dissimilar to Auntie May's. But I was bundled through the front door in seconds, though not before noticing a small brass plate on the door. 'Alfred Mackintosh', it said. 'Dentist'. Sweet Jesus Christ.

They took off my handcuffs and my jacket, but both men kept a firm hold on me. One of my arms was forced upwards behind my back and I was marched across the hall which served as a waiting room and pushed into the lavatory.

"Clean yourself up in there and come out without your clothes on," said Ernie. "We don't want to mess up Mr Mackintosh's nice leather chair."

I took off my shoes and socks, my stinking cords and pants, and my shirt, grateful that my tormentors had spared me the shame of a public strip. I looked at myself in the mirror, my lower face grotesquely bound, my eyes bloodshot, tiny and terrified. There was a hand towel by the basin, and I soaked it and cleaned myself. I couldn't stop my hands from shaking and I was terrified of being sick and choking on my own vomit.

I stumbled out of the loo, and Eric and Ernie looked at me and laughed.

"Fat, isn't he?" said Ernie, scarcely able to contain his mirth.

"Yeah, and such a tiny little willie."

"Well, he's frightened, Eric. Some people really get worked up about a visit to the dentist's. Fear does that to you."

I stared hard at them both, memorising their faces. They didn't actually look anything like Morecambe and Wise, though Ernie was shorter than Eric and had a fuller head of hair. They looked like the kind of scary squaddies you sometimes saw on trains, or bouncers outside a nightclub. Bland, cleanly shaven faces that looked as though they never smiled, only snarled or laughed with derision.

"Right, well, I think we'd better get you into the surgery, Will," said Ernie. He got my arm behind my back, in its now familiar place, and pushed me across the waiting room. There were old copies of *Country Life*, *Hello!* and *The Lady* on the table in the middle of the room. Reminders of a normal world outside that had ceased to exist for me.

When I saw the dentists chair, a long, tan leather recliner, and the drill, and the little silver dish full of surgical instruments, I flipped. I struggled desperately, but it was completely useless. Ernie increased the pressure on my arm to within an ace of breaking point, Eric gave me another of his speciality punches to the stomach, and I ended up on the floor again. They lifted me onto the chair, and though I kicked and punched and wriggled, it was futile. My wrists were bound to the arms of the chair with rope, my legs strapped tightly to the end of the leather recliner with Ernie's long leather belt.

Eric playfully slapped both my cheeks, just like his namesake. "See you later, sunshine," he said.

And then they left and I sweated with fear. There was a clock on the wall, and I watched the minute hand drag its way one and a half times round the dial. With each minute that passed, the fear grew more intense, not less. Perhaps they were waiting for the dentist to arrive. I tried to concentrate on the tank of tropical fish on a table, I tried to concentrate on the neatly kept suburban garden through the windows, I tried repeating my Transcendental Meditation mantra. But all I could think of was my white, out of condition body, and my face, and my mouth, and all the terrible things that could be done to them with the standard equipment in a dentist's surgery. My heart was beating incredibly fast and I found myself longing for a coronary. "Please God, let me die before it starts," I prayed. "Please God, just let me fucking die before the pain gets too bad."

At 1p.m., bang on the dot, the door burst open, and there were Eric and Ernie, both dressed in green, loose-fitting surgical outfits and those caps that seem to be made out of Jay cloths. Ernie had a gauze mask over his face, Eric was wearing a plastic cup on his nose. "I sit at my piano," he sang, imitating Eric Morecambe imitating Jimmy Durante, his hands playing up and down my body as though I were a piano. Meanwhile, Ernie had forced my head up and was viciously unwinding the masking tape. I screamed as it took away the hairs on the back of my neck.

"That's just for starters," he said. "Relax."

"What do you want to know?" I screamed. "I'll talk, I'll talk." As well as panicking, I'd done some thinking. I would tell them exactly how I'd found Henry. I'd tell them everything he had told me. I would tell them about the proposed swap of painting and money at Hampton Court on Christmas Eve. The only thing I would try not tell them about was the covert pictures Henry had taken of Sir Dominic with the heroin. That was the only thing they, or their boss, didn't know, or wouldn't know soon anyway.

"Talk?" said Ernie, as if he was unfamiliar with the word. "I don't think we've got much to talk about have we, Eric?"

"Not yet, anyway," said Eric. "Sir Dominic's instructions, and correct me if I'm wrong, Ernie, is that we should give Mr Benson a thorough check-up first. Sir Dominic was worried about Will's teeth. He thought he might need a couple of fillings. Perhaps even an extraction."

"Have we got the gas for the extraction?" asked Ernie.

Eric slapped his brow in mock horror. "Clean forgot to order a new canister. We'll have to make do without."

Ernie went and switched on the machinery. Then he turned on the rectangular, reflecting light that would illuminate my mouth. I could bite, I thought, I could bite.

"Now which drill shall I use?" pondered Eric. "There's the slow growly one or the fast, high-pitched screamy one?"

"I'd try the growler," said Ernie.

Eric started the drill. "Open wide," said Eric. "There's a good chap." I kept my mouth clamped shut.

"This drill can go straight through teeth and metal fillings," said Eric. "Just think of the mess it might make of your face."

"Or of your willie, Willy," sniggered Ernie, like a five-year-old. "Does the drill reach that far, Eric?" Eric moved the drill to within an inch of my shrivelled member. I could feel the breeze created by the rotating bit.

"No problem." he said. "I'd open wide if I were you."

I opened my mouth, and a lump of rubber was jammed between my teeth on one side, forcing my jaws uncomfortably wide apart. I couldn't bite. Eric went to work with the nasty growly drill. There was the familiar smell of burning tooth, and then he got close to the nerve and the world just became a great shriek of agony. As a child, I'd had a dentist who didn't believe in injections for young children, and at first the pain was familiar, recognisable, just about bearable. But in childhood the horror had lasted five seconds at most. This went on and on, the pain intensifying as Eric got ever closer to the nerve. After thirty seconds, it was unbearable. Why didn't I pass out, how much pain could the body stand before you passed out? After a full minute, Eric stopped and Ernie hurried over with a plastic cup of pink water and the funnel you spit into. He removed the rubber wedge.

"Have a nice rinse, Will?" he said. I swilled the water round my mouth and spat bits of tooth and old filling and rather a lot of blood into the funnel. I should have spat it into his face, but I hadn't got the courage, and I hated my own craven timidity.

"When did you last see Henry Sutton?" asked Eric conversationally.

"Last night in Chester," I said. "At a B&B opposite the station."

"And where is he now?"

"I haven't a clue," I said. "I honestly haven't a clue."

"I'm sure he'd have told you where he was going. An old friend like you."

"He said he was planning to meet Sir Dominic at some kind of do on Christmas Eve. At Hampton Court."

"Yes, we know about that, sunshine." said Eric. "But where is he now?'

"I don't know. You've got to believe me, I really don't know."

"I think you do," said Ernie.

"I don't," I yelled.

"My turn now," said Ernie. "I think I'll have a go with the high pitched screamy one."

He had a go with the high pitched screamy one. Two minutes worth. My body refused to faint. I spat more tooth and filling and blood into the funnel.

"Where's Henry?" asked Eric quietly.

"I don't know," I whimpered. "I don't know where he lives. I haven't seen him for years. He's got a brown VW camper van. Perhaps he sleeps in that."

Eric had another go with the slow growly one to see if I could remember the registration number. His hand slipped and he churned up quite a bit of gum. When I next spat into the funnel there was a huge amount of blood.

"The registration number?" said Ernie.

"I don't know," I said, sobbing now, the whole of the right side of my mouth a raw and throbbing mess of pain. "Surely you know I'd tell you if I did."

"I don't think he knows," said Eric.

"Nor do I," said Ernie. "We'd better ask him an easier one."

"Yes, a nice easy one. What's your wife's address, Will?"

"Sir Dominic's a bit anxious that you might have phoned and told her about your little chat with your old friend Henry."

"Oh Christ," I prayed. "Sweet fucking Jesus Christ not this."

"What's the address, Will? Your wife's called Kim, isn't she? Where does Kim live?"

"I haven't spoken to her. You've got to believe she knows nothing about this. Nothing at all."

"But it would be so much better, Will, if we could make absolutely sure of that for ourselves. In fact, Sir Dominic insisted on it. He was adamant on the point, wasn't he, Ernie?"

"Absolutely adamant, Eric. I don't think I've ever known him more adamant. He wanted us to find out her address, call round, and ask her, politely, if you'd phoned her last night or this morning."

"But I didn't," I yelled.

"Open wide," said Eric.

It took forty-five minutes. I watched the clock. Eric and Ernie took turns with the slow growly drill, and the high pitched screamy drill. I did quite a lot of screaming myself. Then they pulled out three of my teeth. It seemed to cause them a lot of effort and they weren't best pleased. So they inscribed Kim's name just above my left nipple with the slow growly drill. They were just finishing off the "M" when I told them her address.

"Thank you," said Eric and Ernie in unison.

"I think he's earned a little rest," said Ernie.

"Absolutely," said Eric. "And besides, we've got to toddle off to Vauxhall."

Eric went to a cupboard and produced a hypodermic. He filled it with a colourless solution from a small glass vial and slid the needle into a vein in my arm. He pressed the fluid home.

Eric and Ernie went and stood at the foot of the reclining chair. "Bye-bye, Will," they said, waving me off. "Bye-bye."

It was dark when I woke, pitch dark, and I could hear the sound of the sea. It seemed to be immediately below me. I was lying on bare floor-boards, and the sea, gurgling, sluicing, was beneath the boards. And then sensation returned. And the memory of pain. And I wasn't sure which was worse.

I was clothed. I seemed to be in a tracksuit but I was still freezing cold, shivering, more or less uncontrollably, and my teeth were hurting. Not a scream now, a persistent, thunderous throb. My mouth tasted, vilely, of blood. And my chest hurt, and I remembered that it now bore Kim's name. And that was when I allowed myself a small, thin smile. I'd sent Eric and Ernie to the wrong address. I'd sent them to the launderette three streets away from ours.

I don't know what I'd have done if they hadn't believed me. No, that was a lie. I was kidding myself. I'd have told them, spat it out along with the blood, the lumps of filling and broken teeth. That was why I waited as long as I could possibly bear before giving the false address. For a good deal longer than I could bear, in fact. Eric and Ernie had me marked down as the coward I was. If they knew the address had been forced out of me only after forty-five minutes of ingenious torment, there was just a chance they might believe it. And they had. And that was worth a small smile on that freezing night with the sounds of the sea, curiously comforting, just below me. I had found something inside myself I didn't know I had. I felt whole again. I wanted to live.

But staying alive was a problem. I wanted to go back to sleep, but that would be fatal. I was already weak. The temperature was below freezing, though at least I was out of the wind. This must be a pier, I told myself, and I was in a pavilion, or at least a shelter, at the end of a pier. I must stand up, and walk, and grope around in the dark to see if there was a way out. And if I couldn't find any way out, I still had to keep moving.

I lumbered stiffly to my feet and the movement made my mouth and chest hurt. The tracksuit was soft and comfortable, but offered little protection from the cold. I had no underwear on, and my feet seemed to be shod in open-toed sandals though I couldn't actually feel my toes at all. What I could feel was a sharp pain near the bottom of my left leg. With the contrapuntal double concerto of pain playing between my mouth and my chest, this new and unfamiliar pain hadn't registered at first. Now it became insistent. I sat down and there was a clanking sound. I felt my left ankle. There was a ring of metal round it, about three inches wide. It was digging into the flesh at the bottom of my calf. Attached to the manacle was a chain, its links about half an inch across. I got to my feet and held the chain and worked my way along its length to wherever it was secured. It was attached to a column, a rusted iron column, which nevertheless felt exceptionally solid when I pushed against it. The chain had been looped round the column and secured with what felt like a small but strong brass padlock. I was tethered like some wounded animal. I wasn't going to get out of here until someone found me. Or came for me. The thought that it might be Eric and Ernie, that this was just a brief seaside respite from the dentistry or that they might have some new, entirely different treat in store, gave me the terrors all over again. I began to shiver, uncontrollably, and the shivers made what was left of my teeth howl out in protest. The panic seemed to rise inside me, distend my whole being, like an inflating airbag in the gut. "Stop it," I shouted out loud. "You're going to get out of this." My words reverberated in the dark. Was it night, I wondered, or were the windows boarded up? But surely, if the latter, there would be the faintest chink of light?

There wasn't much point in calling for help if it was dark, I thought. Who'd be on a pier, at night, in the dead of winter? Night fishermen, I suddenly realised. My throat was tight and constricted and I realised I must be seriously dehydrated. Nevertheless, I screamed 'Help' until I ran out of breath and spirit, and then I sobbed for a while. And as I was sobbing I heard a distant clock chime. It was midnight. I would have to wait at least seven hours for daybreak. I sat down, curled myself into a ball, and sobbed some more.

After about twenty minutes I began to feel numb. I also felt deliciously sleepy. The pain seemed to be receding. It was at that moment I realised I had to get up again, and move. If I fell asleep there was a real chance I might never wake up. I stood up and decided to walk a few circuits at the furthest extent of my chain. The manacle bit into my flesh and it hurt and I felt almost relieved. It was the pain that was going to keep me alive. I put my hands in front of me and walked slowly, scared that I might bump into something. By my calculation, though it was actually impossible to tell in the blackness, I'd done about half a circle when I knocked something over with my foot. I got down onto my knees and scrabbled around the floor. Eventually, my hand touched something cold and shiny. It was a plastic bottle. I held it in my hands, and fumbled with my stiff cold fingers for the cap. I twisted it off, and raised the bottle experimentally to my nose. No smell. Not paraffin or something noxious then. I could hardly contain my excitement. It must be water. I raised the large heavy bottle to my lips and nothing came out. I felt robbed. Defeated. Incredulous. How could nothing come out of an obviously full bottle? And then I realised that the contents must be even more frozen than I was. I pressed, then shook the bottle. It wasn't entirely solid, there was a definite sloshing. I forced my thumb into the neck and pushed, and to my joy, the ice gave way. I raised the bottle to my lips and took a swig. The intense cold of the fluid set off my teeth, but the feeling of moisture on the back of my throat, which had begun to feel like cracked leather, was intoxicating. I remembered that it was dangerous to take too much water at once in cases of dehydration and I'd had nothing to drink for almost eighteen hours, had indeed been dehydrated with hangover when Eric and Ernie first picked me up. After the first huge slurp, I took tiny sips, which hurt my teeth less. And then I completed the circuit, and did another and another, until the chain was wrapped right round the column. I walked back out again, and in again, and out again, about half a dozen times, and the pain in my lower calf muscle got worse and worse. So I stood still and did physical jerks with my arms. I hadn't done them since I was at prep school and within a couple of minutes, I was puffed out but warmer. Or less cold. And so began the pattern of the long night. Circular walks, round and round to the centre of the column and then back out again. Physical jerks and later bending and stretching exercises. And occasional blissful moments when I'd sit on the floor with my back against the column, panting, exhausted, and took a few sips of the icy water. I kept the bottle with the cap screwed on plumb next to the pole. It was the only way I could be sure of finding it in the dark.

I had a lot to think about that night. I thought of Eric and Ernie at first, and their possible return. The water was a blessing, but it also seemed to indicate that someone wanted to keep me alive. Why? To do what? To find out what? But there was no point in dwelling on fear. The worst thing about fear was that it preyed on itself. Fear gave way to the fear of fear, taking over your whole mind and body, making thought, movement, any kind of hope, impossible. When visions of the dentist's chair filled my mind, I forced myself to think about Vermeer. I'd spent a long time after Natasha's departure on the night before the gaudy looking at the pictures in the book Nicholas had given me, and I tried at first to remember all the paintings. There were thirty-five acknowledged Vermeers, with a further three decidedly inferior items whose authenticity was disputed. I tried to bring them all to mind, in the chronological order in which they appeared in the book. The early, lifeless historical paintings, mere academic exercises. The uneasy tavern and courtship scenes, in which there was a current of tension, unease, suspicion, between two or more figures.

Then, miraculously, came the beautiful studies of women, alone, performing tasks, apparently unaware that they were being observed with such attentive, loving detail. They were paintings that made the everyday seem eternal, and even on that bleak, dark pier their sense of peace, light and balance refreshed my battered spirit if not my aching body. I'd always lazily assumed that I liked everything Vermeer ever painted but as I ran the pictures through my mind like one of the slide shows we used to have in history of art at school, I realised I didn't. There were too many paintings which included representations of other pictures – art about art, if you like, though in Vermeer's case, since he was an art dealer, he was probably using his own paintings as advertisements for other pictures he had to sell. Nor were all his subjects pleasing. There is something faintly disagreeable about the smirking youth, believed to be a self-portrait of Vermeer himself, in *The Procuress,* though it is characteristic of the painter that this traditional brothel scene also exudes a strange tenderness and warmth in the cash transaction between the older man and the strangely contented, homely whore. The pendant paintings *The Astronomer* and *The Geographer* were merely dull, dutiful commissions that also suggested that Vermeer found little inspiration in painting men. And the *Allegory of Faith*, in which a swooning woman clutches her breast with her foot on a globe is frankly dismaying, exuding a sentimental, even melodramatic religiosity that is entirely missing from such a beautiful and profound painting as *Woman Holding a Balance*, in which a young (and pregnant) woman seems to be taking stock of her whole spiritual life.

Yet the duds made the masterpieces seem even more impressive, the relative failures throwing into sharp relief the perfection Vermeer achieved on at least a dozen occasions. As I clanked round and round on my chain, it struck me there was something heroic as well as beautiful about Vermeer. He was born in a pub, and later ran a pub himself, as well as working as an art dealer. He had at least eleven children, several of whom died in infancy. I imagined him escaping to his studio, in flight from screaming infants, a harassed wife and the mother-in-law with whom he lived in the later years of his life. The sense of peace and profundity in his greatest paintings must have been exceptionally hard won, the calm centre in a life of noisy chaos, increasing poverty and terrible grief as several of his large brood were carried off to the graveyard. It has been estimated that Vermeer never painted much more than a couple of pictures a year, and towards the end of his short life, his business as an art dealer and his own career as an artist failed following the 1672 invasion of Holland by the French. "During the ruinous and protracted war he was not only unable to sell any of his art but also, to his great detriment, was left sitting with the paintings of other masters he was dealing in," his unhappy wife testified after his death.

The great painting I had handed over to Eric and Ernie that morning was generally reckoned to have been painted in those last grim years of his life. It made the work's sense of happiness and grace even more remarkable. But who was the woman? As I'd told Henry, Vermeer's wife would have been in her early forties by then and almost certainly prematurely old and careworn; in any case, it was hard to imagine any mother with as many children as her reacting with quite such joy at the prospect of yet another baby as the woman in the picture. And yet I was haunted by that radiant face. I felt as if I knew her, which was absurd. And then suddenly, walking in circles, clockwise in, anti-clockwise out, I made the connection. Not one connection, but two.

The pregnant woman with the Bible was surely the same person as *Girl with a Pearl Earring*, painted some eight years earlier in about 1665. *Girl with a Pearl Earring* is perhaps the most beautiful, and paradoxically troubling, of all Vermeer's pictures. Some think it is an idealised figure, others that it might be Vermeer's eldest daughter, Maria, though the dates seem to rule that possibility out. Maria would only have been eleven when the picture was painted and the girl in the painting is evidently in her early or mid-teens. But what makes it still more unlikely that it's Vermeer's daughter, at least to those who love the artist, is that the relationship between painter and subject is clearly charged with sexuality.

The girl is wearing a blue and gold turban and the beautiful pearl earring which gives the work its title. She is looking over her shoulder towards the viewer with liquid brown eyes and a sensual, half-open mouth. An extraordinary atmosphere of complicity is established between the girl and who ever happens to be looking at the painting. This feeling is enhanced by the work's simplicity. Instead of the usual humdrum domestic surroundings of Vermeer's pictures, the background is entirely black, throwing the beautiful girl into sharp relief.

The painting is also deeply ambiguous, and its meaning seems to change as you look at it. It's not clear, for instance, if the girl has just turned to look at the viewer, or is in the process of turning her head away. Her expression, so alive, so deep, is equally ambivalent. Is it a look of sexually aroused, possibly guilty welcome? Or of regretful, hurt farewell? Are we looking at the beginning of an affair, or its end?

Either way, it is the aching vulnerability of the girl that lingers most resonantly, most painfully, in the memory. And in the darkness and the cold of my imprisonment on the pier, I remembered when I had seen that look before. It had been the afternoon I had parted from Rose for the last time.

During that summer of 1982, Rose and I usually went out with the rest of the gang, though we often managed to slip off for a grope and a snog, the fumbled, secret moments achieving a special sweet intensity because we knew they wouldn't last long. Rose was always desperately worried about being discovered necking, as she quaintly put it, by Henry. But occasionally, we'd have proper dates on our own – a visit to the cinema, a meal out, with Rose riding pillion on my Honda 50. My word, I felt grown-up. Her parents were elderly and anxious, and I always had to promise to bring Rose home by midnight, and since Auntie May rarely went out and I was embarrassed about bringing Rose back there and taking her up to my bedroom, we usually ended the evening at what we called "our" rhododendron in Oxshott Woods. We'd stumble through the dark, tripping over roots, scaring each other with spooky noises, tipsy and giggling. And we usually had a good hour left for "necking", which Rose, the least prudish of girls, interpreted in the broadest possible terms. But while Rose was quite happy to go up to nine, as she put it, she stopped short of ten. She'd let me touch her down below, and she would happily bring me to a climax with her gentle hands. But full sex was out. She was fifteen and she said she'd always made a deal with herself that she'd wait until it was legal.

I should have been happy with this state of affairs, and I certainly never tried to force the issue, thought it often used to hang heavily in the air between us. When you're a virgin at eighteen, the idea of full sexual intercourse assumes the significance of the Holy Grail and coming so close without actually going "all the way" became an almost obsessive source of regret. The packet of Durex, which I'd bought, flushing hotly with embarrassment, from a middle-aged lady in Boots, remained as intact as Rose herself.

Then one day, a few days before the disastrous boat trip, when summer was turning into autumn and Rose was already back at school, she'd whispered in my ear (Rose had a lovely way of whispering in your ear) that she was ready to make love properly. Since I'd just spent myself in her hands and she was busy cleaning us both up with a Kleenex, I was a little surprised by her timing but not unduly worried. In those sappy days, there seemed to be virtually no limit to the number of times you could climax. So I began to make renewed advances and Rose had said, not now, not here, but the Sunday after next. Her parents were visiting a relative on the south coast and Henry was going rock climbing with some chums. We'd have her house to ourselves all day and we could be cosy and warm in bed. Just the thought of it made me erect again, and I kissed her tenderly and said a heartfelt thank you.

But the boat trip and my disappearance with Natasha intervened. Rose had phoned me at the office the following morning during her school break, and I feared she was upset about Henry's behaviour and worrying about how Natasha was feeling. Not a bit of it. She just wanted to make sure I'd escaped Natasha's coils. I said we'd got a taxi and I'd dropped Natasha off at her place in East Molesey and then gone straight home to Thames Ditton. I was surprised and faintly appalled by how easy I found it to tell this lie and wishing to change the subject, I put it to Rose that Nicholas and Henry had behaved disgracefully.

"Oh come on, Will," she said, "that's just boys' games. It's not to be taken seriously. I bet you got up to similar stuff at boarding school." I found myself blushing.

"Yes, but . . ." I spluttered.

"Henry was just being kind to poor old Nicholas," said Rose, "and then that silly stuck-up bitch had to go and throw a wobbly and ruin the whole evening." I had the feeling that Rose had been thoroughly briefed by Henry about just how unimportant 'boys' games' were, and being fifteen and a devoted sister, she'd taken it on trust. I was glad she took such a relaxed view of blow-jobs though. It was something else to look forward to.

Puttering over to Rose's on my Honda on Sunday however, I had a resurgence of guilt. At eighteen, the truth seems more important than kindness or even common sense. I'd had a brief, undesired and entirely unenjoyable bunk-up with Natasha, and she had made it perfectly clear that she saw no future in it by returning straight to university. I had been nothing more than a handy means to revenge. Yet all week I agonised about my infidelity to Rose and whether I should tell her about it. And if I was going to tell her about it, ought I to tell her before or after we had sex?

Of course, I shouldn't have told her about it. I'd known that as soon as I started my confession. The only tiny moral consolation was that at least I'd broken the news before we went to bed rather than after. That really would have been a cad's trick. Rose had opened the door with the sensual, fearful, faintly guilty expression of the *Girl with a Pearl Earring*. As soon as I'd crossed the threshold she'd clamped her mouth to mine and seemed to melt into my body, a delicious foretaste of things to come. And then I'd told her, clumsily, unnecessarily, about Natasha. And it looked as though her world had collapsed around her.

She didn't get angry, she was the least angry person I have ever met, she just cried, quietly, great salt tears rolling down her cheeks. The saddest thing of all was that she let me comfort her, hug her, the very person who had caused her all this misery. I tried to explain that it meant nothing to me, that the experience had indeed been actively unpleasant. And all she could say, through her sobs and snuffles, was that she was sorry, she couldn't make love now, it had all been spoilt for her. "It was meant to be pure," she said. "We were both meant to discover it for the first time together. And now it's all spoilt."

It was me who became angry. I said what Nicholas and Henry had got up to was just as much a betrayal, worse because they had clearly enjoyed it and hadn't given a damn about Natasha seeing them. And Rose had repeated her, or Henry's view, that a blow-job between male friends was unimportant boys' stuff and begged me, heartbreakingly, not to be cross with her. She asked me to get her a drink, and I raided her parents drinks' cupboard and made us both stiff gins and tonic. She wouldn't clink glasses with me, an unfailing tradition we'd developed, and after a couple of sips, she asked me to go. She escorted me to the door, and I asked if I could phone her, and she nodded mutely and brushed away a tear. And as I turned to look at her from the seat of my Honda, she was turning round to go back indoors, but looking over her shoulder at me, with an expression that was hurt, wounded, and loaded with all the terrible complicity the betrayed feel for their betrayer. It was the last time I ever saw her.

The genius of Vermeer's painting, I realised, as I did another series of stretching exercises, was that it was a case of both/and rather than either/or. It showed, simultaneously, the beginning and the end of the affair, the guilty first-passion and its grieving demise. And however you read the picture, there was no mistaking Vermeer's tenderness and regret or the girl's vulnerability and love.

But it had turned out all right for Vermeer's young mistress, if my theory that the *Girl with a Pearl Earring* and the *Pregnant Lady with a Bible* were one and the same person. It certainly wasn't a theory I'd seen propounded in anything I'd read on Vermeer, and, superficially, there was little to identify the two figures as the same. The girl's hair was hidden, the woman's was auburn and abundant and gathered in braids in a loose bun. The woman's cheekbones weren't as sensationally beautiful as the girl's and the look of yearning in those liquid eyes had been replaced by a contentment it didn't seem sentimental to describe as spiritual joy. It was the shared intimacy of the two paintings, despite their different moods, and the position of the head, that made the comparison irresistible. And Vermeer, I suddenly remembered, had left one clue, which seemed to me to clinch the matter. On the table in the foreground of the later picture, something shone, half hidden, in the folds of a thick embroidered tablecloth. It was little more than a faint reflection, and I would need to look at the picture again to be sure. But if memory served, it might well be a large pearl, identical to the one in the painting of the girl.

It was, of course, impossible to deduce the complete history of their relationship from the two paintings; it might even be sentimental to try. But it seemed to me the basic pattern was clear. The young girl had sat for Vermeer in her teens. She had probably been the daughter of a rich merchant, perhaps, to judge by her exotic turban and the pearl, the daughter of a man who travelled east in his trade. And something had developed between them as he painted her. Perhaps it was no more than desire on Vermeer's part for his subject, but it seemed impossible to me, judging from the painting, that his feelings weren't returned. And that those feelings had included a tangle of guilt.

Had it been merely a mutual *tendresse*? Or had it gone further? Had Vermeer deflowered the girl, gently, lovingly, on the studio couch, while his large family ran riot downstairs? After his death, Vermeer's wife described her own life as an endless round of domestic preoccupation. The affection of a young woman must have been precious to Vermeer, who so evidently loved female beauty and whose domestic circumstances were so busy, so anxious, and so often shadowed by infant mortality. Every time he and his wife had sex, there must have been the worry in the back of both their minds that it might produce yet another demanding, possibly sickly child. But as a devout Catholic – he had converted when he married his Catholic wife, and several of the paintings reflect his faith – he must also have been keenly aware that in loving the young girl physically, he was committing a mortal sin. The portrait seems to show both desire and regret, sexual intimacy and its termination. My guess was that the relationship probably only lasted for as long as it took Vermeer to paint the picture, that it might indeed have ended before the painting was finished. There was something valedictory about the *Girl with a Pearl Earring.*

And then eight years passed. Perhaps the artist and the young woman had remained friends. And eventually, the girl, now a young woman, had fallen in love with a more suitable, younger man, married him and become pregnant. And she wanted Vermeer to record the happiness she felt, so different from the troubled mood of the earlier painting. If a sin had been committed, it had clearly been forgiven, on both sides, and by God. Instead of sadness, happiness. Instead of guilt, grace. A happy ending. The happiest possible ending. And perhaps the girl, now a woman, had given Vermeer the earring as a keepsake of their earlier love, and he had incorporated it, almost hidden, in his painting as a clue to posterity.

But if Henry was to be believed, Rose had endured a more harrowing time before achieving her own happy ending. The following evening, the Monday night, when I knew she would be doing her homework, I'd phoned again to be told, curtly, by her elderly father, that she was too busy to come to the phone and he would appreciate it if I troubled his daughter no further. His few words, dignified and icily polite, somehow conveyed the message that he thought I was an utter shit, and I wondered just how much Rose had told him. I wrote a couple of times, but my letters went unanswered, and in our last few days together at the office, Henry had airily brushed off my inquiries about her welfare, though it was impossible not to notice that his manner, too, was noticeably cooler than it had been. And then I'd set off for a fortnight's holiday with my Auntie May, happily exploring Florence and Siena together, and a couple of days after our return, I'd gone up to the great anti-climax that was Oxford. By the following Christmas, Henry had gone to Hong Kong and though I'd sent Rose a card and expressed the hope of seeing her during the holidays, I'd received no reply. By then, if Henry was to be believed, she'd already started going off the rails.

But was Henry to be believed? It was the question that had been nagging away at the edge of my mind ever since I'd woken up on the pier. No, it had been nagging for longer than that, though I hadn't wanted to acknowledge it. During the hungover journey down from Chester, the sheer implausibility of Henry's long tale in the B&B had begun to trouble me. I could certainly imagine Sir Dominic taking custody of a stolen Vermeer, particularly if it meant him receiving yet another generous slice of personal publicity and acclaim. It was also easy to accept that he might have participated in a scam for importing Indian works of art. English collectors had after all been looting the world for centuries. It was just that export licenses made it more difficult these days. If Sir Dominic thought he could get away with a basically venial crime – the *objets d'art* weren't stolen after all, and their owner had wanted to sell – then he might well have gone ahead. But it was the James Bondish aspects of Henry's narrative that beggared belief. The idea of Sir Dominic as the Mr Big of a big heroin operation. The sudden switch of contraband in Bombay. The brutal beating-up of the antiques' dealer. Sir Dominic was certainly powerful, indeed ruthless when it suited him, as his vigorous libel action against *Theatre World* demonstrated. But even there we had no proof that he had actually manufactured the libel himself, and it could all be the kind of conspiracy theory to which journalists are notoriously prone, particularly towards the end of a long session down the pub.

Considered rationally, what possible reason was there for Sir Dominic to be a heroin smuggler? Each year, HappiSnax turned in massive profits. He had no need of the money, and if there was one dominating need in his life, it was his almost childlike hunger for approval and applause. And if he really did run the kind of shit-hot criminal organisation Henry described, why on earth would he have sent his wife and a shambolic journalist in pursuit of the man who had double-crossed him? He would have more efficient, more ruthless lieutenants than that. Eric and Ernie, for instance.

Just the thought of Eric and Ernie brought the memory of the dentist's chair back into vivid focus. The pain, numbed by the cold, returned with a vengeance, and so did the fear. I ordered myself to be calm, forced myself to walk, and the more I walked, the clearer it all became. Henry was a self-confessed drug smuggler. Who knew if he confined his operation to cannabis? There were fatter profits to be made with the hard stuff. And weren't Eric and Ernie exactly the kind of people a drug smuggler, with dodgy clients and bad debts to collect, might find exceptionally useful? Might they not also be the ASMs he said he always took with him on his foreign tours? But the key, surely, was where Eric and Ernie had picked me up. Sir Dominic would know from Natasha exactly where I now lived in Pimlico. Henry had no idea. I hadn't told him where I used to live with Kim. I hadn't told him where I was living now. I hadn't told him where my 'safe house' in the suburbs was. Even as I'd lapped up Henry's preposterous story, under his spell, as we'd all been under his spell in the old days, I'd retained an instinctive sense of caution. Henry was a liar. Everything I'd learnt about him in the last few days suggested that he was addicted to deceit in the way other people are addicted to cigarettes or alcohol or heroin. He loved lying. He had lied at the beginning of that glorious night in Oxshott Woods, pretending he had to do a job for the *Esher Herald.* He had been lying ever since.

The only person who knew I'd be on that train was Henry. He had been insistent that I'd caught the first train, had even left me an alarm clock to make sure I didn't oversleep. It was conceivable, just, that Sir Dominic was keeping a watch on trains coming from the nearest mainline station to Buckley. But he wouldn't have needed to, with access to my Pimlico address. It had to be Henry.

The last thing Henry would have wanted was for me to resume contact with Natasha and Sir Dominic. When I heard their side of the story, Henry's would doubtless collapse as the ludicrous fiction most of it was. What I did believe was that Henry was blackmailing Sir Dominic, though not, I fancied, from the Robin Hoodish motives he had described. Henry really did have photographs of Natasha and Sir Dominic beaming smugly in front of the missing Vermeer. It would, at the very least, be embarrassing if those photographs were handed over to the police, or the press, and Sir Dominic had to explain that he had intended to hand the painting back to the nation but had somehow contrived to lose it before he had a chance to do so. Even if he wasn't accused of criminal conspiracy, he would be the object of ridicule. The publicity-seeker who'd let a masterpiece slip through his hands. It would be unbearable to him. I fancied Sir Dominic would pay a lot to retain his dignity, a fact of which Henry, too, would be keenly aware.

So I had to be kept away from Natasha and Sir Dominic. But why the appalling cruelty in the dentist's surgery first? Why this remote and freezing pier when a nice anonymous house and a couple of dim but basically decent minders would have done just as well? There was, I realised, another way of looking at it. I was at least being allowed to live. It would have been quite possible for Eric and Ernie, or even Henry himself, to have killed me. But perhaps Henry hadn't progressed as far as killing yet. Just torture without bloodying his own hands. I wondered if the dental treatment was mere gratuitous cruelty, or perhaps delayed revenge for my betrayal of Rose all those years ago, a betrayal which had apparently caused her and her family so much misery. But there was a more pragmatic reason for it. Henry had no idea how regularly I was in contact with Kim. It was entirely possible that I might have phoned her after Henry's departure the previous night in Chester or from the train the following morning. With me missing, Henry might have reckoned that Kim, too, might want to make urgent contact with Natasha and Sir Dominic. He might well have instructed Eric and Ernie to find out where she lived and go on a little fact-finding mission to discover just how much she knew. The thought of Kim suffering what I'd been through was unbearable. I'd been right to hold my tongue for as long as I had. I just wished it didn't hurt so much now.

And so the long night wore on, marked by the chiming hours and half hours of the clock. It sometimes seemed inconceivable that thirty minutes could take so long to pass, and I'd kid myself that I'd missed a chime, that the wind had blown it in the other direction, though there didn't seem to be much wind. And then, after I was convinced at least an hour, perhaps two, had gone by, the bell would chime and I realised that only thirty minutes had dragged their weary painful way.

At last, the dawn came. The first smears of grey light appeared in high windows and gradually I began to make out my surroundings. I was in what appeared to be an empty hall, and the column to which I was tethered was just one among several, supporting the roof. There was a raised stage at one end, and I was in what had once been the auditorium, though all the seats had been removed. And as the winter light grew feebly stronger, I saw something that made my heart sink. My bottle of mineral water hadn't been the only one, something to get me through the night until rescue or worse the following day. I was surrounded by 1.5 litre plastic bottles, arranged in a neat circle round the column beyond my length of chain but easily within reach if I lay down. I counted them. There were thirty of them. I went closer to investigate. Next to each bottle was a circular pack of Laughing Cow processed cheese and a Mars Bar. I also discovered a couple of plastic buckets and two rolls of lavatory paper. Enough to survive on, and somewhere to evacuate the waste, for a month. Eric and Ernie clearly weren't planning a return visit for a while. And the intention appeared to be to keep me alive. But how on earth was I going to survive this cold for a month? Eight hours had been hell, thirty days and nights were surely a complete impossibility. I walked wretchedly around, surveying the food and drink that numbered the days of my confinement. I sucked forlornly at the Mars Bar, and it set my teeth screaming, and gnawed one triangle of cheese on the side of my mouth Eric and Ernie had left more or less intact, and carefully stored the rest of the food by the pillar. They would have to last me all day. And then I realised I wanted a pee, and reached wearily for one of the two buckets. It contained a Threshers carrier bag and I opened it. Two bottles of Famous Grouse whisky. "I'll have a double Grouse waiting your pleasure," Henry had said as he left me at Chester. And he had. An exceptionally generous double. Enough, I realised, to kill yourself with.

Only I wasn't going to kill myself, or I wasn't going to kill myself yet. Standing up to Eric and Ernie had given me a measure of faith in myself which I'd been lacking for far too long. And I was sick of being a pawn in Henry's game. My affection for him, instantly revived when I'd met him again after so long, had been replaced by a fierce hatred. I wasn't going to let the arrogant bastard, with his lies and his elaborate games, his cruelty and his appalling need to dominate and deceive, get away with it. I was going to survive this, and get even. Not with some melodramatic personal revenge. But by going to the police, telling them all I knew about Henry and what he had done to me. And watching him go down in court.

Of course it might not be that simple. It was Monday morning now. On Tuesday night, Henry was due to make the swap with Sir Dominic at Hampton Court. After that he'd said he was going straight to the airport, heading off for a life in exile he had already planned. But that could all be lies too. If Henry was due to leave the country in less than two days, what was the point of giving me supplies for thirty? I didn't like the answer to that. Perhaps he had no plan to come back for me at all. On the other hand, the supplies for thirty days might just be another of his elaborate hoaxes, to scare me, rattle me, send me scurrying to the Scotch. A single bottle, drunk fast though not fast enough to make you sick, could probably kill you. It was certainly enough to make you crash out for many hours, lower the body's resistance, and give hypothermia time to do its work. Perhaps that was the aim. Henry knew how much I drank. Leaving me alone with two bottles of Scotch, he probably hoped that I'd drink myself to death, saving him the trouble of bumping me off himself, or sending Eric and Ernie to do it. But even in the dark months since my separation from Kim, I knew that while I drank too much and got drunk too often, I wasn't actually an alcoholic. I wasn't totally reliant on the stuff. Or at least I hoped I wasn't. Now, anyway, seemed a good time to prove it, one way or the other. On the other hand, a little voice whispered inside my head, one small drink, every now and again, wouldn't do much harm. It might actually do some good, warm me up. But I told the voice to shut up. I needed to keep my wits about me, needed clarity to endure. I would however keep the bottles to hand. A painless means of oblivion might be extremely handy if the ordeal became intolerable.

I continued my exercises, continued my circular walks. Though the light strengthened outside, the inside of the theatre remained murky. The high windows were small and dirty. I could just about make out an old pinball machine in one corner, a few slot machines abandoned near the stage. Was the theatre merely closed for winter, or had it been abandoned for years? Impossible to know, but the desolate atmosphere, and the lack of seats, suggested to me that it might well be permanently closed.

During the hours of darkness, I'd occasionally given vicious tugs to my chain, more from frustration than from any real hope of release. Chaining people up, I thought gloomily, was exactly the kind of practical job Henry would be extremely good at. Now there was some light, it was depressingly certain that I stood no chance of freeing myself at all. The manacle that bit uncomfortably into my lower calf was made of solid steel, though luckily the edges were rounded rather than sharp. Otherwise, it would have cut my leg right open. It was hinged, with a keyhole on one side. Had I had a paperclip to hand, I might have tried jiggling it about in the lock, but it looked a strong, uncompromising item and in any case, the pier wasn't exactly cluttered with paper clips. Or anything else that might prove remotely useful in an attempt at escape. I surveyed the floor area I could reach in minute detail. Even an old nail might have been handy but there was nothing. Just the water bottles, the food and the two plastic buckets with flimsy plastic handles.

The chain, although made of a surprisingly light metal, was sturdy, the links sealed, and the brass padlock that secured the chain, once it had been looped round the column, looked equally unyielding. I tried twisting the links against the steel loop of the padlock, but it was a fruitless exercise. There wasn't even enough play in the chain to bash the padlock against the metal column. I hurt my hands and fingers wrestling with the solid metal, but didn't make the slightest impression on either chain or lock. I'd just have to hope for a rescue.

Occasionally, I could hear the sound of a car horn outside, or the distant grumbling of a lorry, but the noises from the mainland were exceptionally faint, compared with the gulls whose constant cries became a kind of company. I couldn't even hear the chimes of the clock any more. There was little chance that my shouts would be heard by anyone on the beach, still less the promenade of whatever resort I happened to be imprisoned in. My only hope was that fishermen might use the pier, the only likely visitors in the dead of winter, and I might hear them, and they me.

Although it seemed futile, I shouted, "Help" as loudly as I could for a long time, six cries in a row, and then a break to get my breath back and to listen in case there was any response. I kept hoping to hear the sound of footsteps on the boards outside, perhaps talk or even laughter as anglers arrived. But a cold Monday morning was hardly likely to be a popular time for fishing anyway and all I heard was the gulls and the gentle murmuring of the sea beneath me. At eleven o'clock, I heard the clock again – the wind must have changed direction, and the chimes seemed like old friends. I had half of the Mars bar, a triangle of cheese and another drink of water.

The day dragged slowly by, and as the clock struck two, watery sunlight came in through the windows. The temperature was still freezing, or at most, a couple of degrees above, but the sun seemed like a good omen. Perhaps it would encourage people to take a walk on the pier. I continued with my own circular walk and my exercises, and watched the lozenge-like patches of light that came through the windows move slowly across the floor and up the wall. And it was when they were about half way up, turning gold as the sun set, that I received yet another horrid surprise. I'd been vaguely aware that there were pictures or posters on the walls, but had been unable to make them out in the sepulchral light. But now the sun caught one of them. It was a a poster advertising a show. 'Full supporting cast' were the first words to be illuminated. Then in much larger letters: 'Laughter Show'. Whose laughter show? I wondered idly. 'Little and Large's Laughter Show' it turned out, as the sun moved a few further inches up the poster. I belatedly realised that the top of the poster was almost certain to contain the name of the venue where I now found myself trapped. It was obviously somewhere on the south coast, for the sun sank in the west and was casting its dying light onto one of the side walls of the theatre, the east wall. And then I knew I was in even more trouble than I'd previously thought. As the light rose higher I saw the words 'Pavilion Theatre, Lympington', and at last knew why no one had been on the pier that day, and why no one was likely to come in the foreseeable future.

We'd carried the story in *Theatre World* some three years earlier. A small exploratory oil rig mounted on a massive floating pontoon had broken free of its moorings in a fierce January storm and smashed its way through the middle of Lympington pier on the south Devon coast. Fortunately, there had been no one on either the pontoon or the pier at the time – the oil-men had been evacuated by a coastguard helicopter as the weather turned really rough and no one was going to go on the pier in that kind of weather at two in the morning. But the Pavilion, locally celebrated and much loved for its summer shows, had been left isolated in the sea, with a twenty-yard gap between it and the remains of the pier on the shore. There had been much talk about repairs, but the local council was strapped for cash and an appeal had raised nothing like the sum required. With each passing winter, the condition of what was left of the pier grew worse, and it was now believed to be only a matter of time before the demolition experts were sent in to blow up the precarious structure, particularly now an application for lottery cash had failed. No wonder I'd heard no one walking outside on the pier that day. It was inaccessible from the land.

It was then that I began to give in to despair. At the back of my mind, glowing like a fitful beacon of hope, was the thought that Henry seemed to have chosen a really duff spot to hide his victim. Piers, after all, were public places. But not this one. The Pavilion Theatre might just as well have been Alcatraz. And now I had another night to get through, and if the food supplies were to be believed, another twenty-nine days and nights after that.

Darkness fell quickly and I began to fear it like a child. The thought of another fifteen or sixteen hours without sight, without hope, became unbearable. I began to hyperventilate, and my body was seized with another uncontrollable attack of the shakes. I began to pray. "Please God, get me out of this. Please God get me out of this. Please God get me out of this". I said the words over and over again, like a mantra. The physical symptoms of my distress began to subside, but not the great ache of despair within. I hadn't got the inner resources for this, I told myself bleakly. I was no John McCarthy. I was a coward. I forced myself to eat another triangle of cheese and a bite of Mars bar.

The clock chimed away. Six o'clock, seven, eight, and the temperature dropped. I kept thinking of the two bottles of Famous Grouse that I'd placed conveniently to hand near the pillar. By nine o'clock, the desire for a drink had become unbearable. By ten, I knew I had got to have one, have several. I couldn't make it through the night. What was the point of trying to make it through the night anyway? It would only lead to another day, another night of abject misery. Not just the physical discomfort and the fear. But the knowledge of the weakness, the terror, the loathsome jelly that lurked within. I was going to blot it all out.

I walked to the column and groped blindly for one of the bottles. Unscrewed the cap, and smelt the sweet familiar smell. If I took one sip, I knew, I would have another and another and another. And eventually, I would pass out and probably die. So I took a sip. And another. Just small ones. And then, without quite knowing what I was doing, still less why I was doing it, I screwed the cap back on and threw the bottle hard, in what I imagined to be the direction of the stage. It smashed, very satisfyingly. I was about to do the same with the other, when I realised that a heavy glass bottle might be useful. In self defence, should Eric and Ernie or even Henry himself come back. But it would also make a fairly useful noise if I banged it against the metal column in the remote possibility of anyone arriving on my end of the pier. But I couldn't trust myself to keep a full bottle within reach. So I walked to the furthest limit of my chain, unscrewed the top and sprayed the scotch all over the floor. The smell of whisky in the air was curiously satisfying. It was no longer the smell of death. I did a few more exercises and prayed some more. The old refrain at first. God, get me out of here alive. But then my prayer changed. I thanked him for giving me the courage to get rid of the Scotch. And then I thanked him for Kim, and for my Auntie May, and JB and all the other people I'd loved or liked. It was a long list, and it kept getting longer. I began to realise just how fiercely I wanted to live. But at the same time, I realised that if I was going to die, I wanted to die forgiven. I muttered what I could remember of the General Confession from *The Book of Common Prayer*, old phrases coming back comfortingly to mind from my schooldays and my rare, too rare, visits to church since then. I acknowledged and bewailed my manifold sins and wickedness. "The remembrance of them is grievous unto us." I recited in the dark, "The burden of them is intolerable. Have mercy upon us, have mercy upon us most merciful father: for thy son, our Lord Jesus Christ's sake, forgive us all that is past." I asked Kim to forgive me too, for the rows and the bitterness that had grown between us in our barrenness. And I remembered all the good times we had had together and began to feel, miraculously, a sense of peace. In those dire circumstances, there was no reason to feel peace. It was the grace of God.

And then I heard the chugging of a motor boat, distant at first but getting closer. And then it stopped just beneath me. It must be tying up at the pier itself. But who would visit a derelict pier at night? The thought that it might be Henry, or, even worse, Eric and Ernie, working under cover of night was appalling. They might have been coming to free me, of course. Or they might be coming to kill me. And now I wanted, wanted more than I could ever have imagined, to live. But there was no point in keeping quiet. Eric, Ernie and Henry knew where I was. They could find me whenever they liked. And if it was my tormentors, and their manner even verged on the threatening, I was going to smash the bottle and do as much damage with it as I possibly could. At that moment the idea of ramming broken glass into Henry's face was obscenely attractive. There was, however, a chance it was someone else. So I screamed help at the top of my voice and bashed my empty bottle against the metal column, hard but not so hard that it would break. And then I heard the most wonderful sound of my life. It was a shout, almost a scream, and I knew it was Kim. "Will," she cried, "Will, are you all right?"

"I'm all right," I bellowed back. "Thank Christ you've come." And then I began to cry.

"We're coming up," yelled Kim. "We've found a ladder," I could hear footsteps on metal rungs, footsteps on the boards of the pier, and then there was a tremendous crashing sound at the landward end of the theatre and a beam of torchlight raked the room.

A shadow ran towards me, and Kim dropped to her knees and hugged me to her a breast. She was crying too.

"Natasha and that husband of hers got a message. It said you'd been tortured," she said at last through her tears.

"Just a bit," I said. "How the hell did you find me?"

"Tell you later," she said. "Let's get out of here."

"There's one small problem," I said. "I'm chained to a post."

"Trev," she called.

"Don't say Trev the bloody Rev's with you?" I said, suddenly light-headed with elation.

"Course I am," he said in his reassuring, sensible, grown-up voice. "What the hell have you been up to in here, Will?" he added. "It smells like a sodding distillery." He laid his torch down on the ground, and I picked it up and shone it first at Kim and then at Trev. They both grimaced in the glare, so I put it back on the floor but I'd needed to be sure they were really there, that they weren't mere phantoms of my imagination.

"I was left a couple of bottles of whisky," I said. "I thought I'd better not drink it so I got rid of it."

"Blimey," said Kim. "Are you sure you're feeling all right, Will?"

I pulled her to me and buried my face in her neck, and breathed in her familiar clean, wholesome and, to me, wonderfully sexy, smell.

"I've missed you so much." I said. "Can I come home?"

"I'll be bloody angry if you don't," she said. "Despite what Natasha's been telling me."

"Ah, you've heard about that?"

"I've heard," she replied.

She pointed the torch at the chain, then at the pillar. "Will's tied up, Trev. I don't suppose there's any chance of you asking that nice fisherman if he's got anything to cut Will free with?"

"Of course," he said. "Do you mind if I take the torch?"

I told him I didn't mind. I minded even less when he reached into his pocket and passed me a packet of Camel, a quarter bottle of Bells and a disposable lighter.

"Kim bought them on the way down, only she hasn't got any pockets," he said, and toddled off.

"You really are an angel of mercy, aren't you?" I grinned, and fired the lighter to look into her eyes.

She was crying again and I kissed the tears away. I opened the cigarettes, lit one and took a deep and blessed drag. It was odd. I hadn't missed smoking at all while I was in fear. Now I couldn't understand how I'd survived without it. Then I opened the whisky, took a delicious swig that bit at the back of the throat and combined blissfully with the taste of fag and passed the bottle over in the direction of Kim.

"Here," I said. "If anyone's earned a drink, it's you."

"I'm not supposed to be drinking at the moment," she said. "But I don't suppose a small one would do any harm." She took a sip, and handed the bottle back.

Her words hung in the air between us. Kim only gave up drinking, and not always then, when she was trying to get pregnant, or praying that she might be pregnant after an IVF treatment. But I hadn't been around to supply the sperm for the last three months. I remembered her and Colin walking together from the Festival Hall, the remains of the cosy meal for two in Rita Road, her fury when I'd arrived, unannounced, the following morning.

"I'm pregnant, Will," she said. "I got the result on Saturday morning."

"Congratulations," I said. My voice was icy, though I'd yearned for several years to hear those words. "Colin must be very pleased."

"What do you mean, Colin?" she said, her voice hurt, puzzled, angry.

"I saw you on the South Bank together," I said glumly. "And when I turned up to your huge displeasure the following morning, it was clear you'd had someone round for dinner that night." It didn't make much difference to me whether Kim had had sex with Colin or he had merely usurped my role of wanking into a plastic pot. The idea that he might be the father of her child was unbearable.

"I was angry because I thought you were spying on me. And I was tense about whether I really was pregnant. And yes, I had had Colin round the previous night. He'd invited me out to that flashy concert because his sister had to cancel and he guessed I might be feeling lonely, and giving him supper seemed the least I could do. And yes, the boring little creep did make advances, as well as bad-mouthing you, but I had him out of the house double-quick."

"He's not the father then? You promise he's not the father?" I thought I could bear it if anyone rather than Colin was the father.

"Of course he's not the father, Will."

"Who is then?" I'd take it like a man I told myself. "If you don't want to tell me I'll understand," I added.

"You're the father, Will," she said softly, tenderly. "I'm just sorry it's taken me so long."

I assumed she meant that I'd bring the child up as my own, and that she'd actually used donor sperm from someone else.

"I asked them to freeze some of your sperm," she continued. "That last time we tried it together. The ninth. They don't need the whole lot for every attempt. I had a hunch that if that last treatment failed, you'd insist on calling a halt. As you did. And then you walked out on me."

"Hardly walked out. We both agreed that we needed a respite from the endless rows."

"No, you're right. And I was glad you went. I thought I'd give it one last chance on my own. Without all that terrible burden of expectation and anxiety between us. You'd signed all the forms of consent as a matter of routine when we started and I just told them you'd gone abroad on business for a few months."

"And it worked?" I still couldn't really believe it.

"It's worked. It's still precarious. You know as well as I do that with IVF there's a strong possibility of losing the baby in the first three months."

"But we're not going to lose it, are we?" I said with utter confidence. I felt the same kind of peace, the same feeling of rightness, I'd felt earlier after saying my prayers.

"No, we're not going to lose it," said Kim. "He'll hang on in there. Now we've got this far at last, I just know it's going to work."

"What do you mean he?" I said. "It's going to be a girl."

"A little chap" she said.

"A girl. Like her mum."

"Do you really mind either way?"

"No, of course I don't."

We were holding hands but I moved closer to her for a proper hug. But before I could, she had lashed out in the dark, and punched me smack on the wound on my chest that bore her name.

"That's for Natasha," she said. "And for your paranoid suspicions about Colin. The very idea"

I couldn't answer. I was too busy gasping with pain.

"What's the matter, Will? I didn't hit you that hard," she said with concern.

"Er, I've just been given a tattoo," I said. "Your name as it happens. It's still a bit tender."

We kissed and made up, and we were still kissing and making up when Trev, who with typical tact had given us a few minutes alone together, returned with his fisherman, armed with a pair of industrial strength wire-cutters. It was time to go home.

# 7: Christmas Eve 1996

*Demand me nothing. What you know, you know*
*From this time forth I never will speak word.*

*Othello*

Natasha had sent round the Roller, complete with my old friend Hastings. We were off to Hampton Court. As we struggled through heavy traffic down the Embankment, I found the Wombles record, the smoked salmon sandwiches and the champagne. All three went down very nicely indeed. I gazed happily at Kim. She was dressed as Ophelia and looked a treat in a plain white dress with flowers in her hair and wild garlands round her neck. She had spent a small fortune in the florist's. Trev the Rev, who'd stayed the night with us in Vauxhall, was wearing black tights, a black jerkin and carried a skull. Hamlet with a pipe in his mouth, defiantly clenched between his teeth though Kim had banned him from smoking the noxious weed inside the car and indeed even inside the house, dispatching him instead to our scrubby patch of garden. He had taken these orders in a true spirit of Christian humility.

I, in contrast, looked like an old tramp, though I was actually meant to be Gloucester in *King Lear.* I was wearing ragged clothes and an enormous amount of false facial hair that tickled like hell. Kim had applied it with sadistic glee and vast quantities of glue. I also had a shaggy old wig with bits of twigs in it and a vile-looking bloodied bandage for wearing over my eyes once we'd reached our destination. In this disguise, I was completely unrecognisable. Which was just as well because Henry would have got a very nasty surprise indeed if he discovered me at Hampton Court when he thought I was on the pier.

Initially, the police had insisted I shouldn't go to the Christmas Eve Shakespearean Revels, as the night was threateningly billed. I, however, had pointed out that without me there would be little chance of copping Eric and Ernie who might turn up as well as Henry. When Kim, Natasha and Sir Dominic had all sworn faithfully that I would be in total disguise the police had finally agreed to my presence and Kim and Trevor had scooted off to the theatrical costumier's after forcing me into the dentist's by main force and making sure that I didn't freak out completely when I was finally placed in the chair. It had been a bad hour. The dentist reported that Eric and Ernie had made a right mess of the teeth they'd left me with and they hadn't been in exactly pristine condition in the first place. A long course of treatment was threatened but he had temporarily covered the worst of the holes, which gave the screaming nerve endings a rest, as well as giving me some terrific painkillers. After that, I'd looked in at the St Thomas's Casualty department, who dressed the wound on my chest. There was no sign of infection and the injuries, said the nurse, were not serious. To judge by the funny look she gave me I had the nasty suspicion that she thought that I'd inflicted the wound on myself. You do, after all, get all kinds of weirdos in the accident and emergency department. I hadn't got the energy to explain how I'd actually come by my home-made tattoo but I aroused her suspicion still further when I asked if the word Kim would be legible when the wounds had healed. "Yes," she'd said sternly. "You'll probably have a faint scar for life." I'd felt curiously pleased about this. I'd then sauntered into a locksmith's, who, after several tries with an assortment of keys, finally found one that fitted the manacle round my leg. The young man there had given me some odd looks too. I was getting used to them and couldn't keep a fatuous grin off my face.

As the Roller struggled on, and the Wombles blasted out, I sipped my champagne and thought about the last eighteen hours. There hadn't been much sleep the previous night, like the nights before it, but adrenaline, the sheer joy of survival and Kim's wonderful news were keeping me buoyantly afloat. That and quite a lot of booze, of course. It seemed to go very well with the painkillers despite the dentist's stern injunctions about mixing them.

The big, shaggily bearded sailor had easily cut through my chain, and then I'd climbed down into his fishing boat with Kim and Trev. We'd sailed about twenty miles east to the harbour at Lyme Regis, sitting in his tiny cabin and drinking strong tea with plenty of sugar and condensed milk. He was a taciturn chap, who gave the impression that rescuing people from derelict piers was all part of a day's work, and his presence restricted our conversation.

Kim gave him a kiss as we climbed out of the boat, and the old tar blushed. Trevor attempted to hand over a tenner, but it was brusquely refused, and the fisherman shook my own ice cold hand with his warm one. "How long were you out there?" he asked.

"About twenty-four hours, I think."

"Lucky they found me in the pub just before closing time then. It's five degrees below now and expected to get colder." I wondered how long I'd have survived if Kim and Trev hadn't mounted their rescue mission. Another night or two? Probably not much longer.

"Happy Christmas," he said, as we parted on the great wall of the Cobb. I'd completely forgotten that we were this close to the festive season.

Trev kindly leant me his Barbour – it was bitingly cold, though mercifully there was little wind – and led the way to the car park. Kim's battered Mini was there, and as we approached it, someone leapt out of the passenger seat. It was Natasha, and she ran towards me and hugged me, a most un-Natasha-like display of affection.

"Thank Christ you're all right, oh thank Christ," she said.

"Yeah, well you can let him go now," said Kim, unusually bitchily for her. I thought I might try getting locked up on derelict piers more often. It seemed to do wonders for my sex appeal. Trev volunteered to drive, Natasha sat next to him in the front, and Kim and I cuddled up on the back seat.

"Now, for God's sake tell me how you found me," I said, offering the whisky around and relieved to find there were no takers. "But just a couple of questions first. Sir Dominic isn't a big heroin smuggler is he, Natasha?"

"No, of course he isn't," she said, bridling.

"And as far as you know, he hasn't got a couple of thugs on his payroll called Eric and Ernie?" Natasha was adamant that she'd never heard of Eric and Ernie.

"But Henry did offer him the Vermeer for thirty grand and also suggested another little deal involving smuggling *objets d'art* from India?" I guessed.

"Yes," said Natasha. "I knew all about the Vermeer, of course, when you came round with the news that Henry had turned up at Nicholas' with it. Henry had actually come to the house for dinner on the very night he and that beastly butler stole the painting. But Dommo didn't tell me anything about his smuggling arrangement until later. Very sheepish he was about it too. I told him he was a damned idiot."

I bet you did, I grinned to myself. I was also relieved to learn that I had been right to ditch my suspicions about Sir Dominic and realise that Henry was my real adversary. Though the whisky bottles suggested that Henry had been quite happy to make that known himself, provided he thought I was *hors de combat.* But I wasn't any longer. It was a good feeling.

"It might have been helpful if you'd told me some of all this when we set off after Henry," I said mildly. "You just gave the impression you were coming along for the ride because you were an old friend and didn't like to think of Henry in trouble."

"I know, and I feel awful about it," Natasha said. "But you had good reason to feel hostile to Dominic after that libel business. Be honest, Will. If you'd known he'd been in possession of a stolen Vermeer that had gone missing again without us having a clue where it was, you'd have been tempted to write something about it and make him a laughing stock at the very least."

I had to admit that this was true. "But it could have saved us an awful lot of time if you'd told me Henry was working in the lighting business. You must surely have asked him what he did for a living when he came for dinner?"

"Henry told Dominic he was in the antiques' trade when he first approached him about the Vermeer. There was no reason to disbelieve him."

It was so easy to forget that Henry never told the truth when he could think of a lie instead. "Fair enough," I said. "So what happened from the moment Henry and I did our vanishing act?" I asked.

"Well, I was furious, naturally," said Natasha. "I was stuck at that bloody venue with the Metal Motherz and a load of underage groupies with nowhere to stay for the night. So I drove straight home. Frankly, I thought you'd been bought off. It was clear that Henry had shown the picture to Nicholas in the expectation that the news would get back to me, his sister, and to Dominic. In fact, Nicholas told you about it first, and as soon as you came to me with the news, I guessed that Henry was going to ask some kind of ransom for its return. Unfortunately, we'd been foolish enough to pose for some photos with the painting."

"I know," I said. "I saw them."

"Yes, well, as you can imagine, it would be embarrassing at best if Henry went public with them. At worst, Dominic could have been suspected of being involved with the theft himself. So I thought it would be a good idea to tag along with you."

And have a bit of a sexual adventure on the side, I thought, though since Kim was sitting next to me it didn't seem a sensible idea to bring the matter up.

"The plan was that if you and I succeeded in finding Henry, I'd do my best to sweet-talk him and get the painting back. Frankly, I thought it was probably little more than another of Henry's stunts, and I was sure that if I pleaded with him he'd do the decent thing. If he didn't, Dominic had authorised me to offer up to two hundred grand for the picture's safe return, together with the photographs and the promise of complete silence. So, when you disappeared, I thought you'd simply decided to go along with his blackmail plan."

"Gee, thanks."

"Well, you were clearly short of money and Henry's famously persuasive."

He was indeed. While I was with him, I'd bought all the claptrap about Sir Dominic being an international drug-dealer.

"Anyway," Natasha continued. "I got home and told Dominic I'd caught up with Henry, and then lost both him and you. He was exceptionally worried. The previous day, he'd received a couple of photographs. No message."

"Sneak pictures of Sir Dominic watching the unloading of the smuggled *objets d'art* from India?" I guessed. "Henry told me a slightly different version. He said he had pictures of Sir Dominic supervising the unloading of heroin he had himself forced Henry to smuggle in from India. Henry persuaded me that both he and I were in grave danger from Sir Dominic, and his thugs. Like the fool I was, I believed him."

"Well, when Dommo showed me the pictures of the Indian stuff, and confessed to his foolhardy scheme to get round export licenses, it was clear that we were in even more trouble than I'd thought we were. Dominic was all for going to the police and confessing. I begged him to give me another twenty-four hours. I didn't want him to be disgraced, a laughing stock." Natasha may have had unconventional sexual morals, but she was clearly loyal to her man outside the bedroom. I admired her for it.

"I thought there was a chance that you might have gone back to your place in Pimlico," continued Natasha. "It was worth a try anyway. But I kept phoning all day and only getting the answering machine, and then I realised that the one person you might have contacted was your wife. Unfortunately, I didn't have her number or address, so I went to see Maxie."

"I bet he was thrilled," I said, remembering his earlier enthusiasm for her.

"He was vile," said Natasha, wrinkling her nose. "He kept hedging, saying you'd told him never to pass on your Vauxhall address and phone number, and he suggested that he might just be persuaded to change his mind in return for, in return for . . ."

"It's all right, Natasha," said Kim kindly. "I'm sure Will can guess."

"You didn't, did you?" I said. Needless to say, I'd never told Maxie to keep my address and number a secret.

"I was desperate to find you and discover what was going on," she said. "He suggested all kinds of disgusting things. I managed to beat him down to oral sex. With a condom. Compared to what he was asking for earlier, it was nothing."

"Christ, I'm sorry," I said. I was ashamed to think of how many hours I'd wasted drinking with the creep. I'd always known he was repellent. I just hadn't realised he was quite that repellent.

"Anyway, I went round to Kim's. It was about nine o'clock at night by now, and told her the whole story. She said she was convinced that you wouldn't be acting dishonourably and thought you might be in some kind of danger from Henry. I thought she was over-reacting. You see part of me still wanted to believe all this was some kind of elaborate prank." Natasha began to cry a little. She'd had a terrible few days, I thought. Just as bad as mine in some ways. Kim patted her shoulder and Trev the Rev squeezed her knee.

"I could punch that Maxie," he said.

Kim took up the narrative from the distressed Natasha. "The trouble was, we couldn't think of how to get a trace on you. Natasha phoned her brother, and he rather aggrievedly said he'd heard nothing from you." I had, I remembered, promised to keep in touch with Nicholas. But things had happened so fast and so hectically once we were on Henry's trail that I'd never found the time. "We kept trying the old number you had for Henry and Rose but there was no reply."

"His parents are dead, according to Henry," I said, "Not that he's to be trusted."

"Then Natasha remembered you'd put in a call to the former editor of the *Esher Herald*, and he might have left a message on your answering machine," continued Kim. "The only trouble being that your answering machine is so old you can't access the messages remotely. And neither Natasha or I fancied confronting Maxie and asking to borrow a spare key."

"Very wisely," I said. Once I'd got even with Henry, I planned to get even with the peroxide-blond twerp.

"We'd have risked it if we thought we were likely to get anything useful out of the editor. But it seemed such a long shot that we decided to wait till morning and get his number from the *Esher Herald* like you'd done.

"The nice Brummie girl?"

"Yes," said Kim. "I phoned him and told him I was your wife. I said you were still anxious to trace Henry but had been called away for a few days. And he said he'd left a message and was surprised not to have heard from you. I must say he sounded very sweet."

"He always was. We called him Old Moley."

"I remember you mentioning him, now I come to think of it," said Kim. "Anyway, he said he'd not heard from Henry for years. There was something about 'that regrettable business with the craft fair . . .'"

"I should have mentioned that earlier," said Trev. "I'll explain later."

"Right," said Kim. "Anyway, what Moley did have was news of Rose. She still lives locally and apparently she's got a long history of petty crime and drug addiction and was always appearing before the local magistrates. Moley had looked up the latest case when he got your message. Apparently, she'd been up before the beaks yet again for trying, very ineffectually, to break into a chemist's shop. Moley said Rose lost a child a few years ago and the magistrates never wanted to send her down, but all the probation orders and community service never seemed to do any good. This time, she was sent to a rehab centre, with the stipulation that she was to attend the local psychiatric day centre after getting off the drugs for the umpteenth time. The magistrates warned that this was her last chance and if she was up before them again they would have no choice but to send her to prison."

This was desperately depressing. "Henry said she'd kicked the drugs and was running a rehab centre herself," I said in some distress. I couldn't bear to think of sweet little Rose wrecking her life like that. Still less that I might have been the cause.

"I had to work yesterday," continued Kim, "so I phoned Natasha with Rose's address and the address of the day centre. I said if she got any hard information she was to ring me at once and I'd make some excuse and leave the office."

And Natasha, still shaken by her experience with Maxie, and with Sir Dominic tied up all day in business meetings, had phoned Trev the Rev and asked him to meet her at the psychiatric centre. She couldn't face it on her own, she said tearfully, and she thought Trev, a friendly face from the past, might help to reassure Rose. So the faithful Trev had set off in his van, and Rose had met him outside the psychiatric wing of Kingston Hospital at noon.

"Unfortunately," said Trevor, "They wouldn't let us see her. I'd put on the old dog collar to try to look trustworthy, but it didn't wash. They said the policy at the day centre was that there were to be absolutely no distractions from the outside world. They also said that while they couldn't stop it, they would be grateful if we didn't trouble her when she left at the end of the day. I got the impression that they were acutely anxious about her.

"I was worried about disturbing her but Natasha, rightly as it turned out, was insistent. I'd discovered by glancing at the noticeboard that the day centre kicked out its clients at 5p.m. so we had some time to kill, and, as it happened, Natasha had the *Good Food Guide* with her and we had a most agreeable meal at Chez Max. You wouldn't expect to find a really first-class restaurant in a little shopping parade in Surbiton, but it was terrific. I kicked off with magret of duck . . ."

"Trev," said Kim, with a dangerous sweetness in her voice that I recognised from past experience. It always meant trouble. "If you don't shut up about your lunch I'm going to strangle you and I don't care if you are driving the car." She closed her fingers round his dog collar.

"Right, of course, sorry," he said. "It's just that the next bit is a bit distressing. I was trying to put it off. After lunch, we went for a walk along the river, and then we drove back to the hospital and lurked. There was a risk, you see, that she might not go home and we'd miss her. In fact, she came out at five sharp and walked to the bus stop. We went up to her and said hello and she didn't recognise either of us at first. She was almost unrecognisable herself. Dull grey skin, greasy hair, and this aura of terror and despair. She was like one of the damned."

My poor Rose, I thought.

"It was strange. When she'd finally worked out who we were, as though dimly remembering something from a dream, she was at once relieved and terribly distressed. She clung round my neck and cried and the people in the bus queue started tutting, so we went back to the van. She said you were in terrible danger, Will. Apparently, Henry had visited her the night before and told her he'd imprisoned you on the pier. Just the thought of the pier terrified her, and she said he'd put her there once, a few years earlier, to do cold turkey."

I imagined withdrawing from heroin in that terrible isolation, and shivered.

"Which pier?" Trevor had asked her, and Rose kept saying "The pier where we used to go for our holidays. Spoilt now, broken now."

"But which one?" Trev asked again, "Where?"

"For ages it looked as though she'd completely forgotten where it was, and then it suddenly came to her," said Natasha. "Lympington, she said at last, in Devon. We asked her where Henry was and if he'd got a picture with him but she just kept shaking her head and crying whenever we mentioned him. "You've got to find Will," she said. "They tortured him. Go now."

"And then," said Trev, "before I could stop her she jumped out of the van and crossed the road. A car almost hit her, but she seemed oblivious. She must have seen the bus at the stop and she climbed on board just before it pulled out. We thought about following her but feared we'd probably do more harm than good. And besides, it looked as though we'd better get down to Lympington fast."

Natasha had phoned Kim at work and she'd pleaded a migraine, gone home and driven down to Kingston to meet them. And since even Kim's old Mini was faster and more reliable than Trev's van, they'd left the van in Kingston and driven down to Lyme together.

"We looked at the atlas and although Lyme's about twenty miles east of Lympington, we thought it was the one place nearby where we could be reasonably certain of finding someone with a boat late at night," said Kim. "We drove down to the pub by the Cobb, racing to get there before last orders, and asked the landlord if there were any fishermen there. He pointed out the chap you've just met. I think he thought we were mad at first when we said we thought there might be someone held hostage on the pier. But he could tell from our faces we were in deadly earnest and Trev's dog-collar helped."

"It does have its uses sometimes," he said.

As we drove back towards London, they asked me exactly what had happened to me since I'd gone off with Henry and I told them the story while trying to underplay the more gruesome moments. It was strange. It was me that had been the victim but I felt humiliated by the experience, almost guilty, as though I had been involved in some kind of pornographic obscenity. I couldn't bear to remember it, still less describe it. Kim must have read between my bland words, because she began to cry and squeezed my hand so hard it hurt. And then I fell asleep. It was enough to know she was there, and the quarter bottle of Scotch helped. When I woke up, we were driving along the Embankment past the Chelsea Hospital. Natasha was at the wheel and there was no sign of Trev. Kim explained that we'd dropped him off in Kingston so he could pick up his van and he'd be spending the night with us.

Natasha drove up to her house in Belgrave Square and asked us if we wanted to come in to talk to Sir Dominic. I couldn't face it. I was dog tired, my teeth ached and it seemed to me that I'd done quite enough running around on his behalf. Natasha now knew all that there was to know, and could tell him herself.

"Just make sure he gets in touch with the police." I said. "Give us a ring in the morning when he's made an appointment. I'll come along too." I was looking forward to seeing Sir Dominic in the doghouse.

We drove home, and Trev arrived soon afterwards, and charitably announced he'd like to go straight to bed. I showed him into the spare room, and imagined a child sleeping there in less than nine months' time. It was almost too wonderful to believe. Then I took a long, much needed bath and Kim came and sat on the edge and watched. She looked horrified at the gauze and elastoplast Eric and Ernie had applied to my chest while I was unconscious, but with a large malt in my hand, three neurofen down the neck, and the knowledge that Kim was pregnant, I felt just fine. I just hoped she'd think the other scratches on my body were also Eric and Ernie's work, rather than Natasha's. Kim insisted on washing me herself, as she'd done when we'd first started going out and I'd taken another beating, and I was astonished to find myself becoming sexually aroused. I'd half feared that the experiences of the last few days would have put me off sex for months.

"Let's go to bed," she said.

"But won't it disturb . . ."

"Not if we're gentle," she said.

We were very gentle and it was lovely. Afterwards, as we curled around each other, snug as spoons in a drawer, I began to apologise about Natasha.

"It's OK," she said. "From what Natasha told me, I gather that you put up a fairly valiant show of resistance."

"Yeah, but I can't quite claim I was raped."

"You didn't enjoy it though, did you? When Natasha came round on Sunday night after her foul time with Maxie she became embarrassingly frank over the second bottle of wine. I gather her sexual tastes are somewhat unorthodox. Having seen the state of your back I'd say that was an understatement."

"I still shouldn't have gone along with her though, Kim."

"No, you shouldn't. But you were under a lot of pressure and we weren't actually together at the time. And I've got to admit, I had a terrific time with Colin."

"But you said . . ." I began explosively, then realised she was winding me up. "Sorry," I said, and kissed the nape of her neck. She was giggling happily. "Shut up, fatty, and go to sleep," she said. "It's almost four o'clock." So I did as I was told.

The phone rang at nine the following morning, summoning us to Scotland Yard. By the time we got there, with Trev the Rev in tow, we'd missed most of the fun. We were escorted to the office of a CID superintendent, with a couple of other lesser ranks in attendance. Sir Dominic and Natasha were already there and had told most of the tale. I got the impression from his subdued and deferential manner that Sir Dominic had received a terrific ticking off for not going straight to the police when he was first approached about the Vermeer. Poor Natasha and Kim got a further dressing down for mounting their own rescue operation rather than going to the cops. I got off remarkably lightly, but then Natasha had told them about Eric and Ernie. I had to tell them about this again in some detail – the superintendent seemed to be familiar with their *modus operandi* – and didn't like it a bit.

The big news of the morning was that Henry was clearly determined to carry out his plan to extract cash from Dommo in almost exactly the same way he'd outlined to me in the Chester B&B. A typewritten letter had been shoved through the letter box in Belgrave Square a few hours after Natasha had set off on her rescue mission with Kim and Trev the previous day. It said Sir Dominic was to bring £200,000 (how typical of Henry to exaggerate the ransom) in used notes to the Shakespearean Revels. In return, he would receive the Vermeer, the compromising photos of the Indian art treasures and Henry's promise – whatever that was worth – that he would then keep quiet and trouble Sir Dominic no further. Henry's letter added that he would also reveal the location where "Will Benson, that fat, tiresome, gullible hack" was being held. If there was any funny business, or any sign of a police presence, Henry concluded, he would destroy the Vermeer and make sure that by the time I was found, if I was found, I would be dead. As far as Henry was concerned, I thought bitterly, I was just another bargaining counter. So much for our friendship. Fat and gullible I undoubtedly was, but I was glad he found me tiresome too. All that business about him hoping I'd find him and placing announcements in *Theatre World* was clearly a load of lies too.

The letter supplied no details about how the transfer was to be arranged, so I told them about Henry's proposed swap of cases in the cloakroom.

"Right, we'll have someone there," said Superintendent Gross. "It would be helpful if we could arrest him at the exact moment of the exchange. We'll supply the briefcase and make sure the contents look authentic enough for a quick examination."

"Knowing Henry, he'll change his plan," I said.

"We'll have other people at Hampton Court too," he assured me.

Sir Dominic was evidently recovering from his ticking-off. "You will be careful, won't you?" he said. "If he suspects there are police around, he might really destroy the picture. Or simply disappear."

Superintendent Gross, who I was warming to, gave Sir Dominic a look that seemed like a dictionary definition of the word 'baleful'.

"If you had come to us earlier we would almost certainly have the picture safely recovered and Henry Sutton under lock and key by now," he said. "As it is, we're going to have to spend Christmas Eve poncing around in fancy dress with the real possibility that the whole operation could go hideously pear-shaped." It was unclear whether it was the dressing-up, the ruined Christmas Eve or the possibility of failure that annoyed Gross most.

Sir Dominic looked abashed. "I could certainly help with the costumes . . ."

"We'll manage," said Gross. "I'm sure the Met's amateur dramatic society will be able to provide." It was at this point that he suggested that I ought to stay away from the event and Natasha and Kim had protested on my behalf. Grudgingly, he conceded, though he stressed that if I saw Henry, or Eric and Ernie, I was to steer well clear of them and simply tip off one of the police who would be there. I nodded. Part of me wanted to smash my tormentors to a pulp, personally, but I knew that vengeance usually did the perpetrator as much harm as the victim. It was agreed that the superintendent and his fellow officers would meet Sir Dominic in Hampton Court's Great Hall at 6p.m., in full disguise, a good two hours before the revels were due to commence. They'd do a recce together, and establish means of discreet communication should Henry show up.

Out on the street, Trev, who had been waiting for us, was trying to keep himself warm with his pipe. I lit up a Camel and Sir Dominic, heaving a deep sigh, flamed a modest Hamlet cigar. I'd been hoping for the full twelve-inch tycoon number with which he was sometimes photographed.

"Christ, I've not had a dressing-down like that since I was caught drinking with a few chums at Wellington," he said engagingly. He put one arm round my shoulder, and another round Kim's. "I owe you both a debt of gratitude. And apologies for getting you into this mess. I'm truly sorry." You could see why he had become such a success. Even in his present chastened mood, there was no mistaking the power of his personality. Or, surprisingly, his warmth. I already knew he could be a dangerous adversary. I now realised that he would probably be a formidable friend. Natasha's marriage to a man thirty years older than herself began to make a sense that went beyond the merely financial. I just trembled to think of what they got up to in bed. The thought that he might also know what I and his wife had got up to in bed was even less reassuring, and I felt distinctly alarmed when he asked Kim if he could have a word in private with her "brave husband".

She nodded and Sir Dominic led me a few paces down the road.

"I suppose Natasha got you into bed?" he asked, an entirely unexpected note of sympathetic concern in his voice.

I nodded. "Yes, I'm terribly sorry. I honestly didn't have that much choice."

"My dear fellow," he said, patting my arm. "You're very far from the first. The fact is that I've never been terribly interested in sex, and after a few nights with Natasha after our wedding I speedily concluded that I'd much prefer to give it up all together. So I feign impotence, which I'm afraid leaves other chaps exposed to her advances. She's a lovely girl, a deeply conventional girl in many ways . . ."

"But absolutely terrifying in the sack," I said.

"Quite," he replied. "More terrrifying now than ever, I gather. The mixture of guilt and sexual frustration, I suppose. You weren't badly hurt, I hope?"

I shook my head.

"Good," said Sir Dominic. "A former business associate threatened to prosecute for common assault. It took quite a lot of smoothing over. After he'd come out of hospital that is."

"You're joking?"

Sir Dominic shook his head. "She bit him rather badly in a sensitive place," he said. "But it's all blood under the bridge now."

I shuddered and gave thanks that I'd got off relatively lightly, and we rejoined the others and made our farewells. We'd gone our separate ways, Sir Dominic and the vampiric Natasha to finalise arrangements at Hampton Court; Kim, Trev and I to the dentist's. And now here we all were in the Roller, the Wombles now replaced by Bowie's Station to Station, cruising down the A3 toward Hampton Court. A thought suddenly occurred.

"Shouldn't you be in your parish, Trev, preparing for midnight mass with your flock?" I asked.

He gave one of his lupine grins. "Of course I should, only I could hardly miss this, could I? My curate's doing it. Natasha's arranged that after the chauffeur's dropped you off in Vauxhall he'll drive me all the way home. I'm doing early morning Communion for her instead."

"When I was on that pier . . ." I said, awkwardly.

Trev nodded.

"I prayed," I said. "And I think my prayer was answered."

"He does that sometimes," smiled Trev. "Just when you think the sod's gone away for good."

We were crossing Hampton Court Bridge now and I remembered my visit to Nicholas' house that had started the adventure. It seemed hard to believe it was less than a week earlier. Hastings swung the Roller through the lion and unicorn gate, fondly remembered from childhood, and joined a queue of expensive looking cars headed for the carpark behind the stables.

"Where are you going to spend the evening?" Kim asked him as he opened the door for us.

"There's a small do for chauffeurs in the Orangery," he said. "Sir Dominic always thinks of the drivers. But I'll be back here from 11p.m. ready to take you home."

We thanked him, and walked through thin sleet over the bridge to the first of the great courts. There was a desk where we had to hand over the thick, engraved invitation cards Sir Dominic had provided that morning. They were worth £150 each. It had been warm in the Roller, and I shivered now. But my Gloucester rags were warmer than my tracksuit on the pier. Kim had put on her astrakhan coat and floppy hat over her Ophelia costume but Trev, in his tights, looked almost ill with cold, and clasped his hands over his crotch like a small boy who wanted to go to the loo. There were fire-eaters and other fellows of infinitely tedious jest performing by the light of braziers and flaming torches in the Clock Court, but the steady stream of revellers scurrying towards the royal chambers were too frozen to stop and watch. Kim checked in her coat at a temporary cloak-room at the bottom of the staircase leading up to the apartments on the first floor, and I was amused to see one of the policemen who'd been at our interview that morning looking an absolute wally in baggy woolly tights, a white ruffled dress shirt, and a cloak that looked like an old dog blanket. A red rose was pinned to the blanket as if he were a member of the Labour Party.

"Who are you?" I asked pleasantly as he took Kim's coat.

"Sodding Romeo," he said mournfully, then pointed at his forehead. I thought he was commenting on the lunatic nature of the whole affair and was just about to agree that it was indeed preposterous when I realised that I had my bandage wrapped round my forehead, like a bloodied rugby forward, and he was telling me to cover my eyes. I pulled it down and could just about make out his satisfied nod through the gauze.

We climbed the stairs and I realised that with the bandage and the scratchy beard it wasn't going to be the most comfortable of nights. There was, however, the promise of lashings of alcohol and Kim's company and that was compensation enough. I told Kim she'd have to be my eyes. I could see people as vague shapes, but couldn't make out their features, or what they were wearing.

"Right," she said, as we entered the weapon-festooned guard-room, where the reception was taking place. "Well, there's a line-up. And all the waitresses are topless."

"You what?" I said, resisting the temptation to push the bandage up onto my forehead again with a fierce effort of will.

"Just my little joke," said Kim. "They're actually dressed like the fairies in *A Midsummer Night's Dream.* Sir Dominic and Natasha have come as Antony and Cleopatra by the look of it. And they're with another couple. She consulted the programme we'd been handed as we entered the room.

"It's Mr and Mrs Adrian Noble, the artistic director of the RSC and his wife," said Kim. "Apparently this bash is being thrown by Sir Dominic to raise funds for a double-bill of Edward Bond's Shakespeare plays, *Lear* and *Bingo.*"

"They'll need the money then," I said with a shudder, remembering those two noxious plays by perhaps the most unendurable of all living playwrights. "No one empties a theatre quite as efficiently as Edward Bond."

"Be fair," said Trev. "There's always Howard Barker."

We reached the handshaking stage. Natasha squeezed my hand very thoroughly and whispered into my ear about how much she liked Kim. Sir Dominic gave me a manly clasp and whispered "no sign of him yet" without moving his lips. I told him that if HappiSnax ever went bust I could probably get him a job as a ventriloquist. He leant forward, close to my ear. "All the cops are wearging gred groses," he said.

"The booking's cancelled," I told him.

I'd interviewed Adrian Noble a few weeks earlier but he was having one of his facial spasms when we shook hands, so his failure to recognise me was no real test of my disguise. He was dressed as Autolycus, out of his own production of *The Winter's Tale*, Kim told me later. She hadn't been sure about his wife, Joanne Pearce, but thought she was probably meant to be Perdita.

The large room was crowded and it was annoying not to be able to indulge in my favourite hobby of celebrity spotting. Apparently, the star of the *tout ensemble* was Rolf Harris blacked up as Othello, closely followed by Elaine Paige *en travesti* as Richard III. When Trev came back from getting huge Scotches for him and me and an orange juice for Kim, he swore he'd spotted Michael Fish in a toga and Andrew Lloyd Webber as King Lear.

Suddenly, Kim let out a little squeal, and chased across the room to accost someone. It turned out to be Kevin, her former subordinate on the subs desk at *Theatre World* and my only real ally there now. Unable to face talking to Colin myself, I'd cravenly got Kim to ring Col at home that morning before we set off for Scotland Yard to explain why I hadn't been at work the day before. She'd said she'd only given him the briefest details, but insisted he'd been sympathetic and concerned and had magnanimously agreed I needn't come in that afternoon after I'd visited the police, the dentist's and the casualty department. Since Christmas Eve at *Theatre World* always turned into a piss-up at lunchtime anyway with everyone staggering home when they felt like it, we both knew this wasn't quite as generous as it sounded. But at least he wasn't planning to fire me. Or not yet, anyway.

"Colin gave us the edited highlights of your adventures," said Kevin with a big grin on his face. He'd always adored Kim and been a good friend to me. "I gather you've been a bit of a hero, Will." I blushed and Kevin, perceptive as always, changed the subject. "There's good news about JB too," he added. "He phoned Mr Torrington today. He's back at home and apparently the doctors reckon he'll be well enough to come back to work by Easter. Torrington said he sounded so keen he wouldn't be surprised to see JB back a lot sooner. Which is just as well, as Col is very much out of favour at the moment. Indeed, poor old Colin is feeling so sorry for himself he sent me here instead of him."

It was hard to decide which piece of news gave more pleasure, JB's recovery or Col's decline.

"Why's Colin out of favour?" said Kim, with an entirely unnecessary note of concern in her voice.

Kevin produced a sheet of newsprint from his back pocket. "Col told me you'd probably be here tonight so I brought it along." He handed me the page but I couldn't read it, so Kim took it from me and studied it in silence for a few moments. Then she burst out laughing.

"It's the Many Happy Returns column," she said. "With Ian McKellen engaged to a Spice Girl and Melvyn Bragg presenting topless darts. You wrote this didn't you, Will?"

"Er, yes," I said. "But surely it's me that ought to be in trouble, not Col?"

"It was obviously a joke not intended for publication and it wouldn't have made the paper if I hadn't played a malicious trick," said Kevin. "Since you were off on Monday, when you usually help out with production, Col said he'd do some subbing. Among other tasks, I asked him to revise page nine, and specifically mentioned that I hadn't had time to read either the Production News or Many Happy Returns columns. Needless to say, Col was too busy phoning up his contacts to wish them a grovelling Merry Christmas to do much work and he didn't get round to reading properly. Worse than that, he initialled a proof and then sent the page down the line to the printers. The paper hit the shops this morning, and the phone's been red hot all day. Colin was hauled in to see Torrington and nobly admitted that it was entirely his fault. Which was just as well since I'd have gone straight up and told the boss myself if he hadn't. Needless to say, Col was furious with me afterwards, but there was absolutely nothing he could do. I made damn sure I'd held on to the page-proof with his initials on it. A little notice went up just as were getting into the Christmas spirit in the staff room, with the good news about JB and a curt postscript saying that Col was to revert to the post of deputy editor forthwith.

"I'm still going to be in trouble," I said gloomily. "I lost the Birthday Bible in a pub. That's why I made the column up."

Kev slapped me on the back. "For Christ's sake, Will, have you been worrying about that?"

"Amongst other things," I admitted.

"We've got it all on a back-up file in the system" he said. "And Julie's got a spare printout in her desk."

I sighed with relief. Worry really was an unproductive waste of time. Then I squinted at Kev through my bandages.

"Are you wearing sunglasses?" I said.

"Yes. I'm meant to be sand-blind Old Gobbo in *The Merchant of Venice.*"

"You couldn't lend them to me? For reasons I won't go into I'm meant to be completely unrecognisable and this bloody bandage is driving me mad."

"Of course," said Kev, handing them over. I put them on, and it was bliss to be able to see properly again, albeit through glasses, darkly. Apart from anything else, the waitresses looked sensational, even if they weren't topless. One of them arrived now with another loaded tray. I helped myself to another Scotch, Kim stuck to the orange juice. Then someone pinched my bottom. I turned round and it was Nicholas, looking frighteningly gaunt, but less ill and a great deal more cheerful than when I'd last seen him. He was wearing a mud-spattered cream suit and carrying a dandyish cane, which I guessed he also needed.

I hugged him, Trev hugged him, and I introduced him to Kim and Kevin.

"Who are you supposed to be?" I asked, then guessed, certain that I was right; it was perfect casting. "Melancholy Jaques in a modern-dress production of *As You Like It*?"

"Spot on," he said. "Unfortunately, as far as the Seven Ages of Man speech goes, I seem to be in some kind of limbo between the lover and mere oblivion. But I feel OK today." He smiled bravely. "Natasha's told me all about your exploits," he added. "I've toured the room but there's no sign of Henry." At that moment, Natasha came over herself. She looked magnificent in a white sheath dress, a jewelled necklace in the shape of an asp and a simple golden crown. There was a small figure dressed in clouds of gauze and fairy wings besides her and at first I assumed it was a waitress. But it wasn't. It was Rose. She was wearing a lot of make-up and her eyes were far away but she wasn't the terrified figure Trev had described. She came over and stood on tiptoe and kissed me on the cheek.

"The old gang's reassembled," said Trev. "Apart from you know who."

"I've had a long chat with Rose," said Natasha. "She says Henry's definitely coming. He came round to her place this morning with the ticket and the costume and wanted her to be here."

"He said he wanted to say goodbye," said Rose. Her voice was husky and slurred, and I guessed she was calm because she was smacked out of her head. I gazed into the eyes I had once loved and the pupils were huge.

"I'm sorry I didn't make the reunion," she said. "I was someplace else." No one else seemed to know what she meant, but I did.

"It's OK, Rose," I said. "None of the others made it either."

Trev slapped a hand to his forehead. "Midsummer night, 1992, you mean? We were all going to meet up again. I did remember but Judy was having Tom. I was in the maternity unit at the time. He was born early on midsummer's day."

Natasha and Nicholas both admitted that they'd completely forgotten the plan.

"Fatty here didn't," said Kim. "We'd only just got married and he insisted on trekking out to Oxshott Woods. I said I'd come with him to keep him company because I had a hunch no one else would turn up but he said I'd be *de trop.* It was just meant to be the gang."

"It was silly of me really," I said. "You can't bring back the past." But at that moment I wanted to bring back the past so much I knew I was going to cry. I didn't want them to see me weep, it would seem like a rebuke to their own forgetfulness, and there was no reason why they should have remembered after all those years. Instead, I said I'd got to go to the gents.

There was a sign pointing to the loos and I wandered, my dark glasses misting up with tears, through a succession of William and Mary's state apartments which had bored me rigid as a child. I'd arrived at Oxshott Woods at 9.30 that night, just as the dusk was deepening, with two cold boxes full of booze. I wasn't really surprised that no one had turned up, it was sentimental of me to think they might, but I drank far too much, became maudlin and fell into an alcoholic slumber under a pine tree on the lip of the sandpit. I'd woken at dawn, hungover and cold, and staggered down to Oxshott station to wait for the first train back to town. As I sat on the platform, drinking yet another Scotch I knew I didn't need, I'd thought that was the end of the old gang, and that I'd never see them again. And now I'd seen them all, and a lot of me wished I hadn't. It was great to see Trev happy in the priesthood and blessed with his improbably large brood, and in a different, more complex way, good to see Natasha again, alarming, perverse, but her own woman and oddly endearing underneath the frigid exterior. But then there was Nicholas. We'd lost so many years of friendship and now he was facing up to a cruel, obscenely early death. His mischief, his wit, his intelligence all doomed, as he said, to mere oblivion. And Rose, who had wrecked her life and was, unless I was much mistaken, back on the smack again and destined for prison. And finally, perhaps most painfully of all there was Henry, our leader, our hero, who had turned out to be the most devious and destructive man I had ever met. We were, I realised, all still dancing to his tune that night, just as we'd been dancing to his tune on the ghetto-blaster at Oxshott Woods. Three lives had turned out OK, mine included, despite some precarious moments. Kim had rescued me from more than the pier. By taking me back, by loving me, she'd rescued me from a half-life as a drunk, lonely, increasingly desperate waster. And, miraculously, I was going to be a dad now too. It was time to grow up. But my happiness was shadowed by poor Nicholas and Rose, and the contemptible Henry. Three ruined lives. I thought of all that joy, all that exuberant untested youth on that miraculous midsummer night. We'd suffered a fifty per cent casualty rate, through chance, malice, the thousand natural shocks that flesh is heir to. It seemed like lousy odds to me.

I found the loo, off a staircase leading down to the gardens. I had a pee, and washed the bits of my face that weren't covered with false beard. And when I came out Rose was waiting for me. She had a glass of Scotch in each hand, and she handed one of them to me, solemnly, like a gift. "Happy Christmas," she said.

We sat on the steps together, and I put my arms round her shoulders and we cuddled up close as we'd often done in the old days. There were a few fresh needle marks in her arms, and the faded tracks of many more.

"I'm sorry it all went wrong between us," I said, gesturing at her arms, which she made no attempt to conceal. "Henry said it all started to go rotten for you after we split up."

"He was lying as usual," she said, in that slurred, distressingly detached voice. "I was miserable for a while, like any teenage girl would be, but only for a few weeks. And then I just got on with my life. I went to Cambridge, got an OK degree in English and became a librarian, got married, had a kid." She sounded as though she was describing someone else's life and in a way, of course, she was.

"The baby died. Three months old. Cot death. No one's fault," she said, no trace of emotion in her voice. "I got very down and my husband Jules fucked off. I couldn't blame him. And then my parents died, within months of each other, and Henry turned up after years abroad. He had a load of heroin and we spent three months together at my parents old house having a ball with it.

"And then one day, Henry said it was time to stop. We did cold turkey together, and he found it easy and I didn't. Then he buggered off on one of his world tours and I went straight back on the stuff and it's been like that, on and off, ever since."

"You're using again now, aren't you?" I asked gently.

"Yeah. Henry came round on Sunday with fifty grams. He does that most times when he's brought a load in. I was determined to keep clean, but it's hard when you've got a bag of bliss on the mantelpiece. He told me about what he'd done to you. I shot up as soon as he'd gone."

"Does he bring in a lot of heroin?" I asked. "He told me he only dealt in grass and ecstasy."

"It's mostly heroin now," she said.

"But how can he deal in heroin when he's seen what it's done to you?" I asked, as much to myself as to her. "And even if he can get his head round that, why keep tempting you with the stuff when you're clean?"

"Henry's got this theory," she said, lighting a Gitane *sans filtre* from the stub of another and stamping out the butt on the concrete step. I just prayed there weren't any smoke detectors. Hampton Court was understandably nervous about fire since the conflagration a few years earlier. "Henry says in this world there are weak people and strong people, and the weak deserve anything that's coming to them. He got himself, and me, addicted to heroin quite deliberately, just to see if we could get off it, test our courage, as he put it. And because he managed it, he thinks anyone worth caring about can kick it too. He brings me the stuff because he wants to find out if I can really kick, have the stuff around and still not use. He says he'll love me again if I can manage it. Most of the time, I know he's a sick, sadistic bastard, Will. But he was so good to me when I was young. And . . ." she gnawed on her lower lip. "I so much need someone to love me."

I squeezed her tight. "Would you like to come and stay with Kim and me for a while?" I asked her. "I might even be able to get you a job." There was currently a vacancy in the advertising department and Mr Torrington, a devout Catholic, was always a sucker for a hard luck story. He'd taken me back, after all.

"It's too late, Will," she said. "It's all fucking Rothmans now."

I smiled grimly at the old joke. "It's not too late, Rose. You were clean until a few days ago. You can get clean again. It's a pretty junior job in the advertising department, but it's fun at *Theatre World.* And you could stay with us until you're sorted out." Kim, I knew, wouldn't object to having a junkie former girlfriend about the house. It was one of the reasons I loved her and I knew if anyone could help Rose, it was her.

"No, it's too late," she said again. Then almost inconsequentially she added: "You met Eric and Ernie then?"

"I met Eric and Ernie," I said grimly.

"Dentist's?"

"Yeah. Not you too?"

"No. Henry sometimes threatens me with it. They use it mostly for bad debts. The only time I met Eric and Ernie was when they took me out to the pier a couple of years ago. Henry wasn't there but we went on the boat he lives on when he's not abroad or touring with a band. They chained me up in that godforsaken theatre and took it in turns to rape me. Then they left me there and Henry didn't come and get me for a couple of weeks. Not much fun is it?"

From her flat tone of voice, she might have been describing a disappointing holiday.

"Did Henry know they raped you?"

She nodded. "I think he told them to," she said. "He'd just discovered that I'd been working in a Surbiton massage parlour. You wouldn't think there were massage parlours in prim little Surbiton but there are. Henry wasn't pleased when he heard about my job."

Christ, I thought. He wasn't human. Rose was fiddling nervously with her handbag. I guessed the reason why.

"I've got to go to the loo," she said. "It takes a bit of time. I'll see you back at the party."

"I'll wait," I said. She nodded and disappeared into the ladies. She was back by the time it took to chain-smoke a couple of cigarettes. Her eyes were further away than ever but she clearly wasn't suffering any more. The heroin had taken away the pain. She was happy, almost, or as close as she probably ever got to happiness.

"I feel Capstan Full Strength," she giggled, and we walked back through the oppressive rooms to the reception.

"You'll think about coming to stay with us?" I said.

"It's too late, Will, like I said." I decided I'd get Kim to have a word with her. Presumably, we'd have to get her into rehab again before she came home with us.

We rejoined the group. Trev was reading from the programme. "Apparently several of Shakespeare's plays were performed in the Great Hall in front of Queen Elizabeth," he said. "And blimey, listen to the menu. Thick pease pottage, swan stuffed with quails, spit-roasted venison and apple moise, whatever that it. It's all being prepared in the original Tudor kitchens."

"I wish they'd get on with it," said Kim grumpily. "I'm bloody starving." There's nothing worse than being sober at interminable receptions when everyone else is getting happily pissed.

I know. I tried it once and vowed never to repeat the experience. A waitress passed and I helped myself to another Scotch. So did Rose. She clearly liked to accompany the heroin with a chaser or two. Janis Joplin did too, and look what happened to her.

Trev continued his catalogue of revelry. "After dinner, there's going to be a Shakespeare revue performed by members of the RSC. There'll be a bit of *Kiss Me Kate*, a couple of sketches, Kenneth Branagh doing an extract from Henry V and Sir Alec Guinness will be reading . . ." But I never heard what Alec Guinness would be reading. Out of the corner of my eye, I'd seen a couple of chaps in bright jesters' outfits, complete with caps and bells and bladders on sticks. Eric and Ernie had arrived.

"I'm just going to slip away for a while," I whispered in Kim's ear. "Will you look after Rose and make sure she doesn't get too close to the two bods in the jesters costume? She's high as a kite and they could freak her out. Don't look round but it's Eric and Ernie." Kim nodded and I glided round the room. There were several people in bad fancy dress wearing red roses, but eventually I found Gross. He looked distinctly uncomfortable in turquoise doublet and hose with a huge white hat with a preposterous pink feather in it. And a red rose, of course.

"Osric?" I said, and gave my name in case my disguise was as impenetrable as I hoped it was.

He nodded glumly. "I was set up by the lads," he said. "It was the only naffing costume left."

"Eric and Ernie are here," I said. "The clowns over by the window." He nodded almost imperceptibly when he'd discreetly clocked them. "I've trawled the room," I added. "There's no sign of Henry."

"I know," he said. "I'd like to pull in those two sadists now but they're probably checking the place to make sure it's all clear. You wait. One or both of them will go out in a minute and bring him in. Provided they haven't spotted a police presence."

"You know quite a lot about Henry, don't you? More than you were letting on this morning? You never asked any of us to do a photofit for one thing. Just a quick verbal description."

He nodded. "We've pulled in people who have had dealings with him over the years. Not to mention the people who have had dealings with Eric and Ernie they're never likely to forget. We know he's brought in vast amounts of heroin, but never heard how. Your account of the theatrical tours this morning made a lot of sense. What we do know is that he distributes the stuff on those rock tours but we've never got an undercover man onto the right tour. People don't like talking about Henry much, even when we're exerting as much pressure as we can get away with."

"But how do you know what he looks like?"

"We received a couple of photos, anonymously, a couple of years ago. Very clear pictures of him sitting in the garden of a country pub. Looking happy. They just said 'Henry Sutton, drug-smuggler', on the back." Rose, I thought. She'd probably sent them, fearfully, after her terrible experience on the pier. She must have been living in constant dread that Henry would one day find out.

"We've shown them to a lot of people who've gone down on drugs charges. He's been repeatedly identified as a major player, and we know he uses a couple of thugs called Eric and Ernie. His surname changes, depending on who you're talking to but he always calls himself Henry or Harry or Hal. But we've never got a trace on him till now."

Because he's either abroad, or touring or drifting around on a boat, I thought. But I didn't want to mention the boat to Gross. He might have asked me who'd told me, and Rose was carrying. She was in enough trouble as it was. Just then, Sir Dominic came hurrying over in his toga. His brow was beaded with sweat, and for so authoritative a man he looked seriously rattled. He was also carrying a briefcase, which presumably contained the ransom. "I've just had Henry on the mobile," he said. "He's in the kitchens and he's armed."

Gross snapped his fingers at a passing waitress and I took my hat off to the man. Here was the night approaching crisis point and he was going to have a drink before he got down to sorting it all out. I don't think even I'd have done that. But since he was having one I thought I might as well keep him company. In fact, Gross helped himself to a Perrier. I stuck to the Scotch. Then I noticed that the waitress was wearing a red rosebud on her breast. Another cop. Presumably, he just wanted her there to relay his instructions. All this flashed through my mind in less than the time it took to take a large slurp.

"Henry said Eric and Ernie are here," said Sir Dominic.

Gross and I both nodded. "In a couple of minutes, they're going to make contact with me and escort me over to the kitchens. I'm to take the money with me. He said he also wants to see any other members of what he calls the old gang who happen to be here. He says if there's any sign of police involvement, he'll have no qualms about using his gun."

"Right," said Gross, taking the bad news on the chin. "We'll have those comics out of the equation right away. Do your stuff, Susan. And do stop looking wildly round the room, Sir Dominic," added Gross curtly. "I don't want them to see you're rattled." Actually, I thought Sir Dominic was doing pretty well under the circumstances. But then Gross probably still bore him a grudge for fucking up his Christmas Eve.

From where I was standing, I could see what happened without staring too obviously. Susan stopped at a group of men looking unhappy in tights. They were all very big. The put their glasses on her tray and strolled over to Eric and Ernie. There weren't any pleasantries, still less police cautions. The two biggest men punched my torturers as hard as they could in the stomach, and they both went down on their knees. There were gasps from those standing nearby, but by now Eric and Ernie had the cuffs on and Susan and another fairy were calming the guests down. "Just a couple of gate-crashers," they said airily as Eric and Ernie were led out of the door leading to the state rooms. You could see at least some of the guests wondering what kind of party it was where gate-crashers were treated quite so roughly. Personally, I felt like letting out a loud cheer.

"Everything OK?" Gross asked me.

"Yeah, they're out of the room," I said.

Gross looked round and snapped his fingers and yet another adorable cop-fairy flutttered over at his command. "I want three men at each of the two exits to the kitchens, at least one of them armed at each end. They're to position themselves outside without drawing attention to themselves." She nodded and fluttered purposefully off.

"Right. Did you detect any sign of panic in the kitchens, Sir Dominic? Do you think Sutton's actually threatened anyone with his gun yet?"

"There was quite a lot of noise, the kind of noise you'd expect to find in a busy kitchen preparing for a banquet. People shouting orders. A clatter of pans. Not the kind of tense hush you'd get when you've got a madman waving a gun around the place."

Gross nodded.

"I don't think taking Eric and Ernie out like that was altogether wise," added Sir Dominic, mopping his brow with a red silk handkerchief. "As well as his threats about the gun, he said that if his instructions weren't carried out to the letter, he'd destroy the Vermeer." You had to admire the tycoon's guts. He'd already been ticked off twice by Gross that day. And now here he was coming back for more, telling the policeman how he ought to be running the operation. I expected another angry outburst from Gross. But this time he just smiled seraphically.

"It's the only bargaining counter he's got. He won't get rid of it in a hurry."

"So what do we do now?" asked Sir Dominic. "He definitely wants to see me, Natasha and his sister, Rose, who he says he knows is here. And I'm afraid he's guessed that you're here too, Will. I denied that you were but he said he'd been back to the pier and discovered you were gone. He was certain you'd have come along, and that you'd have brought your wife with you. He said he was looking forward to meeting her."

"I can't let any of you go in," said Gross firmly. "He'd probably take one or more of you hostage as a way of getting out of here."

I got the impression that the superintendent was beginning to realise the whole operation was in danger of going hideously pear-shaped, just as he'd feared. A simple matter of picking up a drug-smuggler with a stolen painting looked as though it might be turning into a siege.

"Go and get the 'old gang' he mentioned," the policeman said to Sir Dominic. The tycoon hurried over to our little group on the other side of the room and Gross consulted, *sotto voce*, with one of his colleagues. When Natasha, Trev and the rest came over, the cop seemed surprised to see so many of us.

I made brief introductions. "This is Superintendent Gross," I said. "We're all old friends of Henry's apart from Kim, who's my wife, Rose, who's Henry's sister, and Kevin, who's a colleague of mine. Rose looked totally spaced out and more than a little alarmed. As well she might. She'd presumably had a lot of bad times with the cops and she knew exactly what was in her handbag.

"Right," said Gross. "I think we'll go and have a little conflab outside. No point in alarming the rest of the guests though I fear they could have a long wait for their supper." He told the policeman he'd been talking to earlier to watch the doors and to let no one outside the reception room.

We stood on the landing outside and I belatedly realised I could take my sunglasses off now. The walls were covered with *trompe l'oeil* pictures of shields and swords and elaborate crests, all painted in a drably unattractive beige.

"You all know about the Vermeer?" he asked the others.

Everyone nodded.

"Your friend Henry is in the Tudor kitchens with the painting and he's asked for most of you to go in and see him. But you're not going to. He's armed and the whole situation is far too dangerous and volatile. A colleague is calling the siege experts and I hope they will be here within half an hour. There's just a chance, however, that it might be helpful if he knows you're outside and can hear your voices. Something to keep him occupied until the reinforcements arrive."

We all nodded again. Henry certainly had a knack for turning a party into a surprise, I thought grimly.

"Right. Well, we'll go over to the kitchens now. Be as quiet as you can and don't go within twenty feet of the door unless I tell you to. There will be several men outside wearing fancy dress. Don't get in their way. They're policemen."

We went down the stairs. The policemen who had been there earlier had gone and so had all the coats and bags. Presumably, the staff had transported them to the exit of the Great Hall for people to pick up as they left at the end of the evening. We stepped out into the Clock Court and a figure slipped out from behind one of the pillars of the colonnade and ran to a brazier that was still burning brightly in the cobbled yard. The entertainers all seemed to have packed up and gone home. It was Henry, wearing an army sergeant's uniform. The bright yellow flames illuminated his face and he looked eerily diabolical in the flickering glare. He had a gun in one hand, a rolled up canvas in the other. We'd fallen for his misdirection yet again.

"No one move," he said. "Whoever moves gets shot and the picture goes straight onto the brazier." He was brilliant. He must have known that if there were any cops with guns, they'd all have taken up their position outside the Tudor kitchens as soon as Sir Dominic relayed the contents of his phone call. But by the same token, Henry couldn't fire his gun without alerting them. The kitchens, as I remembered from umpteen visits since childhood, were down a passage on the other side of the courtyard. Any shot would be clearly audible. With luck, his voice might be audible, too.

"Is Will Benson there?" he asked. I realised that he probably couldn't make out our faces with only the light of the flames. Not that he'd have been able to recognise me anyway. I was standing next to Gross. "Say yes," he hissed in my ear, "and follow his instructions. If you can keep him distracted, I should be able to radio the boys outside the kitchens."

"Is Will Benson there?" Henry repeated.

"Yes" I shouted back, loudly in case there was anyone within earshot. "I'm here."

"No more shouting. Right, Will, walk very slowly to the brazier. Hands on your head."

I stepped forward and moved towards him. When I reached the brazier, Henry held the pistol to my head. My mouth was dry and my heart was pounding but after the dentist's and the pier, this somehow didn't seem as frightening. At least I wasn't on my own.

"No one move." He said. "If anyone does, the painting goes first. Then Will. And I wouldn't want to kill my dear chum Will, would I?"

"Who's there, Will?" he asked quietly.

"Natasha and Sir Dominic. Your sister. Trev and Nicholas. My wife Kim and Kevin who works *for Theatre World.*" I hadn't thought fast enough and Henry was counting the silhouettes.

"There are eight people there Will. Who's number eight? It's a cop, isn't it?"

I said nothing. "It's a cop, isn't it?" He held the canvas close to the flames. "Yeah, it's a cop," I said.

"Take two steps forward, cop," said Henry. Gross took two steps forward.

"Throw your radio over here and don't even think about turning it on," said Henry, the gun at my temple, the painting near the flames. Gross chucked over the radio. It lay on the ground a couple of feet from us.

"Now, Kim," said Henry. "I want you to walk slowly over to the radio, pick it up and give it to me. One hand on your head all the time. "Don't let him hurt Kim," I prayed, "don't let him hurt Kim." She stepped forward and she had never looked more beautiful than in the light of those dancing flames. My lovely, eminently sane Ophelia. She picked up the radio and handed it to Henry. "Don't move for a moment," he said. He looked at the radio and seemed satisfied that it wasn't switched on. Then he looked at Kim. "She's nice, Will. Much better than you deserve. I can see now why you held out so long at the dental surgery. It surprised me that."

He stared hard at her. "What's it like being married to a fat piss-head, Kim?" She said nothing. "I asked you a question, Kim. What's it like being married to a fat piss-head?"

"I love him," Kim said simply, and I could see that there were tears in her eyes. "Please don't hurt him any more. He's suffered enough."

"Sweet," said Henry contemptuously and I'd never hated him more, not even on the pier when I discovered the thirty bottles of water that seemed to measure the days of my confinement. "Right, Kim. Now I want you to go back to the policeman and ask him, ever so nicely, for his gun. I want you to stand right in front of him while he's giving it to you so he can't try any target practice, and then I want you to hold it high above your head and walk slowly back to me."

"Who've you come as?" I asked Henry as Kim walked slowly towards Gross. "The bloody sergeant in *Macbeth*?" I thought if I tried to make some kind of conversational contact he might be less disposed to use his gun. Not that he had shown the faintest flicker of mercy in the past.

"Shut up, Will," he said, his eyes fixed on Kim. She was standing a couple of feet in front of Gross and more or less completely obscured him. After a couple of tense seconds she raised the gun above her head and turned round. She walked over to the two of us and took up a position about three feet from Henry, to his right.

"Take the painting, Will," said Henry, passing me the portrait tied up with a piece of string. I held out my hand and grasped the painting gently. He kept the gun resting on my temple but now turned to look at Kim. "Give me the gun," he said. "You hold the barrel and I'll take the handle." Once he'd got the gun, he kept pointing it directly at Kim's head. "Now walk towards the barrel and rest your head on it like Will. She stared levelly back at him for a few seconds. Her eyes were dry now, her courage incredible. Then she took a couple of small steps and rested her forehead against the barrel. I smiled at her and she smiled back.

Henry had both his arms outstretched, like a crucifixion scene with handguns. The others stood stock-still, watching this hideous little pageant. Then Henry called Sir Dominic over, and told him to place the briefcase just next to the brazier. He ordered him to open it. I don't know if the money was fake or not, but the bundled tenners looked realistic to me and seemed to satisfy Henry. He told Sir Dominic to shut the case and to walk slowly back to the others. Henry now decided it was time for a little lecture on literature.

"You asked me who I'd come to the revels as, Will. Well, I'm Iago. You may remember that the excellent Shakespeare critic, John Wain, compared Iago to a typical sadistic warrant officer in that book of his. I can't remember what it was called. Can you, Will?"

"*The Living World of Shakespeare.*"

"Ah yes. And what did Coleridge have to say about Iago, Will?"

"He spoke of the 'motive-hunting of motiveless malignity'," I said. Motiveless malignity struck me as being a superb description of Henry.

"But Coleridge, poor addled, laudanum-addicted Coleridge, a weak man, Will, a weak man, was wrong. What he didn't realise is how much fun this sort of thing is. It is fun, isn't it?"

Kim and I remained silent. "Come on, say it," he said, increasing the pressure of the guns on our foreheads.

"It's fun," we both said.

"And we're going to have a little bit more fun before we go," he said. "I think this Vermeer has caused us all quite enough trouble. So I'm going to count to ten, Will, and if you haven't put it into the brazier by then, I'm going to blow your brains out."

"One, two . . ."

I felt panic get me in its grip but it was a familiar visitor now and I could just about think through it. I didn't think Henry would pull the trigger. He must have known it would alert the policemen outside the kitchens. It was just a cruel bluff. I was damned if I was going to destroy that Vermeer. It meant too much to me, especially now Kim was pregnant too.

"Eight, nine, ten," said Henry. I stood stock-still, wondering if you'd feel anything when a bullet entered your brain. There was a long tense silence. I sweated buckets and concentrated on my sphincter. I was determined not to foul myself in front of Henry as well as Eric and Ernie. It would be a humiliation too far.

Eventually, Henry broke the silence. "Not quite as flabby as I thought," said Henry. There was a note of approval in his voice that I despised. "So, we'll play it another way now," he continued. "I'll count to ten again, and if the painting's not on the brazier by the time I've reached it, lovely Kim's a dead woman."

"Don't do it, Will," said Kim. I couldn't take a risk with her. I couldn't keep her in suspense for ten seconds. Particularly not with that tiny foetus inside her. By the time Henry had reached two, the Vermeer was burning merrily on the brazier. I thought of that beautiful woman, and something died inside me.

"Very sensible," said Henry. "Right, Kim, you can go back to the others now." She seemed reluctant to leave me alone. Henry tapped her skull a couple of times with the barrel of the black automatic. Lightly, teasingly.

"Just go, Kim," I said. She walked slowly back to the others, back straight, head erect.

"Right," said Henry. "Well, you can all go back to the party now. Have a wonderful time."

No one moved. "Back inside or I shoot Will. Then I start shooting at the rest of you."

"I'm afraid we must do as he says," said Gross. They turned and started walking back to the entrance to the staircase. All except Kim. And Rose. "Off you go, Rose. Off you go, Kim," said Henry.

Kim started to follow the others, after giving me a nervous wave with a look of terrible anguish on her face. I gave her a thumb's up sign and tried to smile. But Rose stood rooted to the spot. There were another few seconds of silence. And then Rose made her dash. She ran straight toward her brother, and he swung the gun away from me towards her. Presumably, he wasn't so accurate with the gun in his left hand with which he'd held Kim hostage. I ought to have moved then, rushed to the safety of the shadows behind the pillars but I found my legs wouldn't work. Rose kept running and though he had his gun trained on her, Henry didn't pull the trigger. She had something in her hand and I saw it was a small silver revolver. A lady's gun, I've heard them called. She probably took it with her when she was out scoring in rough areas. Henry must have seen it too but still he did nothing. There were tears streaming down Rose's face. She stopped about six feet from Henry, her gun pointing at him. Henry dropped both his guns on the ground.

"You won't do it, Rose. You're spineless, remember," he said. Rose just stood there, the gun outstretched, crying silently. She must have heard him call her spineless so many times before. This would be the last. She shot him in the stomach and he fell to his knees, with an expression of surprise on his face. And then Rose took two steps forward and shot him in the head.

"I'm sorry about my brother, Will, and I'm sorry it's too late," she said calmly. "Fucking Rothmans." Then she put the barrel of the little gun into her mouth and as I lunged wildly towards her, she pulled the trigger. Too late, just like she'd said.

# Author's Note

I am greatly indebted to Charles Hill and Peter Gwynn, who shared some of their considerable experience and expertise in the world of art crime with me. Both, I hasten to add, operate on the right side of the law. The theft of a Vermeer outlined in this novel is loosely based on a real life case, but the stolen painting I describe is as imaginary as the characters portrayed in these pages. The painting of the *Girl with a Pearl Earring* does exist, of course, and its beauty alone justifies a trip to the Mauritshuis in the Hague. Will and Kim went to see it a couple of weeks after the adventures described in Under the Influence, as well as spending a bleary day in Amsterdam where Will, needless to say, fell into a canal after unwisely combining excessive quantities of Purple Haze in the coffee houses with lashings of Nicholas's favourite Dutch gin in the bars. The book's thinking about Vermeer, if it can be so dignified, has been greatly influenced by the magnificently authoritative catalogue that accompanied the great Vermeer exhibition presented in Washington and the Hague (1995–1996) and Edward Snow's beguiling *A Study of Vermeer*. Finally, a word of apology to David Bowie, whose later work is heavily criticised in these pages. Since the typescript was completed he has released *hours*... which marks an entirely unexpected return to (almost) vintage form. It's great to have him back.

Charles Spencer
Claygate, Surrey
June 2000